Also by G. M. Best

Non-Fiction
Seventeenth-Century Europe: Documents and Debates
Continuity and Change: A History of Kingswood School 1748-1998
Charles Wesley: A Biography
Shared Aims
Transforming Lives
A Tragedy of Errors: the story of Grace Murray
John Cennick: The Forgotten Evangelist
The Cradle of Methodism: A History of the New Room
In Their Words

Historical Guides
John Wesley: a tercentenary commemorative study
Wesley and Kingswood in Methodism and Education: From Roots to Fulfillment
The Seven Sisters
Susanna Wesley
Charles Wesley

Children's Book
Gospel's Story

Musical
Marley's Ghosts

Novels
Oliver Twist Investigates
Wuthering Heights Revisited
The Jacobite Murders
The Barchester Murders

Part of the slavery exhibit in the Museum at The New Room in Bristol

SLAVERY AND BRISTOL

G.M.BEST

NEW ROOM PUBLICATIONS
BRISTOL

NEW ROOM PUBLICATIONS

Bristol and Slavery
First published 2020

New Room Publications is an imprint of Tangent Books
Unit 5.16 Paintworks
Bristol BS4 3EH
0117 972 0645
www.tangentbooks.co.uk
Email: richard@tangentbooks.co.uk

ISBN 978-1-910089-95-8

Author: Gary Best

Design: Joe Burt (www.wildsparkdesign.com)

Copyright: New Room Publications/Gary Best All rights reserved

Gary Best has asserted his rights under the Copyright, Designs and Patents Act of 1988 to be identified as the author of this work. This book may not be reproduced or transmitted in any form or by any means without the prior written consent of the publisher, except by a reviewer who wishes to quote brief passages in connection with a review written in a newspaper or magazine or broadcast on television, radio or on the internet.

A CIP record of this book is available at the British Library.

Printed on paper from a sustainable source

Printed in Poland
www.lfbookservices.co.uk

All the proceeds from this book will go to help maintain the New Room in Bristol and its many educational activities, particularly its work in telling the story of Bristol and slavery to young people.

To The Reader

You may choose to look the other way but you can never say again that you did not know.
William Wilberforce, abolitionist campaigner in speech to Parliament in 1791

This is a story that everyone in Bristol should know. It is a story of how the city came to play a major role in the transatlantic trade that enslaved generations of Africans and helped generate a racist legacy that is still with us.

The new Room was built by John Wesley in 1739 and from the outset he voiced his opposition to the social injustices that he saw in Bristol and denounced the city's role in the slave trade. Some of the visitors who come to the New Room today like stand in the pulpit from which some of his denunciations were made and it is therefore very apt that the New Room should produce this book. Wesley passionately believed that everyone was of equal worth in the eyes of God and that enslaving a fellow human being could never be justified. His single biggest contribution to the early abolitionist movement was his pamphlet *Thoughts on Slavery*, published in both Britain and America in 1774 and repeatedly reprinted until the time of the American Civil War. In it he conveyed the story of the slave trade accurately and historically whilst challenging his readers to make a personal response. How could anyone remain silent in the face of such monstrous inhumanity? It was a pamphlet designed to engage head and heart and it was a call to action. I have modelled this book on that approach. It conveys as accurately as I can the history of the slave trade but it also contains much that is deliberately designed to engage the heart as well as the mind – hence the many thought-provoking quotations that intersperse the text and the profuse number of illustrations. Pictures often say far more than words can. Reference to what costs then meant in today's values are based on the National Archives currency converter.

The first section of the book provides a brief history of how most societies have chosen to embrace slavery, how Europeans became increasingly involved in enslaving Africans, and Bristol's early connections with the slave trade up to 1700, including the role of the Merchant Venturers.

The second section of the book uses as its basis a first-hand account of what it was like to be enslaved. This is taken from the autobiography of Olaudah

Equiano, which was first published in 1796. Wesley was one of the people who subscribed to have it printed. Equiano's story really does convey what it was like to lose one's freedom and be taken away from not just one's family but the culture in which you grew up. It also provides a deep insight into the horrors inflicted on those who were enslaved. I have divided the extracts from his autobiography into six chapters. Within each of the chapters I provide evidence of the truthfulness of his story and, wherever possible, that evidence includes examples drawn from Bristol's participation in the slave trade. It makes for harrowing reading at times, but Equiano's story also shows how the human spirit can overcome suffering and rise above prejudice and greed and all the other evils that lie behind enslavement. Equiano does not permit himself to be a victim. Nor does he just look to white men to bring about an end to slavery. He works hard to achieve his own freedom and, once free, he becomes a leader of 'the sons of Africa', encouraging freed slaves to engage directly in the abolitionist movement.

The third section of the book looks at the eighteenth century, the heyday of Bristol's role in the slave trade. It has been called Bristol's 'golden age' but there was nothing golden about the source of the wealth. Rather than just provide a chronological account I have chosen to adopt a themed approach in the hope that will make the story clearer. The first two chapters deal with the slave traders and the slave captains and their crews. There would have been no slave trade if no one had wanted to buy slaves, and so the next chapter looks at the slave owners, particularly those involved in the sugar plantations in the Caribbean. Often books on slavery focus on the perpetrators rather than the victims so I have deliberately devoted a chapter to the slaves who actually came to Bristol. Their stories have a lot to say to us about the nature of enslavement. The final chapter in this section looks at what the money from the slave trade was spent on and how it transformed the city and the surrounding area. If you want to know the truth behind many of the historic buildings that still delight us today, this is where you'll find it.

The fourth section of the book shows humanity at its best and its worst because it examines the abolition movement and the determination of merchants and plantation owners to defend what they were doing. Traditionally it is the Quakers who are normally credited as being the first Christian denomination to oppose the slave trade, but I have tried to show why the Methodists have an equally strong claim in that respect. From the outset the New Room enjoyed positive links with the Quakers. Its first housekeeper, Sarah Perrin, was a Quaker and, when the New Room was expanded and rebuilt into its current form in 1748, it was George Tully, the man who had built Quakers Friars, that was chosen for the task. John Wesley was a great friend of Anthony Benezet, the leading Quaker abolitionist, and the two men worked closely with the lawyer Granville Sharp, who was so instrumental in placing abolition on the political agenda. Some of those who campaigned for the abolition of slavery could not divorce themselves entirely from the culture in which they grew up and so at times they could say or do things that we would regard as racist. However, many of the abolitionist leaders were, like John Wesley, truly remarkable in their capacity to put human worth beyond all other considerations. Their story reminds us that individuals can make a difference and that change often has to come from the bottom up rather than the top down.

Histories of Britain's role in the slave trade and of slavery often end in 1833 with the Abolition of Slavery Act. The fifth section shows why this is a mistake. It explores how slavery has survived and the appalling legacy of racial prejudice that the transatlantic trade engendered not only in the world as a whole but here in Bristol. It takes the story up to 2020 and the Black Lives Matter campaign that saw the destruction of Edward Colston's statue. I hope this book will show why John Wesley's call for people of all races to recognise each other's worth is as relevant today as it was then.

G.M. Best
Historical Consultant at the New Room, 12 June 2020

Knowing this history better, understanding the forces it has unleashed, and seeing oneself as part of a longer story, is one of the ways in which we can keep trying to move forward.
David Olusoga in *Black and British: A Forgotten History* in 2016

CONTENTS

SECTION ONE

13   A Brief History of Slavery and of Bristol's role in the Slave Trade up to 1700

SECTION TWO

37   **The Slave Trade from a Slave's Perspective**

43   How Equiano became a slave
57   How Equiano was taken to Barbados
69   Equiano's first taste of life as a slave
79   Equiano's life as a sailor in the Royal Navy
97   How Equiano saw the full extent of slave owner cruelty and earned his freedom
117 How Equiano became a missionary
133 Equiano's life as a campaigner for the abolition of slavery

SECTION THREE

151 **Bristol's role in the Slave Trade in the eighteenth-century**

159 Edward Colston
171 The Rivalry with Liverpool
185 The Slave Traders
199 The Slave Captains and their Crews
217 The Slave Owners
239 The Slaves in Bristol
259 The Transformation of Bristol

SECTION FOUR

281 **The Anti-Slavery Movement in Bristol**

287 Slavery and the right to be free
301 How the idea of abolition came to Bristol
317 How the right to be free was legally tested
329 John Wesley's 'Thoughts Upon Slavery'
345 The Society for effecting the Abolition of the Slave Trade
371 The battle to end the slave trade
391 The Victory of 1833

SECTION FIVE

417 **The Survival of Slavery and Racist Attitudes into the Modern Era**

449 **Further Reading**

456 **Index**

Left: Nubians enslaved by Egyptians in c1750 BCE, Greek slaves working in a mine in c500 BCE, Roman collared slaves in around second century, and slave market in Yemen from 13th century illustration. Above: Section from painting by Rubens of Roman philosopher Seneca and a nineteenth-century engraving of St Paul with the runaway slave Onesimus. Paul asked the slave to return to his master but asked the master to free the slave.

SECTION ONE

A Brief History Of Slavery And Bristol's Role In The Slave Trade Up To The Eighteenth-Century

From the hour of their birth some are marked out for subjection, others for rule… The use of slaves and of domestic animals is not very different because both minister to human need

Aristotle, ancient Greek philosopher in his book *Politics*

For most of human history enslavement has been viewed as perfectly acceptable. Some people were born enslaved but many more had slavery thrust upon them. An individual or a small group might be seized by raiders out to make a quick profit but it was particularly common for the the victor in a war to enslave the entire population of a village or a town or even an entire region. As a consequence slaves were often people of a different religion, nationality, or ethnic background from their owners. It was easy to justify this by stating they were 'inferior' to their conqueror. All ancient civilisations, regardless of their differing religions, had forms of slavery – the Sumerians, the Egyptians, the Chinese, the Assyrians, the Babylonians, the Iranians, the Indians, the .pre-Columbians, and so on. It is estimated that over 80% of the people living in ancient Athens were slaves and over 25% of the people living in ancient Rome.

Slaves are the excrement of mankind

Marcus Cicero, statesman and philosopher who defended the rights of Roman citizens

Slaves were at the whim of their owner and they had no redress for any barbarities inflicted upon them. One of the first voices to speak in favour of treating slaves humanely was the Athenian Zeno of Citium, who founded a philosophy known as Stoicism three hundred years before the birth of Christ. This promoted a life based on wisdom, morality, courage and moderation. Seneca, a Roman Stoic wrote to a friend in around 64 A.D:

> Kindly remember that he whom you call your slave sprang from the same stock, is smiled upon by the same skies, and on equal terms with yourself breathes… Treat your inferiors as you would be treated by your betters… Associate with your slave on kindly, even on affable, terms; let him talk with you, plan with you, live with you.

The emphasis on good treatment was something taken up by the apostle St Paul, but he also told slaves that it was their duty to obey their masters 'with fear and trembling, and with sincerity of heart, just as you would obey Christ'. The early Church that he helped create clearly did not like the institution of slavery because it believed Christ died for all and that therefore all were equal in the eyes of God. It campaigned hard for slaves to have the right to marry and not be separated from their children, it encouraged owners to set their good slaves free, and it offered protection to any maltreated slave who took refuge in a church. However, the Church stopped short of demanding the abolition of slavery in part because some Christians saw it as a God-given institution. Only occasionally did a Church leader voice total opposition to any form of enslavement.

Is there any difference between the slave and his owner? Do they not draw in the same air as they breathe? Do they not see the sun in the same way? Do they not alike sustain their beings by consuming food? Is not the arrangement of the guts the same? Are not the two one dust after death? Is there not one judgment for them?... If you are equal in all these things... how can one person judge himself to be the master of another human being, and say, 'I own slaves and slave-girls' like 'I own herds of goats or pigs'
    Gregory of Nyssa, a fourth century bishop, in *Fourth Homily on Ecclesiastes*

When William the Conqueror conquered England in 1066 he inherited a country where 10% of the population were slaves. None of the clergy questioned this except Wulfstan, Bishop of Worcester, the one Saxon bishop permitted to stay in office. He expressed concern to William about Bristol's 'shameful trading' of white slaves to Ireland:

> You might well groan to see the long rows of young men and maidens whose beauty and youth might move the pity of a savage, bound together with cords, and brought to market to be sold.

When the King listened and banned the slave trade, the Irish responded by kidnapping people from the area around Bristol in order to acquire the slaves they wanted. Their raids were only stopped when William's great-grandson, Henry II, conquered Ireland and, in 1171, made Dublin temporarily a colony of Bristol.

By the twelfth century full-blown slavery had fallen out of favour across most of Northern Europe, partly as a consequence of demographic and economic factors, but mainly because the Church had started to take a much stronger line against slavery, arguing it was wrong to enslave anyone who was a Christian. It upheld that only 'pagans' should be enslaved and, once they were converted to Christianity, they should then be also freed. Slavery was replaced by 'serfdom', which has been described as a kind of 'slavery with limitations'. Serfs could be bought, sold, or traded and could not leave the land they were bound to, but they had some rights. For example, they had the right to cultivate certain fields to maintain themselves and, through the feudal courts system, they had the right to be heard if they received unfair treatment. Serfdom proved relatively short-lived across most of Europe because of the impact of the Black Death in the fourteenth century. It killed perhaps as much as 60% of the population in some areas and serfs who survived were far too valuable to retain a semi-slave status. Only in parts of central and eastern Europe did serfdom continue. In Russia it was to survive until 1861 and the treatment of Russian peasants in some areas often remained barbaric long after that.

Things cannot go well in England… until there will be neither serfs nor gentlemen, and we shall be equal
John Ball, the people's leader during the Peasants Revolt of 1381

Slavery continued to flourish unabated in most of Africa, in South and Central America, and in China, Japan, India, Australia and New Zealand. It also remained a feature of society in Southern Europe because of the political and economic power of the Muslim world. The Muslims viewed all black Africans as

Left: St Wulfstan in stained glass window in Worcester Cathedral. Above: Russian peasants chained together to pull a barge c1900. Below: Serfs operating a plough in 14th century Luttrell Psalter and nineteenth-century engraving of Muslim slavers.

uncivilised and inferior and so destined for enslavement and they saw nothing wrong in enslaving any non-Muslim, regardless of the country from which they came. It is estimated that over the centuries Muslim raiders and traders have been responsible for enslaving at least eighteen million Africans and one million Europeans drawn from Spain, Portugal, Italy, Greece, the Balkans, and Russia.

I have not bothered to describe the country of the African blacks… because, as I naturally love wisdom, ingenuity, religion, justice, and regular government, how could I even notice such people as these?
Ibn-Hawkal, tenth century traveller from Baghdad

When the Christians of Southern Europe took back control of the lands that bordered the Mediterranean from the Muslims, they saw nothing wrong in retaining slavery as a legally recognised institution. Spain, Portugal, Italy, and southern France were all happy to enslave Muslims and to copy the Muslim practice of acquiring black slaves from Africa. As a result Barcelona, Cadiz, Palma de Mallorca, Naples, Palermo, Arles, Montpellier, Nice, and Narbonne all gradually became important slave markets. Northern Italy embraced the slave trade for commercial reasons and so black slaves were also sold in Genoa, Venice, Florence and Rome. All this helps explain (but not justify) the decision of the Papacy to give its approval for Christians to enslave all non-Christian races. It was thus with the Church's approval that between 1415 and 1460 Prince Henry the Navigator began opening up new slave markets as a commercial offshoot of Portuguese ships initiating what became known as the Age of Discovery. Portugal was particularly keen to acquire slaves because of the shortage of labourers in that country.

Slavery is a weed that grows on every soil
Edmund Burke, philosopher and politician in a speech in 1775

The Portuguese mastered the use of the trade winds that blew from the east near the equator and the returning westerlies in the mid-Atlantic. This enabled them to explore the islands in the Atlantic and the coast of Africa. They did three things that established the pattern for the later transatlantic slave trade operated by all of Western Europe. First, they entered into deals with Muslim traders so they could purchase Africans from them. Secondly, they paid for the Africans they wanted by providing European goods, thus making the slave trade attractive to manufacturers. Thirdly, they began using Africans as slave labour in the new colonies that they created. Enslaved Africans were used to produce sugar cane on Madeira and to grow cotton on the Cape Verde Islands. Only occasionally did a Portuguese sailor express concern at treating the Africans in this way:

> What heart could be so hard as not to be pierced with piteous feeling to see that company? For some kept their heads low, and their faces bathed in tears... Others stood groaning very mournfully, looking up to the height of heaven ... crying out loudly as if asking help from the Father of nature; others struck their faces with the palms of their hands, throwing themselves at full length upon the ground, while others made lamentations in the manner of a dirge after the custom of their country... But to increase their suffering there now arrived those who... parted fathers from sons, husbands from wives, brothers from brothers. No respect was shown to either friends or relations.

In nothing was slavery so savage and relentless as in its attempted destruction of the family instincts of the Negro race ... Individuals, not families; shelters, not homes; herding, not marriages, were the cardinal sins in that system of horror
    Fannie Barrier Williams, African-American nineteenth-century women's rights activist cited in *Black Women in Nineteenth-Century American Life* published in 1990

Spain rapidly followed Portugal's example, linking exploration with exploitation. In 1480 it won Portugal's agreement to it taking control of the Canary Islands and a stretch of African coast from whence slaves could be acquired. At the same time it commenced its war to retake Granada, the last remaining area of Spain controlled by the Moors. Grenada's conquest ten years later was followed by a massive enslavement of Muslims. In 1492 King Ferdinand and Queen Isabella commissioned an Italian, Christopher Columbus, to seek a western sea passage to the East Indies, hoping to profit from the lucrative spice trade. He crossed the Atlantic and discovered first the Caribbean islands and then a continental landmass beyond them. He named the islands 'the West Indies' because of his mistaken belief that he had reached India. It was left to the Portuguese explorer Vasco da Gama to discover a route to India by rounding the southern tip of Africa in 1497-8. This opened up contact with the Muslim slave traders of East Africa. One merchant who became a leading purveyor of black slaves was an

Slavery Up To 1700

Left: 1684 engravings of Muslims enslaving white Christians. One shows a clergyman on the left and a Turk on the right. Bottom left: 19th century art often chose to depict Arab enslavement of white women. Above: Prince Henry the Navigator. Below: Christopher Columbus

Italian from Florence called Bartolommeo Marchionni and he promoted the mapmaking skills of his fellow Florentine, Amerigo Vespucci, who gave his name to the continent that Columbus had discovered, calling it 'America'.

> ***Your Highnesses may see that I shall give them as much gold as they need… and slaves as many as they shall order to be shipped***
> Christopher Columbus writing to the King and Queen of Spain in 1493

In around 1495 Giovanni Cabota, a naturalised Venetian originally from Genoa, settled in Bristol and adopted the English name John Cabot. He and a Bristol merchant called Willian Weston obtained a commission from King Henry VII in 1496 to undertake voyages across the Atlantic in search of new lands and trade routes. Weston had been engaging in trade with the Portuguese in Lisbon and Madeira and elsewhere since 1480, and he knew all about the commercial advantages that could stem from colonisation and enslavement. It was a condition of the royal patent that the ships used would be from Bristol and it is reasonable to assume the voyage had financial backing from other merchants. One of those was undoubtedly Robert Thorne, whose business was based not just in Bristol but Seville and he had first met Cabot in that city. The Thorne family had originally come from Florence and it had been trading with Genoese merchants in the Mediterranean for at least three generations. Like Weston, Thorne had seen at first hand the money to be made out of slavery because Genoese merchants supplied Seville with enslaved Muslims, enslaved natives from the Canary Islands, and enslaved Africans. He also had an interest in exploration because the main Genoese traders with whom he worked were the Catonos, who had close links with Christopher Columbus. Some historians argue that Weston and other Bristol merchants had already started exploring sections of the American coastline even before Cabot's project.

After one abortive effort, Cabot, accompanied by Weston, successfully crossed the Atlantic in 1497 in a ship called the *Matthew*. They explored part of the coastline of North America, discovering an island which Cabot called 'New-found-land' off what is now Canada. In 1498 Cabot undertook another voyage, this time with a fleet of five ships from Bristol. This was definitely a trading as well as exploratory expedition but it is not clear what happened to it. It is thought Cabot may have explored the North American coastline as far south as the Caribbean. Recent research seems to indicate that Weston undertook a voyage in 1499 or shortly afterwards that went far up into the North West Atlantic, possibly reaching as far as the Hudson Strait. Cabot's son, Sebastian,

Above: Statue of John Cabot, Narrow Quay, Bristol and replica of his ship 'The Matthew' constructed to commemorate 500th anniversary of his journey to Newfoundland; and copy of part of the Royal Charter . Right: portrait of Sebastian Cabot based on a Holbein portrait and Cabot Tower built in 1897 in the parkland of Brandon Hill in Bristol. Below: Cabot Circus, city centre shopping area named after him in 2008.

also acted as both explorer and commercial entrepreneur, working alongside Bristol's merchants so that the port could become the main one involved in transatlantic voyaging. Those who chose to name Bristol's new shopping complex 'Cabot Circus' in 2008 might not like to know that Sebastian Cabot left England in 1512 to work for Ferdinand II of Spain and, as a consequence, became both a slave trader and a slave owner.

We shall take you and your wives and your children, and shall make slaves of them, and as such shall sell and dispose of them as their Highnesses may command; and we shall take away your goods, and shall do all the harm and damage that we can

The Spanish Requirement of 1513

In 1513 Ferdinand II issued a 'Requirement' that authorised a war of conquest in Central and South America. It stated that God had divinely ordained that Spain should take possession of the territories of the New World in order to force the native inhabitants to abandon their pagan faiths and to accept the authority of the Catholic Church. Anyone resisting conversion would be enslaved. The Spanish Requirement was read to the native inhabitants without even being translated into their language. Entire civilisations were destroyed. Some of the soldiers used by Spain in that process were enslaved Africans. Spanish soldiers sent to colonise the West Indies discovered that when it came to developing sugarcane plantations one African was worth four enslaved native Indians in terms of output so the King authorised the enslavement of Africans to work in the Americas. As European diseases began to ravage the native population of the new colonies, the reliance on imported Africans increased.

Plantation estates were initially usually about a hundred or so acres in size but by the eighteenth century some of the larger estates spread over 750 acres or more. A plantation of around two hundred or so acres would require a workforce of around one hundred slaves because sugar cane production was highly labour intensive. The slaves were assigned the task of planting the sugar cane from October onwards. This involved clearing ground, hoeing it into squares, and pushing a piece of cane into each square. The planted cane then had to be manured and kept weeded. The sugar cane was ready to be cut with machetes after about fifteen months or more and so workers began harvesting normally from January onwards, often working eighteen-hour days. The cut cane was loaded onto carts and taken to sugar mills, where it was crushed so its fresh juice could be extracted. This was then immediately boiled until it was

Colonisation as depicted in the engravings of the Dutchman Theodor de Bry in the 1590s. Right: Christopher Columbus as the harbinger of European civilisation. Below: the natives depicted as savage cannibals and shown being made to dig for gold. Bottom: scenes of the cruelty of the Spaniards towards the natives.

the consistency of honey. Any delay led the juice to sour and spoil. Sugar boiling was dangerous work because accidents were very common. If it was not done properly the resulting sugar would not crystallise properly. The honey-like sugar that boiling produced was left in barrels until a brown syrup called molasses could be drawn off. This was then distilled to make rum. The remaining dark brown crystal or 'muscavado' sugar was packed for export into large barrels, each holding about 272 kilos of sugar. The English called these barrels 'hogsheads'.

> *They give us a pair of linen drawers for our whole garment twice a year. When we work at the sugar-canes, and the mill snatches hold of a finger, they cut off the hand; and when we attempt to run away, they cut off the leg; both cases have happened to me. This is the price at which you eat sugar in Europe*
> Voltaire, French philosopher in his novel *Candide* in 1758

The demand for more African slaves quickly soared as more and more sugarcane plantations were created to meet the ever-growing demand for sugar in Europe. Indeed such was the demand that European Muslims were also sent out as 'white slaves'. In 1532 Portugal established its first permanent settlement in the Americas at Sao Vicente in Brazil. It was not long before it also began a war of conquest and it used enslaved Africans as part of its colonisation process. Any English merchant trading in Southern Europe had opportunities to invest in the growing slave trade. Bristol's grammar school and, to a lesser extent, Bristol Cathedral, may well owe their existence to the decision of the sons of Robert Thorne to do exactly that. The two brothers, Robert and Nicholas, were primarily dealers in soap, leather, cloth, and wine but they also traded with a merchant called Thomas Malliard who was very much involved in the sugar trade.

Most historians assume Robert and Nicholas increased the family's wealth by investing in the slave-markets of Southern Europe. Both the brothers had a huge sense of civic responsibility and served for a time as M.P.s for the city. Robert was responsible for creating a fund to offer interest-free loans to businesses in Bristol and a fund to buy corn and wood when they were cheap so that they could then be sold to the poor at cost price whenever prices rose. He and Thomas used some of their wealth to provide the endowment for Bristol's new grammar school, which was created in March 1532 under a charter granted by King Henry VIII as a school for the sons of Bristol merchants and tradesmen. The new grammar school began its work in premises at St Bartholomew's Hospital, near the bottom of Christmas Steps, and the school's motto of 'Ex Spinis Uvas'

Above: Roger Thorne by unknown artist and Nicholas Thorne by E. Cashin. Right: St Bartholomew's Hospital, the original location of Bristol Grammar School when it was founded in 1532. Below: the memorial plaque to Nicholas Thorne and his two wives in the school. Bottom right: a 1655 print of the Augustinian abbey that Nicholas Thorne encouraged Henry VIII to make into Bristol Cathedral in 1542.

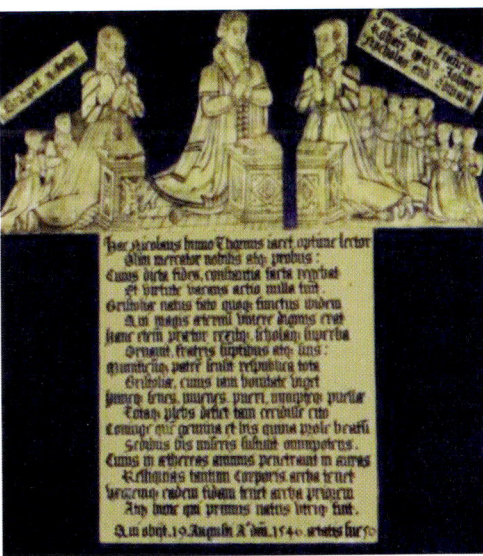

('Grapes from Thorns') reflected their patronage. In 1539 Henry VIII appointed Nicholas Thorne and another merchant to supervise the dissolution of Bristol's three monastic houses, following the King's decision to break away from Roman Catholicism and create the Church of England. Thorne (alongside others) lobbied King Henry to have Bristol given cathedral city status. As a result the former Augustinian abbey was saved so it could became Bristol Cathedral in 1542.

Slavery was established by decree of the Almighty God
Jefferson Davis future President of the Confederate Staes of America in a speech in 1750

The emergence of Protestantism did not curb Europe's growing involvement in black slavery. Too much money was to be made and it was far too easy to argue from the Old Testament that slavery was acceptable. In Leviticus 25 v44-45, for example, there is a specific decree that enslaving foreigners is acceptable:

> You may purchase male or female slaves from among the foreigners who live among you… You may treat them as your property, passing them on to your children as a permanent inheritance.

If you read the Biblical accounts of the lives of Abraham, Jacob, and others then it is obvious sexual slavery in particular was accepted. Solomon had hundreds of concubines. Jews and Muslims thought black Africans were destined for slavery because they believed them to be the descendants of Canaan, the grandson of Noah cursed by God to become 'the lowest of servants' in Genesis 9 v 25 in order to punish Ham, Canaan's father.

In 1552 Bristol's traditional merchants guild acquired a Royal Charter and thus became the Society of Merchant Venturers with the right to develop commercial links with West Africa. It is thought that some of its members were part of the syndicate which funded three slave-trading voyages by the Plymouth-born merchant John Hawkins and his young cousin, Francis Drake, in the 1560s. On the first voyage they sailed to Sierra Leone, captured three hundred Africans and took them to the Caribbean where they were exchanged for sugar, ginger, pearls, and animal hides. On that occasion Hawkins and his crew were among the first Europeans to try smoking tobacco, a product that was soon to encourage England to create the colony of Virginia. On the second voyage Hawkins captured and sold four hundred slaves and, on his third, a further five

Above left: Sir John Hawkins 1580 by unknown artist. Above right: Sir Francis Drake who accompanied Hawkins on two of the three slave trading voyages. Below left: very early portrait of an African woman holding a clock c 1580 attributed to Annibale Carracci. Below right: Coat of arms of the Guinea Company. Bottom right: Coat of arms of the Society of Merchant Venturers.

hundred. At lest one of these may have been brought back to Bristol because there is a reference to a 'blacke moore' gardener working in the city in the 1560s. Portugal and Spain saw these voyages as an infringement of their monopoly on trading Africans and dubbed the English 'pirates'. This was a factor in Spain's decision to send an Armada to conquer England in 1588.

The Armada's defeat forced Spain to concede that England could trade along parts of the African coast, although it continued to refuse permission for English ships to trade in slaves. A handful of English sea captains ignored this, including doubtless some from Bristol. A few black slaves were brought as trophies to Bristol and a black woman named Katherine ended up working in one of the city's pubs in 1612. A weakened Spain increasingly looked to Portugal to provide its colonies with slaves. Colonial development drove first Catholic France and then the Protestant Dutch Republic to engage fully in the slave trade. France, which had long established slave markets in Marseilles and Nantes, showed no qualms about using slaves in the various new colonies it was establishing in Canada and the Caribbean. The Dutch Republic was initially more hesitant about engaging in slavery and for a time Amsterdam and other ports refused to permit human cargo. However, the combination of religious and commercial rivalry changed the Republic's attitude because the colonies it created in Africa, the Americas, and India faced bitter opposition from the established colonies of Catholic Spain and Portugal. Dutch ships began seizing enemy slave ships and using the slaves thus acquired in their colonies. By 1626 the Dutch government was promising its settlers in New Amsterdam (now New York) that it would supply as many black Africans as it possibly could.

> **[I told him] we were a people who did not deal in such commodities, neither did we buy or sell one another , or any that had our shapes**
> Richard Jobson, an English sea-captain reporting his words to an African slave-trader in *The Golden Trade* in 1623

England was last to embrace the slave trade because it was slower to create effective colonies. All its early efforts, such as the tobacco plantations in Virginia and the sugarcane plantations in Guiana, St Lucia and Grenada, failed. In 1607 Virginia was successfully restarted with the creation of the new settlement of Jamestown, but it sought no black slaves because it preferred to use white indentured labour. This was a form of semi-slavery for whites. An indentured labourer was bound by a signed contract to work for a particular employer for a particular length of time (usually around ten years). In that time he was fed, clothed and housed but received no pay. Signing an indenture was often a way for the poor to emigrate because their employer paid the cost of their ship's passage. Technically immigrants were free to work for themselves after their indenture expired, but many unscrupulous employers found ways of ensuring their workers remained permanently in servitude and some sold indentured workers to others just as they might sell slaves. Though British merchants saw no reason as yet to embrace the slave trade, they were happy to profit from the trade in slave-produced Caribbean sugar cane. In 1612 two of Bristol's merchants, Robert and Thomas Aldworth, established the city's first sugar refinery. Most of the sugar would have come from plantations using slave labour.

The situation changed almost overnight as soon as England created its own successful colonies in the Caribbean, beginning with Barbados in 1627, Nevis in 1628, Montserrat and Antigua in 1632, and Jamaica in 1655. The plantation owners quickly discovered that the economics on sugar plantations favoured black slaves over indentured white labourers. There was little difference in initial cost layout between purchasing a slave and paying the travel cost for an indentured white worker but Africans were easier to acquire and they survived tropical diseases better. And, of course there was no limit set to their servitude. England commenced providing small but ever increasing numbers of enslaved Africans for its sugar plantations. Crucial to this was the creation in 1631 of 'the Company of Adventurers of London Trading to the Ports of Africa'. This was commonly known as 'the Guinea Company' because Guinea was the name the English gave to the stretch of West African coast they used. The slave trade was termed the Guinea trade. That is commemorated in one of Bristol's streets being called 'Guinea Street'.

The creation of the Guinea Company owed much to the English desire to emulate the success of the Dutch East India Company, which had been founded in 1602. The latter had become a hugely successful government-backed military-commercial enterprise. It issued bonds and shares of stock to the general public and, in foreign countries, it had quasi-governmental authority because it negotiated treaties, waged wars, funded explorations, created its own colonies, employed people from various nations, and even struck its own coins. The Guinea Company was very much a poor relation because at its height the Dutch East India Company was to have 25,000 employees and operate in Mauritius, India, Indonesia, Japan, Taiwan, Malaysia, Thailand, Vietnam, and South Africa. However, the Guinea Company was only England's first step. The commercial companies it subsequently created were to play a key role in the ever-growing exploitation of Africa, Asia and the Americas.

> *This settlement has been made and upheld by negroes and without constant supplies of them [it] cannot exist*
>
> Sir John Yeamans, Governor of South Carolina 1672-4

The Guinea Company was London-based and it seems likely that any direct involvement by Bristolians in the slave-trade was at this stage slight. The historian Madge Dresser has suggested that the Bristol-born Admiral Sir William Penn, the father of the famous Quaker who founded Pennsylvania, may have supplemented his naval salary by engaging in the slave trade in Jamaica. Certainly both he and his son developed plantations using slave labour. However, a far greater contributor to the nation's embracement of slavery was John Yeamans, who was probably the most influential of the early merchants encouraging English slave ownership. The son of a prosperous Bristol brewer, Yeamans had become a colonel in the royalist army during the Civil War and in 1650 he fled with other royalists to Barbados, where his family owned land, keen to escape the persecution of a victorious Parliament and create a new life. One of his cousins, Robert Yeamans, had been sentenced as a traitor in 1643 and hung, drawn and quartered outside the family home in Wine Street. Yeamans developed large sugar plantation estates that were heavily reliant on African slave labour and he became the leading figure on the island's Council. Such was his ruthless and tyrannical approach that he has been described as 'a pirate ashore'. He was, for example, accused of murdering his former business partner so he could marry the man's wife, although he used his power to have the Council set the case aside.

In the 1660s Barbados experienced an economic downturn and so Yeamans decided to diversify and help create the colony of South Carolina. He was named as its Lieutenant-General and Governor and he organised the initial settlement in 1665 before returning to Barbados. The London backers of the colony ensured that Charles II rewarded him with a knighthood and he was made a baronet. The initial settlement failed but a second attempt in 1670 succeeded and Yeamans is seen today as one of the key founders of Charlestown. He sent two hundred slaves to create his own plantation in the new colony and thus set in motion the process by which South Carolina eventually acquired the largest slave population in North America. He became the colony's governor in 1672 but his determination to enrich himself at the colonists' expense made him very unpopular. It says much for his mercenary nature that he exported food during a food shortage so he could obtain extra profit. At the time of his death in 1674 the

Left: 1885 engraving of John Cary's workhouse before its destruction in 1940. Below left: Admiral Sir William Penn by Peter Lely and his memorial in the church of St Mary Redcliffe. Below right: William Helyar holding designs for the extension to Coker Court, paid for in part by profits from slave-worked plantations: a process initiated by his ancestor, Cary Helyar, in the 1670s when he acquired slaves from the Royal African Company. Bottom: Sir John Yeamans and his home, St Nicholas Abbey, built in the 1650s in Barbados.

colonists were sending petitions to London for his removal. John's considerable wealth passed to his sons and the link between Barbados and Bristol remained a strong one. The Yeamans name was given to a large block of flats built in 1965 in Redcliffe. At that time the issue of Bristol's role in the slave trade was not so controversial.

Yeaman's story reflects the significant change in England's attitude towards slavery following the restoration of the Stuart monarchy in 1660. By then the country had significant colonial possessions in the Caribbean, including Barbados and Jamaica, and six colonies in mainland North America and, thanks to the work of Oliver Cromwell, a powerful navy sufficient to give the country great power status, especially at a time when for various reasons Spain, Portugal and many Italian states were in decline. Charles II saw nothing wrong in slavery because his years of exile in France had given him a continental approach to the issue. He thought the slave trade made commercial sense and that it was better for Africans to be enslaved in other countries under Christian masters than to remain at home in a pagan state and be at the mercy of Muslim slave traders.

We hereby for us, our heirs and successors grant… that it shall and may be lawful to… set to sea such as many ships, pinnaces, and barks as shall be thought fitting… for the buying, selling, bartering, and exchanging of, for, or with any gold, silver, negroes, slaves, goods, wares and manufactures
Charles II's Charter of the Royal African Company in 1672

In 1661 Charles created a company called 'the Royal Adventurers into Africa' to replace the old Guinea Company and he gave it a monopoly over all English trade with Africa. It was envisaged that 25% of the company's profits would come from selling slaves. Badly organised and facing intense competition and opposition from the Dutch, the company failed and was wound up in 1672. It was replaced by the much more effective 'Royal African Company', which had four plantation owners among its directors. The Royal African Company firmly embedded England in the slave trade. Between 1690 and 1700 its members traded over 16,000 slaves as part of a three-stage process that has become known as 'the triangular trade'. The first stage was for ships to transport English manufactured goods to Africa for sale. These goods included a wide variety of items, ranging from pots and pans made of copper to weapons, clothing and cheap jewellery. The export trade explains why there were countless petitions from manufacturers to extend England's role in the slave trade. The goods were profitably exchanged for slaves, who became the new cargo for what was called 'the middle passage'. This was the journey to the Caribbean or to the Americas. Once the slaves were sold, the ships were cleaned and loaded with goods that could be sold in England and Wales : mostly sugar, rum, and molasses if the slaves were sold on islands in the Caribbean and tobacco, rice, hemp, and some manufactured goods if the slaves were sold in the Americas.

> *Over the period of transatlantic slavery, Africa helped to develop Western Europe in the same proportion as Western Europe helped to underdevelop Africa.*
> Walter Rodney, Guyanese political activist in *How Europe Underdeveloped Africa* in 1972

The Royal African Company and its European equivalents enabled exploitation on a much grander scale than had been possible by small groups of merchants just as many big multi-nationals do today. One of the London merchants who had estates in the Caribbean and who made a fortune as a member of the Royal African Company was Edward Colston, whose name is now associated more with Bristol because of his philanthropic generosity to the city. The controversy that now centres around his role will be examined in the third section of this book. The only objection raised to the slave-trading operations of the Royal African Company was that the Company operated solely out of London. This did not suit other ports, especially Bristol, which by this stage had four large sugar-refining partnerships based in the city as a result of its merchants trading in the Caribbean and developing their own slave-run plantations. Why should they let London merchants profit from selling them slaves when they could just as easily operate within the triangular trade pattern? In her book *Slavery Obscured* the historian Madge Dresser has suggested that Bristol's merchants began illegally trading in slaves and that explains why one of the Bristol ships at this time was known as the *Blackamore* and why part of the north of Barbados became known as 'Little Bristol'.

A more substantiated proof comes from Jamaica. A large estate on the island was owned by a Somerset landowner called Cary Helyar, whose family had strong commercial links with Bristol. Just before he died from a tropical disease, Cary invited his younger brother, William Helyar, to help him develop his estate. Not wishing to also die, William decided to rely on agents to run the family's estate and documentary evidence suggests that in 1684 he entered into an agreement with his nephews, Anthony and William Swymmer, who were merchants in Bristol, and another merchant called John Napper, to provide him with slaves. At the time Anthony Swymmer was in Jamaica and acting as the official representative of the Society of Merchant Venturers whilst his brother William was running a sugar refinery and other family businesses in Bristol. Three years earlier the Swymmers had built two warehouses on the Bristol docks to house sugar imports from Jamaica and Barbados and possibly also Antigua.

It is possible that Napper and the Swymmers were just acting as intermediaries and purchasing Helyar's slaves from the Royal African Company but it is much more likely, as Helyar paid for them in Bristol, that they were bringing them illegally on an English ship. Napper, Helyar and William Swymmer were certainly not beyond shady deals for all three were involved in the kidnapping of white men in Bristol so they could be sold as indentured labourers. The black slave deal did not end well as far as Helyar was concerned because William Swymmer had to report that forty of 'our negroes' had died and the remaining eighty had been rendered so unfit by the journey that they were unfit for purpose. He offered to compensate Helyar for the loss by getting his brother Anthony to buy replacements in Jamaica 'from the first ship that arrives whatever they cost'. In 1686 William's son, John Helyar, went out to Jamaica to personally supervise what was going on and correspondence from that year indicates there was a similar failure to deliver another consignment of slaves. Interestingly John appears to have negotiated the deal with William Swymmer's wife, Elizabeth. Anthony Swymmer compensated for the loss by providing money to Helyar so he could purchase what was required. These slaves were bought from illegal traders and not from the Royal African Company.

Clearly all this did not significantly damage the Swymmers because they invested in the building of a new quay and cranes in Bristol in 1692. Nor did it ultimately damage the Helyars because they sold their Jamaican estate for a profit in 1713. However, it made much more sense to seek an end to the Royal African Company's monopoly on trading slaves than to rely on illicit slave-trading expeditions. This explains why the merchants of Bristol and other ports were constantly petitioning Parliament to be allowed to officially join in the slave trade. A key figure behind that demand was the Bristol-born John Cary. His father was a wine merchant who also had sugar plantations in the West Indies. John was an avid churchgoer and an advocate for social reform and today he is best remembered for his philanthropic role in promoting the creation of a workhouse for the poor in Bristol. His vision was to create a place that could offer work to the unemployed and a home to those who were no longer fit enough to work. To create it the Bristol Corporation of the Poor took over a sugar refinery which had become the temporary base for the Bristol

Slavery Up To 1700

The Transatlantic Slave Trade Database estimates 12.5 million Africans were enslaved.between 1500 and 1870 and two million of these did not survive to be sold. The chart on the right details how many Africans were enslaved by the seven countries most involved and the chart below where the enslaved were sold. The map shows the Triangular Trade system that developed among the British slave traders.

USA	305,326
Netherlands	554,336
Denmark	111,040
Spain	1,061,524
France	1,381,404
GREAT BRITAIN	**3,259,441**
Portugal	5,838,266

Europe	9,000
Danish West Indies	100,000
Other parts of Africa	150,000
North America	400,000
Dutch Americas	400,000
French Caribbean	1,120,000
Spanish Americas	1,300,000
British Caribbean	2,300,000
Brazil	5,000,000

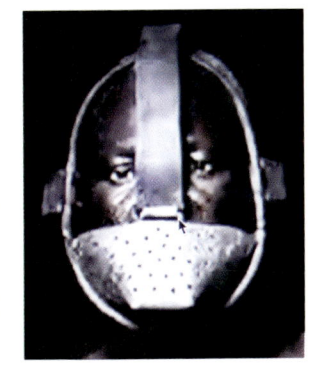

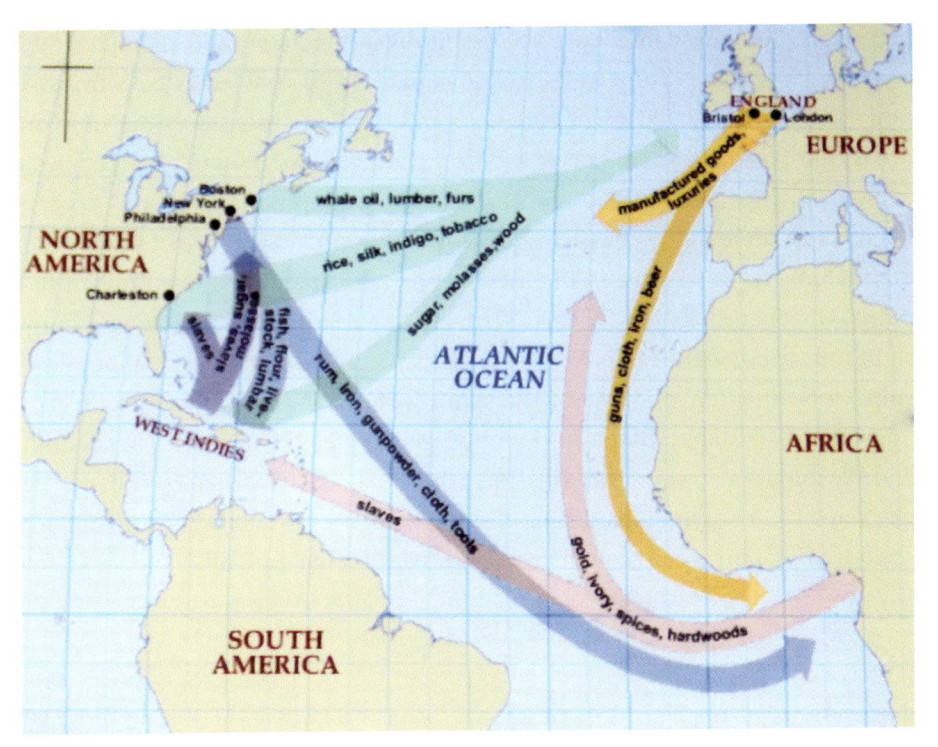

Mint. It was therefore known as the Mint Workhouse until it was renamed St Peter's Hospital. Cary is also regarded as a key figure in establishing economics as a scientific study that requires 'proof' and 'evidence' and in encouraging the country to develop new manufacturing methods. However, this gifted and kind man had no doubt whatsoever that slavery was not just permissible and acceptable but also essential. He wrote about how 'the African trade' was vital to the nation's prosperity and that the Crown should permit all traders to engage in it if they wished.

> *The African trade is a trade of the most advantage to this kingdom of any we drive, the first cost being little more than small matters of our own manufactures, for which we have in return gold, teeth (i.e. ivory), wax, and negroes, the last being… the best traffick the kingdom has*
> John Cary in *A Discourse on the Advantage of the African Trade to this Nation* in 1695

John Cary's arguments easily persuaded Bristol's two M.P.s, Thomas Day and Robert Yate, to lobby Parliament to end the Royal African Company's monopoly. Both these men were successful sugar merchants and, like Cary, had a strong civic pride. They had strongly supported his moves to help Bristol's poor. In 1698 the government agreed to end London's monopoly but only on the condition that traders not in the Company paid a 10% tax on all exports to Africa. This was judged reasonable because, unlike the Royal African Company, they were not having to contribute towards the cost of creating and maintaining fortified slave trade bases on the African coast. The ending of the monopoly opened the floodgates. Virtually any maritime city or town of any significance joined the ranks of 'the Ten Percenters' and started to send out slave ships, including, for example in the south-west, Falmouth, Plymouth, Exeter, Topsham, Barnstaple, Bideford, Lyme Regis, Poole, Dartmouth, Portsmouth and Weymouth. However, heading the pack was Bristol, assisted by the fact the city was a centre of manufacturing. The stage was set for it to become the major slave-trading port when Britain's role in the slave trade took off.

SECTION TWO

THE SLAVE TRADE FROM A SLAVE'S PERSPECTIVE

A prodigious odyssey from enslavement to hard-won emancipation, from unlettered anguish to articulate rage, and from spiritual desolation to a state of grace

Simon Schama, American historian on Equiano's autobiography in *Rough Crossings* in 2005

This section explores the slave trade and slavery primarily through extracts from the autobiography of an African called Olaudah Equiano whose slave name became Gustavus Vassa. Born the son of an Igbo chief in what is now part of southeastern Nigeria, Equiano's first experience of slavery was from the other side because his father was rich enough to own slaves. However, whilst still a boy he was seized in a raid in 1753 and enslaved first in North America, then on the seas, and finally in the Caribbean. He saw at first hand all the brutality associated with slavery and faced many trials and dangers before managing to eventually buy his freedom. He settled in London, where he became the leading spokesman for the city's black community and created the 'Sons of Africa' to lobby for the abolition of the slave trade. He joined the Methodists and their leader John Wesley was one of many abolitionists who subscribed to enable the publication of his autobiography, *The Interesting Narrative of the Life of Olaudah Equiano or Gustavus Vassa, the African, Written By Himself* in 1789.

I might say my sufferings were great; but when I compare my lot with that of most of my countrymen, I regard myself as a particular favourite of heaven, and acknowledge the mercies of Providence in every occurrence of my life

Olaudah Equiano in his autobiography in 1789

Equiano's book is an amazing story of personal endurance and of economic and moral survival as he struggles to persuade white men to view him as a rational, intelligent human being. It caused a sensation, not just because of its powerful and graphic indictment of slavery but because of the quality of the writing from a black man, and it was subsequently published in other countries, including Russia, Germany, Holland, and the United States. It founded a new literary genre known as 'the slave narrative', personal stories of enslavement and emancipation. Famous examples of subsequent nineteenth-century slave narratives can be found listed in the further reading section of this book. Equiano's autobiography went out of circulation until a reprint in 1967. Since then it has been repeatedly published. It still generates controversy because not everyone approves of what he did once he became a free man. Some argue he sold out his African heritage in order to become as much like a white man as possible. Aspects of this debate will feature in some of what follows though it is not the main focus.

In recent years a record of Equiano's baptism was discovered in South Carolina dating from 1759 and it stated that he was born as a slave in America. This has led some historians, notably Vincent Caretta, to believe the book's account of his early life and kidnapping in Africa is just a fabrication drawn from what he had read and what he had heard. Other historians disagree and point out that eighteenth century slave baptism records are notoriously unreliable. They believe all other evidence points to the book being an accurate and totally truthful account of his life. Even if they are wrong, Equiano had plenty of opportunity to listen to first-hand experiences and his book is a very accurate and moving portrayal of the slave experience. His African name can be aptly translated as meaning 'when he speaks, others listen'.

I wish I could give you my pain just for one moment. Not to hurt you, but so that you could finally understand how much you hurt me

Anonymous

In Equiano's book and in many of the extracts from the writings of others you will find the word *negro* and it is perhaps worth explaining at this juncture how this word arose and why it is no longer used. The Portuguese and Spanish slave traders first used the word negro because it means 'black' and the French had their version, which was *negre*. Some old maps refer to West Africa as 'Negroland'. The British and Americans adopted the word, initially applying it to anyone whose skin was dark (including the native Americans) and to both males and females. Only very occasionally was the word *negress* used. From the eighteenth century onwards negro was considered the normal word to use for people of

THE TRADE FROM A SLAVE'S PERSPECTIVE

Above: an eighteenth-century portrait said to be that of Olaudah Equiano in Royal Albert Memorial Museum in Exeter, although it has been suggested it may be of another famous African, Ignatius Sancho. Left: portrait of Equiano with his daughter Joanna by Mervyn Weir for cover of Joanna's biography by Dr Angela Osborne in 2007.

black African origin. Hence its use by Equiano. A Negro Code produced in South Carolina in 1848 said the word should not be used to cover the free inhabitants of Africa, such as the Moors and Egyptians, and so it was implied that a negro was not just black but an inferior African for whom enslavement was natural. Nevertheless, negro remained for most people a totally accepted word until the 1960s. It was considered to be less offensive than using either the word *black* or the word *coloured* (a word coined originally for slaves who had been freed).

> ***If thought corrupts language, language can also corrupt thought***
> George Orwell, journalist, novelist and critic in his novel *1984* in 1946

A variation on negro was the word *niger or nigger* because the Latin for black is *niger*. It was first used by the English in the sixteenth century and by the nineteenth century it was often used instead of negro, particularly by the less well-educated. It became the word used if you wanted to imply an African or African-American was inferior. This can be seen in Mark Twain's famous novel *Huckleberry Finn*, written in 1884, because Twain, who opposed racism, always used the word negro but he has a number of his characters use the word nigger. By the twentieth century nigger had become such a word of abuse in the United States and elsewhere that its use, even for the sake of realism, was understandably hated by anyone wanting to see racial equality. As early as 1940 the African-American writer Langston Hughes was saying it was a word that required banning:

> Used rightly or wrongly, ironically or seriously, of necessity for the sake of realism, or impishly for the sake of comedy, it doesn't matter. Negroes do not like it in any book or play whatsoever, be the book or play ever so sympathetic in its treatment of the basic problems of the race. Even though the book or play is written by a Negro, they still do not like it. The word nigger, you see, sums up for us who are coloured all the bitter years of insult and struggle in America.

'The N-word' is now declared taboo and it has been a source of intense controversy that a variant of it – *nigga* – is used within rap and hip-hop. There it is used to express black solidarity and affection but only if the word is sung by black people. If a white person sings the song and uses the word it is regarded as offensive. Most organisations that are concerned with civil rights and racial integration regard the use of the word in this way as most undesirable.

After the Second World War the use of the word negro globally declined as more and more African independent nations were established. It became much more common to refer to which country a person came from (Nigerians, Kenyans, Ugandans, South Africans, etc) and to use the collective continental word *Africans*. However, within the United States the word negro was still being used widely in the 1960s (as can be seen, for example, in the speeches of the civil rights activist Martin Luther King). Nevertheless, by then its use was being seriously questioned. Some felt it was associated too much with slavery and segregation and a second-class status. It was therefore suggested it would be preferable in America to replace the word negro with *Afro-American,* a word that had been in use since 1831 to describe Americans of African descent. Those who had come to America from the West Indies could use *Afro-Caribbean*. It was felt this terminology better expressed the dual background of most black Americans and many accepted the change. Alongside this change in terminology many black Americans in the 1960s and 1970s adopted the hairstyle that became known as 'the afro'. This was a conscious rejection of the hairstyles favoured by white Americans and which until then negroes had been largely copying.

However, the Muslim civil rights activist Malcolm X urged black Americans to reject American culture altogether and to reassert their racial pride by describing themselves as *blacks*. After his assassination in 1965, a black power movement emerged and the slogan was created 'Black is beautiful' to end once and for all the view that black people were somehow inferior. As a consequence many did not accept the word Afro-American. The situation changed again when the very militant behaviour of the Black Panther movement in the early 1970s led to a decline in support for the black power movement as a whole. In 1988 the popular civil rights activist Jesse Jackson suggested whilst he was running for the American presidency that it would be preferable to start using the words *African-American* and *African-Caribbean* to put the emphasis back onto integration rather than on black and white separation. It was an apt choice because the first ever use of the word African-American was in 1783 during the American War of Independence and it was used in a document designed to encourage Africans to embrace the new nation that was being created. Jackson's suggestion proved very popular, although some preferred not to abandon the word black and chose to describe themselves as *Black Americans*. By 1997 the United States was offering Americans with an African heritage the option of declaring themselves negro, black, or African American in any future census.

Since then the number of Americans wanting to call themselves negro has steadily declined and the 2020 United States census has ceased to even offer the word. It uses only the category of *Black or African American* for 'Americans with an African heritage'. Surveys have shown that African-American has become the preferred term for historical and formal public usage, but that Black American remains the far more popular term in a social setting with one poll suggesting that 78% of black Americans prefer to be called 'black' rather than 'African American'. It has become apparent in the last decade or so that for some black Americans the reference to an Africa past has become an unhelpful distraction, and they would like to see African-American applied only to those Americans who have an African parent or parents (as was the case with the ex-president Barrack Obama). A good example of this approach can be found in the article *Black American or African American,* written in 2011 by a medical consultant in Atlanta, Melody McCloud:

> It is my position—and one shared my millions—that the term 'African-American' is a misnomer when describing native-born Black Americans. If you were born in New York... New York is in America, not in Nigeria or Nairobi. If you were born in Kentucky, that's not in Kenya, and Boston isn't in Botswana... I proudly tell people I am an American... Did my ancient African ancestors come to America by force over 400 years ago? Absolutely. And it was an atrocious crime of mammoth proportions. But since then, all of my ancestors were born on American soil. They worked this soil. Their blood, sweat and tears watered this soil, and I was born on this soil... I'm an American. A Black American. Period... If you were born in America, you don't have to adopt, or assimilate to, the American way-of style, language, manners and public decorum. It is naturally yours. Embrace it. Love it. Succeed in it... Looking back 400 years isn't going to advance your position today.

However, others Americans fear that to cease any reference to Africa would simply encourage people to forget what happened, and they say it is vital that injustice and cruelty on such a scale should not be forgotten.

Africa to me... is more than a glamorous fact. It is a historical truth. No man can know where he is going unless he knows exactly where he has been and exactly how he arrived at his present place
    Maya Angelou, African-American poet and memoirist quoted in *New York Times* in April 1972 after exploring her African roots

---

1.
How Equiano Became A Slave

People say that slaves were taken from Africa. This is not true. People were taken from Africa and were made into slaves

Twentieth- century poster

In his autobiography Equiano states he was born in 1745 in the Igbo village of Essaka in the kingdom of Benin (which today is southeastern Nigeria) and be begins his story with an account of how he was kidnapped and enslaved at the age of ten. Modern research has pinpointed that he arrived in Britain in December 1754 so his memory must be adrift – either he was younger than ten when he was kidnapped or he was born earlier than he says. Such an error is hardly surprising at a time when people often did not know their precise age. Here is his account:

> I had never heard of white men nor of Europeans nor of the sea… My father … [who was one of the elders or chiefs of my tribe had] many slaves… As I was the youngest of the sons, I became, of course, the greatest favourite with my mother, and was always with her; and she used to take particular pains to form my mind. I was trained up from my earliest years in the art of war; my daily exercise was shooting and throwing javelins… One day… all our people were gone out to their works as usual, and only I and my dear sister were left to mind the house. Two men and a woman got over our walls, and in a moment seized us both, and, without giving us time to cry out, or make resistance, they stopped our mouths, and ran off with us into the nearest wood. Here they tied our hands, and continued to carry us as far as they could, till night came on, when we reached a small house, where the robbers halted for refreshment, and spent the night. We were then unbound, but were unable to take any food; and, being quite overpowered by fatigue and grief, our only relief was some sleep, which allayed our misfortune for a short time. The next morning we left the house, and continued travelling… My sister and I were then separated… It was in vain that we besought them not to part us; she was torn from me, and immediately carried away, while

I was left in a state of distraction not to be described. I cried and grieved continually; and for several days I did not eat any thing but what they forced into my mouth. At length, after many days travelling, during which I had often changed masters, I got into the hands of a chieftain… [who] used me extremely well… This first master of mine, as I may call him, was a smith, and my principal employment was working his bellows… [After I tried to escape and return home] I was again sold. I was now carried to the left of the sun's rising, through many different countries… While I was journeying thus through Africa, I acquired two or three different tongues.

In this manner I had been travelling for a considerable time, when one evening, to my great surprise, whom should I see brought to the house where I was but my dear sister! As soon as she saw me she gave a loud shriek, and ran into my arms—I was quite overpowered: neither of us could speak; but, for a considerable time, clung to each other in mutual embraces, unable to do any thing but weep… When these people knew we were brother and sister they indulged us together; and the man, to whom I supposed we belonged, lay with us, he in the middle, while she and I held one another by the hands across his breast all night; and thus for a while we forgot our misfortunes in the joy of being together: but even this small comfort was soon to have an end; for scarcely had the fatal morning appeared, when she was again torn from me for ever! I was now more miserable, if possible, than before.

Enslavement in Africa was sometimes a punishment for crimes committed but it was more commonly a product of inter-tribal rivalry. It was deemed perfectly reasonable to kidnap men, women, and children from other tribes and to enslave entire defeated villages. Equiano was kidnapped so he could be sold to another tribe. Historians think the smith who bought him may have belonged to the Akwa, who were well-known for working in brass. His attempted escape led to him being handed over to slave traders who then took him much further away from his home. Almost all the long distance slave traders were Muslims. That is not surprising because the prophet Muhammad was a slave owner and trader and, just as there are passages in the Old Testament that endorse slavery, so there are passages in the Quran that do so. The Muslims provided slaves not just for Africans but for markets in Europe, the Middle East, the Arabian peninsula, the Persian Gulf, and India. To meet demand they obtained slaves from many parts of the world and so not all of the enslaved were black. For example, they drew white slaves from the Ukraine and the Caucasus. This book does not examine this wider Islamic slave trade but its existence should not be forgotten.

> *The slave trade is the ruling principle of my people. It is the source and the glory of their wealth... the mother lulls the child to sleep with notes of triumph over an enemy reduced to slavery*
>
> King Ghezo, nineteenth century ruler of Dahomey

There was African resistance to the Muslim slave traders but it is difficult to judge its scale because of the lack of records. Before returning to Equiano's account it is worth mentioning one case that is recorded because it relates to an African resistance leader sold to a Bristol slaver. His name was Tomba and he was a leader of the Baga people, who lived in a swampy coastal region of what is now Guinea in West Africa. 'Baga' means 'people of the seaside'. In 1720 Tomba formed a resistance movement to the slave traders who had been raiding his people and he led attacks on their homes. After a few months he was defeated and the Muslims took him and others to Bance Island in the Sierra Leone River where there was a slave-trading fort built by the Royal African Company as a depot to which the enslaved could be brought for sale. Such depots were created all along the coasts of the lands that now comprise Ghana, The Gambia, Nigeria, Cameroon, Benin and Angola, because Europeans rarely went on slave hunts. They preferred to either purchase what they wanted from local chiefs or to tap into the Muslim slave market.

We know about Tomba because he attracted the interest of a Royal Navy surgeon called John Atkins, whose ship was in the island's large natural harbour:

> I could not help taking notice of one fellow among the rest, of a tall, strong male... [who had a] bold, stern aspect. As he imagined we were viewing them with a design to buy, he seemed to disdain his fellow slaves for their readiness to be examined, and... scorned to look at us, refusing to rise or stretch out his limbs as the [slave] master commanded... [He was given] an unmerciful whipping... with a cutting manatee strip... all of which the negro bore with magnanimity, shrinking very little, and shedding a tear or two, which he endeavoured to hide as though ashamed... All the company grew curious at his courage.

Tomba had been bought from the Muslims by John Leadstone, better known as 'Captain Crackers', a former official of the Royal African Company turned pirate. He sold him and others to the Bristol slaver Richard Harding, the captain of the *Robert*. What happened next was later told to Atkins when he met up with Harding months later. Still resistant to his fate, Tomba persuaded a female slave to release him and another slave from their chains just before the *Robert* set sail and she procured an axe for him. He murdered two sailors before the alarm was raised and he injured a third before Harding, brought on deck by the noise of the struggle, managed to knock him out with an iron hand-spike. Because he knew he could get a good price for Tomba and the other attempted escapee, Harding did not kill them. Instead he had them whipped and 'scarified' (i.e. scarred using a knife). However, to deter further resistance, he brutally tortured and slaughtered the less valuable woman and two poor quality slaves who were judged to have helped her. According to Atkins:

> He sentenced them to cruel deaths, making them first eat the heart and liver of one of ... [those they had] killed. The woman he hoisted up by her thumbs [and] whipped and slashed her with knives before the other slaves till she died.

No-one knows what subsequently happened to Tomba but it is highly unlikely that his story had a happy ending.

My back is thick with scars for protesting my freedom
Solomon Northrup, African-American author of *Twelve Years A Slave* in 1853

Most African chiefs were keen to obtain European manufactured goods and so they were happy to either supply the Muslim slave traders or, if they lived near the coast, deal direct with the white captains of European slave ships. In 2009 the Civil Rights Congress of Nigeria very controversially tried to recognise the African role in the slave trade. It sent out a letter to tribal chiefs asking them to issue an apology:

> We cannot continue to [just] blame the white men...In view of the fact that the Americans and Europe have accepted the cruelty of their roles... it would be logical, reasonable and humbling if African traditional rulers ... [could also] accept blame and formally apologise to the descendants of the victims.

The response was very mixed. Some agreed, some refused, and some saw no

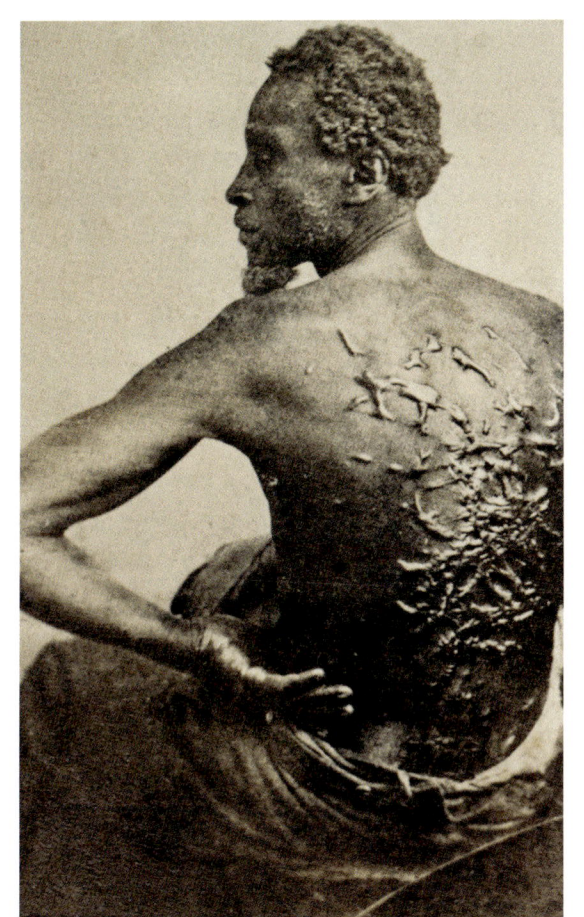

Whipping, scarifying and branding were common punishments. Dogs were used to hunt down escaped slaves. Left: photo of scarred back of Peter Gordon, an African American slave, sent by an army surgeon to his brother in 1863 with these words: 'I have seen hundreds of such sights—so they are not new to me; but it may be new to you. If you know of any one who talks about the humane manner in which the slaves are treated, please show them this picture.'

reason to pander to the angst of descendants of the enslaved abroad when it was not a burning issue among their own people.

There were, of course, a few African leaders who resisted supplying slaves to the Europeans. A notable example was Nzinga Mbande, the queen of the Ndongo in Angola. She fought a long war of resistance against the Portuguese demand for slaves between 1623 and 1657. However, her resistance did not have a happy ending. Towards the end of that conflict she had to seek Dutch military aid. The price of that aid was for her to provide them with slaves. The European practice of offering guns as part of the payment for slaves made selling almost irresistible because a chief who possessed guns was far better placed to defeat his rivals. The deaths caused by the resulting inter-tribal conflict are impossible to quantify but they must run into many thousands. Once a chief had commenced providing slaves it became difficult to resist the opportunity to acquire other manufactured goods from Europe. Greed then overcame any moral scruples. Bristol provided its share of the guns required. That is why a 1790 business card of the Bristol gunmaker, William Heard, depicted not just an Englishman with a gun but also an African.

I verily believe that the far greater part of wars, in Africa, would cease, if the Europeans would cease to tempt them, by offering goods for sale
John Newton, former slave ship captain in *Thoughts Upon the African Slave Trade* in 1788

Once Equiano was in the hands of Muslim slave traders escape was virtually impossible. The enslaved were usually forced to march tied together in a line and sometimes they were given ivory or other trading goods to carry on their heads. These lines were known as 'coffles' from an Arabic word for 'caravan'. Up to forty of the enslaved would be joined either by light chains or by a rope with a leather thong tied round every neck. Sometimes a slave trader would take extra measures for those judged likely to attempt an escape. For example, he might join two slaves together by securing the right leg of one slave and the left leg of another in a pair of irons. This meant they could not take any individual action and they could only walk if they held up the fetters that bound them with a provided cord. Another method was to make the enslaved Africans wear very heavy shackles. Denied the opportunity to run away, it was not uncommon for the enslaved to eat dirt in the hope of killing themselves. In 1797 the Scottish explorer Mungo Park travelled for five hundred miles across Africa with a coffle and was deeply shocked at the way the enslaved were treated and very surprised

How Equiano Became A Slave

Top: Engraving of a slave raid on African village printed in Rene Claude Geoffrey de Villeneuve's book 'Africa' 1814. Above: engraving of a coffle in 'The Last Journals of David Livingstone in Central Africa' 1874. Right: business card of Bristol gunmaker from c 1795 showing an African with one of his guns. This would have been bought with money obtained by providing slaves.

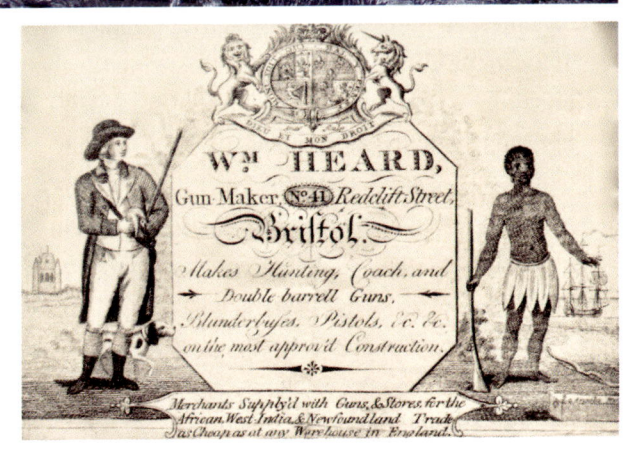

at their readiness to show him kindness:

> These poor slaves, amidst their own infinitely greater sufferings, would commiserate mine; and frequently, of their own accord, bring water to quench my thirst, and at night collect branches and leaves to prepare me a bed in the wilderness.

I didn't know I was a slave until I found out I couldn't do the things I wanted
Narrative of the Life of Frederick Douglass, an American slave *published in 1845*

As the Muslims sold and acquired slaves as they travelled it was still not certain that Equiano would end up on the coast for sale to Europeans. He says after much travelling he was sold to a rich widow as a companion for her son and that she lived in a town called Tinmah, where he tasted coconuts for the first time. Some historians think this may be Teinma, a town on the delta of the Niger River not far from the port of Bonny, which was a major centre for providing slaves for the British slave trade. That part of the coast was known as the Bight of Biafra. Others disagree because Equiano records further extensive travelling after the widow changed her mind and resold him:

> All the nations and people I had hitherto passed through resembled our own in their manners, customs, and language: but I came at length to a country, the inhabitants of which differed from us in all those particulars… I came among a people who… [cooked] in iron pots, and [who] had European cutlasses and cross bows, which were unknown to us, and fought with their fists amongst themselves. Their women were not so modest as ours, for they ate, and drank, and slept, with their men… [In some places] the people ornamented themselves with scars, and likewise filed their teeth very sharp. They wanted sometimes to ornament me in the same manner, but I would not suffer them; hoping that I might some time be among a people who did not thus disfigure themselves…

> At last I came to the banks of a large river, which was covered with canoes, in which the people appeared to live with their household utensils and provisions of all kinds. I was beyond measure astonished at this, as I had never before seen any water larger than a pond or a rivulet: and my surprise was mingled with no small fear when I was put into one of these canoes, and we began to paddle and move along the river… Thus I continued to travel,

sometimes by land, sometimes by water, through different countries and various nations, till… I arrived at the sea coast.

> ***I have seen hundreds of escaped slaves, but I never saw one who was willing to go back and be a slave***
> Harriet Tubman who escaped from slavery in 1849 and helped others to escape

Equiano's account is a useful reminder that African culture was very varied. Across Africa hundreds of different languages were spoken and ethnic groups had different ways of dressing, eating, and living. Some lived in relatively simple villages and others in large towns and there was a rich variation of skills in working with wood, clay, leather, textiles, and metals. There is still a common misconception today that all enslaved Africans were uncivilised 'primitives' – a view that was promoted by the slave traders – but in various parts of his autobiography Equiano makes clear that his own tribe, the Igbos, were a civilised people. It is true that many African tribes engaged in practices that were cruel and barbaric but so too did Europeans at this stage. Indeed on the issue of slavery it can be argued that Africans had a superior approach to the Europeans because it was customary in many African cultures for the children of slaves to be automatically regarded as being free. Europeans did not do that.

It is also worth noting that Africa over the centuries had possessed its fair share of empires, ranging from the New Kingdom of Egypt that lasted over five hundred years to the powerful medieval kingdoms of Benin, Ghana, Benin, Mali and Songhai. The latter, which was at its peak between 1450 and 1580, had a very structured government, a developed currency, and traded extensively with Europe. It was the European demand for slaves that crippled the development of Africa not the alleged 'primitiveness' of its peoples.

> ***dis poem***
> ***shall speak of the wretched sea***
> ***that washed ships to these shores***
> ***of mothers crying for their***
> ***young swallowed up by the sea***
> Allan Hope (known as Mutabaruka) Jamaican poet in 1992

Equiano says his total journey involved six to seven months of travelling. Most historians believe that over the centuries millions must have died either travelling in the coffles or when they reached the coast. There was a high death rate at

It is not surprising that Equiano found those enslaved alongside him strange people. Over forty-five distinct ethnic groups, each with its own distinct culture, suffered at the hands of the slave traders. The largest number of those enslaved came from the Bakongo of Angola and the Congo, the Mande of Upper Guinea, the Gbe speakers of Togo, Ghana, and Benin, the Akan of Ghana and the Ivory Coast, the Wolof of Senegal and the Gambia , the Igbo of southeastern Nigeria, the Mbundu of Angola, the Yoruba of southeastern Nigeria, the Chamba of northern Nigeria and Cameroon, the Makua of Mozambique, and the Falani who were scattered across most of West Africa. The cultural differences are still evident below as these modern photographs illustrate.

the coastal forts because the enslaved had to be imprisoned until a European ship arrived and docked. The holding enclosures were known as 'barracoons' (after the Spanish word for a hut) and they were usually terribly crowded and insanitary. Equiano was lucky that there was a ship docked when he arrived at the coast so he did not have to spend any time in a barracoon:

> The first object which saluted my eyes when I arrived on the coast was the sea, and a slave ship, which was then riding at anchor, and waiting for its cargo. These filled me with astonishment, which was soon converted into terror when I was carried on board. I was immediately handled and tossed up to see if I were sound by some of the crew; and I was now persuaded that I had gotten into a world of bad spirits, and that they were going to kill me. Their complexions differing so much from ours, their long hair, and the language they spoke (which was very different from any I had ever heard), united to confirm me in this belief.

Most of the enslaved were terrified because they had never seen a white man before and they were unable to speak the language of the white traders. Various accounts indicate that it was normal for rumours to circulate among the enslaved about why the white men might want to obtain so many black people. One suggestion was that the white men made gunpowder out of their ground bones, but the most common belief was that the white men were cannibals. This view was reinforced by the Africans witnessing the white men drinking wine. They assumed the red liquid was blood. Equiano says he was examined and that was normal practice. Europeans only bought slaves if they judged they were worth having. It was normal practice to strip each individual naked so that the inspection process could be thorough. Many accounts indicate that purchasers often used such examinations as an opportunity to grope the female slaves.

Alexander Falconbridge, a surgeon on slave ships from Bristol, wrote this about the examination process:

> When the negroes whom the black traders have to dispose of are shown to the European purchasers, they first examine them relative to age. They then minutely inspect their persons, and inquire into their state of health; if they are inflicted with any infirmity, or are deformed, or have bad eyes or teeth, if they are lame, or weak in the joints, or distorted in the back, or of slender make, or are narrow in the chest; in short, if they have been afflicted in any manner, so as to render them incapable of much labour, they are rejected.

Left: Fort at Bance Island in the Sierra Leone River by J.Corry 1805. Below: 19th century drawing of a barracoon and an example of the forts that can still be seen today. Bottom: 18th century map of the slave forts along the African coast.

It is estimated that between 50% and 66% of those brought to the coast for sale were rejected. What happened to them is largely a matter of surmise but Falconbridge records instances where the slave providers simply beheaded the unwanted slaves in front of the captain.

The measure of a man is what he does with power
  Attributed to Pittacus of Mytiene, a Greek general in the sixth-century B.C.E.

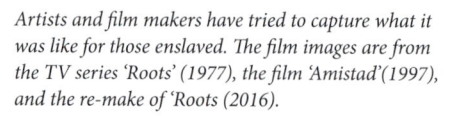

Artists and film makers have tried to capture what it was like for those enslaved. The film images are from the TV series 'Roots' (1977), the film 'Amistad' (1997), and the re-make of 'Roots (2016).

2.
HOW EQUIANO WAS TAKEN TO BARBADOS

Alas! I had not then learned the measure of 'man's inhumanity to man' nor to what limitless extent of wickedness he will go for the love of gain
  Solomon Northup, African-American author of *Twelve Years A Slave* in 1853

Equiano does not name the ship that took him away from Africa but the historian Vincent Caretta has suggested it may have been the *Ogden* under the command of a captain called Walker. If so, he travelled on a ship from Liverpool rather than from Bristol. The *Ogden* held 243 slaves. Equiano vividly recounts the terror he experienced on first boarding his ship and waiting for it to set sail:

> When I looked round the ship… [I] saw a large furnace or copper boiling, and a multitude of black people of every description chained together, every one of their countenances expressing dejection and sorrow… Quite overpowered with horror and anguish, I fell motionless on the deck and fainted. When I recovered a little I found some black people about me, who I believed were some of those who brought me on board, and had been receiving their pay; they talked to me in order to cheer me, but all in vain. I asked them if we were not to be eaten by those white men with horrible looks, red faces, and loose hair. They told me I was not; and one of the crew brought me a small portion of spirituous liquor in a wine glass; but, being afraid of him, I would not take it out of his hand. One of the blacks therefore took it from him and gave it to me, and I took a little down my palate, which, instead of reviving me, as they thought it would, threw me into the greatest consternation at the strange feeling it produced, having never tasted any such liquor before. Soon after this the blacks who brought me on board went off, and left me abandoned to despair. I now saw myself deprived of all chance of returning to my native country…
>
> In a little time after, amongst the poor chained men, I found some of my own nation, which in a small degree gave ease to my mind. I inquired of these what was to be done with us; they gave me to understand we were to

be carried to these white people's country to work for them... I asked how the vessel could go? they told me they could not tell; but that there were cloths put upon the masts by the help of the ropes I saw, and then the vessel went on; and the white men had some spell or magic they put in the water when they liked in order to stop the vessel. I was exceedingly amazed at this account, and really thought they were spirits... While we stayed on the coast I was mostly on deck; and one day, to my great astonishment, I saw one of these vessels coming in with the sails up.

The fact he was allowed on deck indicates he must have been very young – perhaps only seven or eight years old. The worst was yet to come. Most of the British slave traders crammed as many Africans as they could into their ships for the journey to the Caribbean. This process was called 'tight packing'. Each African adult male was allocated a space that was about eighteen inches wide and they were forced to lie on their backs with their heads resting on another's legs. There was often barely more than two or three foot space above them because another tier of slaves was placed above them on racks. This meant there was no standing space except in the actual entrance to the hold. Women and boys were given even less space, although sometimes, as in Equiano's case, they were permitted more time on deck. In the case of the women this made them vulnerable to being raped by the sailors unless the captain objected because it lowered their sale value.

With our ships, the great object is, to be full. When the ship is there, it is thought...she should take as many as possible. The slaves lie close to each other, like books upon a shelf
John Newton: hymn writer and ex-slave trader in *Thoughts Upon the African Slave Trade in 1788*

Equiano's response to being taken down into the hold was to wish he was dead:

I was not long suffered to indulge my grief; I was soon put down under the decks, and there I received such a salutation in my nostrils as I had never experienced in my life: so that, with the loathsomeness of the stench, and crying together, I became so sick and low that I was not able to eat, nor had I the least desire to taste anything. I now wished for the last friend, death, to relieve me; but soon, to my grief, two of the white men offered me eatables; and, on my refusing to eat, one of them held me fast by the hands,

How Equiano Was Taken To Barbados

Below: the famous eighteenth-century drawing which first tried to show how little space was given to slaves. Left: a reconstruction in Charles Wright Museum of African American History in Detroit showing how a bunk level was often used so more slaves could be carried. The bottom picture is of a model of a slave shop at the Smithsonian showing how the slaves were normally kept in the level immediately below the deck. This level was above the hold, which contained supplies and other cargo.

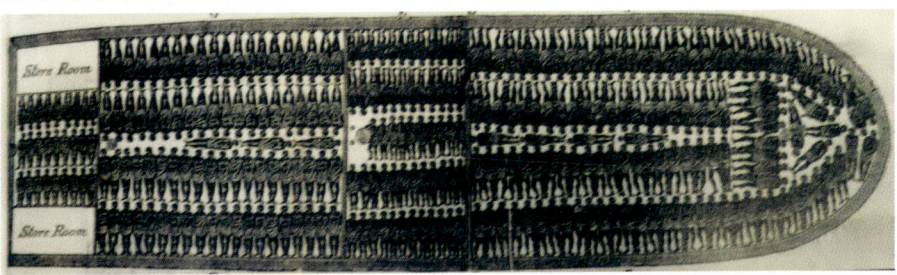

and laid me across I think the windlass, and tied my feet, while the other flogged me severely. I had never experienced any thing of this kind before; and although, not being used to the water, I naturally feared that element the first time I saw it, yet nevertheless, could I have got over the nettings, I would have jumped over the side, but I could not; and, besides, the crew used to watch us very closely who were not chained down to the decks, lest we should leap into the water: and I have seen some of these poor African prisoners most severely cut for attempting to do so, and hourly whipped for not eating. This indeed was often the case with myself.

But still I feared I should be put to death, the white people looked and acted, as I thought, in so savage a manner; for I had never seen among any people such instances of brutal cruelty; and this not only shown towards us blacks, but also to some of the whites themselves. One white man in particular I saw, when we were permitted to be on deck, flogged so unmercifully with a large rope near the foremast, that he died in consequence of it; and they tossed him over the side as they would have done a brute. This made me fear these people the more; and I expected nothing less than to be treated in the same manner.

Equiano's comment about the ill-treatment of the crew is accurate and this will be looked at in a later chapter. Being permitted on deck for exercise was strictly limited for adults because of the understandable fear that the enslaved Africans might seek to escape or attempt to rebel. For the same reason they were usually kept chained together in pairs in the hold. The Bristol slave trader Isaac Hobhouse told one of his captains that it was vital to 'keep them shackled and hand bolted ' to prevent danger. The chains would gradually produce running sores because the transatlantic journey could take two to six months dependent on weather conditions. The heat was so intense below deck that the enslaved were usually kept naked. They were fed once a day with beans, corn, yams, rice and palm oil. Water was given more frequently to avoid death through dehydration from the heat. Those who tried to commit suicide by refusing to eat or drink were brutally force-fed, using a device called a 'speculum orum', which kept the mouth open. Some ships provided wooden tubs in which the enslaved could relieve themselves but most provided no toilet facilities. This was partly because of the cramped conditions but mainly because the enslaved had to be released from their fetters to access a tub. This meant it was normal for the Africans to have to lie in their urine and faeces and this resulted in the spread

How Equiano Was Taken To Barbados

Right: Reconstruction in Charles Wright Museum of African American History in Detroit showing 'tight-packing' with slaves forced to lie on their sides. Below: an early drawing showing the limited height space as well as the overcrowding. Below right: leg shackles used on ships. Bottom: A painting in Itau Cultural Institute, San Paulo, by Johann Rugendas based on a visit to a slave ship headed to Brazil in c 1830.

of amoebic dysentery.

> *A charnel stench, effluvium of living death*
> *spreads outward from the hold,*
> *where the living and the dead, the horribly dying,*
> *lie interlocked, lie foul with blood and excrement*
>   Robert Hayden, African-American poet in *Middle Passage* in *A Ballad of Remembrance* in 1966

The following extract is from the 1763 logbook of Captain William Miller, who worked for the Bristol slave merchant James Laroche. It recounts the impact of dysentery on his 'cargo' of 438 Africans on board a ship called *The Black Prince*. In it he uses the words 'victuals' for food, 'gripings' for stomach pains and 'fluxes' for severe diarrhoea in which blood is also passed, and he uses the phrase 'falls away' to describe significant weight loss:

> '*8 March*. One woman is very bad. Many of them [suffer] with purging and some falls away [because they are] not eating…
> *14 March*. The slaves fore and aft in both holds falls away very much although [they make] no visible complaint [and] eat their victuals very well…
> *1 April* The slaves still fall away and complain of gripings and fluxes…
> *10 April* Slaves is much worse and this dirty weather can't get them up [on deck] …
> *19 April* The slaves still complaining of griping and falls away…
> *29 April* Washed all the slaves fore and aft [for] the first time since we left the [African] coast.

By the time his ship reached Antigua on 7 May forty-four Africans had died and the rest were in a terrible state.

> *I think that in terms of hell on earth… [the Middle Passage] must have been as near as anyone ever comes*
>   Barry Unsworth, author of the Booker-prize winning novel *The Sacred Hunger* in 1992

This is Equiano's account of the conditions he experienced:

> When the ship we were in had got in all her cargo, they made ready with

many fearful noises, and we were all put under deck, so that we could not see how they managed the vessel… The stench of the hold while we were on the coast… [had been] intolerably loathsome… but now that the whole ship's cargo were confined together, it became absolutely pestilential. The closeness of the place, and the heat of the climate, added to the number in the ship, which was so crowded that each had scarcely room to turn himself, almost suffocated us. This produced copious perspirations, so that the air soon became unfit for respiration, from a variety of loathsome smells, and brought on a sickness among the slaves, of which many died…

This wretched situation was again aggravated by the galling of the chains… and the filth of the necessary tubs, into which the children often fell, and were almost suffocated. The shrieks of the women, and the groans of the dying, rendered the whole a scene of horror almost inconceivable. Happily perhaps for myself I was soon reduced so low here that it was thought necessary to keep me almost always on deck; and from my extreme youth I was not put in fetters. In this situation I expected every hour to share the fate of my companions, some of whom were almost daily brought upon deck at the point of death, which I began to hope would soon put an end to my miseries… Every circumstance I met with served only to… [show] the cruelty of the whites. One day they had taken a number of fishes; and when they had killed and satisfied themselves with as many as they thought fit… rather than give any of them to us to eat as we expected, they tossed the remaining fish into the sea again, although we begged and prayed for some as well as we could…

One day, when we had a smooth sea and moderate wind, two of my wearied countrymen who were chained together… preferring death to such a life of misery, somehow made through the nettings and jumped into the sea. Immediately another quite dejected fellow, who, on account of his illness, was suffered to be out of irons, also followed their example; and I believe many more would very soon have done the same if they had not been prevented by the ship's crew, who were instantly alarmed. Those of us that were the most active were in a moment put down under the deck, and there was such a noise and confusion amongst the people of the ship as I never heard before, to stop her, and get the boat out to go after the slaves. However two of the wretches were drowned, but they got the other, and afterwards flogged him unmercifully for thus attempting to prefer death to slavery.

> In this manner we continued to undergo more hardships than I can now relate, hardships which are inseparable from this accursed trade. Many a time we were near suffocation from the want of fresh air, which we were often without for whole days together. This, and the stench of the necessary tubs, carried off many.

Some slaves developed scurvy because of their restricted diet and it was not uncommon for other diseases, such as smallpox or measles, to spread, usually with fatal consequences. The crew did not like going among the stench-ridden 'cargo' so it was not uncommon for a dead slave to remain chained to a living slave for hours or sometimes days before his or her body was taken and thrown into the sea. Sharks, growing accustomed to being thus fed, learnt to follow the slave ships.

But, oh, the living look at you
with human eyes whose suffering accuses you,
whose hatred reaches through the swill of dark
to strike you like a leper's claw.
You cannot stare that hatred down
or chain the fear that stalks the watches
and breathes on you its fetid scorching breath;
cannot kill the deep immortal human wish,
the timeless will
>   Robert Hayden, African-American poet in *Middle Passage* in *A Ballad of Remembrance* in 1966

The constant fear that the Africans might rebel and seek to take over the ship was not without foundation. It is estimated that a revolt of some kind took place on at least one in every ten voyages across the Atlantic. Usually these were brutally suppressed but occasionally the slaves won. That happened in the case of a ship from Bristol called the *Marlborough* in October 1752. According to a newspaper account the rebellion occurred because its captain, Robert Codd, inadvisedly used twenty-eight of the 400 slaves on board to help navigate his ship, having been deceived by their civil behaviour into thinking it was safe to do so. However, it is more likely that he used a few slaves and they freed the rest because it would have been unheard of to release so many. The Africans managed to get hold of some weapons and they slaughtered or injured most of the ship's crew of forty-two. A survivor, John Harris, later recorded:

How Equiano Was Taken To Barbados

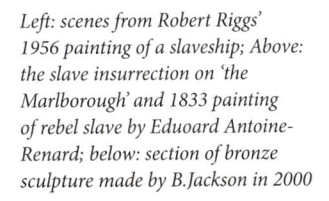

Left: scenes from Robert Riggs' 1956 painting of a slaveship; Above: the slave insurrection on 'the Marlborough' and 1833 painting of rebel slave by Eduoard Antoine-Renard; below: section of bronze sculpture made by B.Jackson in 2000

> They shot the doctor... and then struck him over the head with the butt end several times; but perceiving he was not quite dead, they... beat his brains out... Our chief mate was stabbed in the body, and the second mate's throat cut from ear to ear... [The third mate was] cut limb from limb... I was shot in my right arm and belly.

Codd, Harris and eleven others survived the attack by climbing up the rigging. It is not known how many Africans were killed in the fighting. Lack of food and water forced the surviving crew members to descend to the deck after two days. The Africans then cut Codd's belly open and tossed him and three others overboard to drown. The remaining nine sailors were kept alive so they could handle the ship. Four of the nine were just young boys. The *Marlborough* was not far off the African coast at the time of the rebellion and all the slaves wanted to get ashore as soon as possible so they could escape recapture. The leadership for the rebellion had come from Africans from the Gold Coast (now part of Ghana) and they began boarding the ship's small boats first. The other Africans, who were mostly from the kingdom of Bonny (now part of Nigeria), feared that these boats would not return for them and so also began clambering into them. As a consequence the overloaded boats began to sink and in the resulting chaos about a hundred of the slaves were drowned. When order was restored, it was agreed the sailors would sail the ship nearer to shore in order that the one remaining small boat could commence ferrying the remaining Africans ashore.

The strange ship movements of the *Marlborough* were witnessed by Thomas Jones, the captain of the *Hawk*, another ship from Bristol. He realised there must be a problem and so he pulled his ship alongside the *Marlborough* and saw that it had been captured by the slaves. He chose not to immediately engage in an open battle, probably because he hoped to retake the ship undamaged, thus making it more valuable as salvage. Instead he tried to board the ship by night. However, he and his men were unexpectedly repulsed by the Africans, who proved far more adept at using guns than Jones had expected. During the fighting Harris and another sailor managed to jump overboard and cross over to the *Hawk* before the two ships separated. The *Marlborough* then sailed off into the night manned by the remaining seven crew members and with an estimated 150 Africans still on board. What happened to her is not known, but most assume the ship was probably lost at sea.

The horrors of the Middle Passage were often glossed over by the slave traders and they excused their behaviour by saying that they were freeing the Africans from barbarity and introducing them, once landed in new countries, to Christianity. Christians who joined the abolition movement were incensed by this justification which, in the words of the famous novelist Harriet Beecher-Stowe, made out slavery to be 'a missionary institution, by which closely-packed heathen are brought over to enjoy the light of the Gospel'. In reality most plantation owners did not want to have their slaves converted to Christianity because it was harder to justify having slaves who were Christians. Some islands passed laws to make clear that no slave who became a Christian should expect that to lead to their freedom. This issue will be looked at later in more detail.

This slavery breeds ugly passions in man
Herman Melville, American novelist in *Benito Cereno* in 1856, a novella about a slave ship revolt

Today most white people register how horrific the Middle Passage was, but they tend to see it as something that happened a long time ago. Colin Palmer in the Smithsonian Institute's *Captive Passage* rightly makes clear that white people need to remember that for many black people it is still a hugely significant event:

> The Middle Passage was more than just a shared physical experience for those who survived it. It was and is a metaphor for the sufferings of the African peoples born of their enslavement, of severed ties, of longing for a lost homeland, of a forced exile. Its meaning cannot be derived solely from the tonnage of the slave ships, the cramped quarters of the human cargo, the grim catalogue of disease and death, or even the dramatic tales of resistance. It is a living and wrenching aspect of the history of the peoples of the African diaspora, an inescapable part of their present, impossible to erase or exercise. A gruesome reminder of things past, it is simultaneously a signifier of people's capacity to survive and to be refuse to be vanquished.

These pictures help show why some regard Christianity as hypocritical and paternalistic and 'the white man's faith'. Left: conversion used as an excuse for enslavement. Below: a black African shown dependent on white kindness and 'Uncle Tom' and other slaves submissive to abuse in the hope of heaven after life. Bottom: a painting of George Washington falsely showing happy slaves working on his estates in idyllic conditions.

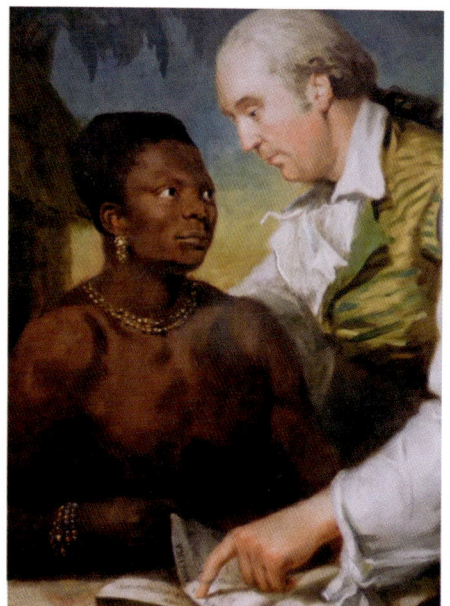

3.
Equiano's First Taste Of Life As A Slave

There was a lot of stigma attached to having been a slave. The shame was placed on the people who were enslaved, rather than the slavers
Hannah Durkin a lecturer at Newcastle University in *Slavery and Abolition* in 2020

Here is Equiano's account of what happened when his ship reached its Caribbean destination:

> At last we came in sight of the island of Barbados, at which the whites on board gave a great shout, and made many signs of joy to us. We did not know what to think of this; but as the vessel drew nearer we plainly saw the harbour, and other ships of different kinds and sizes; and we soon anchored amongst them off Bridge Town. Many merchants and planters now came on board, though it was in the evening. They put us in separate parcels, and examined us attentively. They also made us jump, and pointed to the land, signifying we were to go there. We thought by this we should be eaten by these ugly men, as they appeared to us; and, when soon after we were all put down under the deck again, there was much dread and trembling among us, and nothing but bitter cries to be heard all the night from these apprehensions, insomuch that at last the white people got some old slaves from the land to pacify us. They told us we were not to be eaten, but to work, and were soon to go on land, where we should see many of our country's people…

If he was on the *Ogden* it reached Barbados on 9 May 1754. The inspection process he describes was normal because it was not unknown for slave traders to try and disguise how ill the surviving slaves were when they reached their destination. For example, they would cover the wounds made by the chains with a paste and they would 'cork' slaves who had dysentery. For that reason buyers always subjected their potential purchases to a very close – and often humiliating – inspection. Those who were judged too ill were rejected and these were sometimes referred to as 'refuse slaves'.

The demand for slaves in Barbados and the other Caribbean islands was high not just because of the ever-increasing number of sugar plantations but also because of the high death rate. It is estimated that about 25% of the enslaved died within the first three years from tropical diseases and that the rest (the so-called 'seasoned' slaves) rarely lasted more than seven years. The mortality rate among the Europeans was even higher because they were more susceptible to tropical diseases. Being constantly surrounded by disease and death encouraged a 'life is cheap' attitude. There was also a relatively low birth rate among the enslaved. In part that was because the sugar plantation owners had a preference for male slaves (which meant they took fewer women) bit it was also that slaves were worked so hard that it reduced the sex drive. Only when the cost of purchasing slaves began to rise did some planters begin looking at breeding the slaves they required.

That, I decided, was what it meant to be a slave: your past didn't matter, in the present you were invisible and you had no claim on the future
　　　　　　　Lawrence Hill in award-winning novel *The Book of Negroes* in 2007

The new arrivals were soon taken on shore:

> Soon after we were landed, there came to us Africans of all languages. We were conducted immediately to the merchant's yard, where we were all pent up together like so many sheep in a fold, without regard to sex or age. As every object was new to me every thing I saw filled me with surprise. What struck me first was that the houses were built with stories, and in every other respect [they were] different from those in Africa: but I was still more astonished on seeing people on horseback. I did not know what this could mean; and indeed I thought these people were full of nothing but magical arts…
>
> We were not many days in the merchant's custody before we were sold after their usual manner, which is this: on a signal given (as the beat of a drum), the buyers rush at once into the yard where the slaves are confined, and make choice of that parcel they like best. The noise and clamour with which this is attended, and the eagerness visible in the countenances of the buyers,

serve not a little to increase the apprehensions of the terrified Africans... In this manner, without scruple, are relations and friends separated, most of them never to see each other again. I remember in the vessel in which I was brought over, in the men's apartment, there were several brothers, who, in the sale, were sold in different lots; and it was very moving on this occasion to see and hear their cries at parting... Why are parents to lose their children, brothers their sisters, or husbands their wives? Surely this is a new refinement in cruelty... [All the enslaved went] different ways, and I never saw one of them afterwards.

Yonder they do not love your flesh. They despise it. They don't love your eyes; they'd just as soon pick em out. No more do they love the skin on your back. Yonder they flay it. And O my people they do not love your hands. Those they only use, tie, bind, chop off and leave empty
     Toni Morrison, African-American author of Pulitzer-Prize winning novel
Beloved in 1987

Those new to buying and using slaves soon learnt to ignore whatever initial moral qualms they might have had about enslaving Africans. The one-time cost of purchasing a slave was much cheaper than paying someone a regular wage and, of course, any child born to a slave was automatically judged to be the property of the owner. The moral ambiguity of the slave owners can be seen in a poem called *Sugar Cane*, written in 1759 by James Grainger, a Scottish doctor who had settled on the island of St Kitts. The poem says it might be preferable to employ workers rather than slaves but then goes on to advise the reader how to choose the best slaves:

> Must thou from Afric reinforce thy gang! -
> Let health and youth their every sinew firm;
> clear roll their ample eye; their tongue be red;
> broad swell their chest; their shoulders should expand;
> not prominent their belly; clean and strong
> their thighs and legs, in just proportion rise.
> Such soon will brave the fervour of the clime...
> an useful servitude will long support.

It also describes how best to obtain maximum work from the enslaved in order to maximise one's profits. Dr Samuel Johnson, famous eighteenth-century creator

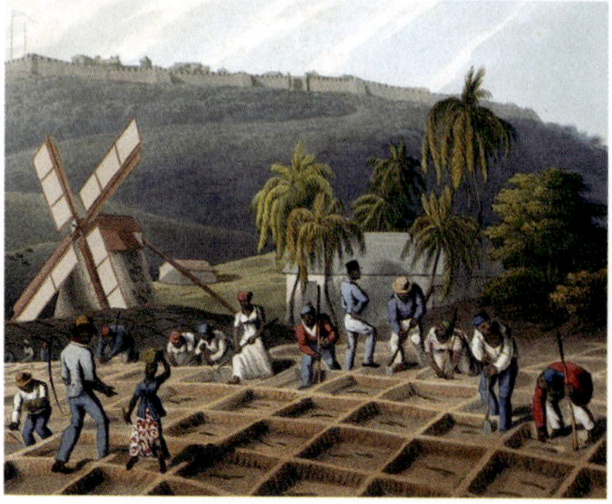

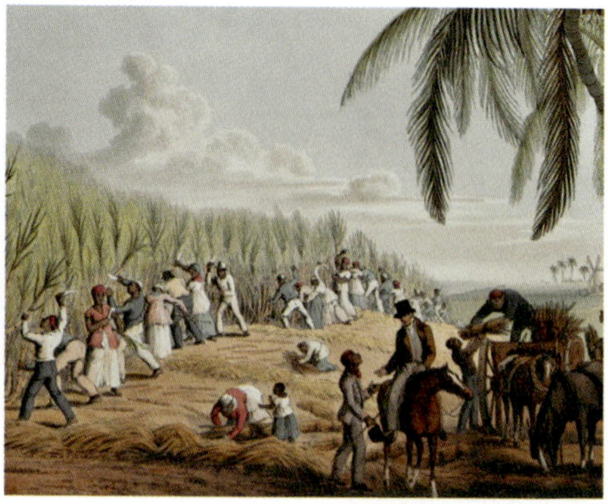

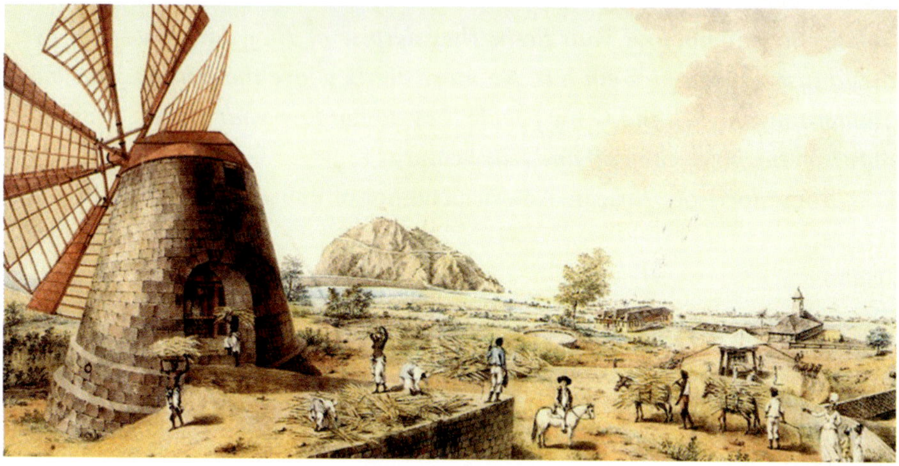

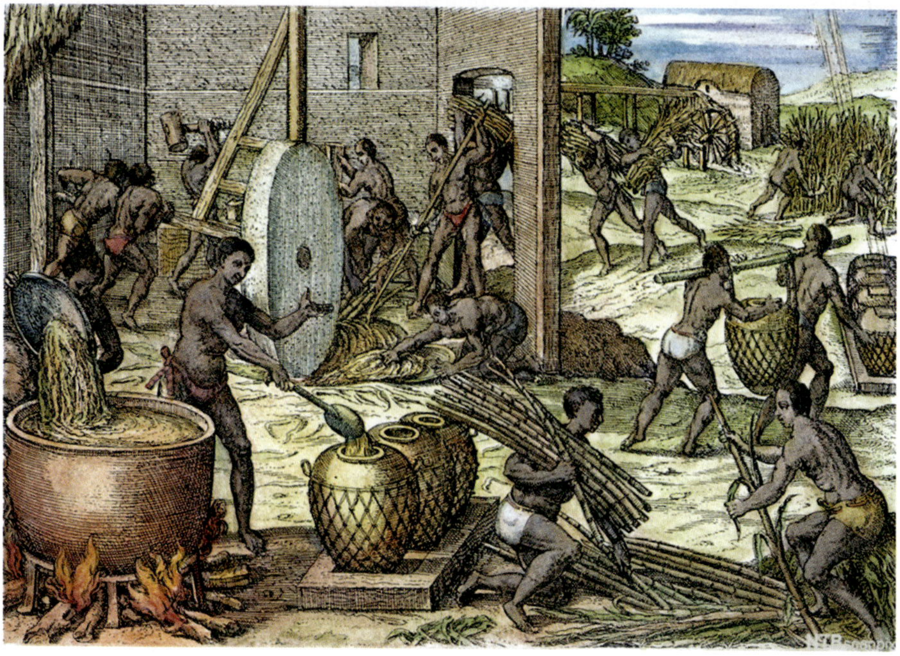

Equiano's First Taste Of Life As A Slave

Opposite page: slaves planting and cutting sugar cane in Antigua by William Clark 1823, bringing canes to a mill in Barbados by Agostino Brunias c 1795; and processing the cane to make sugar by Theodor de Bry 1595. Above: slaves working in tobacco shed by unknown artist c1670 and engraving of slaves producing tobacco in Virginia 1759. Right: an 1840 tobacco box designed by the abolitionist movement and nineteenth century Bristol trade cards advertising cigarettes by using images of African-Americans.

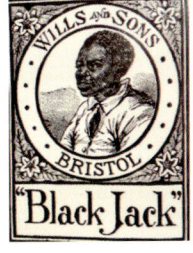

of the first English dictionary, could not help but note the hypocrisy of the poet, commenting that he was encouraging slaveowners to purchase slaves 'with the same indifference that a groom would give instructions for choosing a horse'. This was an apt analogy because it was not uncommon for masters to brand their newly purchased slaves in the same way as they did horses and cattle.

My natural elasticity was crushed, my intellect languished, the disposition to read departed, the cheerful spark that lingered about my eye died; the dark night of slavery closed in upon me; and behold a man transformed into a brute!
Narrative of the Life of Frederick Douglass, an American slave published in 1845

Equiano records how he was judged too ill to sell on Barbados:

> [I] and some few more slaves, that were not saleable amongst the rest, from very much fretting, were shipped off in a sloop for North America. On the passage we were better treated than when we were coming from Africa, and we had plenty of rice and fat pork. We were landed up a river a good way from the sea, about Virginia county.

It was normal for the slaves judged too old, too young, or too sick to be taken on to North America and Vincent Caretta has shown that a sloop called the *Nancy* left Barbados on 21 May 1754 with thirty-one slaves on board for Virginia . It is a popular misconception that most slaves were taken to the American colonies. Over a period of two hundred years around 400,000 slaves were sold to the colonies but that represents just between 4% and 5% of the total enslaved. Equiano was purchased by a plantation owner called Campbell. He vividly conveys how difficult it was to adjust to the strange new world in which he found himself:

> I was a few weeks weeding grass, and gathering stones in a plantation; and at last all my companions were distributed different ways, and only myself was left… I had no person to speak to that I could understand. In this state I was constantly grieving and pining, and wishing for death rather than any thing else… [When Mr Campbell was taken unwell] I was one day sent for to his dwelling house to fan him. When I came into the room where he was I was very much affrighted at some things I saw, and the more so as I had seen a black woman slave as I came through the house, who was cooking the dinner, and the poor creature was cruelly loaded with various kinds of iron

machines. She had one particularly on her head, which locked her mouth so fast that she could scarcely speak and [she] could not eat nor drink. I was much astonished and shocked at this contrivance, which I afterwards learned was called the iron muzzle.

Soon after I had a fan put into my hand, to fan the gentleman while he slept; and so I did indeed with great fear. While he was fast asleep I indulged myself a great deal in looking about the room, which to me appeared very fine and curious. The first object that engaged my attention was a watch which hung on the chimney... I was quite surprised at the noise it made, and was afraid it would tell the gentleman any thing I might do amiss. And when I immediately after observed a picture hanging in the room, which appeared constantly to look at me, I was still more affrighted, having never seen such things as these before... In this state of anxiety I remained till my master awoke, when I was dismissed out of the room, to my no small satisfaction and relief for I thought that these people were all made up of wonders. In this place I was called Jacob; but on board... [the ship I had been] called Michael.

A slave must move by the will of another, hence the necessity of terror to coerce his obedience
> Jamaican plantation owner in 1763 cited in the International Slavery Museum in Liverpool

The American colonists had a reputation for being more humane towards slaves than the Caribbean plantation owners. However, as Equiano's account of the cook forced to wear an iron muzzle shows, they had no compunction about resorting to cruelty for even the tiniest offence or mistake. The profit margins for producers of tobacco were not high and some historians argue this often led producers to vent their frustrations on their slaves by using increasingly barbarous punishments. Of course to the outside world the plantation owners constantly projected a false image of happy slaves singing and dancing. In the nineteenth century African Americans were to develop what became known as 'negro spirituals'. These were more aptly described as 'sorrow songs' by the African-American writer William Du Bois. By using Biblical imagery that often centred on the story of Moses the slaves were able to express their desire for escape and freedom. A song like *Michael Rowed the Boat Ashore* was not just about ending an unhappy existence by dying and crossing the River Jordan to have a better life with Jesus. It was also a symbol of crossing the river that marked the border between the slave states of the south and the free states of the north. Some experts believe that a number of the spirituals contain explicit instructions to slaves on what routes to take and how to avoid capture. Frederick Douglass, who wrote the most famous of all the nineteenth-century slave autobiographies, had this to say on the subject of slave-singing:

> Slaves sing most when they are most unhappy. The songs of the slave represent the sorrows of his heart; and he is relieved by them, only as an aching heart is relieved by tears… They were tones, loud, long and deep, breathing the prayer and complaint of souls boiling over with the bitterest anguish. Every tone was a testimony against slavery, and a prayer to God for deliverance from chains. The hearing of those wild notes always depressed my spirits, and filled my heart with ineffable sadness. The mere recurrence, even now, afflicts my spirit, and while I am writing these lines, my tears are falling. To those songs I trace my first glimmering conceptions of the dehumanising character of slavery… Those songs still follow me, to deepen my hatred of slavery, and quicken my sympathies for my brethren in bonds.

Through all the sorrow of the… songs there breathes a hope… that sometime, somewhere, men will judge men by their souls and not by their skins. Is such a hope justified?
William Du Bois, African-American civil rights activist in *The Souls of Black Folk* in 1903

Equiano's reference to his name being changed shows how it was entirely up to white people to decide what an African should be called. A change in ownership often produced a change in name and Equiano was to later acquire the very unusual name of 'Gustavus Vassa' from a subsequent owner. This was the name of a sixteenth-century king who had given Sweden its independence by defeating the Danes. To give a slave the name of a freedom fighter may have been a joke. Most owners provided their slaves with just ordinary names. The men were given names such as Ben, George, and Oscar, and the women names like Elizabeth, Susan, and Margaret. Very often the name choice was Biblical in origin – hence names like Paul, Ruth, Abraham, Rebecca, Daniel, Abigail, James, etc. At a time when a gentleman's education was centred around learning Latin, some gave their house slaves Roman names, such as Caesar, Venus, Pompey, Dido, Scipio, etc. If a slave was given a surname as well, then that was usually kept simple – something like 'Jones' or 'Smith'. Occasionally the surname might be derived from the place where the slave worked. Hence one of the slaves baptised in Bristol was given the name 'William Bristol'.

X is not my real name, but if you study history you'll find why no black man in the western hemisphere knows his real name. Some of his ancestors kidnapped our ancestors from Africa, and took us into the western hemisphere and sold us there. And our names were stripped from us and so today we don't know who we really are. I am one of those who admit it and so I just put X up there to keep from wearing his name

Malcolm X, African-American human rights activist in Oxford Union Debate in Dec 1964

All of this naming normally totally ignored the various African tribal languages, but the historian Pip Jones in her book *Satan's Kingdom* provides an exception among a group of slaves in Bristol from the Gold Coast (now Ghana). These were from the Fante tribe (a sub-group of the Akan people) but they were commonly known as Cormantins or Coromantese. The coastal fort from which they were purchased was Fort Cormantin and this was frequently used by Bristol slave ships. Gold Coast slaves were initially much in demand because they were good workers although that later changed as it became clear they were more prone to rebel. The case of the revolt on the *Marlborough* mentioned earlier is a typical example. The Coromantins tried to retain some link with their African past by giving each child born into slavery a tribal surname based on the day of the week in which he or she was born:

	Boy's name	*Girl's name*
Sunday	Quashy	Quasheba
Monday	Cudjo	Juba
Tuesday	Cubbenhah	Beneba or Benebo
Wednesday	Quaco	Cuba
Thursday	Quaw	Abba
Friday	Cuffee	Phibba
Saturday	Quamin	Mimba

Research into church records in Bristol have found references to the baptism of a child whose mother was named Benebo in 1704, to the baptism of a girl called Sarah Quasabrack (a variation on Quasheba) in 1720, to the burials of a Thomas Quaco in 1735 and a Phillis Quaco in 1740, and to the baptism of a John Coffee in 1747 (a possible variation on Cuffee unless the name was given to reflect the colour of his skin). A reference has also been found to a Henry Coffee, who was imprisoned in Newgate Prison in 1769. Later church records also list the baptism of Harriet Quyman (another possible variation) in 1785 and the burial of Joseph Cudjoe in 1803. The best documented individual is to a seaman called John Quaco. His marriage to a black wife called Penelope is recorded in St Michael's Church in 1743 and we have his application for a pension from the Seaman's Hospital Fund in1763. it describes him as 'a free man above one and twenty years and never out of employ'.

I am
the offspring of their sacrifice,
the fruit of a freedom tree
planted by the enslaved
and watered with the tears
of the shackled,
the daydream of slave minds drunk
with precious thoughts of liberty,
the answered prayer
of an oppressed people.
Because they were,
I am
Marcus Granderson, podcaster and writer in *Timestamp: Musings of an Introverted Black Boy* in 2019

It is worth saying that at varying times in his book Equiano compares the slavery he had grown up knowing in Africa with the white man's version. His main conclusion was that the Africans had been more benign until the Europeans had appealed to their greed. Those enslaved had not faced the erosion of their basic identity or the destruction of family life that was so much part of the white way of doing things. One of the things that he resented most was the way the British totally denied their slaves a voice. They were never listened to and any slave who spoke out was ruthlessly punished. Only in one respect did he think the white man's operation of the slave trade was 'better'. Black Africans were prepared to enslave their fellow blacks but he knew of no example where whites were prepared to enslave their fellow whites. He wrote: 'In this I thought they were much happier than we Africans.'

4.
Equiano's Life As A Sailor In The Royal Navy

To make a contented slave ... he must be made to feel that slavery is right; and he can be brought to that only when he has ceased to be a man
Narrative of the Life of Frederick Douglass, an American slave published in 1845

Equiano was soon resold because he caught the eye of Michael Henry Pascal, an officer in the Royal Navy. Igbo slaves were quite popular among the British because they had a reputation for being very loyal and affectionate if treated well and Pascal was on the look-out for a suitable slave that he could take back to London as a present to his relatives. Pascal had reached the rank of lieutenant whilst fighting against Spain in the War of Jenkin's Ear between 1739 and 1748 but peace had led to him and many other officers being placed on extended leave at half-pay. He had therefore taken up commercial shipping work and he was in Virginia as the captain of a merchant ship called the *Industrious Bee*:

> I was sent... to the place where the ship lay ready to sail for England. I now thought my condition much mended; I had sails to lie on, and plenty of good victuals to eat; and every body on board used me very kindly, quite contrary to what I had seen of any white people before; I therefore began to think that they were not all of the same disposition... By this time... I could smatter a little imperfect English; and I wanted to know as well as I could where we were going. Some of the people of the ship used to tell me they were going to carry me back to my own country, and this made me very happy... My captain and master named me Gustavus Vassa... by which I have been known ever since... The ship had a very long passage; and on that account [by the end of the voyage] we had very short allowance of provisions... The captain and people told me in jest they would kill and eat me; but I thought them in earnest, and was depressed beyond measure, expecting every moment to be my last.

> *If I say you are not free to associate with me, it also means that I am not free to associate with you. I might call you the slave but I am not less bound by the slavery I have created*
>
> Ray Anyasi, Nigerian author in *Broken Cloud* in 2015

It is clear from the above passage that there were times when his ignorance made him the butt of jokes and that caused both false hopes and false fears but sharing the dangers and hardships involved in a sea crossing also led to the formation of some inter-racial friendship. It made him realise, as he says, that not all white men were the same. Prejudice is based on assuming that a person can be judged by their skin colour or their hair texture or their language or whatever else is 'outward'. Equiano increasingly was to appreciate that what mattered more than anything else was a person's character, his or her morality. Being a good person was of more importance than being black or being white. Critical to him appreciating that was the friendship that developed between him and a young lad called Dick Baker, a friendship that was to endure until Dick's death in 1759:

> There was on board the ship a young lad who had never been at sea before, about four or five years older than myself: his name was Richard Baker. He was a native of America, had received an excellent education, and was of a most amiable temper. Soon after I went on board he showed me a great deal of partiality and attention, and in return I grew extremely fond of him. We at length became inseparable; and, for the space of two years, he was of very great use to me, and was my constant companion and instructor… Although this dear youth had many slaves of his own, yet he and I have gone through many sufferings together on shipboard; and we have many nights lain in each other's bosoms when we were in great distress. Thus such a friendship was cemented between us as we cherished till his death… an event which I have never ceased to regret, as I lost at once a kind interpreter, an agreeable companion, and a faithful friend; who… [had] a mind superior to prejudice; and who was not ashamed to notice, to associate with, and to be the friend and instructor of one who was ignorant, a stranger, of a different complexion, and a slave!

Modern research has shown that the *Industrious Bee* reached Falmouth on 14 December 1754. Docking there provided Equiano with his first taste of a new and fascinating world:

I have crossed an ocean
I have lost my tongue
From the roots of an old one
A new one has sprung
   Grace Nichols, Guyanese poet in The Fat Black Woman's Poems in 1984

Every heart on board seemed gladdened on our reaching the shore, and none more than mine. The captain immediately… [had brought] on board some fresh provisions… and our famine was soon turned into feasting… I was very much struck with the buildings and the pavement of the streets in Falmouth; and, indeed, any object I saw filled me with new surprise. One morning, when I got upon deck, I saw it covered all over with the snow that fell over-night. As I had never seen any thing of the kind before, I thought it was salt; so I immediately ran down to the mate and desired him, as well as I could, to come and see how somebody in the night had thrown salt all over the deck… I went to church; and having never been at such a place before, I was again amazed at seeing and hearing the service. I asked all I could about it; and they gave me to understand it was worshipping God, who made us and all things…

[I] soon got into an endless field of inquiries, as well as I was able to speak and ask about things… My little friend Dick used to be my best interpreter… and he always instructed me with pleasure… I was astonished at the wisdom of the white people in all things I saw; but was amazed at their not sacrificing, or making any offerings, and eating with unwashed hands, and touching the dead. I likewise could not help remarking the particular slenderness of their women, which I did not at first like; and I thought they were not so modest and shamefaced as the African women. [Having] seen my master and Dick employed in reading… I had a great curiosity to talk to the books, as I thought they did; and so to learn how all things had a beginning. For that purpose I have often taken up a book, and talked to it, and then put my ears to it, when alone, in hopes it would answer me; and I have been very much concerned when I found it remained silent.

Equiano's description of his first response to a world of books is touching. Some black critics have chosen to criticise him for being so obviously attracted to the white man's way of life. However, it is a natural human reaction to be fascinated by things that are new and, as he grew older, Equiano's basic take on life became that all cultures, including his own, had something to learn from other cultures. From subsequent passages in his autobiography it is evident that the 'wisdom of the white people' that he admired lay in their technical mastery as evidenced by so many amazing inventions, their creative diversity as displayed in their art, music, and literature, their philosophical thinking about human rights (especially the right to be free), and their religious ideas as found in the Bible.

Equiano goes on to say:

> My master lodged at the house of a gentleman in Falmouth, who had a fine little daughter about six or seven years of age, and she grew prodigiously fond of me; insomuch that we used to eat together, and had servants to wait on us... After I had been here a few days, I was sent on board of the ship; but the child cried so much after me that nothing could pacify her till I was sent for again. It is ludicrous enough, that I began to fear I should be betrothed to this young lady... [I] said I would not leave her... [but] one night I was sent on board the ship again and in a little time we sailed for Guernsey, where she was in part owned by a merchant, one Nicholas Doberry... My master placed me to board and lodge with one of his mates, who had a wife and family there... together with my friend Dick... [I tried] by washing [to] make my face... white, but it was all in vain.

Clearly a black African had a novelty value and at this stage Equiano found it difficult to assess what was intended for him. The last sentence is particularly moving because it shows just how much already his life had taught him to think being white was superior to being black. His belief that he might wash himself white may have been naive but it was a belief shared by others. Down in St Ives in Cornwall there is a former ale house named *Labour in Vain*. Tradition says that a black man was rescued from a shipwreck and taken to the pub where the townspeople tried to wash him white.

All blacks are white when born but presently change their colour
William Spavens, seaman in *Memoirs of a Seafaring Life* in 1796

In January 1755 Pascal was recalled into the Royal Navy to serve as a second or third lieutenant on *H.M.S. Roebuck*. This was a transport ship for moving troops and a major war was in the offing between Britain and France. This put an end

EQUIANO'S LIFE AS A SAILOR IN THE ROYAL NAVY

Top: Falmouth Harbour by J.W. Turner 1816. Above left: the plaque on the Labour In Vain house in St Ives. Above: etching of the execution of Admiral Byng in 1758. Left: the Guerin family home in Maze Hill in Greenwich as it is today. Below: a 1784 etching of St George's Hospital at Hyde Park Corner where Equiano was treated.

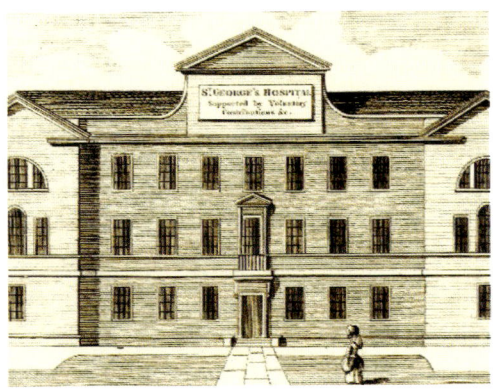

to any thought Pascal had of giving away Equiano to his relatives. Instead he had the mate from the *Industrious Bee* bring both him and Dick Baker to join him on the *Roebuck*. The ship's muster books show Baker and Equiano became crew members in June 1755. Baker is listed as Pascal's servant and Equiano as the servant of the ship's captain, Matthew Whitwell. All servants on ships were young boys. It was a way for the Navy to acquire and train its sailors at a time when recruitment was notoriously difficult. In the course of the Seven Years' War it is estimated 4,500 servants were trained to become sailors. They were usually promoted to the rank of an ordinary seaman when they were aged between seventeen and nineteen and to the rank of an able seaman when they were aged between eighteen and twenty-one. As a lieutenant Pascal would have been entitled only to bring on board one servant but a captain could bring on board four servants. By assigning Equiano to Whitwell Pascal was basically cheating the system. Servants were not paid – their salaries went to their master and, more importantly, so also did their share in prize money if the ship captured an enemy vessel. Almost certainly Pascal was claiming two wages with the connivance of the captain.

Ship records usually only provide a list of crew's names and not their ethnicity so the exact number of black sailors, both enslaved and free, on board Royal Navy ships is not known. However, it is generally accepted that the figure ran into thousands in the course of the eighteenth century. Most of the black sailors, as in Equiano's case, served in a low capacity, often as cabin boys or cooks. Interestingly the first ever slave narrative to be published was a pamphlet written by a naval cook in 1760. It was entitled *A Narrative of the Uncommon Sufferings and Surprising Deliverance of Briton Hammon, a Negro Man*. Briton Hammon was owned by a British army major-general called John Winslow, who was working in Massachusetts. In 1747 he hired out his slave to work as a cook on an American ship headed for Jamaica and he did not see him again until thirteen years later when, on boarding a ship in London, he discovered its cook was Hammon. In the intervening years Hammon had been shipwrecked, captured by Indians, and imprisoned by Spaniards before finding his way into the Royal Navy. Unlike Equiano, Hammon does not go into any detail about the ships on which he served, except to mention that he once contracted a serious fever and once was badly injured in the head and arm during a sea battle against the French. The main thrust of the pamphlet was his delight at being able to become his master's slave again. The 'surprising deliverance' in the title is a reference to his release from 'the dreadful captivity' of working for the Navy.

A sailor's life was both difficult and dangerous so perhaps it is understandable why Hammon saw a return to Massachusetts as preferable, but, in the modern era, slaves who appear to like their slavery are often decried. It is no accident that Hammon's narrative is often not mentioned in books on slavery. However, it is perfectly possible that Hammon had no choice but to return to his master once he was found. The publication of the pamphlet must have been funded by Winslow. Was that because he admired the survival power of Hammon and was delighted at his safe return or was it because he felt he could produce a piece of useful propaganda to show that slaves were safer and happier with their masters?

I learned that courage was not the absence of fear, but the triumph over it. I felt fear myself more times than I can remember, but I hid it behind a mask of boldness. The brave man is not he who does not feel afraid, but he who conquers that fear
    Nelson Mandela, President of South Africa in *Long Walk to Freedom* in 1994

Equiano was initially very happy with his new life in the Royal Navy:

> I was… [no longer] afraid of any thing new which I saw… My griefs too, which in young minds are not perpetual, were now wearing away; and I soon enjoyed myself pretty well, and felt tolerably easy in my present situation. There was a number of boys on board… [and] we were always together, and a great part of our time was spent in play. I remained in this ship a considerable time, during which we made several cruises, and visited a variety of places. Among others we were twice in Holland, and brought over several persons of distinction from it, whose names I do not now remember… One day, for the diversion of those gentlemen, all the boys were called on the quarter-deck, and were paired proportionably, and then made to fight; after which the gentleman gave the combatants from five to nine shillings each. This was the first time I ever fought with a white boy; and I never knew what it was to have a bloody nose before… [We fought for more than an hour and] I had a great deal of this kind of sport afterwards, in which the captain and the ship's company used very much to encourage me.

It was customary for those who were under the age of fourteen to be trained as 'powder monkeys' and Equiano says that he was so instructed. A powder monkey had to ferry gunpowder either in bags or cartridges from the ship's hold to the ship's cannon. This role was normally given to the young boys because they were small enough to move quickly round the limited space below deck and because their lesser height made them less vulnerable to sniper fire as their heads were below the level of the ship's gunwale. Being young and naive about the nature of war at sea, he longed to experience a sea-battle, but that did not happen. The main role of the *Roebuck* was transportation not battle and that explains why he mentions in his autobiography the ship on one occasion going up the Scottish coast as far as the Orkneys and then returning full of Scottish soldiers for the war effort. In the winter of 1756 the *Roebuck* sailed into Portsmouth just in time for the famous court martial of Rear-Admiral John Byng, Commander-in-Chief of the Mediterranean Fleet, for having failed to defend the British-held island of Minorca.

Slavery is so intolerable a condition that the slave can hardly escape deluding himself into thinking that he is choosing to obey his master's commands when, in fact, he is obliged to do so. Most slaves suffer from this delusion
            W.H. Auden : poet in *Writing* in *The Dyer's Hand* in 1973

Equiano says that Pascal was summoned to London 'for promotion' and, in his absence, he and Dick Baker were assigned to a sloop of war called the *Savage*, which was sent with other ships to help rescue Byng's flagship, *H.M.S. St George*, which had run aground. The *St George* was then anchored in Portsmouth Harbour as the venue for Byng's court-martial. Equiano says he saw the Admiral 'several times' during his trial, which lasted from 28 December 1756 to 27 January 1757. Byng was found guilty and, after a failed appeal, he was shot on the quarterdeck of *H.M.S. Monarch* in Portsmouth Harbour on 14 March in the presence of all the crews from other ships of the fleet in boats surrounding it. By then Pascal had been assigned to a new warship, *H.M.S. Preston*, which had just been built in Deptford. Equiano and Baker were summoned to London to join him on the new ship.

Illness caused Equiano's naval career to come to a temporary halt. Exposure to Britain's much colder climate had given him chilblains and the blisters on his feet suddenly became badly infected to the point where he could no longer stand up. Pascal asked his relatives, the Guerins, who had a house in Maze Hill in Greenwich, to look after him. Maynard Guerin was an attorney who acted as an agent for naval and military officers and it is thought that his wife was a sister of Pascal's mother. It soon became obvious that Equiano required hospitalisation and Maynard arranged for him to be treated at St George's Hospital. This was sited at Hyde Park Corner and it catered for around 250 patients in its fifteen wards. It was thought at one stage that Equiano might have to have a leg amputated. Whilst he was still recovering he fell seriously ill with smallpox and that required more weeks in the hospital. Fortunately he survived and his convalescence was then spent inside the Guerin's home. He was looked after by Maynard's two daughters, Elizabeth and Mary, who were then aged thirty-six and twenty-nine. It is thought these were the women for whom Equiano had been originally intended as a gift. They took the young boy under their wing and began teaching him to read and write and to understand some of the basics of Christianity. Their interest in him and his regard for them was to become lifelong.

My humanity is bound up in yours, for we can only be human together
Desmond Tutu, South African former Archbishop of Cape Town in *Dignity: In Honour of the Rights of Indigenous People* in 2010

Once he had fully recovered, Equiano rejoined Pascal and his friend Dick on *H.M.S. Preston* in the November of 1757. It sailed to Holland and, whilst it was there, Pascal was transferred onto the *H.M.S. Royal George*, the largest ship in the Royal Navy. Its size amazed Equiano:

> When I came on board of her I was surprised at the number of people, men, women, and children, of every denomination; and the largeness of the guns, many of them also of brass, which I had never seen before. Here were also shops or stalls of every kind of goods, and people crying their different commodities about the ship as in a town.

Dick Baker was not transferred and so he stayed on board the *H.M.S. Preston*. In January 1758 Pascal was appointed as sixth lieutenant on the *H.M.S. Namur*, which was then at Spithead. This was the flagship of the highly experienced Vice-Admiral Edward Boscawen, who had been given the task of organising a naval siege of the French fortress of Louisbourg on Cape Breton Island off the coast of Nova Scotia. Thus Equiano found himself part of a very large fleet headed for North America. On board the *Namur* was Britain's most famous military commander, General James Wolfe:

> [His] affability made him highly esteemed and beloved by all the men. He often honoured me, as well as other boys, with marks of his notice; and saved me once a flogging for fighting with a young gentleman.

The fleet, comprising forty men-of-war and 150 transport ships, reached Cape Breton in June 1758. The first task was to land the British soldiers on the island:

> My master had some part in superintending the landing; and here I was in a small measure gratified in seeing an encounter between our men and the enemy. The French were posted on the shore to receive us, and disputed our landing for a long time; but at last they were driven from their trenches, and a complete landing was effected. Our troops pursued them as far as the town of Louisbourg. In this action many were killed on both sides… I saw… a lieutenant… giving the word of command, and, while his mouth was open a musket ball went through it, and passed out at his cheek. I had that day in my hand the scalp of an Indian king, who was killed in the engagement: the scalp had been taken off by a Highlander.

The fortress surrendered after a two month siege. This victory effectively ended French power in North America and led to the subsequent campaign to capture Quebec in 1759. This was successful but at the cost of Wolfe's life.

On the voyage home back to Britain Equiano experienced his first sea fights and his skills as a powder monkey were put to the test. All this fighting experience made Equiano appreciate that white men were not masters of the universe. None entered a battle knowing whether he would be injured or not, whether he would survive or not, and white sailors and soldiers were just as subject to the other vagaries of life, such as sickness or barbarous punishment, as any black man. He says this made him less fearful of white men and more determined to put his faith in the God that the Guerin sisters had talked about.

The fleet arrived back in Britain at the end of 1758 and the *Namur* then had to be overhauled and repaired so Equiano once more went to live with the Guerins and he says he took pleasure in attending the sisters around London. They resumed his religious education and Equiano become increasingly receptive and agreed to their wish that he should be baptised as a Christian. Elizabeth Guerin told Pascal that it was vitally important he should permit this to happen before he took Equiano back to the war again. Pascal objected, saying it would give a slave ideas beyond his station. However, to Equiano's delight, he bowed to her continued pressure:

> I was baptised in St. Margaret's Church, Westminster, in February 1759, by my present name… Miss Guerin did me the honour to stand as godmother, and afterwards gave me a treat… [When the *Namur* was ready for sea] I

Equiano's Life As A Sailor In The Royal Navy

Left: a black sea-cook in 1831 cartoon by T. Maclean. Below: General Wolfe by J. Highmore c1760, the figurehead from 'H.M.S Namur now in Museum of Haifax in Canada and Admiral Edward Boscawen by J. Reynolds 1825. Bottom: troops landing at Louisbourg 1758

> parted from those amiable ladies with reluctance; after receiving from them many friendly cautions how to conduct myself, and some valuable presents.

Equiano is sometimes criticised for hanging onto the name 'Gustavus Vassa' and not reverting to his African name when he later became a free man, but his slave name had become his baptism name and his baptism mattered hugely to him. It was not, as some have alleged, just an act undertaken in the hope that it would guarantee freedom. Nor was it, as others have suggested, an act to show he was prepared to abandon his African heritage by adopting the white man's faith. That accusation ignores the fact that Christianity was not in its origins white and that Equiano never lost his pride in being an African or his belief in the ability of Africans to make a unique contribution to human society. Looking back on his life in the 1790s he wrote about his African heritage:

> The manners and customs of my country...had been implanted in me with great care, and made an impression on my mind, which time could not erase, and which all the adversity and variety of fortune I have since experienced, served only to rivet and record: for, whether the love of one's country be real or imaginary, or a lesson of reason, or an instinct of nature, I still look back with pleasure on the first scenes of my life.

What Equiano refused to do was elevate Africa into a utopia that it was not. He accepted that he could learn from other cultures. In the case of religion his Igbo upbringing had taught him there was only one God. Christianity seemed to offer him greater insights into the nature of that God. Obviously at this early stage his understanding of Christianity was fairly superficial but his autobiography shows he constantly sought to deepen it. Some researchers have analysed the many Biblical quotations that Equiano uses within his autobiography and they have found that his main focus was clearly on passages that were about oppression or liberation. Not surprisingly he became increasingly a critic of the white man's corrupted version of Christianity. It is worth quoting in this context Katherine Gerbner's book *Christian Slavery*, published in 2018:

> Older scholarship tended to view Christianity as… a method of slave control [but] more recent studies have moved in the opposite direction. Some historians have argued that Christianity provided an important theological impetus for rebellions on both sides of the Atlantic, while others have argued that spiritual practices among slaves made them persistently resistant…

Equiano's Life As A Sailor In The Royal Navy

Above: St: Margaret's Church, Westminster. Left: contrasting images of Christianity: a 19th century drawing of an African bowing to what is obviously a white Christ and the head of the Black Christ, a 17th century wooden image washed ashore at Portobelo in Panama. Below: a black sailor among whites in 1822 cartoon by G. Cruikshank. Bottom: Battle of Lagos 1759 by R. Perret. The 'Namur' is on the left.

By joining churches and participating in Protestant rituals, enslaved and free black Christians implicitly undermined the ideology of mastery and religious exclusivity… [and they] read and interpreted scripture in new ways that challenged white Christian culture. Their eagerness to learn how to read and write was particularly troublesome… [because] literacy gave black Christians a powerful tool to advocate for themselves and their communities.

In a secular age Equiano's conversion, when not criticised, is often ignored. Yet it was to be critically important in shaping his future life. As he grew in his faith he talked freely about Christianity's 'inestimable benefits'. It gave him a light to guide him and a hope to live for and the strength to endure and persevere. At this early stage what he drew most from it was that he was just as important in the eyes of God as any white man and therefore he should not be enslaved.

It was his strong religious beliefs that were the foundation from which all of his actions emanated
Marie-Antoinette Smith, American professor in From Tribal Spirituality to Christianity: Olaudah Equiano's AfroEnglish View of Christians *in 2001*

In April 1759 Boscawen's fleet headed off to the Mediterranean and the island of Gibraltar. It was not a good time for Equiano. Pascal was refusing to set him free and, in Gibraltar, the news of his friend Dick's death reached him:

[They] brought his chest, and all his other things, to my master: these he afterwards gave to me, and I regarded them as a memorial of my friend, whom I loved, and grieved for, as a brother.

In August the *Namur* participated in the Battle of Lagos, a major sea battle against the French. Once again Equiano had to be a powder boy:

My station during the engagement was on the middle-deck, where I was quartered with another boy, to bring powder to the aftermost gun; and here I was a witness of the dreadful fate of many of my companions, who, in the twinkling of an eye, were dashed in pieces, and launched into eternity. Happily I escaped unhurt, though the shot and splinters flew thick about me during the whole fight. Towards the latter part of it my master was wounded, and I saw him carried down to the surgeon; but, though I was much alarmed for him and wished to assist him, I dared not leave my post… Our ship suffered very much in this engagement; for, besides the number of our killed and wounded, she was almost torn to pieces, and our rigging so much shattered, that our mizen-mast and main-yard, etc. hung over the side of the ship; so that we were obliged to get many carpenters, and others from some of the ships of the fleet, to assist in setting us in some tolerable order; and, notwithstanding, it took us some time before we were completely refitted; after which… we, with the prizes, steered for England.

Every now and then a man's mind is stretched by a new idea or sensation and never shrinks back to its former dimensions.
Oliver Wendell Holmes, American writer and poet in *The Autocrat of the Breakfast Table* in 1858

The following year Pascal was appointed to command a fireship called the *Aetna*. Fireships were filled with explosives and combustibles and, if deemed necessary, they could be set on fire and allowed to drift into the enemy ships. This was to be Equiano's place of work for almost three years. He says that during that time one of the crew taught him to write and the basics of arithmetic and that he used what little leisure time he had to constantly improve his level of education. That, and his participation in a number of sea battles and greater age, probably explains why Equiano was promoted to the rank of able-seaman in 1762. This was the highest paid rank below that of an officer. It would have pleased Pascal because he was continuing to claim Equiano's share of prize money and, as an able-seaman, that share would have increased.

Very few black sailors were given able seaman status so Equiano's promotion was quite an achievement. The most famous picture of a black able-seaman is found in the painting made of Admiral Nelson's death on the flagship *H.M.S. Victory* at the Battle of Trafalgar in 1805. A black sailor is shown pointing towards where the lethal bullet had been fired from. He was one of ten black sailors on board the *Victory* and some of these were later rewarded by being given a retirement alongside their white crew-mates in the relative comfort of the Royal Hospital for Seamen at Greenwich. One such pensioner, Richard Baker (not to be confused with Equiano's friend of that name), was photographed in 1854 as one of the last Trafalgar survivors. Such recognition was extremely rare. If the press mentioned a black sailor it was usually only because they had earned a notoriety based on freakish behaviour. Billy Waters won fame in the 1780s as an eccentric one-legged street entertainer. William Brown won a brief notoriety in 1815 after it was belatedly discovered that he was a female. Joseph Johnson achieved fame by singing patriotic songs with the model of a ship on his head.

> *Naval and maritime service were not… based on a meritocracy. Black mariners were confronted not so much with a glass ceiling but a wooden deck above which they were not expected to serve*
>
> Douglas Hamilton, Head of History at Sheffield Hallam in *A most active, enterprising officer* in 2017

It was virtually impossible for a black sailor to acquire officer status. The most notable exception was John Perkins and the press coverage of his exploits never mentioned he was black. Perkins was born in Jamaica in around 1750 and he was what was called a mulatto (i.e. of mixed race). His mother was a slave but he had a white father. At the age of nine he went to sea as the slave of a naval carpenter called William Young and, like Equiano, found himself fighting in the Seven Years War. It is not known how he earned his freedom but it may have been by fleeing his American owner and joining the British forces in the American War of Independence. In 1775 he commenced serving as a local pilot in the Royal Navy. Such was his usefulness that he was commissioned as a lieutenant and placed in command of a schooner called the *Punch*. He earned himself the nickname 'Jack Punch' by capturing at least 315 ships and boats belonging to the rebel colonists. Perkins had similar success against the French in the West Indies when he was promoted in 1781 to command a sloop of war called the *Endeavour*. Reports of his achievements featured in London's press.

Perkins briefly visited Britain in 1784 and 1786 and in the years of peace he became a useful spy for the Navy, working in Cuba and Saint-Dominique (now Haiti). It took the intervention of the British government to prevent the French hanging him. Perkins resumed the command of ships and reached the rank of post-captain during Britain's war with France between 1792 and 1802. His contribution to the British success in the Caribbean was noted by the Governor of Jamaica, Sir Archibald Campbell:

> By the gallant exertions of this officer some hundred vessels were taken, burnt, or destroyed … in favour of Britain… [and] the character and conduct of Captain Perkins were not less admired by his superior officers in Jamaica, than respected by those of the enemy.

Once again the press reports of his deeds never mentioned his colour. No

EQUIANO'S LIFE AS A SAILOR IN THE ROYAL NAVY

Above: 1822 cartoon of Billy Waters busking. Below: detail from 'Death of Nelson by Daniel Maclise and 1854 photo of veterans from the Battle of Trafalgar, showing the black sailor Richard Baker. Right: 1815 etching of Joseph Johnson wearing his special hat. Black entertainers increasingly became figures of fun and from 1830 some white comedians and singers began to 'blackface'.

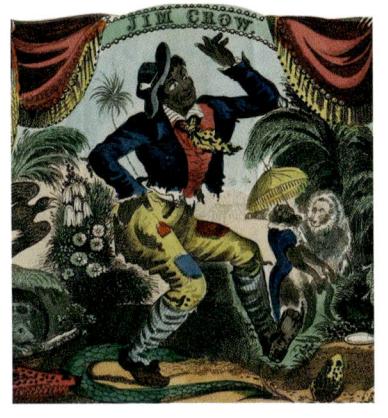

95

one wanted to publicise that a black man had authority to impose his will on white sailors. Towards the end of the war when the fighting had more or less stopped, some lieutenants began formally complaining at the 'cursed disgrace' of having to obey a 'coloured captain'. The start of the Napoleonic Wars in 1803 temporarily silenced his opponents and Perkins was given the role of dealing with the newly independent state of Haiti. However, someone in authority must have decided in 1805 that it was time to end his career. It was known that he had chest problems so he was ordered to take command of a ship in Nova Scotia. This was tantamount to a death sentence and it forced Perkins to resign. He retired to Jamaica and, with the money he had earned from the capture of so many enemy ships, he purchased large estates. Thus the ex-slave ended his life as a slave-owner – perhaps one reason why his story has received relatively little attention until recently.

The moment the slave resolves that he will no longer be a slave, his fetters fall. He frees himself and show the way to others Freedom and slavery are mental states
 Mahatma Gandhi, Indian anti-colonial nationalist in *Non-Violence in Peace and War in* 1949

The Seven Years' War came to an end in February 1763. Pascal knew it would be only a matter of time before he and many other officers would be once more placed on extended leave. What would he then do with Equiano, who had faithfully served him for nine years? His answer to that question was conveyed to Equiano when their ship neared London in December . He would sell him.

5.
HOW EQUIANO SAW THE FULL EXTENT OF SLAVE OWNER CRUELTY AND EARNED HIS FREEDOM

Is it not enough that we are torn from our country and friends to toil for your luxury and lust of gain? Must every tender feeling be likewise sacrificed to your avarice?

Oluadah Equiano

Pascal's sale of Equiano was brutally done and undertaken before the *Aetna* docked, presumably to avoid any arguments over his entitlement to all the prize money and so there was no chance of his slave running away. He may also have wanted to present the Guerin sisters with a fait accompli so as to avoid having to face their opposition. One cannot help but feel that he had also become very angry at Equiano's assertions that his baptism had set him free:

> He forced me into the barge, saying… he would take care I should not [escape from him]. I was so struck with the unexpectedness of this proceeding, that for some time I did not make a reply, only I made an offer to go for my books and chest of clothes, but he swore I should not move out of his sight; and if I did he would cut my throat… Plucking up courage, I told him I was free, and he could not by law serve me so. But this only enraged him the more; and he continued to swear, and said he would soon let me know whether he would or not… for he was resolved to put me on board the first vessel he could get to receive me… [Some of] the boat's crew… strove then to cheer me, and told me he could not sell me, and that they would stand by me, which revived me a little; and I still entertained hopes…

> But, just as we had got a little below Gravesend, we came alongside of a ship which was going away the next tide for the West Indies; her name was the *Charming Sally*… My master went on board and agreed with… [its captain

the price] for me; and in a little time I was sent for into the cabin. When I came there Captain Doran asked me if I knew him; I answered that I did not; 'Then', said he, 'you are now my slave'. I told him my master could not sell me to him, nor to any one else. 'Why', said he, 'did not your master buy you?' I confessed he did. 'But I have served him', said I, 'many years, and he has taken all my wages and prize-money, for I only got one sixpence during the war; besides this I have been baptised; and by the laws of the land no man has a right to sell me'... Upon this Captain Doran said I talked too much English; and if I did not behave myself well, and be quiet, he had a method on board to make me. I was too well convinced of his power over me to doubt what he said...

I immediately left the cabin, filled with resentment and sorrow. The only coat I had with me my master took away with him, and said if my prize-money had been £10,000 he had a right to it all, and would have taken it. I had about nine guineas, which, during my long sea-faring life, I had scraped together from trifling perquisites and little ventures; and I hid it that instant, lest my master should take that from me likewise, still hoping that by some means or other I should make my escape to the shore... My master, having soon concluded his bargain with the captain, came out of the cabin, and he and his people got into the boat and put off; I followed them with aching eyes as long as I could, and when they were out of sight I threw myself on the deck, while my heart was ready to burst with sorrow and anguish... I wished I had never been born.

Perhaps the most telling sentence in this account is: 'I was too well convinced of his power over me to doubt what he said'. Equiano knew that if he resisted the outcome would be brutal punishment. Captain James Doran's comment about him speaking 'too much English' probably indicates he felt Equiano had been corrupted by spending so much time with white men into wrongly thinking he deserved the same freedom they possessed.

Doran's intended destination in the Caribbean was Montserrat. The first sight of the island filled Equiano with fear:

At the sight of this land of bondage, a fresh horror ran through all my frame, and chilled me to the heart. My former slavery now rose in dreadful review to my mind, and displayed nothing but misery, stripes, and chains; and, in the first paroxysm of my grief, I called upon God's thunder, and his avenging power, to direct the stroke of death to me, rather than permit me to become a slave, and be sold from lord to lord. In this state of my mind our ship came to an anchor, and soon after discharged her cargo. I now knew what it was to work hard; I was made to help to unload and load the ship… I had been so long used to an European climate that at first I felt the scorching West India sun very painful, while the dashing surf would toss the boat and the people in it frequently above high water mark… and I was day by day mangled and torn.

Better in th' untimely grave to rot,
the world and its all its cruelties forgot,
than, dragged once more beyond the Western main,
to groan beneath some dastard planter's chain,
where my poor countrymen in bondage wait
the slow enfranchisement of ling'ring fate.
Oh! my heart sinks, my dying eyes o'erflow,
when mem'ry paints the picture of their woe!
For I have seen them, ere the dawn of day,
roused by the lash, begin their cheerless way;
greeting with groans unwelcome morn's return,
while rage and shame their gloomy bosoms burn…
No eye to mark their suff'rings with a tear,
no friend to comfort, and no hope to cheer;
then like the dull unpitied brutes repair
to stalls as wretched, and as coarse a fare;
thank heav'n one day of misery was o'er,
and sink to sleep, and wish to wake no more

Thomas Day and John Bicknell in the first significant anti-slavery poem, *The Dying Negro* in 1775

Doran completed his business on the island by the May of 1764. Equiano had hopes that he might return with the ship to Britain but these were dashed once the ship was ready to sail:

Captain Doran sent for me ashore one morning, and I was told by the messenger that my fate was then determined. With fluttering steps and trembling heart I came to the captain, and found with him one Mr. Robert King, a Quaker, and the first merchant in the place. The captain then told me my former master had sent me there to be sold... [and] he could not venture to take me to London, for he was very sure that when I came there I would leave him. I at that instant burst out a crying, and begged much of him to take me to England with him, but all to no purpose... I took leave of all my shipmates; and the next day the ship sailed. When she weighed anchor I went to the waterside and looked at her with a very wishful and aching heart, and followed her with my eyes and tears until she was totally out of sight.

In fairness to Dolan he chose to sell Equiano to a merchant named King who was known to treat his slaves well. His home lay in Philadelphia and he came from a Quaker family. The role of the Quakers in opposing slavery will be looked at in the fourth section of this book and many Quakers would have disapproved of King's involvement with slavery. What his faith had generated was a belief that it was incumbent on him to behave as humanely as possible in his dealings with slaves. His business lay primarily in purchasing and selling sugar and rum from many of the Caribbean islands and he bought Equiano partly on Dolan's recommendation of his good character and partly because he wanted an educated slave whom he could train to undertake administrative tasks. Equiano fitted the latter role perfectly:

> I had the good fortune to please my master in every department in which he employed me; and there was scarcely any part of his business, or household affairs, in which I was not occasionally engaged... [My labour] saved him, as he used to acknowledge, above a hundred pounds a year.

Equiano was used as a mercantile clerk, as a courier, as a useful assistant on some of the voyages made by King's trading ships, and as an inspector of estates.

The travelling element was the part that concerned King most because it provided plenty of opportunities for Equiano to escape, but his fears on the matter were overcome by Thomas Farmer, his leading sea captain. At first Equiano was permitted to only go on very short trips, but once King and Farmer's trust in him had grown, he went on the long trips to America. One of King's trading activities was to purchase and sell slaves for use on the plantations and Equiano was expected to help in that work. Equiano did not find that easy, especially as King's kindness was not shared by the white agents who worked for him:

> I went with... [King] on board a Guinea-man to purchase some slaves

to carry with us, and cultivate a plantation; and I chose them all my own countrymen… It gave me no pleasure to help enslave my own people… I was often a witness to cruelties of every kind, which were exercised on my unhappy fellow slaves. I used frequently to have different cargoes of new negroes in my care for sale; and it was almost a constant practice with our clerks, and other whites, to commit violent depredations on the chastity of the female slaves; and… [I was] unable to help them.

When we have had some of these slaves on board my master's vessels to carry them to other islands, or to America, I have known our mates to commit these acts most shamefully, to the disgrace, not of Christians only, but of men. I have even known them gratify their brutal passion with females not ten years old… And yet in Montserrat I have seen a negro man staked to the ground, and cut most shockingly, and then his ears cut off bit by bit, because he had been connected with a white woman who was a common prostitute: as if it were no crime in the whites to rob an innocent African girl of her virtue, but most heinous in a black man only to gratify a passion of nature, where the temptation was offered by one of a different colour, though the most abandoned woman of her species.

Scenes of blood and cruelty are shocking to our ear and heart. What man has nerve to do, man has not nerve to hear
    Harriet Beecher Stowe, American abolitionist in *Uncle Tom's Cabin* in 1852

Some critics have accused Equiano of collaborating in the slave trade but it is hard to see what choice he had. He was at this juncture still a slave himself. The trading trips exposed him to the horrors of what was happening on fifteen of the Caribbean islands:

In many of the estates, on the different islands where I used to be sent for rum or sugar… I had all the opportunity I could wish for to see the dreadful usage of the poor men; usage that reconciled me to my situation, and made me bless God for the hands into which I had fallen… It was very common in several of the islands, particularly in St. Kitt's, for the slaves to be branded with the initial letters of their master's name; and a load of heavy iron hooks hung about their necks. Indeed on the most trifling occasions they were loaded with chains; and often instruments of torture were added. The iron muzzle, thumb-screws, etc … were sometimes applied for the slightest faults. I have seen a negro beaten till some of his bones were broken, for even letting a pot boil over... Is not this... enough to bring down God's judgment on the islands? He tells us the oppressor and the oppressed are both in his hands; and if these are not the poor, the broken-hearted, the blind, the captive, the bruised, which our Saviour speaks of, who are they?

He rightly identified that one of the problems was that many plantations had absentee landlords in Britain. This meant they relied on overseers and most of the overseers were very brutal men:

These overseers are indeed for the most part persons of the worst character of any denomination of men in the West Indies. Unfortunately, many humane gentlemen, by not residing on their estates, are obliged to leave the management of them in the hands of these human butchers, who cut and mangle the slaves in a shocking manner on the most trifling occasions, and altogether treat them in every respect like brutes. They pay no regard to the situation of pregnant women, nor the least attention to the lodging of the field negroes. Their huts, which ought to be well covered, and the place dry where they take their little repose, are often open sheds, built in damp places; so that, when the poor creatures return tired from the toils of the field, they contract many disorders, from being exposed to the damp air in this uncomfortable state, while they are heated, and their pores are open... I can quote many instances of gentlemen who reside on their estates in the West Indies, and... [where] the negroes are treated with lenity and proper care, by which their lives are prolonged, and their masters are profited.

If any man shall out of wantonness... or bloody-mindedness or cruel intention wilfully kill a negro or other slave of his own, he shall pay into the public treasury fifteen pounds sterling
  Act of the Assembly of Barbados (but fines were never in practice imposed or collected)

It particularly distressed Equiano that he saw no attention paid to keeping family together and that those Africans judged not worth much were just put onto scales, weighed and then sold 'from three pence to six pence or nine pence a pound'. This is the equivalent in today's values of between £3.30 and £10 per kilo- i.e. less than animal flesh. In his book he says that it was not surprising that some slaves fought back and rebelled because what they faced bred only

SLAVE OWNER CRUELTY AND EARNING FREEDOM

Top left: face mask to prevent slave eating and drinking. Top right: 'Master buy me, he won't kill me…he whip me regular' -slave song in Barbados as recounted by Dr William Dickson to abolitionist Granville Sharp (Gloucester archives) .Left: slave whipping post 1822. Below: branded hand of a slave 1845 and runaway's punishment collar c. 1820. Bottom: engraving from 1830s of House of Correction in Jamaica.

'hostility and hate'. However, any slave who resisted or tried to escape could only expect the worst possible punishment:

> [A] negro man was half hanged, and then burnt, for attempting to poison a cruel overseer. Thus by repeated cruelties are the wretched first urged to despair, and then murdered because they... retaliate on their tyrants!... While I was in Montserrat I knew a negro man, named Emanuel Sankey, who endeavoured to escape from his miserable bondage by concealing himself on board of a London ship, but fate did not favour the poor oppressed man... [and] he was delivered up again to his master. This Christian master immediately pinned the wretch down to the ground at each wrist and ankle, and then took some sticks of sealing wax, and lighted them, and dropped it all over his back. There was another master who was noted for cruelty; and I believe he had not a slave but what had been cut, and had pieces fairly taken out of the flesh: and, after they had been punished thus, he used to make them get into a long wooden box or case he had for that purpose, in which he shut them up during pleasure. It was just about the height and breadth of a man; and the poor wretches had no room, when in the case, to move.

Congregations are lifeless because dead men preach to them
> George Whitefield, Methodist preacher cited in *Life and Memoirs* in 1772

On the trading trips to the American mainland Equiano got to see a number of cities, including Philadelphia, Charleston, and Savannah. In Philadelphia he records how by accident he heard George Whitefield, widely regarded as the greatest preacher of the eighteenth-century:

> I came to a church crowded with people; the church-yard was full likewise, and a number of people were even mounted on ladders, looking in at the windows. I though this a strange sight, as I had never seen churches, either in England or the West Indies, crowded in this manner before. I therefore made bold to ask some people the meaning of all this, and they told me the Rev. Mr. George Whitefield was preaching. I had often heard of this gentleman, and had wished to see and hear him; but I had never before had an opportunity. I now therefore resolved to gratify myself with the sight, and pressed in amidst the multitude. When I got into the church I saw this pious man exhorting the people with the greatest fervour and earnestness, and sweating as much as I ever did while in slavery... I was very much struck

and impressed with this; I though it strange I had never seen divines exert themselves in this manner before, and was no longer at a loss to account for the thin congregations they preached to.

Born in Gloucester and with strong family connections to Bristol, Whitefield has been described as the first modern celebrity. It was said that wherever he travelled in Britain and America the one thing that people could not do was stay away from him. He was critically important in creating the Methodist movement that Equiano was later to join. What made his preaching so unique was that he acted out Biblical stories, making the listeners feel they were actually there. The following account is Whitefield's description of how Bristolians responded to his preaching:

> It was wonderful to see how the people hung upon the rails of the organ loft, climbed upon the leads of the church, and made the church itself so hot with their breath that the steam would fall from the pillars like drops of rain. Sometimes almost as many would go away from want of room as came in, and it was with great difficulty that I got to the desk to read prayers or preach. Persons of all denominations flocked to hear. Persons of all ranks not only publicly attended my ministry but gave me private invitations to their houses.

In Philadelphia it was calculated that he spoke to open-air crowds of up to 30,000 people. He is credited with being a significant influence on the generation that later fought in the American War of Independence because he often spoke of the importance of liberty and freedom. That's why during that war soldiers dug up his body and cut pieces of cloth from his corpse so they could wear them as talismans going into battle. Whitefield was not an abolitionist – unlike his friends, John and Charles Wesley, the other two Methodist leaders – but he did regularly campaign for the better treatment of slaves and he purchased a 5,000 acres estate in Pennsylvania to create a school for African-Americans. His role will be looked at in more detail in the fourth section of this book.

Acting as King's agent whether on the islands or in the mainland colonies was always potentially dangerous because some of the white colonists objected to dealing with a black man. On one occasion in Savannah Equiano was almost murdered:

> One Sunday night, as I was with some negroes in their master's yard in the

town of Savannah, it happened that their master, one Doctor Perkins, who was a very severe and cruel man, came in drunk; and, not liking to see any strange negroes in his yard, he and a ruffian of a white man he had in his service beset me in an instant, and both of them struck me with the first weapons they could get hold of. I cried out as long as I could for help and mercy; but, though I gave a good account of myself, and he knew my captain, who lodged hard by him, it was to no purpose. They beat and mangled me in a shameful manner, leaving me near dead. I lost so much blood from the wounds I received, that I lay quite motionless, and was so benumbed that I could not feel any thing for many hours. Early in the morning they took me away to the jail.

As I did not return to the ship all night, my captain, not knowing where I was, and being uneasy… made inquiry after me; and, having found where I was, immediately came to me. As soon as the good man saw me so cut and mangled, he could not forbear weeping; he soon got me out of jail to his lodgings, and immediately sent for the best doctors in the place, who at first declared it as their opinion that I could not recover. My captain on this went to all the lawyers in the town for their advice, but they told him they could do nothing for me as I was a negro. He then went to Doctor Perkins… and menaced him, swearing he would be revenged of him, and challenged him to fight. But cowardice is ever the companion of cruelty and the Doctor refused… [The captain] nursed and watched me all the hours of the night; and I was, through his attention and that of… [a local doctor called Brady] able to get out of bed in about sixteen or eighteen days.

Captain Farmer attempted to seek legal redress for this brutal attack on Equiano but got nowhere because there was no legal protection for slaves. All a white colonist had to say was that the slave had acted in a rebellious manner and any punishment – even death – was judged an acceptable response.

Every day I longed to be a free man

Olaudah Equiano

Equiano knew he was lucky to be working for men like King and Farmer, but that did not prevent him yearning for his freedom. What kept him going was a mix of the sacred and the secular. His faith helped sustain him and so too did the ability to earn money for himself on the trading trips. He started with just a

SLAVE OWNER CRUELTY AND EARNING FREEDOM

Above: View of 18th century Philadelphia. Below: George Whitefield preaching and the famous portrait of him by J.Russell 1770. Bottom: view of Savannah from 19th century print and a slave manumission document from 1780.

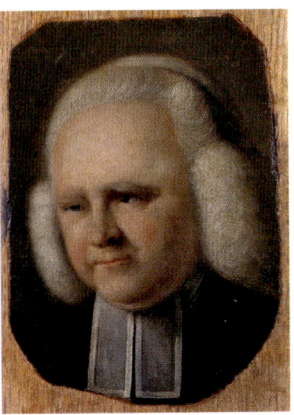

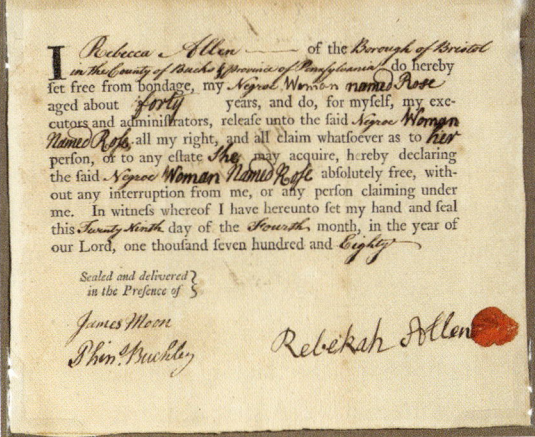

107

few coins and used these to buy small items in one place that he knew he could sell elsewhere at a profit. Over a period of four years he gradually accumulated the money required to purchase his freedom. However, he knew that in the Caribbean freed Africans were often seized and enslaved again. In his book he cites examples and comments:

> Hitherto I had thought only slavery dreadful; but the state of the free Negro appeared to me now equally so at least, and in some respects even worse, for they live in constant alarm of their liberty.

Some know the value of education by having it. I know its value by not having it
Frederick Douglass, African-American abolitionist in speech *On the blessings of Liberty and Education* in 1894

Equiano decided it made sense for him to acquire navigational skills before requesting to purchase his freedom so that, once free, he could speedily find employment on a ship back to Britain, where the risk of re-enslavement would be far less. To that end he began taking secret lessons and this proved disastrous. King discovered about the lessons and wrongly assumed Equiano was planning to run away. His response was to inform Equiano that he was going to sell him to a new master. Fortunately Thomas Farmer intervened and calmed King down, saying he should recall there had been many opportunities for Equiano to escape and he had never taken any of them. A desire to improve his education was part of Equiano's nature. After this crisis had blown over Farmer suggested he should accompany Equiano on the occasion when he formally requested to purchase his freedom from King:

> When I went in I made my obeisance to my master, and with my money in my hand, and many fears in my heart, I prayed him to be as good as his offer to me, when he was pleased to promise me my freedom as soon as I could purchase it. This speech seemed to confound him; he began to recoil: and my heart that instant sunk within me. 'What,' said he, 'give you your freedom? Why, where did you get the money? Have you got forty pounds sterling?' 'Yes, sir,' I answered. 'How did you get it?' replied he. I told him, very honestly. The Captain then said he knew I got the money very honestly and with much industry, and that I was particularly careful. On which my master replied, I got money much faster than he did; and said he would not

have made me the promise he did if he had thought I should have got money so soon. 'Come, come,' said my worthy Captain, clapping my master on the back, 'Come, Robert,… I think you must let him have his freedom… I know Gustavus has earned you more than an hundred a-year, and he will still save you money, as he will not leave you. Come, Robert, take the money.'

My master then said, he would not be worse than his promise; and, taking the money, told me to go to the Secretary at the Register Office, and get my manumission drawn up. These words of my master were like a voice from heaven to me: in an instant all my trepidation was turned into unutterable bliss; and I most reverently bowed myself with gratitude, unable to express my feelings, but by the overflowing of my eyes, while my true and worthy friend, the Captain, congratulated us both with a peculiar degree of heartfelt pleasure… My imagination was all rapture as I flew to the Register Office, and, in this respect, like the apostle Peter (whose deliverance from prison was so sudden and extraordinary, that he thought he was in a vision) I could scarcely believe I was awake. Heavens! who could do justice to my feelings at this moment! Not conquering heroes themselves, in the midst of a triumph. Not the tender mother who has just regained her long-lost infant, and presses it to her heart. Not the weary hungry mariner, at the sight of the desired friendly port. Not the lover, when he once more embraces his beloved mistress, after she had been ravished from his arms! All within my breast was tumult, wildness, and delirium! My feet scarcely touched the ground, for they were winged with joy, and, like Elijah, as he rose to Heaven, they 'were with lightning sped as I went on'. Every one I met I told of my happiness, and blazed about the virtue of my amiable master and captain.

What is noticeable in this account, apart from its wonderful account of Equiano's joy at acquiring his freedom, is how dependent he was on obtaining his master's assent. Without Farmer's input the whole business might have gone badly wrong. It is also noticeable that King demanded he should be given exactly what he had paid. None of the profits Equiano had brought his master were considered. Equiano's Certificate of Emancipation was signed on 11 July 1766. He was twenty-one years old. Such was Equiano's gratitude that he did not seek to immediately leave. He continued to work for both King and Farmer but as a paid employee. However, that soon changed for two reasons. The first was that Farmer, whom he had come to look on as friend, died in the November:

When this dear friend found the symptoms of death approaching, he called me by my name; and, when I came to him, he asked (with almost his last breath) if he had ever done me any harm? 'God forbid I should think so,' I replied, 'I should then be the most ungrateful of wretches'... He expired without saying another word; and the day following we committed his body to the deep. Every man on board loved this man, and regretted his death; but I was exceedingly affected at it, and I found that I did not know, till he was gone, the strength of my regard for him. Indeed I had every reason in the world to be attached to him; for, besides that he was in general mild, affable, generous, faithful, benevolent, and just, he was to me a friend and a father; and, had it pleased Providence that he had died but five months before, I verily believe I should not have obtained my freedom when I did.

In an age when it seemed that the light of human kindness had all but gone out, at least a spark appears to have remained
… ..Ray Costello, historian on Thomas Farmer in Black Salt: Seafarers of African Descent in 2014

The second was that there was an attempt to murder Equiano after King announced he was going to give him Farmer's job, effectively making him a business partner:

> I now obtained a new appellation and was called Captain. This elated me not a little and it was flattering to my vanity to be thus styled by as high a title as any man in this place possessed.

Equiano did not want to remain in a permanent state of danger, and, after escaping the murder attempt, he paid his passage to go to London a ship called the *Andromache,* which set set sail in January 1767. He vowed never to return to the West Indies. What little evidence we have suggests King's business went into a rapid decline without his and Farmer's input. Equiano took with him all his savings, which amounted to thirty-seven guineas (the equivalent today of around £3,500), and a testimonial provided by King:

> The bearer hereof, Gustavus Vassa, was my slave for upwards of three years, during which he has always behaved himself well, and discharged his duty with honesty and assiduity.

SLAVE OWNER CRUELTY AND EARNING FREEDOM

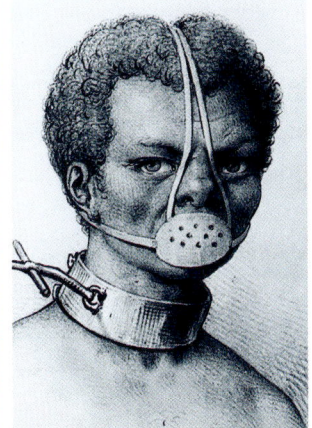

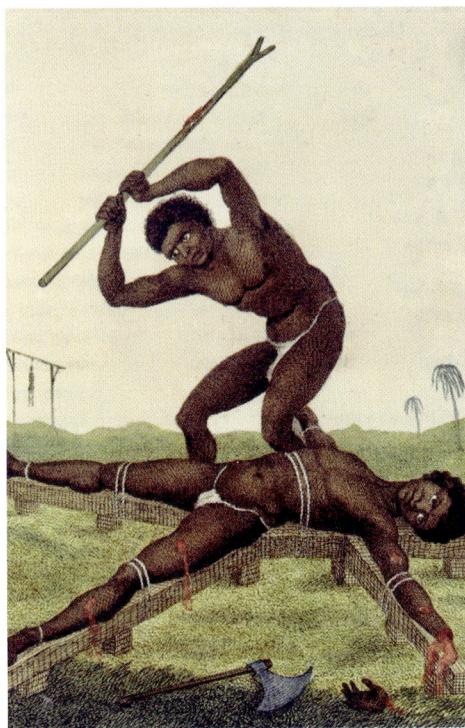

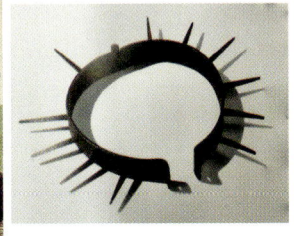

Burn marks on 13 year old girl's back in Virginia 1866; punishment mask in Brazil 1860; hanging by the ribs and mutilation on the rack in Surinam 1776; flogging on the wheel in Antigua; slave collars to restrain and punish slaves and a slave whip from South Carolina.

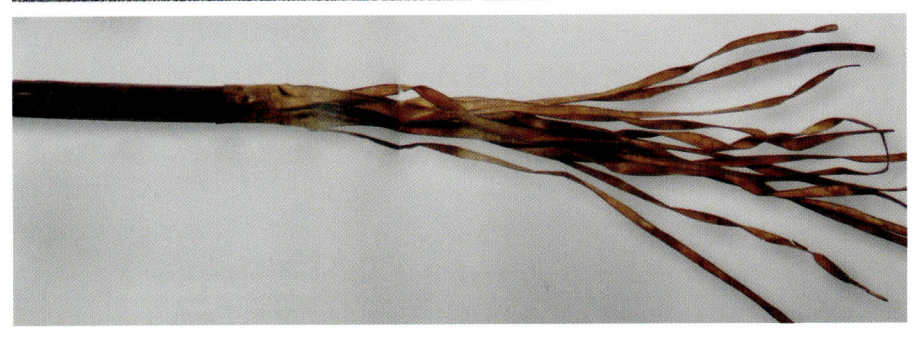

He was delighted at the thought of returning to Britain:

> I embarked for London, exceedingly glad to see myself once more on board of a ship; and still more so, in steering the course I had long wished for. With a light heart I bade Montserrat farewell… and with it I bade adieu to the sound of the cruel whip, and all other dreadful instruments of torture; adieu to the offensive sight of the violated chastity of the sable females, which has too often accosted my eyes; adieu to oppressions (although to me less severe than most of my countrymen); and adieu to the angry howling, dashing surfs. I wished for a grateful and thankful heart to praise the Lord God on high for all his mercies!

Remember not that we were bought, but that we were brave… not that we were sold, but that we were strong
William Prescott, former slave in Born in Slavery *in 1937*

The first thing Equiano did on arriving in London was to seek out the Guerin sisters in Greenwich:

> They were most agreeably surprised to see me, and I quite overjoyed at meeting with them. I told them my history, at which they expressed great wonder, and freely acknowledged it did their cousin, Capt. Pascal, no honour.

A few days later he met his former master Michael Pascal. The meeting did not go well:

> I met him four or five days after in Greenwich Park. When he saw me he appeared a good deal surprised, and asked me how I came back? I answered, 'In a ship'. To which he replied dryly, 'I suppose you did not walk back to London on the water'. As I saw, by his manner, that he did not seem to be sorry for his behaviour to me, and that I had not much reason to expect any favour from him, I told him that he had used me very ill, after I had been such a faithful servant to him for so many years; on which, without saying any more, he turned about and went away.

The weak can never forgive. Forgiveness is the attribute of the strong
Mahatma Gandhi, Indian anti-colonial nationalist in Young India *in 1931*

As Pascal was a frequent visitor to the Guerins, he could not avoid seeing Equiano again. Equiano was willing to forgive Pascal but their next meeting became heated when Equiano demanded that Pascal should give him all the prize-money he had earned in the Navy and Pascal refused to give him a penny:

> He said there was none due to me; for, if my prize money had been £10,000, he had a right to it all. I told him I was informed otherwise; on which he bade me defiance; and, in a bantering tone, desired me to commence a lawsuit against him for it.

The dispute made the sisters realise that they could not offer employment to Equiano within their house and so, in September, they arranged through a family friend that he should be given lodgings with a hairdresser in the Haymarket so he could be given training to become a barber. However, Equiano was not content just to learn about cutting hair and cleaning, powdering, and repairing wigs. One of the hairdresser's neighbours ran a local Academy and Equiano paid for lessons to widen his education, and he also took music lessons from another neighbour, who played the French horn. Learning an instrument was another way of trying to find future employment. There is evidence, for example, to show that regimental bands made use of black musicians and we know that a black man who lived in the St Paul's area of Bristol was teaching the fife to a white boy called Benjamin Ford in the yard of *The Full Moon* public house in 1773. Learning the French horn was the subject matter for an incident involving two slaves in Tobias Smollett's famous novel *Humphrey Clinker*, published in 1771:

> Two negroes that belonged to a Creole gentleman, who lodged in the same house... began to practice upon the French horn... [and] produced such discordant sounds as might have discomposed the organs of an ass... [My uncle Mr Bramble] desired the musicians to practice in some other place... They [referred him to their master and]... continued their noise, and even endeavoured to make it more disagreeable, laughing... at the thought of being able to torment their betters with impunity... Snatching his cane... [Mr Bramble] began to labour them both, and exerted himself with such astonishing vigour and agility that both their heads and horn were broken in a twinkling, and they ran howling down the stairs to their master's parlour.

The money that Equiano had brought with him was virtually gone by the February of 1768 so Equiano took a job as a servant to a naval surgeon called

Charles Irving, but the wages were too low to make this a long-term solution. In May he reluctantly returned to the sea. He took employment on a ship called the *Delawar* under a sea captain called John Jolly, 'a neat smart good humoured man, just such a one as I wished to serve'. Over the next two years he went on trading voyages to Portugal and the Mediterranean, where he got to see many places in France, Italy, and Turkey. In the process he saw other forms of slavery:

> I was surprised to see how the Greeks are, in some measure, kept under by the Turks, as the negroes are in the West Indies by the white people… On of the finest cities I saw was Genoa… but all… [its] grandeur was in my eyes disgraced by the galley slaves, whose condition both there and in other parts of Italy is truly piteous and wretched.

In 1771 he sailed under a new captain to Madeira, Barbados and the Grenadines. As usual Equiano was supplementing his low pay as a sailor by purchasing goods in one place and selling them in another. He recounts how he was saved from being cheated by his fellow crew members:

> A white man, an islander, bought some goods of me to the amount of some pounds, and made me many fair promises as usual, but without any intention of paying me. He had likewise bought goods from some more of our people, whom he intended to serve in the same manner… When our ship was loaded, and near sailing… I asked him for my money [and] he threatened me and another black man he had bought goods of, so that we found we were like to get more blows than payment. On this we went to complain to… a justice of the peace… but being negroes, although free, we could not get any remedy… Luckily for us however, this man was also indebted to three white sailors, who could not get a farthing from him; they therefore readily joined us, and we all went together in search of him. When we found where he was, I took him out of a house and threatened him with vengeance; on which, finding he was likely to be handled roughly, the rogue offered each of us some small allowance, but nothing near our demands. This exasperated us much more; and some were for cutting his ears off; but he begged hard for mercy, which was at last granted him, after we had entirely stripped him. We then let him go… We then repaired on board, and shortly after set sail for England.

Slave Owner Cruelty And Earning Freedom

> ***There may be times when we are powerless to prevent injustice, but there must never be a time when we fail to protest***
> Elie Wiesel, Holocaust survivor and political activist and writer in his Nobel Peace Prize Lecture in 1986

On a subsequent voyage in December 1771 he went to Nevis and Jamaica. It was his first visit to Jamaica and he was taken aback by the sheer number of slaves on the island. Once again he had to witness appalling brutality:

> There are negroes whose business it is to flog slaves; they go about to different people for employment, and the usual pay is from one to four bits. I saw many cruel punishments inflicted on the slaves in the short time I stayed here. In particular I was present when a poor fellow was tied up and kept hanging by the wrists at some distance from the ground, and then some half hundred weights were fixed to his ankles, in which posture he was flogged most unmercifully. There were also, as I heard, two different masters noted for cruelty on the island, who had staked up two negroes naked, and in two hours the vermin stung them to death. I heard a gentleman I well knew tell my captain that he passed sentence on a negro man to be burnt alive for attempting to poison an overseer. I pass over numerous other instances.

The Jamaican custom of weighting slaves to be whipped was also written about by another visiting sailor, William Spavens, in his an account of his life published in 1796, but he goes on to describe the whips used:

> They are stretched to their full length, so that they cannot shrink from the stroke. They then whip them with platted thongs which they call a cow skin. This… is then succeeded by flogging with ebony brushes, which resemble our gooseberry bushes in England, till their skins are filled as full of pricks as a porcupine is of quills; and when these are extracted, the poor wretch is left full of bleeding wounds.

While on Jamaica Equiano once again faced the problem of a white man taking goods from him and then refusing to pay. The man threatened to have him arrested on charges of attempted arson and attempted rescuing of his slaves if he complained. Not surprisingly, the inability of a black person to access justice was to become one of Equiano's themes when he later became a campaigner for the abolition of slavery.

Where justice is denied, where poverty is enforced, where ignorance prevails, and where any one class is made to feel that society is an organised conspiracy to oppress, rob and degrade them, neither persons nor property will be safe

Narrative of the Life of Frederick Douglass, an American slave published in 1845

6.
How Equiano Became A Missionary

I have often been asked how I felt when first I found myself on free soil. There is scarcely anything in my experience about which I could not give a more satisfactory answer. A new world had opened upon me... I lived more in that one day than in a year of my slave life. It was a time of joyous excitement which words can but tamely describe
Frederick Douglass in *My Escape from Slavery* in *The Century Illustrated Magazine* in 1881

By 1772 Equiano was tired of life at sea and so he took up his former position as a servant to the naval surgeon, Charles Irving. He found himself helping with Irving's experiments to devise a means of distilling seawater so it could be made drinkable. Irving was trying to improve on the work of a Scottish doctor called James Lind. In 1773 Irving accepted a surgeon's post on a naval expedition so he could test out his equipment at sea. Equiano agreed to accompany him and signed up as an able seaman on a sloop called the *Racehorse*. The aim of the expedition, which had been authorised by King George III, was to see if a route to India could be found via Scandinavia and Russia and the Arctic and, in the process, increase both geographical and scientific knowledge. The famous naturalist Joseph Banks provided detailed instructions on how the two ships involved should collect specimens. The expedition was commanded by a young but experienced naval officer called John Constantine Phipps, a humane man known for his good humour, courage, and lively intellect. The accompanying ship was the *Carcass* and it was captained by another able officer, Skeffington Lutwidge.

Both the ships were 'bomb' vessels that had been built to withstand the recoil of heavy mortars and so were very stoutly built and they were further reinforced to resist ice. The *Racehorse* held ninety men and the *Carcass* eighty. Historians have researched the muster list and discovered Equiano's name on it. Spelling and pronunciation were rarely accurate in the eighteenth century and he was listed first as Gustavus Weston and then as Gustavus Feston. The 1773 list states he was twenty-eight and from South Carolina. Why Equiano gave that as his place of origin is unclear. Those who question whether he was actually born in Africa have seized on this list as proof he was not, but there could be other explanations. For example, if Equiano had stated that he was born in Africa then it would have been obvious he must have been a slave and that might have led to questions about his status. By naming an American colony he could claim he was born a free man. He was not the only black sailor on the ship because the muster list contains the names of a Jonathan Syphax from Madagascar and a Richard Yorke from Guinea. Another name on the list is that of Horatio Nelson, then a fourteen year-old midshipman, but later to win fame as an Admiral and the hero of the Battle of Trafalgar in 1805.

The ships set sail in late May. Equiano's determination to keep a journal about this exciting venture almost cost him his life:

> The ship was so filled that there was very little room on board for any one, which placed me in a very awkward situation. I had resolved to keep a journal of this singular and interesting voyage; and I had no other place for this purpose but a little cabin, or the doctor's store-room, where I slept. This little place was stuffed with all manner of combustibles, particularly with tow and aquafortis, and many other dangerous things. Unfortunately it happened in the evening as I was writing my journal, that I had occasion to take the candle out of the lanthorn, and a spark having touched a single thread of the tow, all the rest caught the flame, and immediately the whole was in a blaze… In a moment the alarm was spread, and many people who were near ran to assist in putting out the fire. All this time I was in the very midst of the flames; my shirt, and the handkerchief on my neck, were burnt, and I was almost smothered with the smoke. However, through God's mercy, as I was nearly giving up all hopes, some people brought blankets and mattresses and threw them on the flames, by which means in a short time the fire was put out. I was severely reprimanded… and strictly charged never more to go there with a light… [but] not being able to write my journal in any other part of the ship, I was tempted again to venture by stealth with a light in the same cabin, though not without considerable fear and dread on my mind.

Irving's equipment proved a success and Equiano spent much of his time converting sea water into drinkable water for use by the crew. Equiano says the ships got as far north as 81 degrees north and 20 degrees east 'being much farther, by all accounts, than any navigator had ever ventured before; in which

How Equiano Became A Missionary

Left: Constantine John Phipps by unknown artist 1775. Above: Horatio Nelson killing a bear on the Arctic expedition by R. Westall. Below: engraving of the 'Racehorse' and the 'Carcass' enclosed in ice. Bottom: William Romaine, a preacher mentioned by Equiano and a Methodist love feast.

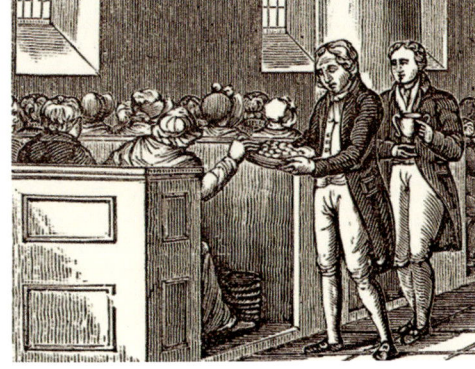

we fully proved the impracticability of finding a passage that way to India'. The Arctic provided him with an entirely new experience and in this section of his autobiography the issue of slavery is largely dropped in favour of Equiano presenting himself as an adventurer. The reference to sea-horses in the following extract probably means he saw walruses:

> We made Greenland, where I was surprised to see the sun did not set. The weather now became extremely cold; and… we saw many very high and curious mountains of ice; and also a great number of very large whales, which used to come close to our ship, and blow the water up to a very great height in the air. One morning we had vast quantities of sea-horses about the ship… [and] we fired some harpoon guns amongst them, in order to take some, but we could not get any… We still held on our course till July the 11th, when we were stopped by one compact impenetrable body of ice. We ran along it from east to west… [and generally the] sunshine, and constant daylight… gave cheerfulness and novelty to the whole of this striking, grand, and uncommon scene; and, to heighten it still more, the reflection of the sun from the ice gave the clouds a most beautiful appearance. We killed many different animals at this time, and among the rest nine bears… I thought them coarse eating, but some of the ship's company relished them very much. Some of our people once, in the boat, fired at and wounded a sea-horse, which dived immediately; and, in a little time after, brought up with it a number of others. They all joined in an attack upon the boat, and were with difficulty prevented from staving or oversetting her…
>
> [On the] 1st of August the two ships got completely fastened in the ice… This made our situation very dreadful and alarming; so that on the seventh day we were in very great apprehension of having the ships squeezed to pieces. The officers now held a council to know what was best for us to do in order to save our lives; and it was determined that we should endeavour to escape by dragging our boats along the ice towards the sea… After two or three days labour, we made very little progress; so that some of our hearts totally failed us, and I really began to give up myself for lost… While we were at this hard labour I once fell into a pond we had made amongst some loose ice, and was very near being drowned; but providentially some people were near who gave me immediate assistance, and thereby I escaped drowning. Our deplorable condition… brought me gradually to think of eternity in such a manner as I never had done before… Pale dejection seized every

countenance; many, who had been before blasphemers, in this our distress began to call on the good God of heaven for his help; and in the time of our utter need he heard us, and against hope or human probability delivered us! It was the eleventh day of the ships being thus fastened, and the fourth of our drawing the boats in this manner, that the wind changed… [and] the weather immediately became mild, and the ice broke towards the sea… This seemed to us like a reprieve from death.

More smiling, less worrying. More compassion, less judgment. More blessed, less stressed. More love, less hate

Roy T. Bennett, writer in *The Light of the Heart* in 2016

Irving and Equiano arrived back in London in October 1773. His experiences in the ice had convinced him that his priority should be to ensure he was saved and not damned before he next faced death. With that in mind he says he had 'a great desire to read the Bible the whole day'. However, he soon realised that he needed guidance to better understand it and so he set about trying to find a group who could help him to become 'a first-class Christian'. He tried attending various Anglican churches but found them all unhelpful because their congregations were largely made up of people who showed little evidence of Christianity in their lives. He then looked to join the Quakers because they showed a more genuine faith but the absence of preaching made that experience unhelpful to his needs. After looking into Roman Catholicism and finding that no better , he turned to considering other faiths, first Judaism and then the Islamic faith:

> I went on heavily without any guide to direct me the way that leadeth to eternal life. I asked different people questions about the manner of going to heaven, and was told different ways… and [I] could not find any at that time more righteous than myself, or indeed so much inclined to devotion… I found none among the circle of my acquaintance that kept wholly the ten commandments… I excelled many of them in that point, by keeping eight out of ten; and finding those who in general termed themselves Christians not so honest or so good in their morals as the Turks, I really thought the Turks were in a safer way of salvation than my neighbours… [and so] experiencing the dishonesty of many people here, I determined at last to set out for Turkey and there to end my days.

Given his African background, it is not surprising that his thoughts should have turned to becoming a Muslim. In the spring of 1774 he signed up to go on a ship called the *Anglicania* and he recommended the captain should employ one of his friends, John Annis, a run-away slave from the island of St Kitts. Unfortunately while the ship was being fitted out for its voyage Annis was seen by his former owner, William Kirkpatrick, and he determined he would have him returned to slavery in the Caribbean:

> Mr. Kirkpatrick came to our ship at Union Stairs on Easter Monday, April the fourth, with two wherry boats and six men… [and they] forcibly took him away from the ship, in the presence of the crew and the chief mate.

Disgusted at his captain's refusal to help Annis, Equiano followed the trail of the captured man:

> I proved the only friend he had, who attempted to regain him his liberty if possible, having known the want of liberty myself. I sent as soon as I could to Gravesend, and got knowledge of the ship in which he was; but unluckily she had sailed the first tide after he was put on board.

For to be free is not merely to cast off one's chains, but to live in a way that respects and enhances the freedom of others
Nelson Mandela: President of South Africa in *A Long Walk to Freedom* in 1994

He obtained a habeas corpus writ to order that Kirkpatrick should appear before a magistrate for kidnapping Annis in the hope a judge would order him to return Annis to freedom. The problem was ensuring that the writ was put into Kirkpatrick's hand:

> I got a tipstaff to go with me to St. Paul's church-yard, where he lived, [but] he, suspecting something of this kind, set a watch to look out. My being known to them occasioned me to use the following deception: I whitened my face, that they might not know me, and this had its desired effect.

Equiano managed to deliver the writ and Kirkpatrick went before a judge but he said Annis was not in his custody. Equiano sought help as to what to do next:

> I proceeded immediately to that philanthropist, Granville Sharp… who received me with the utmost kindness, and gave me every instruction that

was needful on the occasion. I left him in full hope that I should gain the unhappy man his liberty, with the warmest sense of gratitude towards Mr. Sharp for his kindness.

This is Equiano's first mention of Granville Sharp with whom he was later to work closely for many years. Sharp was famous in London because since 1768 he had been engaged in high profile legal cases intended to prove that slavery was an illegal activity under English law. His role in helping create the early abolitionist movement and the legal cases in which he was involved are examined in a later chapter. In this instance his legal advice did not work because Equiano employed a dud lawyer:

Alas! my attorney proved unfaithful; he took my money, lost me many months employ, and did not do the least good in the cause… [and when Annis] arrived at St. Kitts, he was, according to custom, staked to the ground with four pins through a cord, two on his wrists, and two on his ankles, was cut and flogged most unmercifully, and afterwards loaded cruelly with irons about his neck. I had two very moving letters from him, while he was in this situation; and also was told of it by some very respectable families now in London, who saw him in St. Kitts, in the same state in which he remained till kind death released him out of the hands of his tyrants.

Mr. Wesley's people think that they cannot love their neighbour as themselves without endeavouring to find out every possible way by which they may be serviceable to the souls and bodies of their fellow-creatures
James Leckington, a London bookseller in a letter subsequently published in 1804

A devastated Equiano was plunged into despair at his powerlessness and at this critical juncture he had his faith in Christianity restored by talking with an old seaman who was a Methodist and by being invited to attend a Methodist love feast:

I had never heard before the love of Christ to believers set forth in such a manner, and in so clear a point of view… [His] dissenting minister invited me to a love-feast at his chapel that evening. I accepted the offer, and thanked him… When the wished-for hour came I went, and happily the old man was there, who kindly seated me, as he belonged to the place. I was much astonished to see the place filled with people, and no signs of eating and drinking. There were many ministers in the company. At last they began by giving out hymns, and between the singing the minister engaged in prayer... I knew not what to make of this sight, having never seen any thing of the kind in my life before now. Some of the guests began to speak their experience... [and] they seemed to be altogether certain... that no one could ever separate them from the love of Christ, or pluck them out of his hands. This filled me with utter consternation, intermingled with admiration... My heart was attracted and my affections were enlarged. I wished to be as happy as them...

Their language and singing, etc. did well harmonise; I was entirely overcome, and wished to live and die thus. Lastly, some persons in the place produced some neat baskets full of buns, which they distributed about; and each person communicated with his neighbour, and sipped water out of different mugs, which they handed about to all who were present. This kind of Christian fellowship I had never seen, nor ever thought of seeing on earth; it fully reminded me of what I had read in the holy scriptures, of the primitive Christians, who loved each other and broke bread.

The Methodists were a revival movement within the Church of England but the Church authorities viewed them as 'dissenters' because they were not conforming to what the Church deemed appropriate. That explains why Equiano uses the word 'dissenting' to describe the minister that he met. His amazement at hearing hymn-singing was because he probably had not heard it before. The Church of England at this time banned the singing of hymns and it condemned the enthusiastic hymn-singing of the Methodists. The most criticised aspect of Methodism was its use of lay men as well as clergy as preachers. It may be that Equiano's reference to the event he attended having 'many ministers' was because he assumed the lay preachers were ordained. Methodist love-feasts were also condemned by the Church of England because they did not follow the laid down pattern for a communion service.

It is easy to see why Equiano would have been attracted to Methodism. First, there was its social make-up. It had its wealthy members but its main draw was to those whom society judged inferior (notably women) or worthless (notably the working classes). It gave the disadvantaged a sense of their worth in the eyes of God and it proclaimed a gospel message that focused on human equality and the need for social justice. Methodists were very active in visiting the sick and those in prison, in helping the needy and encouraging education. Another offence of the Methodists in the eyes of the Church was that they sometimes held religious meetings in the open air but that would have appealed to Equiano because it would have reminded him of the outdoor worship of his African childhood. Some modern writers have alleged that the religious passages in Equiano's autobiography were just included for a political purpose – to prove to respectable white society that a black man could be a pious Christian. This is nonsense. Not only does it ignore the genuineness of Equiano's faith, it shows an ignorance of the lack of respectability of eighteenth-century Methodism. If he had been politically motivated he would not have attached himself to a branch of Christianity that was looked down upon by those who held power.

I refuse to accept the view that mankind is so tragically bound to the starless midnight of racism and war that the bright daybreak of peace and brotherhood can never become a reality
Martin Luther King, African-American civil rights leader in *Strength to Love* in 1963

The Methodists laid great emphasis on a Christian being 'born again'. Baptism was not enough, nor was trying to live a perfect life because no one could succeed in achieving that. Being 'born again' meant relying entirely on the forgiveness of God and handing your life over to his direction. This greatly puzzled Equiano because he had assumed he would have to earn his salvation by obeying all God's laws much as he had had to earn his freedom from slavery. He records how he tried to discuss the issue with various people and he was told that the price of saving him had been already paid by Christ dying on the cross for him:

> Confusion, anger, and discontent seized me, and I staggered much at this sort of doctrine; it brought me to a stand, not knowing which to believe, whether salvation by works or by faith only in Christ… I weighed all these things well over, and could not help thinking how it was possible for a man to know that his sins were forgiven him in this life. I wished that God would reveal this self same thing unto me.

The need for money drove him in this uncertain state back to the sea. He undertook a voyage to Spain, but found the lack of Christian behaviour on board very difficult: 'I fretted, mourned, and prayed, till I became a burden to others, but more so to myself.' At one point he says he felt like jumping into the sea and ending his unhappy life. Once back in London he sought further advice and he says he was helped to acquire 'a heartfelt resignation to the will of God' by talking with the governor of Tothill Fields prison (sometimes known as Bridewell) in the Westminster area of London. In this mood he returned to his ship for a second voyage to Spain. On the evening of 6 October 1775 he acquired the sense of assurance of salvation he had long sought, and was 're-born':

> As I was reading and meditating… and reflecting on my past actions, I began to think I had lived a moral life, and that I had a proper ground to believe I had an interest in the divine favour… The Lord was pleased to break in upon my soul with his bright beams of heavenly light; and in an instant… I saw clearly with the eye of faith the crucified Saviour bleeding on the cross on Mount Calvary [and] the scriptures became an unsealed book… I saw the Lord Jesus Christ in his humiliation, loaded and bearing my reproach, sin, and shame… It was given me at that time to know what it was to be born again… The word of God was sweet to my taste, yea sweeter than honey and the honeycomb… Now [I saw in] every leading providential circumstance that happened to me, from the day I was taken from my parents to that hour… the invisible hand of God, which guided and protected me when in truth I knew it not… This mercy melted me down… I felt an astonishing change. The burden of sin, the gaping jaws of hell, and the fears of death, that weighed me down before, now lost their horror… I was bathed in tears.

This religious experience was to be a major turning point in Equiano's life:

> Well may I say my life has been
> One scene of sorrow and of pain;
> From early days I griefs have known,
> And as I grew my griefs have grown.
>
> Dangers were always in my path;
> And fear of wrath, and sometimes death;
> While pale dejection in me reign'd
> I often wept, by grief constrain'd…
>
> Oft times I mused, nigh despair,
> While birds melodious fill'd the air:
> Thrice happy songsters, ever free,

How bless'd were they compar'd to me! …

Yet on, dejected, still I went -
Heart-throbbing woes within were pent;
Nor land, nor sea, could comfort give,
Nothing my anxious mind relieve…

Inur'd to dangers, griefs, and woes,
Train'd up 'midst perils, deaths, and foes,
I said 'Must it thus ever be?—
No quiet is permitted me'…

Yet here,'midst blackest clouds confin'd,
A beam from Christ, the day-star, shin'd;
Surely, thought I, if Jesus please,
He can at once sign my release…

O, happy hour, in which I ceas'd
To mourn, for then I found a rest!
My soul and Christ were now as one -
Thy light, O Jesus, in me shone!…

Use me, God. Show me how to take who I am, who I want to be, and what I can do, and use it for a purpose greater than myself
Prayer of Martin Luther King, African-American civil rights leader in the 1960s

---

The first impact of his new found faith was to make him want to convert others: 'I viewed the unconverted people of the world in a very awful state, being without God and without hope'. His preaching to his fellow sailors did not go well: 'I became a barbarian to them in talking of the love of Christ'. When the ship arrived back in London in December, he sought out those 'to whom I could tell of the wonders of God's love towards me'. He was particularly encouraged by listening to a sermon by the Anglican clergyman, William Romaine, at St Anne's, Blackfriars. Romaine was a leading evangelical with strong connections to the Methodist movement. Equiano's thoughts turned towards whether he could become a missionary to his own people in Africa. Dr Marie-Antoinette Smith in her study on Equiano's religious beliefs comments:

> Although he found solace and comfort in western Christianity, he could not come to terms with white Christian duplicity in terms of their proclaimed religious beliefs and their participation in transatlantic slavery. This is where Christian practice fell short for him. Therefore, even after enthusiastically embracing his faith, he longed to… spread Christianity amongst his native people, rather than remain and practice it among Europeans. He believed that Christianity was the true faith to which humans should subscribe and by which principles they should live… It it was the one thing needful to make his people… perfect in all ways. From his perspective, they… would know how to practice Christianity responsibly and according to its true end of living in peace, harmony, and accord with all people.

This made Equiano respond positively when Irving suggested that he should accompany him to the Western Caribbean and help create a new 'model plantation' in which slaves would be well-treated and automatically freed after working for a specified time. The opportunity to do this had arisen because Irving had dealings with a man called Alexander Blair who was wanting to create a castor oil and cotton plantation on the British controlled Mosquito Coast (now part of Nicaragua). Equiano agreed to go as 'overseer' but he clearly saw his role as being also a missionary one. Irving purchased the use of a sloop called *Morning Star* and it set sail for the Caribbean in November 1775.

On board were four representatives of the Miskito (the name give to the natives who lived on the Caribbean coast of Central America). They had been in London to negotiate the release of land for the colony. All four were nominally 'Christian' but they knew nothing about the Christian faith. Equiano's missionary zeal led him to try to remedy that. The most receptive was the youngest, who was known as 'Prince George' because he was a son of the main Miskito chief:

> He was quite attentive, and received with gladness the truths that the Lord enabled me to set forth to him… When I used to go to bed at different hours of the night, if he was in his bed, he would get up on purpose to go to prayer with me, without any other clothes than his shirt; and before he would eat any of his meals amongst the gentlemen in the cabin, he would first come to me to pray.

Equiano taught him not only about Christianity but also how to write English. All went well until the other sailors intervened:

How Equiano Became A Missionary

Left: engraving of Granville Sharp. Below: part of the Mosquito Coast, 1894 photograph of Meskito Indians and Meskito hut from nineteenth century drawing. Bottom: the home of Thomas Hibbert in Kingston built in the 1750s: a sign of the growing wealth of the merchants in Jamaica.

Seeing this poor heathen much advanced in piety, [they] began to ask him whether I had converted him to Christianity, laughed, and made their jest at him… [They] told him never to fear the devil, for there was none existing… so that he would not learn his book any more! … Nor would he be with me, even at prayers. This grieved me very much. I endeavoured to persuade him as well as I could, but he would not come; and [I] entreated him very much to tell me his reasons for acting thus. At last he asked me, 'How comes it that all the white men on board who can read and write, and observe the sun, and know all things, yet swear, lie, and get drunk, only excepting yourself?' I answered him, the reason was, that they did not fear God; and that if any one of them died so they could not go to or be happy with God. He replied, that if these persons went to hell he would go to hell too.'

They may forget what you said but they will never forget how you made them feel
Attributed to Carl W. Buehner, a bishop in the Church of Jesus Christ of Latter day Saints and first cited in anthology published in 1971

The ship reached Jamaica in January 1776 and Irving set about getting a smaller ship to take them to the Mosquito coast. It was left to Equiano to purchase the slaves for the new colony. He deliberately chose Africans from his Igbo tribe. His readiness to become complicit in enslaving his own people has been heavily condemned by many writers. For example Elizabeth Hinds in an article on Equiano in 1998 wrote that his behaviour in Jamaica showed that his religious faith was not able to overcome his mercantile background and that slave buying placed him 'squarely within the dehumanising ideology of capitalism's driving slave market'. In other words he was putting money before people. However, this ignores the fact that there were very few voices demanding an end to slavery at this time and there was not as yet any organisation seeking its abolition. In that context the best Equiano felt he could do was bring the Christian faith to some of the enslaved within a new colony that guaranteed their eventual freedom.

No one is born hating another person because of the colour of his skin or his background or his religion. People must learn to hate, and if they can learn to hate, they can be taught to love, for love comes more naturally to the human heart than its opposite
Nelson Mandela, President of South Africa in *A Long Walk to Freedom* in 1994

Once everything was ready, they sailed to the Mosquito Shore and set about finding an appropriate location for the colony. They selected an area on the Rio Grande de Matagalpa and at first it seemed an idyllic place, despite the hard work involved:

> There was a large lagoon or lake, which received the emptying of two or three very fine large rivers, and abounded much in fish and land tortoise. Some of the native Indians came on board of us here; and we used them well, and told them we were come to dwell amongst them, which they seemed pleased at… They took us to different places to view the land, in order to choose a place to make a plantation of. We fixed on a spot near a river's bank, in a rich soil; and, having got our necessaries out of the sloop, we began to clear away the woods, and plant different kinds of vegetables, which had a quick growth… We used to make fires every night all around us, to keep off wild beasts, which, as soon as it was dark, set up a most hideous roaring… We frequently saw different kinds of animals; but none of them ever hurt us, except poisonous snakes, the bite of which the Doctor used to cure by giving to the patient, as soon as possible, about half a tumbler of strong rum, with a good deal of Cayenne pepper in it… The Indians were exceedingly fond of the Doctor, and they had good reason for it; for I believe they never had such a useful man amongst them…
>
> Upon the whole, I never met any nation that were so simple in their manners as these people, or had so little ornament in their houses… I never saw any mode of worship among them; but … there was not one white person in our dwelling, nor any where else that I saw in different places I was at on the shore, that was better or more pious than those unenlightened Indians… The country being hot, we lived under an open shed, where we had all kinds of goods, without a door or a lock to any one article; yet we slept in safety, and never lost any thing, or were disturbed. This surprised us a good deal; and the Doctor, myself, and others, used to say, if we were to lie in that manner in Europe we should have our throats cut the first night.

However, Equiano's interest in the project waned in the face of the rainy season which commenced in May. Monsoons washed away most of what they had planted. He requested permission to return to London and Irving reluctantly agreed.

George Cruikshank's 1826 cartoon (above) depicts the abolitionists as people who ignore the problems of the working classes in order to focus attention on the enslaved Africans, whom he depicts as living in idyllic conditions. It was essential for the abolitionist cause to counter such propaganda by publishing first-hand accounts like that of Equiano. His autobiography helped encourage other Africans to not only voice their stories but also to campaign for social and political reform. Among those in the early nineteenth century were Mary Price, a slave from Bermuda who wrote her autobiography and became the first woman to present an anti-slavery petition to Parliament, Robert Wedderburn, the mulatto son of a Jamaican slave, who wrote 'The Horrors of Slavery' in 1824 and became a leader of various radical organisations, and William Cuffay, the son of an African naval cook who was a former slave, and who became a leader in the Chartist movement that sought constitutional and social reform for the working classes.

7.
Equiano's Life As A Campaigner For The Abolition Of Slavery

I have a dream that my four little children will one day live in a nation where they will not be judged by the colour of their skin, but by the content of their character
  Martin Luther King: African-American civil rights campaigner in public speech in Washington in 1963

Equiano's return to Britain was fraught with problems because a freed slave constantly ran the risk of re-enslavement. Irving had arranged for him to travel on a ship to Jamaica from whence he could get a ship home, but in the harbour there was another ship belonging to the same company and its captain, a man called Hughes, was short of crew so he asked that Equiano should be made to work for him. When Equiano refused, Hughes said he would sell him back into slavery:

> I begged to be put on shore again; but he swore that I should not… I simply asked him what right he had to sell me? but, without another word, he made some of his people tie ropes round each of my ankles, and also to each wrist, and another rope round my body, and hoisted me up without letting my feet touch or rest upon any thing. Thus I hung, without any crime committed, and without judge or jury; merely because I was a free man, and could not by the law get any redress from a white person in those parts of the world. I was in great pain from my situation, and cried and begged very hard for some mercy; but all in vain. My tyrant, in a great rage, brought a musket out of the cabin, and loaded it before me and the crew, and swore that he would shoot me if I cried any more. I had now no alternative; I therefore remained silent, seeing not one white man on board who said a word on my behalf. I hung in that manner from between ten and eleven o'clock at night till about one in the morning; when, finding my cruel abuser fast asleep, I begged some of his slaves to slack the rope that was round my body, that my feet

might rest on something. This they did at the risk of being cruelly used by their master.

> **Until the colour of your skin is the target you will never understand**
> Attributed to Angela Y. Davis. African-American political activist

The next day Hughes made preparations to leave but Equiano's hanging body was in the way of hoisting the sails so he was cut down. He used the opportunity to lobby the ship's carpenter, a man known to him and Irving. The carpenter took it upon himself to tell both captains that Irving would cause great problems if he heard about Equiano's enslavement. This made the captain of the other ship question whether it was the right thing to do and Hughes angrily told an Indian to take Equiano back to the shore in his canoe. However, just as the canoe was setting off, Hughes had second thoughts:

> When I was not above thirty or forty yards from the vessel… [he ran on] deck with a loaded musket in his hand… and swore heavily and dreadfully that he would shoot me that instant, if I did not come back on board. As I knew the wretch would have done as he said, without hesitation, I put back to the vessel again; but, as the good Lord would have it,… just as I was alongside he was abusing the captain [of the other ship]… and both of them soon got into a very great heat… I then thought it was neck or nothing, so at that instant I set off again, for my life, in the canoe, towards the shore; and fortunately the confusion was so great amongst them on board, that I got out of the reach of the musket shot unnoticed… [and reached the shore] with many thanks to God for this unexpected deliverance.

He agreed to work his passage on another ship that he was told was going to Jamaica. However, the captain had lied to him. Once on board, he found the ship was moving south down the coast cutting and loading mahogany. When he eventually managed to leave that ship and got on another, he found he had again been deceived. It also did not go to Jamaica but headed off elsewhere. Whenever things were not going as well as intended, the captain vented his anger by beating Equiano. On one occasion the captain thought he saw a Spanish vessel and, rather than face capture, looked to blow up his ship by looking to light a barrel of gunpowder. He was only stopped by Equiano threatening him with an axe. When the ship eventually did go to Jamaica Equiano was released but he was given no pay for the work he had done.

In Jamaica he found Dr Irving, who was there to buy replacement slaves. After Equiano's departure he had appointed a white overseer who had so maltreated the Igbo slaves that they had all tried to escape in a large canoe and, not knowing where to go or how to manage the canoe, they had all drowned. Understandably the news of what had happened to his people made Equiano feel very guilty for having left them. Irving did what he could to get Equiano his unpaid wages:

> We went to every magistrate in Kingston (and there were nine), but they all refused to do any thing for me, and said my oath could not be admitted against a white man.

In November Equiano said farewell to Irving and boarded a ship for Britain. He had been helped to find a seaman's post on the *Squirrel* because one of its crew was the African Richard Yorke, who had served with Equiano on the Arctic expedition. Yorke was able to recommend him to its captain. It docked in Plymouth in January 1777 and Equiano travelled from there to London, vowing never again to return to the sea.

Nature created man free and God's grace invites him to assert his freedom
William Warburton, Bishop of Gloucester in speech to the Society for the Propagation of the Gospel in 1766

Equiano became a servant in the household of Matthias Macnamara, who had recently returned to London after serving as the Lieutenant-General and the Acting Governor of Senegal. His continued evangelical zeal led him to invite the other servants to join him in prayers. They just mocked him but Macnamara must have taken an interest in what was going on. He wrote to the Bishop of London, suggesting that the Church should train and ordain Equiano so he could go out as a missionary to Africa. Equiano was delighted but his meeting with the Bishop put pay to his hopes:

> He received me with much condescension and politeness; but, from some certain scruples of delicacy, declined to ordain me.

The big issue dominating most people's minds was the War of American Independence. This had broken out in 1776 and the British forces were not doing well. This would have mattered to Equiano because the British forces in

America were offering freedom to any American slave who joined them. If the British lost the War many African-Americans would face a bitter retribution from their former masters. In 1778 several letters criticising the government's handling of the crisis appeared in a newspaper called the *Morning Post*. They were signed 'Gustavus Vassa'. However, the letters are very different in style from the autobiography. Was that because Macnamara helped him to write them or because, as the historian Vincent Caretta has suggested, they were written entirely by Macnamara and he used his servant's name as a way of hiding his identity? If they were written by Equiano with Macnamara's help it was his first foray into political lobbying and his first published writing. Writing letters to the press was later to become one of Equiano's favourite means of exposing the horrors of slavery.

Equiano left the service of Macnamara in order to engage directly in the war effort. This may have been of his own volition but it may also have been a response to John Wesley's request that all Methodists should support the government's effort to create a new defensive force. France had committed itself to helping the American colonists achieve their independence and there was a widespread fear in 1778 that France might therefore invade Britain. The government ordered the Commander-in-Chief of the Army, General Lord Amherst, to create a massive army camp at Coxheath just outside Maidstone so a huge reserve army could be created by training local militias from all over the country. Equiano became a servant to Colonel George Pitt, the commander of the Dorsetshire militia. He went with him to Coxheath when it was the Dorsetshire militia's turn for training in 1779. Equiano says nothing of note happened in his life at Coxheath to warrant inclusion in his autobiography but we know from other sources that discipline was strict. All men were forbidden to go more than a mile from the camp without a pass.

Equiano is remarkably silent on what he did between 1779 and the ending of the War in 1784. He says his life was less full of incident and he does not wish to bore the reader. All we are told is that he visited Wales in 1783 'out of curiosity' and that he was almost killed when he went down a mine in Shropshire and there was a roof collapse. However, from other sources we know he was moving in those white circles most opposed to slavery, probably because of his earlier contact with Granville Sharp over the abduction of the escaped slave, John Annis. Equiano made an enormous contribution to raising public awareness of the evils of slavery by bringing to Sharp's attention a massacre of slaves on a slave ship called the *Zong*. Sharpe's prominent role in the abolitionist movement and what happened on the *Zong* in 1781 will feature later in this book.

Freedom is unquestionably the birth right of all mankind
John Wesley, founder of Methodism in *Thoughts on Slavery* in 1774

It is not just the *Zong* story that is omitted in his autobiography. So also is the posthumous publication in 1782 of letters written by Ignatius Sancho, an African who for thirty years had held celebrity status in London. Equiano did not move in the society circles in which Sancho had operated so it is highly likely they never met. However, the book of Sancho's letters may well have been influential in encouraging Equiano to consider writing his autobiography. Sancho had arrived in London as a two-year old in 1731. Intended as a gift for the three sisters of the Duke of Montagu, he had become the object of an educational experiment because the Duke, John Montagu, had developed a scientific interest in the question of whether or not Africans were an inferior species. This had happened because of his contact with two educated Africans, Francis Williams and Job Ben Solomon. Their stories will be covered later in this book. Montagu had provided Sancho with an education equal to that of any English gentleman in order to see what that might produce. Sancho had proved an adept student and his manners and learning were so indistinguishable from those of any white man that he soon became known in London circles as 'the extraordinary negro'.

Let it no longer be said by half-informed philosophers and superficial investigators of human nature, that Negers, as they are vulgarly called, are inferior to any white nation in mental abilities'
Ralph Griffiths reviewing *The Letters of Ignatius Sancho* in *The Monthly Review* in 1783

One of Sancho's published letters was an attack on 'the abominable traffic of slaves'. Its main thrust was that Britain had based its commerce with Africa not on brotherly love but on encouraging conflict, not on mutual dependence but on an unbridled pursuit of money. In 1782 it was viewed as controversial. Today his arguments are perceived as shallow, sentimental and cliché-ridden. The letter conveys nothing of the real horror of what was going on. The reason for that is obvious. Sancho's life had been one of more or less constant comfort. After John Montagu's death he had been appointed as the butler to the Duke's widow, the youngest daughter of the famous Duke of Marlborough. She had shown off her husband's talented protégé to the high social circles in which she moved and given him a handsome pension on her death. Between 1751 and 1765 Sancho had spent his time entertaining many famous figures in the literary and artistic circles of London society, composing music, and even appearing on the stage. Domestically he had also had a good life, marrying a West Indian woman, Ann Osborne, and having seven children. His good fortune had continued after his money ran out because George Montagu, the Duchess' son-law, made him his valet and then, in 1774, set him up as a fashionable greengrocer in London's Mayfair. This was sufficiently profitable to give Sancho the right to vote in elections, something no black man had ever achieved.

Equiano's personal experience of the slave trade and of the life of slaves on the plantations left him much better placed than Sancho to voice what slavery meant in practice but as yet he lacked Sancho's status. When the American War of Independence came to an end he opted to work on ships going to the new 'United States'. In 1784 he undertook a voyage to New York and he greatly admired the city. In 1785 he went to Philadelphia, where he was particularly impressed by the educational work of the Quakers among the African-Americans:

> It rejoiced my heart when one of these friendly people took me to see a free-school they had erected for every denomination of black people, whose minds are cultivated here and forwarded to virtue; and thus they are made useful members of the community. Does not the success of this practice say loudly to the planters in the language of scripture – 'Go ye and do likewise?'

For the first time he took on himself to act as the spokesperson for his people. In October 1785 he presented the Quakers with a public thank you:

> Gentlemen… we the poor, oppressed, needy, and much-degraded negroes, desire to approach you with this address of thanks, with our inmost love and warmest acknowledgment; and with the deepest sense of your benevolence, unwearied labour, and kind interposition, towards breaking the yoke of slavery, and to administer a little comfort and ease to thousands and tens of thousands of very grievously afflicted, and to heavy burdened negroes.

He made another voyage to Philadelphia in 1786. On his return in the August of that year he opted to become the voice of the black community in London. By then the city was awash with thousands of African-American refugees. These were some of the former slaves who had won their freedom by supporting the British forces in the American War. The Army had been brought them to London rather than see them re-enslaved and punished, but they were living in terrible

CAMPAIGNING FOR ABOLITION

Above: slave ships in London. Left: Cugoano's signature, giving both his African and his English name of John Stuart. Below left: Ignatius Sancho by Thomas Gainsborough 1768. Below: etching of Ottobah Cugoano serving Lady Maria Cosway 1784

conditions and very few of them could find employment. In this emergency Equiano joined forces with another former slave, Ottobah Cugoano, to form an organisation called 'the Sons of Africa'. Its purpose was to lobby Parliament about the plight of the free Africans. Cugoano was a Ghanaian who had been sold into slavery when he was thirteen. More will be said about him in a later chapter. The Sons of Africa was made up of full time and part time activists but unfortunately virtually nothing is known about them except for their names: Jasper Goree, George Robert Mandeville, James Bailey, William Stevens, Joseph Almaze, Jasper George, Thomas Oxford, John Adams, George Wallace, Cojoh Ammere, Thomas Cooper, Thomas Carlisle, Jorge Dent, Daniel Christopher, John Christopher, James Foster, John Scott, and Thomas Jones.

Change will not come if we wait for some other person or some other time. We are the ones we've been waiting for. We are the change that we seek
  Barack Obama, former American president in speech made in 2008

Equiano became involved in a scheme initiated by Grenville Sharp and backed by the government to create a colony in Sierra Leone to which some of the Africans could go and in which slavery would be illegal. In November 1786 the government hired Equiano to start buying the food and equipment required to give the colony a successful start. He was given the title His Majesty's Commissary for Stores for the Black Poor. Equiano found to his disgust that the government's main agent, James Irwin, was taking money without providing all that what was being paid for:

> I was struck with the flagrant abuses committed by the agent, and endeavoured to remedy them, but without effect. One instance, among many which I could produce, may serve as a specimen. [The] Government had ordered to be provided all necessaries… for 750 persons; however, not being able to muster more than 426 [who were prepared to go to the new colony], I was ordered to send the superfluous… [goods] to the king's stores at Portsmouth; but, when I demanded them for that purpose from the agent, it appeared they had never been bought, though paid for by government. But that was not all… [the Africans waiting to go to Sierra Leone,] suffered infinitely more; their accommodations were most wretched; many of them wanted beds, and many more clothing and other necessaries… [I] remonstrated to the agent in vain, and I could not silently suffer government to be thus cheated, and my countrymen plundered and oppressed, and

even left destitute of the necessaries for almost their existence. I therefore informed the Commissioners of the Navy of the agent's proceeding; but my dismissal was soon after procured.

Equiano's appointment was thus brought to a premature end in March 1787. The Navy Board knew he was telling the truth but he was sacked because too many people did not want to punish a white man on charges brought by a black man. Equiano wrote a letter to a newspaper to expose his wrongful dismissal and to provide evidence of the crimes of Irwin and others. The *Public Advertiser* published a letter that condemned him for uttering 'falsehoods as deeply black as his jetty face'. Equiano correctly assessed that the Sierra Leone project would be doomed by mismanagement. The story of its failure will be covered in a later chapter.

I feel devastation that slavery was humanly possible and absolute pride that so many of my ancestors survived. I think it's a true testament to the spirit of the African people that we have been able to triumph from such adversity
June Sarpong TV broadcaster and BBC's first Director of Creative Diversity in *The Guardian* in December 2006

Equiano decided that his time and that of the other Sons of Africa would be better spent giving the African-Americans skills that would gain them employment in London rather than trying to set up a colony for the few. Cuguano set up an apprenticeship scheme so that those African-Americans who could read and write could pass on those skills to those who lacked them. At the same time all the Sons of Africa began working closely with the Society for the Abolition of the Slave Trade. Those who place an emphasis on the need for violent resistance to overcome oppression sometimes criticise Equiano for looking to the paternalistic benevolence of white men to end slavery rather than supporting black insurrection but this ignores the role of the Sons of Africa. Equiano knew that freedom had to be won by the black as well as given by the white if Africans were to win respect. As far as he was concerned the best way to end slavery lay neither in black insurrection nor in whites persuading other whites but in both white and black campaigning together.

The life of a black man is of as much regard in the sight of God as the life of any other man
Ottobah Cugoano, a Son of Africa in *Thoughts and Sentiments* in 1787.

The Sons of Africa utilised their personal experiences to compile letters to send to the press and to leading politicians, and they organised and sent petitions to Parliament. Equiano also sent his own letters and they had a clarity and directness that made them far, far superior to anything that Ignatius Sancho had ever written. He may also have polished up the draft of a tract written by Cugoano. It was published in 1787 under the title *Thoughts and Sentiments on the Evil and Wicked Traffic of the Slavery and Commerce of the Human Species.*

Equiano thought it would help if he showed slavery was not only morally wrong but also economically nonsensical. He therefore put forward the argument that a whole new market for manufactured goods would open up if the British focused on trading with Africa rather than depopulating it:

> The manufacturing interest and the general interests are synonymous. The abolition of slavery would be in reality an universal good… [The only people to suffer from the abolition of slavery will be] those persons concerned in the manufacturing [of] neck-yokes, collars, chains, hand-cuffs, leg-bolts, drags, thumb-screws, iron muzzles, and coffins; [and] cats, scourges, and other instruments of torture used in the slave trade.

He led delegations and encouraged the Sons of Africa to begin sending letters to the royal family and leading aristocrats. In March 1788 he presented his own petition to Queen Charlotte urging her to encourage her husband, King George III, to support those in Parliament who were seeking to end Britain's role in the slave trade:

> Your Majesty's well known benevolence and humanity emboldens me to approach your royal presence, trusting that the obscurity of my situation will not prevent your Majesty from attending to the sufferings for which I plead. Yet I do not solicit your royal pity for my own distress; my sufferings, although numerous, are in a measure forgotten. I supplicate your Majesty's compassion for millions of my African countrymen, who groan under the lash of tyranny in the West Indies. The oppression and cruelty exercised to the unhappy negroes there, have at length reached the British legislature, and they are now deliberating on its redress; even several persons of property in slaves in the West Indies, have petitioned parliament against its continuance, sensible that it is as impolitic as it is unjust – and what is inhuman must ever be unwise… [I] implore your interposition with your royal consort, in favour of the wretched Africans; that, by your Majesty's

benevolent influence, a period may now be put to their misery; and that they may be raised from the condition of brutes, to which they are at present degraded, to the rights and situation of freemen, and admitted to partake of the blessings of your Majesty's happy government; so shall your Majesty enjoy the heartfelt pleasure of procuring happiness to millions, and be rewarded in the grateful prayers of themselves, and of their posterity. And may the all-bountiful Creator shower on your Majesty, and the Royal Family, every blessing that this world can afford.

Were I to enumerate even my own sufferings in the West Indies… the disgusting catalogue would be almost too great for belief
Olaudah Equiano writing to the press in February 1788

The thing that troubled Equiano most was that Parliament was not prepared to let him personally testify to what he had seen. It seemed to him a denial of justice to prevent him speaking when he could offer information that might influence its decisions. What made the matter worse was that those upholding the slave trade were alleging that any stories of slave maltreatment were fabrications written by the white abolitionists. In an open letter to the press in November 1788 one anti-abolitionist wrote that he challenged the opponents of slavery to 'produce a single man of decent character' who would verify what was being alleged and that any decent black African would 'turn pale in fabricating such assertions'. The publication of his autobiography in 1789 was Equiano's way of giving voice to what Parliament had refused to hear as well as an attempt to change the educated public's attitude and win them over to the anti-slavery cause. It was no accident that he had printed in capitals as part of the book's title WRITTEN BY HIMSELF. He ended his book with these words:

> I am far from the vanity of thinking there is any merit in this narrative: I hope censure will be suspended, when it is considered that it was written by one who was as unwilling as unable to adorn the plainness of truth by the colouring of imagination. My life and fortune have been extremely chequered, and my adventures various… [and] I early accustomed myself to look for the hand of God in the minutest occurrence, and to learn from it a lesson of morality and religion; and in this light every circumstance I have related was to me of importance. After all, what makes any event important, unless by its observation we become better and wiser, and learn 'to do justly, to love mercy, and to walk humbly before God?'

The book's frontispiece portrait is sometimes criticised on the grounds it makes Equiano look too much like a white man. He has a European-style hair cut and he is shown dressed like an English gentleman in a top coat, white waistcoat, and frilled shirt, and carrying a Bible. However, the title of the book makes it clear that Gustavus Vassa is Olaudah Equiano the African. The picture was not about Equiano pretending to be a white man. It was a way of saying to those who denied human equality that a black man was an equal and just as civilised as any white man. The Bible is open at the Acts of the Apostles because in that book Peter declares the gospel is for all, regardless of creed or colour.

Some newspapers immediately tried to discredit the book on its publication. Some argued that Equiano was not born in Africa and so the whole book was a fabrication. Others said it was too well-written to be by a black man and that therefore the book was just propaganda written by a white abolitionist. Equiano's response was to offer witnesses to his African origin and to prove he had written the book by touring the country, signing and selling copies in bookshops and speaking at anti-slavery events. This massive undertaking has been described by the historian John Bugg as 'the first modern-style author tour in British history'. Inevitably his tour included Bristol and Liverpool because of their role in the slave trade. Among the other places he spoke at in the west of the country were Bath, Devizes, Gloucester, Tewkesbury, Worcester, and Shrewsbury. He spoke extensively in the Midlands and in the North, including going going to the great cities of Birmingham, Manchester, Sheffield, Leeds, Nottingham, York, Durham, and Newcastle. It has been suggested that he particularly wanted to speak to miners and other industrial workers, believing that those who were facing exploitation were more likely to sympathise with the enslaved. In the east of the country he went to places like Cambridge. He also went to Scotland and Ireland.

I'm no longer accepting the things I cannot change. I'm changing the things I cannot accept
> Attributed to Angela Y. Davis. African-American political activist

---

Though he faced intense opposition in some places, the overwhelming response of people meeting 'the African' was a positive one. For example, the editorial in a newspaper after his visit to Sheffield in 1790 paraphrased the anti-racist words of Shylock in Shakespeare's *The Merchant of Venice*:

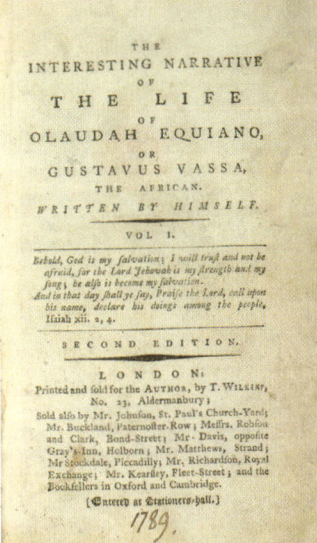

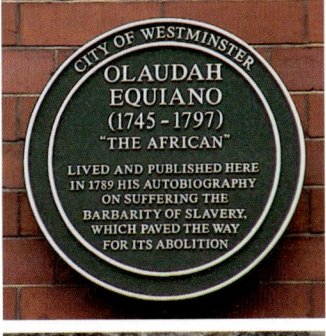

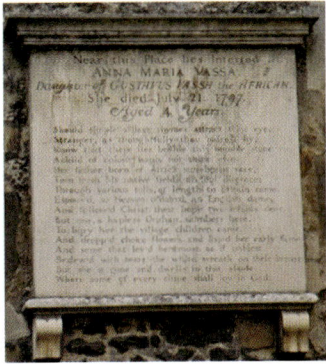

Top: the frontispiece portrait of Equiano and the title page of his book. Left: Youssou N'Dour as Equiano in film 'Amazing Grace'. Above: the plaque in Riding House Street that marks where he lived in London and the memorial to Anna Maria outside St Andrew's Church in Cambridge.

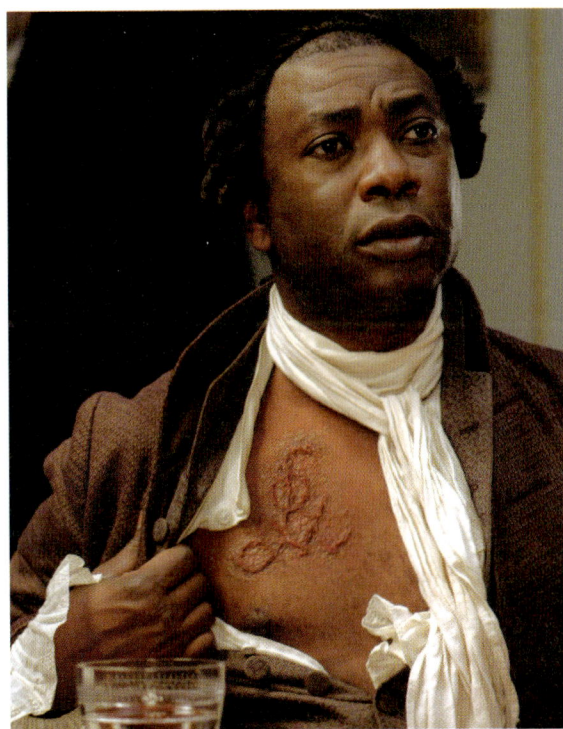

'Hath not an African eyes, hands, organs, dimensions, senses, affections, passions?'... Should any within the circle of our readers doubt the truth of this comparison, let them see Gustavus Vassa, the free African now in Sheffield – his manners polished, his mind enlightened, and in every respect on a par with Europeans.

Equiano was not averse to the use of a Shakespearean image. He promoted himself as a modern day Othello, out to deliver, like the Moor, 'a round unvarnished tale':

> Of moving accidents by flood and field,
> Of hair-breadth scapes i' the' imminent deadly breach;
> Of being taken by the insolent foe
> And sold to slavery; of my redemption thence.

And he soon had his own Desdemona because on 7 April 1792 he married a young white woman named Susannah Cullen, who lived in the Cambridgeshire village of Soham. It is thought he had met her whilst promoting his book in nearby Cambridge. A press report of the marriage states that 'a vast number of people assembled on the occasion'. It also says that Susannah's father was from Ely, but it is now suggested that the Cullen family may have come from Fordham, a village near Soham. The marriage was by special licence at St Andrew's Church in Soham and the parish records show it was witnessed by Thomas Cullen and Francis Bland. Nothing is known about who Bland was but Thomas was obviously a relative, possibly a brother. Was this a love match or Equiano's way of obtaining, in the words of Ronald Paul in the *Journal of Black Studies*, 'the ultimate stamp of approval' to prove he was now racially respectable and had migrated upward 'through the hierarchy of colour'? The latter view harks back to the writing of the French West Indian psychiatrist and political philosopher, Frantz Fanon, who, in the 1960s, advocated that violent resistance was the answer to colonialism and that black people had been traumatised into trying to deny their blackness in a white world. Here is Fanon's take on what a mixed marriage means in his most famous book, *Black skin, White masks*:

> I wish to be acknowledged not as a black but as white... Who but a white woman can do this for me? By loving me she proves that I am worthy of white love. I am loved like a white man. I am a white man. Her love takes me onto the noble road that leads to total realisation... I marry white culture,

white beauty, white whiteness... When my restless hands caress those white breasts, they grasp white civilisation and dignity and make them mine.

And here is what Equiano had to say to those who condemned mixed marriages:

A more foolish prejudice than this never warped a cultivated mind – for as no contamination of the virtues of the heart would result from the union, the mixture of colour would be of no consequence.

After the wedding Susannah accompanied Equiano on a book tour to Scotland, but her ability to travel was curtailed once she became pregnant. In a letter dated 1792 Equiano wrote about the impact his book tours were having:

I trust that my going about has been of much use in the Cause of the accursed Slave trade – a gentleman of the Committee... [of the Society for the Abolition of the Slave Trade] has said that I am more use to the Cause than half the people in the country. I wish to God I could be so.

One day our descendants will think it incredible that we paid so much attention to things like the amount of melanin in our skin or the shape of our eyes or our gender instead of the unique identities of each of us as complex human beings
Attributed to Franklin Thomas, African-American president of the Ford Foundation in the 1980s

All the touring came to an abrupt end in August 1794, almost certainly because Equiano had become a member of a radical political society called the London Corresponding Society and that summer its members faced persecution and arrest. The Society's founder, a London shoemaker called Thomas Hardy, was charged with treason and he and a number of its members were thrown into prison. The L.C.S. had been created by Hardy in 1792 originally just for his friends, one of them being Equiano, who was one of his tenants, but its membership had increased to over 3,000, almost all of them artisans. The prime aim of the L.C.S. was to achieve a radical reform of Parliament and to obtain the vote for all men by using non-violent methods. However, against the backdrop of the violent upheavals occurring in France, this was viewed as threatening the country's stability. One factor that made the L.C.S. seem particularly dangerous was that some of its members, such as Ottabah Cugoano, were known to be defending the right of slaves to rebel. Government agents accused Hardy of plotting to destroy Parliament and planning to have the King assassinated. This was sheer nonsense and Hardy was eventually acquitted but by then Equiano was no longer in a position to renew his former role. A subsequent chapter will look at how the French Revolution also impacted adversely on the country's attitude towards the Society for the Abolition of the Slave Trade.

The revenue from the sales of Equiano's book gave him a comfortable income and he settled down to live with Susannah in Soham. They had two daughters: Anna Maria, born on 16 October 1793, and Joanna, born on 11 April 1795. He gave some of the money to help the families of arrested L.C.S. members but clearly tried to disassociate himself from 'radicalism'. The names of those judged radical, such as Hardy and Cuguano, were removed from the list of those who had subscribed to his autobiography's publication. His wife died after a long illness in February 1796 at the age of just thirty-four and it is assumed that her mother and sister took on looking after the children whilst Equiano returned to London. He did not long survive his wife, dying on 31 March 1797. If his birth date was accurate he was just fifty-two. Granville Sharp went to see him just before he died and wrote afterwards to his niece about how Equiano's illness had deprived him of his voice 'so he could only whisper'.

Equiano's four year-old daughter Anna Maria died not long afterwards on 21 July in Soham, possibly from measles. The plaque outside St Andrew's Church commemorating her burial unintentionally includes the racist lines:

> Know that there lies beside this humble stone
> A child of colour haply not thine own.

Equiano was buried in a cemetery in Tottenham Court Road next to George Whitefield's Tabernacle, a Calvinistic Methodist chapel and one of the places where he had worshipped. His estate, which was valued in modern terms at around £100,000, was left to his surviving daughter, Joanna. She later married a Congregationalist minister called Henry Bromley and the couple ran a chapel in Appledore in Devon for a few years before moving on to other appointments in Essex. She died in 1867 and it is not known whether she and her husband ever had any children.

Until relatively recently the contribution of Equiano and the Sons of Africa did not feature in histories of the British abolition movement because, in the words of one historian:

> They were overshadowed by their white counterparts… [and] their push

towards the abolition of slavery was not seen as significant enough to include.

His autobiography, which on its publication had gone into eight editions, went into obscurity until it was reprinted in 1967. Since then it has never been out of print and there are now numerous editions. As a result of the 2007 bicentenary celebrations of Britain's abolition of the slave trade Equiano's story appeared for the first time extensively, not only in historical works and television documentaries but also in novels, plays, television dramas and films. He is now rightly viewed as a major contributor to the abolition of Britain's role in the slave trade and as the first in a long line of black leaders who, without rancour or violence, have stood up for the right to be treated equally and fairly.

Olaudah Equiano's argument against slavery was his life experience
    Eric Washington, American historian in article in *Christianity Today* in 2019

Left: view of Bristol by John Hassell 1795. Below: Bristol Harbour with the Cathedral and the Quay from Wapping Dock (now site of the MShed) by Nicholas Pocock 1785. Bottom: The Quay with the Tower of St Stephen's by T.H. Shepherd 1830.

SECTION THREE

Bristol's Role In The Slave Trade

The greatest, richest and best port of trade in Great Britain, London only excepted. The merchants of this city not only have the greatest trade, but they trade with a more entire independency upon London, than any other town in Britain... Whatsoever exportations they make to any part of the world, they are able to bring the full return back to their own port and dispose of it there
Daniel Defoe, novelist in his in *A Tour Through the Whole Island of Britain* in 1724-7

The port of Bristol steadily grew in importance in an era when most transport had to be undertaken by water. By the start of the eighteenth century it had become the transport hub for not only the south-west and trade with Wales and Ireland, but also for some of England's international trade with Europe. Every year around 1,300 ships of varying sizes used it facilities. As yet the slave trade hardly featured. It is thought that between 1650 and 1700 there were only about five Bristol ships per year involved in any form of trade with Africa and not all of those were participating in slavery. This very minor involvement reflected the national situation because England's role in the slave trade was as yet very small and almost entirely in the control of London's merchants. In contrast Spain, Portugal and France were transporting around 18,000 slaves per year at this time.

What changed all this was the War of Spanish Succession between 1700 and 1714. This was the war in which the new kingdom of Great Britain (formed by the union of England and Wales with Scotland in 1707) emerged as a great power. Its victory over Spain and France resulted in it acquiring Gibraltar and Minorca, which effectively gave it naval control of the Mediterranean. Britain's interest in developing colonies in the West Indies and the Americas rapidly took off, encouraged by Spain giving it the sole right to supply slaves to all the Spanish colonies. Bristol's merchants were quick to see that huge profits could be made out of the need for slave labour in the growing number of plantations. It is estimated that collectively they began investing on average almost £160,000 a year in the African trade (around £19 million in today's values). As a consequence Bristol's merchants began sending more and more ships to Africa. Between 1725 and 1730 it sent out seventy-nine ships. No other port, except London, could match that. Liverpool, the next biggest competitor, sent out only fourteen ships. By the 1730s Bristol was sending out about forty-five ships each year and virtually all of these were participating to a greater or lesser extent in the slave trade. It was a dramatic turnaround and the profits it brought encouraged even more activity.

One common misconception is that slave ships owed their existence to a small handful of merchants who became slave traders. In reality slave ships required a number of investors because of the costs involved and many merchants and manufacturers were involved. The average cost of preparing a ship for the voyage was about a third of a million pounds in modern money. Most of the slaving voyages that started from Bristol had at least two and often up to six or seven investors. Some had up to twenty-five. Some of these investors were obviously merchants but most were the owners of industries that were keen to export their products to Africa and/or keen to profit from the import of sugar and other products from the Caribbean and Americas. Many of the merchants and manufacturers acquired colonial estates and so became slave owners and the growing demand for sugar was the single biggest driving force behind the growth of the slave trade.

What we call a slave trader was essentially what the investors termed a ship's 'agent' or ship's 'husband' or ship's 'pursar', the person who saw that the ship was properly fitted out and stocked with the initial goods for sale and determined its route. The ship often belonged to him but it might have shared ownership. Some goods were purchased and some were provided because their manufacturer was an investor. Handing over responsibility to 'an expert' was attractive to those who were not merchants because it meant they did not have to have an in-depth knowledge of the trade or take responsibility for the overall management of the voyage. The ship's agent was responsible for appointing the captain and providing him with his instructions. He also wrote the necessary business letters to agents in West Africa, the Caribbean and America. These letters would cover things like the purchase and sale of slaves and the desired produce to be purchased for the return voyage. The success of a voyage depended significantly on the slave trader's understanding of the various markets and on the contacts he had created. Although a number commenced their role when they were still in their

Bristol's Role In The Slave Trade

Top left: Floating dock by Bartlett engraved by Varrall 1830. Top Right: Bristol from the Avon looking north-east by T.H. Shepherd engraved Mottram 1830. Above: Broad Quay in 1785 by Philip Vandyke. The three figures by the barrels include a black man. Right: the Avon at Bristol with Clifton Wood from Sea Banks by Nicholas Pocock.

twenties, most became managers of ventures when they were aged around forty and had built up more contacts.

Singling out slave traders as the sole 'culprits' is therefore wrong. Virtually all of Bristol's merchants and manufacturers were active initiators of the slave trade and that's why the resulting wealth was so widely shared. The need for co-operation explains why the Society of Merchant Venturers was so important to the slave trade. It provided a vital meeting ground for access to the latest commercial information and it acted as a vehicle through which members could agree on deals and assist each other in times of financial difficulty. It also provided its members with certain privileges, such as reduced harbour fees. It was no coincidence that the membership of the Society reached its peak of 132 members in the 1730s when Bristol's role in the slave trade was at its highest. The normal method of joining involved an 'apprenticeship' for five years and this gave existing members an opportunity to monitor a person's suitability. However, it was possible for the son of an existing member or a merchant from outside Bristol to forego this system and simply pay a fee to join. In the first half of the eighteenth century it was very common for the sons of merchants to follow in their father's footsteps just as the sons of manufacturers took on their father's business.

Some families prided themselves on having successive generations of their family as members. This and intermarriage ensured the Society was able to speak with one voice on slavery and most other matters. In the second half of the eighteenth century less sons followed their father and so the Society's ability to attract members from all around the country became increasingly important. Organisationally the Society of Merchant Venturers relied on fifteen people. These comprised four annually elected officials (the Master, two Wardens and the Treasurer), one paid officer (the Hall Clerk), and ten annually elected assistants, whose qualification for office was to be judged 'discreet, wise and worthy' by their peers. Issues were formally discussed at monthly meetings and committees were set up as and when required. Their work involved things like planning improvements to the port, ensuring that the right people were holding positions of power in the city, drafting appropriate petitions, and organising deputations to central government.

The Society's control of the public 'voice' of Bristol should not be underrated. It was easy for it to control Bristol because the city was essentially run by a small Council of just forty-three men : a mayor, two sheriffs, twelve aldermen and twenty-eight councillors. Control of these posts, whether they were by election or appointment, largely rested with the Society of Merchant Venturers. It was

Top: the Merchants' Hall from 1673 Millerd Map and the new Merchants Hall built in 1783 depicted by Hugh O'Neil 1823. Above: the Merchant Hall mansion built for the Society in 1868. Bottom left : the Merchant Venturers Technical College. Bottom right: the Merchant Venturers Almhouses built in 1696 with support from Edward Colston.

very rare for its members to comprise less than half of the Council membership as a whole. Forty-five of the city's eighteenth-century mayors were members of the Society and eleven of these were slave traders. Sixteen slave traders held the office of Sheriff. Similar control existed over the election of Bristol's two M.P.s because the electorate was only a small percentage of the city's population. It was relatively easy for the Society to either bribe or intimidate voters into electing their candidates. Of the twenty-three M.P.s who represented the city in the course of the eighteenth century eight were members of the Society and almost all the rest were men who had its backing. As we shall see in the next section of this book, these M.P.s constantly spoke in favour of the slave trade in Parliament.

> *They exert quite a bit of influence and we, the people of Bristol, don't know much about them and can't hold them to account*
> Paul Burton, Head of Bristol University's School of Policy Studies on the Merchant Venturers cited in *Venue* in 2004

Today the Society of Merchant Venturers tries to forget the role it played in promoting slavery and it focuses instead on its past and present involvement in charitable activities. Its most noteworthy positive input has been in the educational life of the city. That role began in 1595 when the Society set up a school for the children of mariners in the basement room of the Chapel of St Clement, but it really took off once the Society commenced supporting the educational initiatives of Edward Colston and others. In the nineteenth century the Society helped fund many schools and probably its most innovative contribution was to create the Trade School in 1863, the first school in England to aim at teaching the scientific principles upon which manufacture and commerce are based. This later became the Merchant Venturers' School in new buildings in Unity Street in 1885 and then the Merchant Venturers' Technical College. In 1909 its Engineering Department became the Faculty of Engineering for the newly created Bristol University and the Society still is one of the University's sponsors. The Merchant Venturers ceased to fund the Technical College in 1949 but it went on to become Bristol Polytechnic, the precursor of the University of the West of England, and it played a significant role in the creation of Bath University in the 1960s. The Merchant Venturers are currently sponsors to Bannerdown Road Community Academy, Barton Hill Academy, Colston's Girls' School, Colston's School, the Dolphin School, Fairlawn Primary School, the Kingfisher School, Merchants' Academy and the Venturers' Academy.

Alongside this continued educational work the Society currently runs about twelve charities and forty trust funds. It helps fund a number of historic buildings and open spaces and it does much for the young, aged and disadvantaged. However, it would be better if all this positive contribution was not accompanied by a denial of its past. The Society's website proclaims that it has 'no wealth derived directly from the slave trade', that some of its members in the eighteenth century 'may have profited from the slave trade' and it likes to give the impression that its main political concern in the eighteenth and early nineteenth centuries was not defending slavery but promoting free trade. This simply defies historical truth. The early wealth of the Merchant Venturers was rooted in the profits of the slave trade and a very high percentage of its members were involved in some way or other with slavery. The overwhelming majority of the letters, petitions, and delegations it sent to Parliament were in support of Bristol's trade with Africa and the West Indies, and that meant constantly defending both the slave trade and slavery. Much of what the Society subsequently did, including not just its charitable work but investment into the Clifton Suspension Bridge and the Great Western Railway, was paid for by wealth that stemmed either directly or indirectly from slavery.

More than 60% of the Bristol economy was reliant on the brutal commoditisation of human life... The gold and silver... is sown throughout the city... and [in] the endowments of its mercantile benefactors
Article in *The Independent* newspaper in May 2006

This section begins by examining the role played by Edward Colston and why a man who was never a major slave trader has become the focus for the slavery issue in Bristol. The second chapter looks at Bristol's rivalry with Liverpool in the slave trade and why Liverpool gained the ascendancy from the 1740s onwards. The next three chapters are on the three key groups involved in the trade : the slave traders, the captains and crews of the slave ships, and the plantation owners. The chapter on the slave traders focuses mainly on those who organised more than ten slaving expeditions so it does not cover the majority of slave traders, but it deals with all the main players. A sixth chapter looks at the slaves who ended up being brought to Bristol and a final chapter examines the impact the slave trade had on Bristol and the surrounding area.

Above: Edward Colston by Jonathan Richardson the Elder. Left: the 1895 statue by John Cassidy in the centre of Bristol before it was removed; Below: Colston's 1691 almshouses on Michael's Hill.

1

Edward Colston

> *Edward Colston still lives among you, a malevolent presence, more than 200 years after the last terrified black man was stolen from his family, chained, whipped, beaten and tortured by having the initials of Colston's company etched upon his chest with a red-hot branding iron… A statue honouring him still poisons the city centre today*
>
> Mike Gardner retired journalist in *The Bristol Post* in June 2014

Today the name most associated with Bristol's role in the slave trade is that of Edward Colston, who was born in November 1636, the eldest of probably eleven children. There had been Colstons in Bristol from at least the fourteenth century and his father, William Colston, was a prosperous merchant based in Wine Street. The family ran into problems because of their support for the Royalist cause in the English Civil War and William was deprived of his office as alderman and sheriff of Bristol in 1645. The family left the city to live in London and Edward was probably educated at Christ Hospital's School because he later became both a governor and benefactor to it. In 1654 he was apprenticed to the Mercers Company in London and, after his apprenticeship was completed, he worked abroad for a number of years, probably looking after his father's trading interests in Spain. With the restoration of the monarchy in 1660 his family had moved back to Bristol and his father and elder brother Thomas were importing wine and oil from Spain and Portugal and sugar from St Kitts because William had a part share in the St Peter's Sugar House in Castle Precincts. Importing raw or semi-refined sugar and refining it for sale had already become a major part of Bristol's economy with around fifty ships a year involved.

In 1672 Colston set himself up as a merchant in London and over the next eight years built up a prosperous business exporting textiles and importing wine, sherry, oil and fruit. Most of his trade was with Spain, Portugal, Italy and the Canary Islands. In 1680 he joined the Royal African Company and he remained a member of it for twelve years. The decision to do that was probably taken because of his family's commercial interest in the sugar trade. The sugar grown on St Kitts would have come from enslaved labour. Colston served on various committees and in 1689 he became a deputy-governor of the Company. In that capacity he undoubtedly helped to promote greater participation in the slave trade. However, it needs to be remembered that this was happening at a time when society judged slavery to be a perfectly acceptable institution and, like virtually all of his generation, Colston would not have been encouraged to question its morality by the Church. Estimates as to how many Africans were enslaved by merchants associated with the Royal African Company vary but the commonest figure quoted is around 80,000 with 20% of them dying before they were actually sold. However, there is no evidence to prove Colston personally organised a slaving voyage in either London or Bristol whereas it is known that one of the partners in the St Peter's Sugar House, Samuel Jacob, did. Colston left the Royal African Company in 1692 and the St Peter Sugar House was taken over by the Corporation in 1696 for use as a mint. Two years later it became John Cary's work house for the poor.

All this makes Colston an odd choice to be the chief focus of attention. Some historians think the African trade was never a significant part of his business and that his main wealth came from his money-lending. He retired in 1708 before Bristol's role in the slave trade really took off. The slave traders in Bristol who enslaved half a million Africans were not in any sense following his example. They were seeking to improve their profits. The reason for his current notoriety therefore arises not from the scale of his slave trading but as a consequence of the increasing adulation given to him after his death. That adulation did not stem from his role as a merchant but from his role as a benefactor, which put his name into the public eye.

There is no doubting that Colston had a great affection for Bristol. In his words, it was the place where 'I drew my first breath'. He began visiting the city regularly after his father's death in 1681, presumably to help his brother and comfort his widowed mother. Thomas died in 1683 and Colston inherited the family business. He therefore became a burgess of the city and joined the Society of Merchant Venturers in 1684. He provided Bristol's corporation with a much needed loan. However, Colston had no intention of making Bristol his home. His main trading interests lay in London, where he was not only operating a fleet of forty ships but also gaining considerable profits from money-lending to individuals and to the government. It is reasonable to assume he organised agents to run the family business because he returned to living in the mansion he had acquired in Mortlake in Surrey in 1685. However, he continued to regularly visit Bristol in order to check up on his business interests and to see his mother Sarah, who lived to the grand age of ninety-three.

> *I think there's many a slaveholder'll get to Heaven. They don't know better. They acts up to the light they have*
> Sarah Bradford citing words of former slave Harriet Tubman in *Scenes in the Life of Harriet Tubman* in 1869

His mother died in 1701 and by then Colston had become deeply involved in various philanthropic schemes in Bristol. His chief concern was to encourage greater membership of the Church of England in a city which had come to acquire many non-conformist groups. His family's experience in the English Civil War had left him with a horror for religious division. He paid for lectures and sermons to be given in various places, including Newgate Prison, and he provided money to help repair and/or beautify Bristol Cathedral, St Mary Redcliffe, St Werburgh's, All Saints', St James', and St Michael's. He also became a patron of many charities, supporting , for example, John Cary's creation of the Mint Workhouse. Among his gifts was creating almshouses on St Michael's Hill and, working in conjunction with the Merchant Venturers, helping fund almshouses in King Street. On a board in the latter's quadrangle appeared the words:

> Freed from all storms, the tempest, and the rage
> Of billows, here secure we spend our age -
> Our weather-beaten vessels here repair,
> And from the merchants' kind and generous care
> Find harbour here, no more we put to sea,
> Until we reach into Eternity;
> And lest our Widows, who we leave behind
> Should want relief, they too a shelter find.
> Thus all our anxious cares and sorrows cease,
> Whilst our kind guardians turn our toils to ease,
> May they be with an endless Sabbath blest,
> Who have afforded unto us this rest.

Because of his fear of religious dissent Colston made clear that his money should only be spent on those who had a clear connection with the Church of England, which he described as 'the best of Churches'. He became a member of both the Society for the Propagation of the Gospel and the Society for Promoting Christian Knowledge and he said he was not prepared to fund anything that might help the various non-conformist groups in Bristol such as the Baptists and Quakers, or help the Catholics or Jews. It became his expressed desire 'that the youth of the whole city will be educated in the fear of God and in the profession of His true religion, as it is set forth by the Established Church of England'. This led him to want to create schools for orphan boys. An orphan at this time was any child who had lost his or her father. A story circulating just after Colston's death said that on one occasion he was asked why he had not married and his response was 'Every helpless widow is my wife and distressed orphans are my children.'

He helped fund the rebuilding of the Queen Elizabeth's Hospital and then proposed doubling its size on condition it did not take the children of non-conformists. This proposed restriction offended many in the city and in 1705 the corporation refused to work with him on the project. The opposition was not just religious. Not all the wealthy in Bristol shared his concern for providing the poor with a free education. They said a free school was just 'a nursery for beggars and sloths'. Colston decided to create and endow his own school for poor orphans and he received support from the Society of Merchant Venturers. Colston's School for Boys was officially opened on the site where the Colston Hall now stands in 1710. One hundred boys were boarded within the school and each was given a long blue coat and yellow stockings to wear because Colston wanted it to be modelled on the school he had attended in London. They were admitted when aged between seven and ten and were taught reading, writing, spelling and arithmetic up to the age of fourteen and then given £10 each so they could seek an apprenticeship. They were expected to worship in the Cathedral and the punishment for worshipping in any place other than an Anglican church was expulsion.

The school was his single most costly undertaking because he spent well over £30,000 on it (around two million in today's values). It was said that when a grateful widow told Colston that she would pray for Heaven's blessing on him for looking after her son's education, he declined her homage, saying:

> No, we do not thank the clouds for rain, nor the sun for light, but we thank the God who made both the clouds and the sun.

Alongside Colston's School he also created the Temple School for another forty boys, all drawn from the parish in which he had been born, that of the Temple Church. They were taught reading, writing, and basic mathematics so they had the skills to become apprentices. He stipulated that all the boys were to be taught the catechism of the Church and insisted hat none of them should be permitted to be apprenticed to any dissenter. He subsequently fell out with the Rev. Arthur Bedford, the vicar of the Temple Church, over Bedford's readiness to work with dissenters or, as Colston described them, 'fanatics'. Today the Temple School has long been subsumed into the co-educational Church of England St Mary Redcliffe and Temple School

In 1710 the Merchant Venturers ensured Colston's election as one of the city's two M.P.s, even though he was not resident in Bristol. He held that role until 1713 when ill-health forced him to resign it. He died aged eighty-five in 1721 and his body was brought to Bristol for burial at All Saints' Church. His dying wish was that he should be buried without any pomp or ceremony 'in the grave that belonged to my ancestors', but the city insisted on turning the occasion into a grand civic occasion as the *Annals of Bristol* records:

> The funeral procession, which was a week or ten days upon the road, consisted of a hearse with six horses, covered with plumes and velvet, and attended by eight horsemen in black cloaks, bearing banners; and three mourning coaches with six horses to each. At the resting places on the way, a room was hung with black, garnished with silver shields and escutcheons, while upwards of fifty wax candles in silver candlesticks and sconces were placed around the coffin, covered with a silver-edged velvet pall. The gloomy cavalcade reached Lawford's Gate on the night of the 27th October, where it was met by the boys … [from Colston's School and the Temple School], the almspeople in the hospital on St. Michael's Hill, and the old sailors maintained at Colston's charge in the Merchants' Almshouse… The procession, accompanied by torches, with the schoolboys singing psalms, made its way to the church amidst continuous torrents of rain, and the interment took place about midnight, in the presence of as many persons as could crush into the building. The bells of the various parish churches tolled for sixteen hours on the day appointed for the funeral.

Colston bequeathed £100,000 (around six million in today's values) to his relatives, mostly to his niece Mary, who had married Thomas Edwards, his legal representative in Bristol, and £71,000 (around four million in today's values) to public charities across the country but with the bulk going to Bristol. In 1722 an engraving of him was produced and the wording under the portrait described him as 'the brightest Example of Christian Liberality that this Age has produced both for the extensiveness of his Charities and for the prudent Regulation of them'. In 1729 he was given an elaborate memorial tomb in All Saints' Church and it also praised his generosity. By then various stories of his kindness to individuals were circulating so the following sentence was included: 'What he did in secret is believed to be not inferior to what he did in public'.

In the eighteenth century Bristol won a reputation as a 'City of Churches and Charities' and Colston was crucial to that. The creation in 1726 of the Colston Society ensured that his name was not forgotten because it raised money to fund continued work among the poor, the orphaned and the sick, and to institute further educational initiatives, such as the creation of Colston Girls' School in 1891. His generosity also inspired the creation of the Dolphin Society (named after Colston's crest of arms) in 1749, the Grateful Society in 1758, and the Anchor Society in 1768, all dedicated to undertaking charitable activities in the city. The four societies held annual celebrations on his birthday and each organised a parade through the city. Distributing money to the poor became part of these civic occasions. The *Gentleman's Magazine* produced an article on Colston that reflected the growing admiration for him. It praised his 'exalted motives' and his lifelong 'goodness and liberality'. It said he was a quiet, humble, patient, temperate, cheerful, and benevolent man, 'remarkably circumspect in all his actions' and 'a great and exemplary Christian'. It is perhaps worth saying that all four of these societies still exist and still undertake charitable activities, although they are now much smaller and less high profile organisations.

Erected by citizens of Bristol as a memorial of one of the most virtuous and wise sons of their city
Words below statute to Edward Colston in Bristol, erected in 1895

In all this praise Colston's connection with slavery was utterly ignored except for a picture of Colston on his deathbed produced in 1844. This was painted following the exhumation of his body during renovation work at All Saints' Church. The event had caused quite a stir because Colston's body had not shown signs of decomposition when his tomb was opened. Once exposed to the air, decomposition rapidly set in but not before his preserved face had been seen by the artist Richard Jeffrey Lewis. This appears to have inspired him to draw the deathbed scene. In his will Colston had mentioned a servant called 'black Mary' so Lewis drew a black servant woman holding his hand and obviously grieving for her kind master. Nothing is known about who 'black Mary' was but it seems not unreasonable to assume she was a slave brought to England. Lewis was making no political point. His painting says nothing about the horrors of

Edward Colston

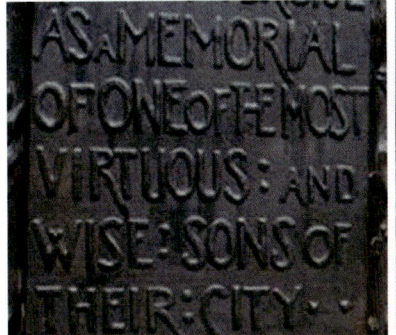

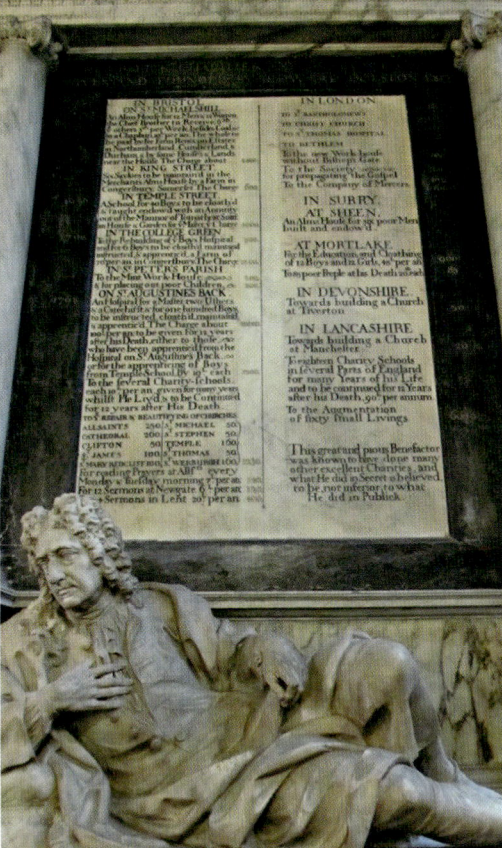

Left: Colston's School on its original site, the offending words on his statue and anti Colston protests in 2017 and 2018. Top: his monument in All Saints' Church which details his generosity. Above: Colston on his deathbed with grieving Black Mary on her knees and holding his hand painted by R.J. Lewis in 1844.

the slave trade and it shows Mary well dressed and very much part of Colston's circle. However, the picture did link Colston with the African trade. Was that why it was put into storage sometime towards the end of the nineteenth century? It only reappeared in 1999 when Bristol's City Museum and Art Gallery put it on display as part of the city's first ever exhibition on the slave trade.

The first detailed and researched biography of Colston was published in 1852. Its author, Samuel Tovey, said nothing about slave-trading. He mildly criticised Colston's attitude towards religious non-conformity, but said it was his only fault:

> It is… no easy task to portray a character which… approaches the ideal perfection of Christian virtue… breathing piety, infusing consolation, healing the broken-hearted, and lifting up those that were down… Benevolence, born of Faith and Hope, influenced and directed all his conduct… There is scarcely a misery incident to mortality which he did not endeavour to alleviate… There is a sacredness in Colston's sublime benevolence… that merits, as it has obtained, our venerated love… [He has] left by his extensive charities a name for thousands yet unborn to rejoice at and to bless… Long may his memory be fostered here.

A focus on an individual in many ways misses the point and leads to a misunderstanding and distortion of the legacy of Transatlantic slavery… The legacy of this trade cannot be pinned to an individual
    Tayo Lewin-Turner, history undergraduate at the University of Bristol in Bristol Museum's *Black History* website in 2019

With this kind of endorsement it is not surprising that the name of Colston was increasingly honoured in Bristol. The parades organised to celebrate his role became ever more spectacular, reaching their peak in the 1880s and 1890s, and over twenty streets and buildings were named after him, including Colston Avenue, Colston Street, Colston Road and the Colston Hall. The last building to acquire his name was the Colston Tower in 1973. Occasionally further societies using his name were created, such as the Colston Fraternal Association and Old Boys' Society in 1853, which aimed to help scholars at Colston's School go to university, and the Bristol University Colston Society in 1899, which aimed to promote scientific research. In 1895 a bronze statue of Colston was erected in the city centre. It was the work of a Manchester sculptor, John Cassidy and on the stone pedestal beneath it was inscribed what had become the unchallenged view of Colston – that he was 'one of Bristol's wisest and most virtuous citizens'.

Once the issue of Bristol's role in the slave trade became a source of shame in the late twentieth century it was inevitable that this inscription would come under attack. How could someone linked to the slave trade be honoured as one of Bristol's wisest and most virtuous citizens? Some people began to demand that Colston's statue should be removed and his name expunged from every street and building to which it had been attached. This led to others defending him. They argued that the Church of his day had not given him reason to see slavery as being immoral, that most of his wealth had not come from the slave trade, and that his philanthropic bequests and the charities which his example had inspired had helped far more people than he had enslaved. They also pointed out that other cities were still happy to commemorate figures from the past whose actions could be judged immoral by modern standards. One obvious example was Washington D.C. named after the first American President, George Washington, who was not only a slave owner but also a key figure in resisting attempts to abolish slavery in the newly-created United States. Was it not better for Bristol to show regret at its role in the slave trade by encouraging greater racial harmony in the city and by doing more to educate children about the city's role in the slave trade?

We all regret that the slave trade happened. Slavery was a trade in which all of Bristol was involved in, but we believe an apology is totally meaningless... It was the business of the city. And of course it was lawful
    D'Arcy Parkes speaking for the Society of Merchant Venturers in *Bristol Evening Post* in Nov. 2006

Despite such arguments, opposition to Bristol's continued recognition of Colston has increased and markedly so in the past decade. In 2013 George Ferguson, Bristol's first modern elected mayor, described any celebration of Edward Colston as 'perverse'. In 2014 Colston was dubbed 'the father of Bristol's slave shame' and the *Bristol Post* held a poll to see if Colston's statue should be removed. 44% of those who responded said 'yes'. In 2017 St Stephen's Church refused to hold the traditional annual thanksgiving service to Colston and Colston Primary School renamed itself Cotham Gardens Primary School. The Colston Hall announced it was also going to change its name and this evoked correspondence in the national press. One person questioned whether Liverpool would now have to rename Penny Lane – a street made famous by the Beatles in the 1960s – because it was named after a Liverpudlian slave trader called James

Penny. Another correspondent wrote to *The Guardian*:

> Airbrushing Colston's name from the Colston Hall would consign his deeds to history rather than make the city permanently aware of the abhorrent reasons for its prosperity… Removing the name would not send as strong a response… as changing the significance of Colston's presence on Bristol's streets… A plaque may not go far enough, but statues to honour the slaves and continuing education of Bristol's children about the city's tainted past would, in my view, do more to show how Bristolian attitudes have changed than wiping the visible trace of Colston from public view… Regardless of which side you are on, no one wants to honour Edward Colston.

In 2018 Bristol's new Mayor Cleo Lake, who described herself as a mix of Scottish, Bristolian and Afro-Caribbean, insisted on having Colston's portrait removed from her office and put in storage. That same year protesters on an Anti-Slavery Day placed one hundred human figures around his statue, laying them out as slaves would have been on board a ship. Many supported a proposal to reword the inscription on the statue's pedestal so it would highlight not only Colston's role in enslaving Africans but his religious bigotry by saying 'local people who did not subscribe to his religious and political views were not permitted to benefit from his charities'. The reworded plaque was controversially abandoned at the last minute in 2019, allegedly because of lobbying by the Society of Merchant Venturers and others. The city council announced it would put a plaque to commemorate the enslaved alongside his statue. This was a big error of judgment because, given the controversy, it would have made more sense to either have immediately done that or to have removed the statue to the M-Shed, where it could have been displayed with an appropriately worded text about Colston's role.

Miles Chambers, the city's poet laureate, understandably commented that Colston's statue had a symbolism that made dealing with it important:

> Some people don't get that black people still feel the full impact of slavery today. We can look at the descendants of the slaves and economically they are still worse off; psychologically they are still worse off; mentally they still feel collectively as inferior; more African-Caribbean males are disproportionately in prison and in the judicial system; they do worse at schools; economically are paid less and are working less. The pattern continues and even though many people say slavery is over, because of those

Edward Colston

The toppling of Colston's statue and casting it into the River Avon as part of the Black Lives Matter protest on 7 June 2020.

legacies we still feel enslaved. A name change or statue move is not going to rectify racism or eradicate the slave mentality that still exists, but it will help to say to black people: 'You are equal to us, you are British, you are valuable and you mean as much to us as any other citizen'.

The callous murder of the African-American George Floyd by a policeman in Minneapolis in May 2020 triggered anti-racist protests not just across the United States but within Britain. Even in the midst of the Covid-19 lockdown enough people felt sufficiently strongly about the continued racism within our society to organise 'Black Lives Matter' protest marches and meetings. The one in Bristol on 7 June almost inevitably gathered around Colston's statue. It was toppled and rolled down to the harbourside and thrown into the River Avon. The action evoked both praise and condemnation and made international news, sparking off a huge debate about the retention of commemorative statues linked to anyone involved in the slave trade. Colston's statue has been retrieved from the river and it is the intention that it will be put on display in its current abused state in the M-Shed. What that action must not do is make it seem as if somehow Bristolians have now dealt with the slavery issue because the irony in all this is that the constant emphasis on Colston has meant that the names of the merchants who actually spearheaded Bristol's role in the slave trade largely go unmentioned, and there is a racist legacy that urgently needs addressing.

All I demand for the black man is, that the white people shall take their heels off his neck, and let him have a chance to rise by his own efforts
William Wells Brown, African-American ex-slave and prominent abolitionist
in *A Demand for the Black Man* in 1862

2

THE RIVALRY WITH LIVERPOOL

Each life was worth 1.6 rolls of cloth, two-and-a-half guns, 72kg of metal and a handful of beads
    Cahal Milmo, journalist writing on slavery in *The Independent* in May 2006

In the years between 1730 and 1746 Bristol merchants became responsible for organising 40% of all British voyages to Africa, sending out more slaving ships than London every year, except in 1733 and 1736. The physical impact of this on Bristol was enormous because the ships using the harbour facilities got bigger – the average tonnage capacity increased from 105 tons to 144 tons – and rapidly increased in number from 240 big ships per year in 1687 to 375 in 1717 and 448 in 1787. Only a comparative few docked at Sea Mills or at what became known as Merchants' Dock and so Broad Quay and its surrounding wharfs were a constant hive of activity with fourteen cranes helping to unload or load not only the big ships but many lesser vessels involved in domestic trade. It took the big ships from seventeen to twenty weeks before they were ready to depart again and some ships stayed even longer if they had to be repaired or refitted. Not surprisingly, the sight of so many ships, both large and small, amazed visitors. The poet Alexander Pope, for example, wrote :

> In the middle of the street, as far· as you can see, [there are] hundreds of :ships, their masts as thick as they can stand by one another, which is the oddest and most surprising sight imaginable. This street is fuller of them than the Thames from London Bridge to Deptford, and at certain times only, the water rises to carry them out;·so that at other times, a long street; full of ships in the middle, and houses on both sides, looks like a dream.

Before the advent of copper bottomed ships in the 1780s the life expectancy of a wooden ship was usually no more than ten years and so merchants worked on the principle that a ship would never do more than about six slave voyages. There were, of course, exceptions. The *Berkeley Gally*, which was built in Bristol in 1705, lasted until 1740 and undertook twenty-five slaving voyages. Obtaining ships as cheaply as possible was a high priority and so only about half of the ships were purpose built in British shipyards. The rest were ships which were second-hand. The commonest source were enemy ships that had been captured in war and then sold off. One advantage of this was that the ships often came already equipped to fight. This was useful at a time when merchant shipping often faced armed attack either from pirates or from Britain's enemies.

All are in a hurry, running up and down with cloudy looks and busy faces, carrying and unloading goods and merchandise of all sorts from place to place; for the trade of many nations is drawn other by the industry and opulence of the people

Thomas Cox, clergyman and topographer on Bristol in *Magna Britannia et Hibernia* published 1720-31

Slaving ships were sometimes named after local places (e.g. the *Bristol*, the *Mary Redcliffe* and the *Oldbury*) or local merchants (e.g. the *Colston* and the *Freke*) or after destinations (e.g. the *Angola*, the *Jamaica* and the *Africa*). Sometimes the name reflected the hopes of its owner that it would prove profitable (e.g. the *Expectation* and the *Delight)* and it was quite common to name ships after a woman (e.g. the *Anna Maria* , the *Bridget* and the *Molly*), members of the royal family or aristocracy (e.g. the *King George*, the *Prince William*, and the *Marlborough*), or a character from the classical world (e.g. the *Hector*, the *Jason* and the *Mercury*). Occasionally the name might reflect participation in the slave trade (e.g. the *Blackamore* , the *Calabar Merchant* and the *Black Prince*).

The master shipwrights most remembered in connection with refitting, repairing or actually building or adapting ships in Bristol in the eighteenth century were a Quaker family called Teast. Sydenham Teast was a merchant who was involved mainly in whaling and in the fur and timber trade until he began investing heavily in the slave trade. The profits enabled him to build a dry dock in 1755 on the Avon at Wapping (now occupied by the housing of Merchant's Wharf). A sketch of the shipyard produced in 1760 shows that Teast was using at least a couple of black workers. He also built the houses on Redcliffe Parade overlooking this shipyard. These were homes for his fellow merchants. His son, also called Sydenham, built a second dry dock in 1790 on the River Frome at Canon's Marsh.

The Bristol slave traders acquired almost half of their slaves from the Bight of Biafra because it was a region that particularly welcomed kettles, basins, and other items made from copper or brass and manufacturers involved in those industries were key investors. Another major slave source was the Gold Coast.

Some historians have suggested that one factor in why Liverpool was able to overtake Bristol was that its merchants showed more enterprise in seeking a wider choice of locations from which to acquire slaves and this mattered when the slave supply in the Bight and Gold Coast began to run dry. Over 70% of the enslaved Africans on Bristol slave ships were destined for sale in the Caribbean. Jamaica alone counted for 50% of the slave sales because, in addition to the demands of the British plantation owners, the island acted as the official centre for selling slaves on to the Spanish American colonies. It is estimated that about 30% or so of the Africans who were disembarked from Bristol ships in Jamaica were sold to the Spanish market. After Jamaica the biggest markets for Bristol merchants were Barbados, Antigua, and St Kitts. The majority of the enslaved Africans taken to the American mainland colonies were sold in South Carolina to work on cultivating and processing first rice and indigo and then increasingly sugar. A significant number were sold to Virginia and a few to Maryland because those colonies also had sugar plantations. The role of slaves on tobacco plantations gradually increased as the century progressed and tobacco imports into Bristol almost trebled.

The slave trade was not without its dangers. Ship losses or bad deals or factors outside any merchant's control, such as the advent of war or a ship loss at sea, could cause the slave trader who had organised a trip to occur heavy losses rather than render him large profits. Five prominent slave traders went bankrupt in the course of the century. One of the first problems that slave traders faced was when the colonial governments of the West Indies and the American colonies began to impose taxes on the sale of slaves in order to raise revenue and, in some cases, to restrict the number of slaves being brought in because of fears that the white populace would be overwhelmed if the slaves chose to rebel. This reduced the slave trader's profit margins. The first to impose taxes was Virginia in 1723. It imposed an import tax of £2 (£232 in modern values) on each slave . In 1731 Jamaica imposed an import tax of £1.80 for every slave sold on the island and £3.60 for every slave that was subsequently re-exported for sale to Spanish or American colonies. In 1735 South Carolina imposed a very high import tax of £20 for each adult and £5 for each child. The Society of Merchant Venturers sent petitions asking the government to stop these taxes but in the end this particular problem was met either by forcing colonial authorities to transfer the tax to the purchaser or by increasing the cost of buying slaves and so effectively passing on the cost of the tax to the purchaser.

Our trade is rendered daily more and more precarious
Petition sent to the government by the Society of Merchant Venturers in 1744

A far greater problem was the hostility of the Spanish. In 1725 Spanish coastguards took possession of a Bristol ship called the *Anna Maria* as it left Jamaica and that set a new trend in which British shipping was targeted. In 1728 the defeat of a Spanish attack on a Bristol ship due to the bravery of its captain, Samuel Pitts, was much celebrated according to the *Annals of Bristol*:

> On her way from Jamaica… [the ship] was attacked by a Spanish rover, with about 100 men, armed with two swivels and abundance of blunderbusses. The Englishmen, urged by Pitts, struggled bravely, but after an hour's fight within pistol shot, the overpowering fire of the enemy forced the little band to take shelter, and about fifty of the Spaniards boarded the galley. The crew then rallied, shot the man who was about to strike the English flag, and fell so furiously on the assailants that in about an hour's time they despatched all the rest but two, who were severely wounded… Hereupon the pirate sheered off, pursued by the galley, which fired three broadsides in the hope of sinking her, but night fell, and her fate was unknown… Captain Pitts had only four or five men wounded, and brought home his ship and cargo in honour and safety.

The Society of Merchant Venturers listed all the Spanish assaults on Bristol ships and the cruelties inflicted on captains and crews and petitioned Parliament to take action. Theirs was not the only complaint. Most famously Robert Jenkins, the captain of *H.M.S. Rebecca*, had his ear cut off when the Spanish accused him of smuggling in 1731. Eventually Britain declared war on Spain in 1739 – the first war to be entered into entirely for colonial reasons. The war became part of a wider European conflict known as the War of the Austrian Succession in which Britain also went to war against France in 1742. Three years later the slave trader Walter Lougher wrote:

> The difference between the trade of this town to Africa before and since the war with France are very great, the numbers before were sixty sail of ships and upwards of an average yearly and I think since only five small vessels have been sent.

Losing ships through enemy attack had led to such huge losses and soaring insurance costs that the trade had been rendered unprofitable. The war lasted until 1748. One of its most famous events was the French-supported invasion of Britain by Bonnie Prince Charlie in an attempt to dethrone King George II. A soldier who dared drink a toast to the Prince's success was publicly whipped with a cat of nine tails in Queen Square.

The hole in the slave market created by Bristol's absence was filled by Liverpool, which took over as the main slaving port, helped by its strong links with the manufacturing industries of Manchester. Its slave traders could afford to continue because they could use safer routes around the north of Ireland to cross the Atlantic, thus avoiding French vessels, and because they had developed ways of selling their slaves illegally to the Spanish and so were less affected by the war's closure of the official slave markets in Jamaica. They also enjoyed much better profit margins than Bristol's merchants. This was partly because they paid their ship captains and crews less but mainly because the shipping using Liverpool enjoyed far better facilities and much lower overheads. Liverpool had created Britain's first commercial wet dock right in its centre in 1715 and the fees to use it were less than Bristol charged to use its inferior facilities. The Society of Merchant Venturers collected the harbour fees but it had done little in the first half of the eighteenth century to improve what was on offer. It had extended the quay along the River Frome in 1712, it had created a wet dock in 1717 but too far away from the centre to be useful, and it had constructed a wharf on Welsh Back for loading goods and built a separate quay on St Augustine's Back for timber and naval stores in the 1720s. This still left Bristol reliant on facilities that were not radically different from what had been created in the thirteenth century.

Though they did not combine to act, Bristol merchants regularly grumbled about the disadvantages they faced. The slaver trader Henry Bright, for example, complained:

> All vessels lie aground supported only by the mud in the bed of the river for fourteen hours out of each twenty-four and large ships are not completely water-borne except at high water except for about six days in every fortnight.

The largest ships could only enter and leave Bristol's muddy dock on the highest tides and that sometimes imposed expensive waits of up to a month. Also adding to the cost was that every ship had to hire a pilot to navigate the twisty River Avon and up to ten boats were needed to tow the big ships. Another factor giving Liverpool an advantage was that its merchants had become adept at avoiding government taxes on imports. They used the Isle of Man as the alleged 'destination' of their returning ships and then smuggled their goods onto the English mainland.

The state of the harbour of Bristol is by nature so far inferior... that ships holders of Bristol are not on an equal footing with the ships holders of other ports

Bristol Corporation in 1792

Ninety of Bristol's merchants banded together to fund the creation of ships that could be used to capture enemy ships, judging prize money obtained from captured enemy shipping was more profitable than trade. This proved a lucrative source of income as this extract from a 1744 newspaper indicates:

> Nothing is to be seen here but rejoicing for the great number of French prizes brought in. Our sailors are in the highest spirits, full of money and spend their whole time in carousing... dressed out with laced hats, tassels, swords with sword knots, and in short all things that can give them an opportunity to spend their money.

By 1747 it was obvious that Britain was going to emerge victorious from the war and that France and Spain's defeat was going to open up an opportunity to expand Britain's role in the slave trade. Between 1747 and 1749 London's merchants made three attempts to reinstate the monopoly they had once held on the African trade by saying that it was essential for the government to protect future shipping by creating and maintaining more military forts. They argued that this required a London-based Company to be set up and that only merchants belonging to it should be permitted to trade. The Merchant Venturers lobbied against this. So, of course, did Liverpool's merchants.

It was economics that determined that Europe should invest in Africa and control the continent's raw materials and labour. It was racism which confirmed the decision that the form of control should be direct colonial rule

Walter Rodney in *How Europe Underdeveloped Africa* in 1972

In 1750 the government created the Company of Merchants Trading to Africa as a vehicle to look after all of Britain's forts and trading posts along the West African coast, but it did not restrict membership to the London merchants.

Images from Bristol's rival. Top left: relief on former Martin's Bank in Liverpool shows manacled slave boys holding money bags and anchors. Above: a Liverpool slave ship by W.Jackson 1780 and some of the street names named after local merchants. Left: a view of Liverpool's wet dock in 1725 showing customs house, exchange and town hall. Below: engraving of Liverpool c 1750.

Any merchant could join and all that was required was a £2 fee for each ship (the equivalent of around £235 in today's money). It was a sign of Bristol's determination to regain its lost position that 237 of its merchants became members of the new Company, compared to 157 London merchants and 89 Liverpool merchants. Liverpool's lesser membership may reflect the readiness of its merchants to avoid any form of 'tax' and to trade illegally. With the war's end there was such a huge surge in Britain's role in the slave trade that it overtook Portugal to become the leading nation involved.

However, Bristol faced a problem in reviving its position. Not only had Liverpool now got the edge but within Bristol's traditional slave trading families there was a lack of sons able or willing to take on the work. Eighteen of the twenty-five or so leading slave traders of the 1720s and 1730s had no sons. Five died as bachelors and, among the married, ten had no surviving son when they died and three others died before their sons had reached maturity. Where there was a son capable of taking on his father's business that seems mostly not to have happened. The uncertainties of the African trade and the obvious advantages possessed by Liverpool seem to have led them to opt for safer forms of investment. They preferred to focus just on direct trade with the West Indies and the American colonies rather than operate the triangular route. Another factor in the reluctance of some was that the merchants who came from a Quaker background were now being told by their leaders that slavery was immoral and they should be abandoning any involvement with it. After 1750 only one slave trader, Richard Farr, was succeeded by his son. In some cases a nephew or son-in-law took over but generally speaking Bristol, unlike Liverpool, had to rely on acquiring a new wave of slave traders.

Two sources provided them. One source were the sea captains who had worked for the slave traders because some of them had acquired the wealth, experience and contacts required to start in business. The other source were merchants new to Bristol, drawn by the opportunities it provided and wanting to enjoy the status of belonging to the Society of Merchant Venturers. Some historians argue that these outsiders lacked the expertise and contacts of their Liverpool rivals, but, nevertheless, they gave a much needed boost to reinvigorate the city's trade and they enabled Bristol to remain as a prominent participator in the slave trade in the second half of the eighteenth century. Between 1755 and 1775 on average there were twenty-five slaving ships leaving Bristol every year, compared to sixty-five from Liverpool and ten from London. This meant that the level of Bristol's involvement in the slave trade almost came close to matching the pre-1740 period. The city fell further behind Liverpool not because it was enslaving less Africans but because Liverpool was continually expanding its role. It has to be remembered that there was plenty of money for investment in this period because it was a time of immense economic growth for Britain. The combination of improvements in farming, the beginnings of an industrial revolution, significant developments in transport, and a growing empire meant that the country was not only able to export an ever-increasing diversity of goods but also able to re-export large quantities of colonial goods drawn from all over the world. Between 1748 and 1770 it is estimated that British imports increased by 500% and exports by 600%.

The war between Britain and its rivals had resolved nothing and so fighting was resumed in the Seven Years' War between 1756 and 1763 – the conflict in which Olaudah Equiano fought as a sailor in the Royal Navy – and so once again there was a slump in Bristol's trade. Apart from shipping losses to enemy action the merchants faced sailor losses because of the actions of newly created press gangs. A press gang, normally a group of about a dozen led by a Royal Navy officer, would seize men, usually when they were inebriated, knock them unconscious, and take them on board a ship. The merchants saw this as unjust, even though they sometimes resorted to similar methods to recruit crews for the slave ships. In Bristol they put up a more successful struggle than was achieved in London or Liverpool. Many sailors would disembark on the Somerset coast before the ship was towed into Bristol and they made Kingswood rather than Bristol their base. The combination of colliers and seamen meant press gangs dared not go there without having military support. Within Bristol merchants did what they could to make the job of the press gangs as difficult as possible, encouraging crowds to behave in a hostile manner and instituting legal suits whenever they could.

Prosperity and luxury gradually extinguish sympathy, and by inflating with pride, harden and debase the soul
                Attributed to William Wilberforce, eighteenth century abolitionist parliamentarian

---

Once again Bristol merchants looked to attacking enemy shipping as an alternative means of generating income. In 1759 one of the agents working for Bristol in Jamaica rightly complained that in the long run this would be counterproductive:

> The great attention to privateering out of your city has much hurted the

trade of it, for their is ten times business carried on from Liverpool to this island [than] from your city.

The Bristol merchants were well aware that their rival Liverpool was yet again using war to outstrip them. 1759 saw Liverpool open a second major wet dock. When the Society of Merchant Venturers renewed its lease to run Bristol's port in 1764 it promised to build and extend quays. Some work was undertaken and plenty of ambitious schemes were discussed, but progress was incredibly slow. A fear of costs and an inability to agree on a scheme meant that nothing of real substance was achieved until 1812. By that time Liverpool had built three more major docks. In 1773 the merchant Lowbridge Bright aptly commented:

The Liverpool people go on with such spirit. I wish we could get more into that track.

His view is not surprising because Bristol's share of the African trade had fallen from its peak of 45% to 15%.

The Seven Years' War inevitably made some people question the desirability of continuing to invest in slave voyages. It is noticeable that the number of investors reduced and slave traders had to rely more on their own money. Over the next forty-odd years the number of slave traders fell to the extent that, as the next chapter shows, just six traders undertook the bulk of the voyages. Another factor encouraging that change in the second half of the eighteenth century was the impact on Bristol of the decision of the American colonists to declare their independence in 1775. The African trade was only about a third of the wider trade with the American colonies and the West Indies and to have that wider trade blocked was catastrophic for Bristol's economy. The number of ships entering Bristol from America and the Caribbean in a year fell from around 125 to 4 and there was a corresponding fall in ships going there. Many manufacturers and merchants went bankrupt and Bristol's plantation owners in the West Indies were also badly hit because the war equally affected their trade with the Americans. In 1778, for example, 247 ships trading among the islands were captured by American privateers. The government's assumption that the economic cost would be acceptable because the war would be short proved disastrously wrong because the American War of Independence lasted from 1776 to 1783. It affected even domestic trade because shipping had relied heavily on American timber and, with that supply ended, wood prices soared. The war was to have other consequences for the slave trade than its temporary cessation because all the American talk of 'liberty' triggered the beginnings of an abolitionist movement in Britain. This will be looked at in the next section of this book.

Bristol's role in the slave trade slowly recovered after the American war. The trade had brought so much wealth to the city that it was hard to relinquish it and there was also an undoubted desire not to simply hand over the trade entirely to rival Liverpool. Jamaica remained the favoured destination. Less slaves were delivered to Antigua, St Kitts, and Dominica (probably because of a decline in their sugar production) and the trade to South Carolina more or less stopped, but larger markets were found in Grenada, St Vincent and Demerara. This shows that the Bristol merchants were prepared to show some initiative. They also had to adapt to changing conditions in Africa. The population in coastal areas had been so reduced by years of slave trading that slaves were increasingly having to be brought from further and further inland and many African slave dealers were no longer prepared to accept low cost goods for them. They wanted to be paid far more. In 1767 unhappiness over 'overcharging' was to lead to the 'Calabar massacre' that will be featured in a later chapter. By 1800 the average cost of purchasing a slave was five times higher than it had been in 1700. Sometimes ships had to sit around for months waiting to acquire the slaves they wanted and this 'wasted' time cost money.

Pounds, shillings, pence appear on every face
Robert Lowell on the people of Bristol in his poem Bristol: A Satire in 1794

Given the problems it is remarkable that the the trade to Africa and the West Indies still comprised over 80% of the total value of Bristol's overseas trade. The amount of money invested annually by Bristol's merchants, manufacturers, and plantation owners was greater by 1788 than it had ever been. As much as £400,000 was invested in 1792 alone (the equivalent today of c.£31 million). However, that investment came from a few. When William Matthews published a *Complete Guide* to Bristol in 1794 he commented:

> The ardour for the Trade to Africa for men and women, our fellow creatures and equals, is much abated among the humane and benevolent merchants of Bristol… while the people of Liverpool in their indiscriminate rage for commerce and getting money at all events, have nearly engrossed this Trade.

What Bristol's remaining slave traders were not doing, with one or two small exceptions, was grasping the opportunity to supply slaves to foreign colonies. Liverpool was doing that and it was therefore continuing to increase its role. Its economic edge was also helped by its creation of a canal network that reduced its transport costs with the manufacturing cities of the north, and by its development of nine shipyards, which meant it could build all the ships its merchants required, including custom-made slave ships. Between 1787 and 1807 Liverpool's ships yards built 469 vessels, averaging about twenty-one a year.

A major war once again hit Bristol much harder than Liverpool. The French Revolutionary War of 1793 to 1801 saw Bristol's role in the slave trade plummet and the almost immediate commencement of the Napoleonic Wars in 1802 provided no opportunity for recovery. Between 1800 and 1807, the year in which Britain ended its role in the slave trade, Bristol only sent out thirteen slave ships compared to Liverpool's 585. What Bristol remained heavily committed to was slave ownership because of the sugar trade. The battle to make the plantation owners abandon their slave labour was to take almost another thirty years.

By 1807 it is estimated that Bristol had engaged in a total of around two thousand slaving ventures and it had been responsible for selling at least half a million slaves. This represents around 20% of Britain's entire role in the slave trade. In comparison Liverpool by the end had engaged in about 4,600 ventures and delivered about 1.3 million slaves. Estimates vary on how much profit was made on a slaving voyage but the return on original investment seems to have been usually between 4% and 20%. Cumulatively this level of return was sufficient to bring in vast amounts of money and this in turn enabled further investment, not just in the slave trade but also in the sugar and other plantations, in the manufacturing industries, in transport improvements, and in farming. This helps explain why between 1700 and 1800 Bristol grew from a city of 21,000 to one of 60,000 and Liverpool increased its population from 5,500 to over 80,000.

No nation in Europe… has… plunged so deeply into this guilt as Great Britain
Speech on the slave trade by William Pitt the Younger in Parliament in 1792

It is not uncommon for the eighteenth-century to be seen as a golden age not just for Bristol and Liverpool but also for Bath, which was transformed into the playground of the rich. What that meant for Bristol will be looked at in a later chapter. Of course more than these three cities benefitted. It has been said that without the African trade and its Caribbean plantation extension the modern world as we know it would not exist. The profits that flowed in from slave trading and from sugar, coffee, tobacco and cotton production transformed the economy and turned Britain into a global power. They encouraged and enabled the development of the industrial revolution and of new banking and insurance and transport systems. Towns and cities across the country grew in response to the direct and indirect stimulus of the slave plantations. The impact on America and many European countries was equally significant and it established what was later to be called 'Western dominance' over the world. The 'golden age', built as it was on human misery and exploitation, bequeathed to the future not just a racist legacy that is still being played out but also a trade legacy. Africa and the rest of the 'underdeveloped' world were seen as being there to benefit the West. A comment made in 1969 by the first president of Ghana is still applicable today:

> If Africa's multiple resources were used in her own development, they could place her among the modernised continents of the world. But her resources have been and still are being used for the greater development of overseas interests.

The white man has no kin; his kin is money
A saying in South Africa

Top: Humphrey Hooke possibly with his son Abraham; Stokes Croft Endowed School in 19th century photograph; and the Lord Mayors Chapel. Above left: sketch of Dukinfield Hall, home of John Duckenfield's uncle in ` North Carolina, memorial to Joseph Iles in Holy Trinity, Minchinhampton; and the hatchment of John Becher in the Lord Mayor's Chapel. Below: John Becher and the houses in Prince Street which he had built.

3

THE SLAVE TRADERS

That which is inhuman cannot be divine
  Narrative of the Life of Frederick Douglass, an American slave in 1845

The first Bristolians to get substantially involved in the slave trade were those who had an existing interest in the Caribbean or the American colonies and all of them would have known Edward Colston. The most active were Edward Saunders, Samuel Jacob, James Day, Richard Henvill, Noblet Ruddock, and William Jefferis. Each of these organised between thirty and fifty-six slave-trading voyages and collectively they were probably responsible for enslaving over 70,000 Africans (i.e. far more people than there were living in Bristol at that time). Edward Saunders commenced his involvement as the captain of a slave ship but went on to become a slave trader. Samuel Jacob was the son of a brewer who became a ship's captain and ended up as a wealthy merchant, profiting from trade in sugar and from the American colonies. He organised a petition to Parliament urging it to stop the colonists in Virginia from imposing a tax on the importation of Africans. James Day, who was a mariner by training, belonged to a prominent Bristol family with strong links to the sugar trade and others in his family were also involved in slavery. Peter Day, for example, organised twelve slaving voyages and John Day, who served as a mayor, was for a time Bristol's spokesman on the African trade in London. Richard Henvill came from the landed gentry in Dorset and, after completing his apprenticeship in Bristol, immediately launched himself into the slave trade in 1709. His family had estates on St. Kitts. Noblet Ruddock, who was Irish, was very involved in trade with Ireland and Europe but his interest in tobacco led him into the slave trade. William Jefferis and his brother Joseph, who was also a slave trader, were Bristol's leading traders in the Carolinas. Joseph was the city's mayor in 1724 and William in 1738.

Alongside these six there were ten others who were collectively responsible for enslaving at least a further 55,000 Africans. Joseph Way, Robert Tunbridge, William Challoner, Philip Harris, Abel Grant, Thomas Freke, Abraham Hooke, John Duckinfield, and John Becher were each responsible for organising between thirteen and twenty-eight slave voyages. The son of a dissenting minister,

Joseph Way became involved in slaving through his brother Benjamin, who had become a prominent merchant in London, having married into a family with estates in Jamaica. A number of Bristol's slave traders were tradesmen and Robert Tunbridge was one of them. He was a soap maker. Others, like William Challoner, came from a maritime background. Philip Harris got involved because he was Noblet Ruddock's brother-in-law. Abel Grant was a merchant very much involved in trade with the colony of Virginia and he usually got his slaves by negotiating with chiefs from Old Calabar in what is now Nigeria. Thomas Freke was a sugar merchant who also had investments in ships, glass, and a very large number of urban and rural properties in and around Bristol. Other members of his family were also slave traders. Abraham Hooke was from a prominent Bristol family. His father built Ashley Court and had a country mansion in Kingsweston. Like Colston, Abraham had an interest in education and he used some of his wealth to help create Stokes' Croft Endowed School and Almshouse.

John Duckinfield had estates in Jamaica and family out in North Carolina. He was unusual in that he tried on at least two occasions to source his slaves from Madagascar. This did not prove very successful. For example, in 1717 his ship the *Prince Eugene* acquired 540 Malagasy slaves but almost half died. According to Duckinfield this was because his captain made the mistake of buying boys and girls rather than adults. The financial loss worried him more than the deaths of the children. His son, Robert, bequeathed a sizeable part of his family's estates in Jamaica to a freed slave, Jane Engusson, and purchased land and slaves from another Bristol merchant to give to the two sons he had had by her, William and Estcourt. He also provided a substantial dowry for Elizabeth, the daughter Jane had given him, but only on condition she married a white man.

John Becher owned plantations in Jamaica so he had a vested interest in becoming a slave trader. He came from a wealthy family in Cork in Ireland and, as a young man, he had been apprenticed to a Bristol merchant and bodice maker called John Duddlestone. Becher had married Duddlestone's daughter and soon became a well-established figure in the city, serving as Sheriff in 1713 and as Mayor in 1721. One of his great-granddaughters was the mother of the famous novelist, William Thackeray. Today Becher is probably best remembered for building a row of terraced housing in Prince Street with his associate, Henry Combe. Three still survive, one being now the Shakespeare Tavern. He was also a key figure in encouraging the Corporation to turn St Mark's Church on College Green into the Lord Mayor's Chapel. This Church, built in 1230, had been in the possession of the Corporation since 1540, following the dissolution

THE SLAVE TRADERS

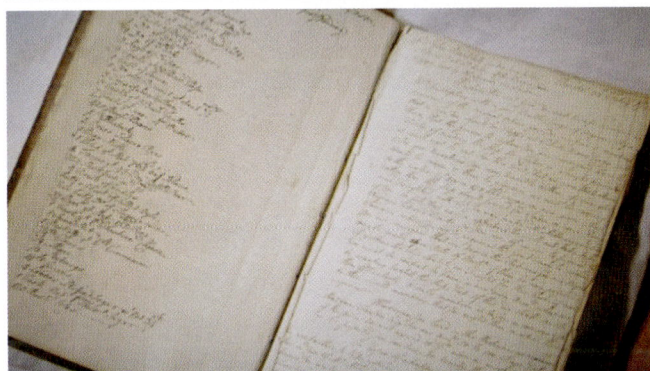

Above: The 'Southwell', one of Michael Becher's slave ships trading off the African coast in the 1740s by Nicholas Pocock. Left: Cranfield Becher's log book for the 'Jason Gally'. Below left: Michael Becher; Below: Hadspen House built by the Hobhouse family largely from the proceeds of the slave trade.

of the monasteries, and it had become the church used by the Huguenots who had fled to Bristol from France. It now is the only municipally-owned church in the country and Becher is buried within it. His hatchment hangs on one of its walls. His sons, Michael, Cranfield, George, and Edward, all became slave traders. Michael alone organised twenty-five voyages. In 2014 Bristol Record Office managed to buy a log book belonging to Cranfield Becher and it vividly tells the story of a transatlantic journey made by the *Jason Gally* between 1743 and 1746. One of the surprises found within it was that women were among the smiths and gunsmiths who supplied goods and services for the ship. The log book leaves no doubt that the enslaved Africans were viewed just as commodities.

So dey lets all but de mean ones come up on deck. Den dey sings. One sings an de rest hum, lak. What dey sing? Nobody don't know. Dey sing lanuguage what dey learn in Africa when dey were free.
Slave known as Uncle Ephraim recalling his grandfather's memory of surviving the Middle Passage cited in Old Massa's People in 1931

In the 1720s and 1730s new slave traders appeared. The ten most significant were Henry Dampier, Thomas Pennington, Walter and Richard Lougher, Thomas Power, Joseph Iles, Henry Tonge, Richard Farr,, William Hare, and Isaac Hobhouse. Collectively these ten men were responsible for enslaving over 100,000 Africans. Dampier, who became Mayor of Bristol in 1755, was related by marriage to James Day and Pennington and the Loughers were from well-established merchant families, but Power and Iles were merchants new to Bristol. Power was the son of a merchant in Bideford and took up trading after being apprenticed in Bristol. Iles was from Minchinhampton in Gloucester and he had married the daughter of a Bristol merchant, Nathaniel Wraxell. He mainly sold slaves to plantation owners in South Carolina. Tonge and Farr were manufacturers. Henry Tonge was a cloth manufacturer and an investor in brass and copper industries. Some of his money also came from his role in the very profitable fire protection service required by Bristol's sugar refineries. He sold slaves mainly to Jamaica. Richard Farr was Bristol's leading rope-maker. His son, also called Richard, was to run several privateers and organise slave voyages between 1746 and 1772 that enslaved probably around 11,000 Africans. He became a major of Bristol in 1763 and Farr Lane is named after the family.

Of the ten men Isaac Hobhouse has probably attracted the most attention. Born in 1685, he was the son of a mariner turned shipwright in Minehead, and, rather like Colston, he was later to show generosity to the place of his birth, although on an infinitely smaller scale. He left in his will a guinea to be paid to each of the poor men and women who lived in the street where he had been born. Hobhouse first invested in a slave voyage in 1711 and within a few years he was a very prominent figure in Minehead. He moved to Bristol in 1717 with his brother-in-law, Christopher Jones, and the two men joined the Society of Merchant Venturers. He created the firm of Isaac Hobhouse and Company by linking up with his two older brothers and five associates. This meant he could take the lead in organising his own slave voyages in 1722. His firm gradually grew richer and richer until he was eventually operating a fleet of thirty-four vessels and their main focus was on the triangular trade. Forty-four of the sixty-eight transatlantic voyages in which his ships were engaged involved carrying slaves. In addition to this he sometimes invested in voyages organised by others and he acquired shares in companies that produced goods for Africa and in a sugar refinery in Redcliffe in Bristol to further enhance his profits.

It is thought that the voyages organised by Hobhouse were responsible in total for enslaving around 19,000 Africans, most of them from what is now Cameroon and eastern Nigeria. He had a reputation for being a harsh and demanding business man and the mortality rate on his ships was higher than the norm. It is estimated 4,000 of the people he enslaved died during the middle passage. The rest were either sold in Jamaica and other Caribbean islands or in South Carolina. Although he suffered, like all merchants, from a slump in the profitability of the slave trade in the 1730s, it is estimated that his total profits probably amounted over the years to at least £400,000 – the equivalent today of c.£47 million. By the end of his career he had various properties in Clifton and, from around 1760 to his death in 1763, he lived in a luxurious house in Queen Square, no longer running but still investing in the slave trade. Hobhouse never married but his nephew Henry took over the business and his son, who became a lawyer, built Hadspen House near Castle Cary in the 1780s. It is now a hotel and spa called the Newt. A number of the Hobhouses became M.P.s, but the most famous family members are probably Emily Hobhouse, who campaigned against the appalling conditions of the British concentration camps in the Boer War, and Sir Arthur Lawrence Hobhouse, who was the architect of the system of National Parks of England and Wales. His son Henry Hobhouse wrote about the impact of sugarcane and five other plants in the 1985 world-famous best-seller *Seeds of Change,* and his daughter-in law was the garden designer, writer and T.V. presenter, Penelope Hobhouse.

If me want for go in an Ebo Me can't go there!
Since dem tief me from a Guinea Me can't go there
If me want for go in a Congo Me can't go there
Since dem thief me from my tata Me can't go there!
Jamaican song yearning for lost homelands cited in Smithsonian's *Captive Passage* in 2002 A tata is a father.

Among Hobhouse's many associates were Henry Bright, Thomas Coster, and James Laroche (or La Roche). The son of a distiller, Henry Bright came to Bristol from Worcester and married the daughter of the wealthy sugar merchant and slave trader, Richard Meyler. More will be said about Bright and Meyler in the chapter on slave owners. The copper manufacturer Thomas Coster, came to co-own six slaving vessels and he also invested in voyages organised by Laroche and others. He was elected as one of Bristol's M.P.s in 1734 and he was one of the men responsible for the erection of the equestrian statue of King William in Queen Square.

James Laroche should be the slave trader that is most remembered in Bristol because he organised more slaving trips than any other merchant. He was a member of the four hundred strong French Huguenot community in Bristol. His father had fled from Bordeaux to London to escape Catholic persecution and he had become the barber to Queen Anne's husband, Prince George of Denmark. Pip Jones in her book *Satan's Kingdom* suggests that James, who was his middle son, might have been the child soprano Jemmie Laroche, who appeared on the London stage. Laroche was apprenticed to a London slave trader and his Huguenot connections then drew him to Bristol. His marriage to Clementia Casamajor assured him of success because her father, Lewis Casamajor, was a major figure among a small circle of Huguenot merchants originally from La Rochelle that included the Peloquins, who became one of the five wealthiest families in Bristol and whose story will feature in the chapter on slave owners. These men had well-established and wide-ranging mercantile connections that ensured Laroche's success. He was probably also helped by his elder brother John's connections in London and Antigua. John Laroche had become the steward to a wealthy Cornish family called the Robartes and they made him the M.P. for Bodmin from 1727 to 1752. The Caribbean links came from John' marriage to an heiress with large estates in Antigua.

James Laroche organised his first slaving expedition in 1729 and by 1731 he had established his reputation as a good organiser. Between 1731 and 1740 he

Above; Thomas Coster by circle of A.Pond c.1750 and 1831 engraving of Overcourt the Elizabethan manor house near Almondsbury purchased by James Laroche. Below left: Sir Abraham Elton by Jonathan Richardson the Elder (undated). Bottom left: Clevedon Court. Below right: Goldney Hall. Bottom right:Thomas Goldney by Richard Phelps 1751.

was responsible for organising forty-two slaving voyages and evidence points to him being pretty ruthless in his pursuit of profit. For example, the records of his ship the *Loango* show that he was engaged in trading children as well as adults from Angola to South Carolina in 1737. In 1738 alone he organised no less than five slaving expeditions that took 1,355 slaves to Jamaica, St Kitts and South Carolina. He continued organising slaving voyages until 1769 and by then he had reached a total of 132. This involved him working in various partnership combinations with seventeen other Bristol traders, including Isaac Hobhouse, Thomas Coster, Noblett Ruddock, Edmund Saunders and Joseph Jefferis, but, such was Laroche's success and resulting wealth that he was able to undertake 87 of the 132 voyages entirely on his own. One of his ships, the *Black Prince*, which undertook eight voyages in the 1760s, has won notoriety for the high levels of sickness and mortality among the slaves.

> *At the savage Captain's beck*
> *Now like Brutes they make us prance:*
> *Smack the Cat about the deck,*
> *And in scorn they bid us dance*
> African poem *The Sorrows of Yaruba* in 1790 cited by K.Hazzard-Gordon in *The Rise of Social Dance Formations in African American Culture* in 1990

Having no children of his own, Laroche chose to develop the career of his nephew James after the death of his brother John in 1752. The nephew, then aged about eighteen, came to live in Bristol as an agent for the Llangyfelach copper works in Swansea but he was soon engaged in his uncle's overseas trade. In 1762 a West Indies agent described him as 'a gentleman of much consequence' and in 1763 he married Elizabeth Yeamans, who owned estates in Antigua. The following year he became Sheriff of Bristol and used some of the family's ever-increasing wealth to purchase an Elizabethan manor called Over Court near Almondsbury.

James Laroche died in 1770. By then it is estimated he had been responsible for the enslavement of probably around 50,000 Africans. His nephew did not personally take over running the family business because by that stage he had inherited Cornish estates from the Robartes family. Instead he opted to become, like his father, the M.P for Bodmin. He held that role from 1768 to 1780. The younger James Laroche's staunch support for the Crown in its dealings with the American colonists led to him being knighted and created Baronet of Over in 1776. However, financial losses incurred during the American War of Independence then caused him to face temporary bankruptcy in 1778. For a couple of years he was reduced to begging former contacts of the family for assistance. By 1782 his business affairs had sufficiently recovered for him to be elected as a Master of the Society of Merchant Venturers. He then remained actively involved in Bristol's trade until his death in 1804. One of the last references to survive about the baronet is an account of how he opposed the abolition of slavery at a public meeting at the Merchants' Hall in 1789. The role of the Laroches is not widely known today in Bristol because there are no images of them and no building or street was ever named after them (although there is a street in Bodmin called Laroche Walk). Their manor house no longer exists. Rumoured to be haunted by the ghost of a white lady who had committed suicide, it was left to fall into neglect after the Second World War and then completely destroyed by fire in 1977. All that remains is a grand archway to the estate and the old coach house and stables, now converted into mews houses. Its parkland has been turned into Bristol Golf Course.

A family that is remembered are the Eltons, thirteen of whom were members of the Society of Merchant Venturers with six of them becoming Masters of it. The fact all of them were involved in the slave trade to a greater or lesser extent is not so well-known. Their family wealth originally came mainly from copper and brass but they had their fingers in other commercial underatkings, including weaving and owning a glassworks in St Philips. Their varied manufacturing interests led the Eltons to participate in the African trade and, in addition to investing in slave voyages, they also organised some voyages themselves. At the height of their wealth the family owned a quarter of the land surrounding Bristol. The first to get really involved in the slave trade was Abraham Elton. A book called the *Annals of the Elton Family*, written in the 1990s by a descendant, Margaret Elton, admits his return profits from slavery were 'enormous'. He was elected as High Sheriff of Bristol in 1702, as a Master of the Society of Merchant Venturers in 1708, and as Mayor of Bristol in 1710. Subsequently he was appointed as High Sheriff of Gloucestershire in 1716 and, after he gave an enormous gift of £10,000 (the equivalent today of around one million) to King George I, he was knighted as a baronet in 1717 and became the M.P. for Bristol from 1722 to 1727. He earned enough money to purchase Clevedon Court in North Somerset and acquire the largest house in Queen Square.

Elton's three sons, Abraham, Jacob and Isaac, had investments in the slave colonies of Maryland and Virginia and they owned the slave ships the *Gardner* and the *Caesar*. Not surprisingly they lobbied parliament about the benefits of the slave trade. Even the salt produced on the Elton estate was used to barter for slaves. The eldest son, Sir Abraham Elton, 2nd Baronet, participated in three slaving ventures between 1713 and 1717 and he served as a High Sheriff and Mayor of Bristol before becoming an M.P., first for Taunton from 1724 to 1727, and then for Bristol from 1727 until his death in 1742. He often spoke on mercantile issues in Parliament and twice lobbied hard against the government doing anything that might harm the slave trade. Jacob, who participated in three slaving ventures in 1711, 1713, and 1715 is now best remembered because he bought and remodelled Elton House in Abbey Green in Bath so he could rent it out to the wealthy. Issac Elton participated in two slaving ventures in 1718 and 1720.

Sir Abraham Elton, 3rd Baronet, proved to be a feckless wastrel and his devotion to pleasure resulted in him ending the family's direct involvement in the slave trade not for moral reasons but out of laziness. He was to die a bankrupt in France in 1781, but the Elton family survived because his uncle Isaac took over the baronetcy. The family was able to partially renew its wealth through having estates in Jamaica and through investing in the sugar refining industry. Like Colston, the Eltons have had streets named after them. There are Elton Roads in Clevedon, Weston-super-Mare, Kingswood, and Bishopston. However, as yet there has been no move to have these renamed and the current guide book to Clevedon Court (now owned by the National Trust) says little about the family's role in the slave trade.

They were exploiting the economic circumstances of their time. All business men do... You could rationally say the whole of Britain's modern wealth is based on the trade. What are we going to do – tear down all our buildings?... This is probably wildly politically incorrect – and I'm not saying we didn't treat slaves disgustingly – but what would have happened to the Africans if they'd stayed in Africa? If you had to choose between living in Darfur and living in America, which would you choose?
Julia Elton, sister of the current baronet, interviewed in newspaper *The Guardian* in December 2006

There is also no move to rename the Bathurst Basin which is between the New Cut and the Floating Harbour. Sir Benjamin Bathurst was a deputy governor of the East India Company and, like Colston, an early investor in the Royal Africa Company for whom he also acted as a deputy-governor. His great grandson, Charles Bathurst, was a member the Society of Merchant Adventurers and the Bristol M.P. who fought to defend the slave trade against the abolitionists between 1796 and 1807. Goldney Avenue and Goldney Hall, which is part of

The Slave Traders

Top: Sir Benjamin Bathurst by circle of J. Riley 1680s and Cirencester Park. Above: Bathurst Basin. Left: Orchard Street, where James McTaggert lived and the site of a Huguenot chapel attended by James Laroche. Bottom: official plaque to the slave trade outside M-Shed and unofficial plaque pinned to a city building.

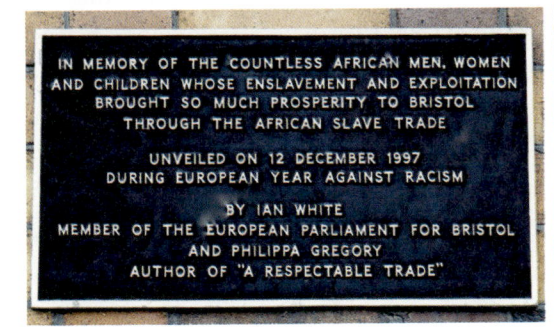

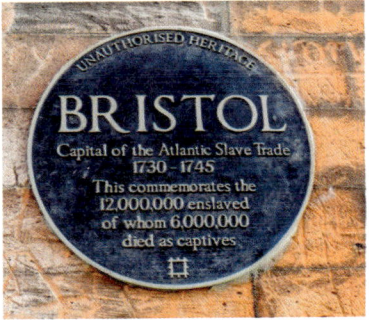

the University of Bristol, are named after Thomas Goldney, who is another unchallenged name. His family were Quakers who had invested heavily in the iron industry and this was what led Thomas to get involved in the Africa trade and, from 1751, in the slave trade. He was one of six partners who created Goldney, Smith & Co, one of the first merchant banks in the country. It later became part of the National Westminster Bank.

Almost 65% of all the slaving voyages organised in Bristol in the second half of the eighteenth century were the work of just six men. The two dominant figures from the 1750s to the 1770s were John Fowler, who organised seventy-seven voyages, and John Powell, who organised fifty-eight. Fowler was a former slave ship captain who had used his money to not just set himself up as a merchant but also to create the banking company of Peach, Fowler & Co based in Wine Street. He became a Master of the Society of Merchant Venturers in 1783-4. Powell was the son of a merchant from Bideford and from 1779 till his death in 1799 he was Collector of Customs, a very profitable but extremely onerous role.

As I expect a cargo of Ebo negroes about this first of March, if you please I will postpone purchasing for you until then. I will have it in my power to give a preference of a pick
   John Fowler to James Stothert, absentee plantation owner in Sept 1789

John Anderson, who organised sixty-six voyages, and Thomas Jones, who organised thirty-four, were engaged in the slave trade from the 1760s to the 1790s. Anderson was a former slave ship captain and, although he had no established links with any of the city's established families, he became a major figure in running Bristol. He was a councillor from 1772 till his death in 1797 and he served as Sheriff in 1772-3 and Mayor in 1783 and as an alderman from 1785 to 1797. Thomas Jones came to Bristol with his brother James from South Wales just prior to the start of the American War of Independence and they set themselves up as merchants. James Jones, who organised sixty-eight voyages, and James Rogers, who organised fifty-one, were the dominant leaders in the slave trade in the 1780s and early 1790s. Rogers had come to Bristol from Haverfordwest where he had been a partner in a marine insurance business and he continued to be involved in underwriting whilst diversifying into trade. One of the men to invest regularly in his slaving voyages was James Laroche, the nephew of Bristol's biggest slave trader. Both Jones and Rogers served for a time as Warden of the Society of Merchant Venturers.

Collectively these six men were responsible for enslaving probably at least a 100,000 Africans. John Anderson, James Jones, Thomas Jones, and James Rogers never worked together in organising a voyage and this may have been in part because they had their own preferred areas of operation. Rogers, for example, liked to source his slave in ports in or near to Sierra Leone whereas John Anderson preferred trading at the Gold Coast. Much of our information about the slave trade comes from the fact that fifteen boxes of Rogers' correspondence have survived. He seems to have been particularly immoral in his attitude towards those he enslaved. He tight packed his ships as much as possible. In 1787 the abolitionist Thomas Clarkson inspected two small pleasure craft that Rogers was intending to sell in Florida but not before first loading them with slaves. To his horror Clarkson worked out that Rogers was only going to allocate three square feet for each slave so there was not even space for them to lie down. In addition the space below deck was only four feet high, This meant the heads of the sitting slaves would have to touch the ceiling.

When the government passed legislation in 1788 to restrict the number of slaves that could be confined within a slaving ship, Rogers devised a scheme to avoid complying. His plan was a simple one: he would pretend the goods on any ship he sent were destined for France not Africa and instruct the captain to hold a mock 'sale' of them in a French port and to replace some of the English crew with Frenchmen. His ship could then proceed to Africa under a French flag, thus negating the need to follow British law. As far as is known his plan was never implemented. The outbreak of the French Revolution prevented it. Rogers' approach may have contributed to his downfall. His ships had the highest death rate of all the Bristol merchants and undoubtedly this must have affected his profits. At least five of his ships in the years 1791 to 1793 suffered extraordinarily high slave losses. The *Rodney*, the *Swift*, the *Fame*, and the *African Queen* all had between 20% and 33% of the enslaved die on the voyage and the *Pearl* had an even more difficult voyage.

It took nine months on the African coast to acquire all the slaves it required and then it lost 65% of them. 260 of the 400 slaves on board died and those who survived were judged unfit for sale. Putting aside the immorality of his behaviour, in business terms such losses were disastrous. The *Pearl*, for example, made a loss of £12,000 (just under a million in today's values). Other evidence points to Rogers often making other bad decisions. For example, he sometimes did not select the right cargoes to make maximum profits and he sometimes advised his captains wrongly and sent them to gutted markets. He also overborrowed. All these factors eventually led to him going bankrupt in 1793. One estimate of his debt places it at £100,000 (almost eight million in today's values).

[The ship's hold was] so covered with the blood and mucus which had proceeded from them in consequence of the flux that it resembled a slaughterhouse
Alexander Falconbridge, ship's surgeon on the impact of severe diorrhoea on Bristol slave ships in Narrative of two voyages to the River Sierra Leone in 1791-3

The next level of involvement in the trade came from seven others: David Hamilton organised twenty-eight voyages, Thomas Sims twenty-five, Charles Anderson sixteen, James McTaggert fourteen, Robert Gordon fourteen, John Chilcott twelve and John Coghlan ten. Collectively these enslaved a further 40,000 or so. Anderson was the nephew of John Anderson and he took on his uncle's business. Sims was the son of a tailor. His father had died whilst he was young and the slave trader Walter Lougher had taken him on as an apprentice out of charity. Hamilton, McTaggert, Chilcott and Coghlan were all former slave ship captains. Gordon came from the landed gentry in Scotland and he had followed his uncle into trade.

Sometimes these later slave traders worked together as had been the pattern in the first half of the eighteenth century. The voyage of the slave ship *Africa* in 1774, for example, was jointly funded by John Anderson, James Rogers and John Chilcott, and the voyage of the *Wasp* in 1780 by Thomas Jones and John Powell. However, research has shown that-that there was an increasing trend after 1790 towards a single merchant funding a voyage. Why? Probably because most investors had decided to disengage from the trade. This was not because it was a risky investment (it had always been that) but because in Bristol more than in Liverpool there was a growing recognition that the abolitionist movement would ultimately be successful. The merchants in Bristol wanted their sons to pursue careers in other less controversial fields of activity.

I am not what I ought to be, nor what I wish to be, nor what I hope to be, [but] I can truly say, I am not what I once was
John Newton, former slave ship captain turned abolitionist cited in *The Christian Spectator* in 1821

4
THE SLAVE CAPTAINS AND THEIR CREWS

You cannot plunder a people non-violently
Ta-Nehisi Coates, an African-American journalist writing in *The Atlantic* in 2014

The slave-ships were not specialist vessels requiring a certain kind of crew to operate them. Most were simply cargo ships that ranged from one hundred to a maximum of two hundred tons. It was not desirable to have a slave-ship too big because it had to be capable of navigating close to the African coast and entering its rivers. The crews for the slave ships were usually quite young. Captains and mates were usually in their thirties. The rest of the crew were normally in their teens and twenties, except for ship surgeons, who tended to be the oldest men on board. Young men tended to cope better with the physical demands of the voyage and older sailors tried if at all possible to avoid serving on slave ships because they did not want to face the close confinement and various dangers inherent in a twelve thousand mile sea voyage that would last between fifteen and eighteen months. Experienced seamen also knew that the chances of being ripped off by the captain of a slave-ship was very high. It was common for the captains to promise good pay but then pay at least half of it in foreign currencies, which were worth far less than the English pound. Worse still, the more unscrupulous captains were known sometimes to leave some of the crew behind in the Caribbean. They saw no reason retain all the sailors for the return journey because a smaller crew was sufficient once the slaves were sold.

Your captains and mates… must neither have dainty fingers nor dainty noses, few men are fit for these voyages but them that are bred up to it. It's a filthy voyage as well as a laborious one
Sir Dalby Thomas, commander on the Gold Coast working for the Royal African Company in 1700

The ships were always in danger of being destroyed by hurricanes or tornadoes or stormy seas or rocky and treacherous coastlines, and there were also human perils to be faced, including attacks from pirates and privateers off the coast of

Africa and in the Caribbean. In 1707, during the War of the Spanish Succession, the government commissioned a Bristol merchant, Woodes Rogers, to act as an English privateer and engage with these enemies. Acting as his sailing master was the highly experienced Somerset-born mariner William Dampier. He had recently achieved national fame by writing two books based on his diaries, one on how he had circumnavigated the world and the other on a voyage of exploration to 'New Holland' (as western Australia was then known). These books had introduced many new words into the English language, such as 'barbecue', 'avocado', 'mango', and 'chopsticks', but, more significantly, they had promoted the idea that all overseas peoples were there to be exploited. Between 1708 and 1711 Rogers and Dampier circumnavigated the world in two warships called the *Duke* and the *Duchess*, capturing or destroying a number of pirate ships and about twenty Spanish ships.

This was a time when ships sometimes changed hands on more than one occasion. A slave ship from Bristol called the *Joseph and Thomas*, for example, was seized by a French privateer in 1709 and used as a French slave ship until it was recaptured by a British privateer in 1710. Rogers had reason to regret going on his expedition because his brother was killed in action and he himself was left seriously disfigured from a musket ball that went through the roof of his mouth. However, investors were pleased because the prize money from the ships he took amounted in today's terms to over £22 million. His voyage is now best remembered for what happened when Rogers sought to re-provision his ships on the little-known island of Juan Fernández. He rescued a Scottish sailor called Alexander Selkirk, whom pirates had marooned four years earlier. Selkirk's story became the source of Daniel Defoe's famous novel *Robinson Crusoe*, published in 1719. Allegedly Selkirk was interviewed by Defoe in the *Llandoger Trow* pub in Bristol, although there is no evidence to prove that.

In 1718 Rogers agreed to become Captain General and Governor in chief of the Bahamas in order to continue the battle against the pirates. Just over 50% of them originated from Britain and about 25% were Americans, whilst the rest, including a significant number of blacks or mulattos, were from all over the world. The pirate problem had become a more serious issue because of the actions of the Bristol-born Edward Teach, better known as 'Blackbeard'. Virtually nothing is known about Teach's early life but it is usually assumed he must have come from a well-off family because he could read and write. It is thought he probably first went to the Caribbean as a sailor on a slave ship. Teach was not anything like as violent as legend later depicted, but he deliberately created a fearsome image for himself to frighten both his crew and his opponents:

> [His] beard was black, which he suffered to grow of an extravagant length; as to breadth, it came up to his eyes; he was accustomed to twist it with ribbons in small tails… and turn them about his ears.

It was said he sometimes tied fuses made of slow-burning twine to his hat and set them alight. In 1717 he had renamed a captured French ship the *Queen Anne's Revenge*, and, after equipping it with forty guns, made it the leading ship in a pirate fleet that was terrorising ships trading in the Caribbean. He gave himself the rank of Commodore and it is estimated he had about four hundred pirates under his command. Teach's ability to blockade the American colonial port of Charles Town in South Carolina in March 1718 was testimony to the danger he posed and the story of Rogers' war against 'Blackbeard' and the other pirates has recently become the basis for the very successful TV series *Black Sails*.

Rogers was able to destroy the pirates' main base – the so-called 'pirate republic' which had operated in Nassau on the island of New Providence. Teach and other leading pirates agreed to stop their activities and Teach was granted a royal pardon. However, he soon sought to resume his piracy and he was killed in November 1718 when his ship was attacked by two British warships. The commanding officer, Lieutenant Maynard, reported that it had taken twenty sword wounds and five gunshot wounds to finish the redoubtable Blackbeard. Sadly Rogers was not properly rewarded for his success, and, on his return to England in 1721, he was put in prison for debt. However, he then wrote a book about the pirates that restored his finances and catapulted him to fame. In 1728 he was re-appointed as Governor of the Bahamas.

'Expulsis Piratis, Restituta Commercia' (the Pirates dislodged, the Trade restored)

Motto of the Bahamas in 1728

The ending of the main pirate threat did not prevent trading ships from having to face attacks from the occasion pirate vessel. In 1719, for example, the *Calabar Merchant* belonging to the slave trader Abel Grant was attacked off the coast of Guinea:

> [The captain of the] pirate ship hoisted a black flag with death's head, and, firing at the *Calabar Merchant*, soon entered on board her, beat and abused the… [captain, Thomas Kennedy] and his men, and kept them as prisoners

for nine weeks, in which time they made use of, destroyed and took away great parts of the ship's cargo, provision, and stores, … often threatening to burn the said ship.

At the end of this time Kennedy somehow not only managed to secure his ship's release but persuaded the pirates to give him 'twenty-one negroes as a satisfaction for the damage they had done him'. These were taken to Virginia but were then confiscated by the authorities because of their pirate origin. Grant had to lodge a legal case to try and get their value as some compensation in what had proved a disastrous voyage.

In June 1721 the *Hambleton* was captured after leaving Jamaica by a pirate ship called the *Good Fortune*. The ship had taken herring from Bristol to be sold as cheap food for the slaves. Its captain Joseph Smith and its crew were held hostage for several weeks before being released with their plundered ship. It is not clear why but the ship was subsequently recaptured by the pirates and this time they set it on fire. Maybe it was felt that Smith had somehow cheated them on the first occasion. Smith and his men were set adrift in a tiny boat. What makes this story particularly interesting is that not all those on pirate ships were there by choice. Many sailors were compelled to work aboard them and one of the pirates who burnt the *Hambleton,* Brigstock Weaver, later became the centre of a legal case that hinged on whether he had or had not been forced into piracy. The case arose because Smith survived and, in 1723, whilst he was back in Bristol, he came across Weaver. He accused him of piracy to the authorities. Weaver was a former sea captain and his defence was that Smith knew from the time he had spent as a captive of the pirates that he was a conscript and not a genuine pirate. He said that Smith had tried to blackmail him into giving four hogsheads of cider in order to avoid an accusation of piracy being levied against him. The mayor did not entirely believe Smith because Weaver, on his arrival in Bristol, had confessed to the authorities how he had been captured and forced into piracy until he had managed to escape. Nevertheless, the courts in London took Smith's word and judged Weaver guilty and he was sentenced to be hung. The fact that he was then pardoned before the execution took place presumably indicates fresh evidence came to light to show that Weaver had been compelled into piracy and that Smith had lied.

Even after piracy declined, the threat remained of being attacked by enemy privateers. For example, a ship belonging to Thomas Pennington, the *Ferdinand*, was captured by Muslim privateers in the 1730s and its captain was held until a ransom was paid to release him. More common were attacks from Spanish

THE SLAVE CAPTAINS AND THEIR CREWS

Top: Blackbeard being captured in 1920 painting by Jean Ferris, William Dampier by Thomas Murray 1698; and an eighteenth century privateer engaged in battle in 1850 painting by Ambroise Garneray. Above: statues of Alexander Selkirk (Robinson Crusoe) in Fife and of Woodes Rogers in Nassau. Below left: William Hogarth's 1729 portrait of Woodes Rogers as Governor of Bahamas being presented with plans of the port of Nassau. Below right: Luke Roberts as Woodes Rogers in the TV series 'Black Sails' in 2016.

and French privateers in times of war. The British government sent ships from the Royal Navy to try and protect its merchant shipping against such foreign privateers but this was not always helpful. For example, in 1737 the Bristol merchants made representation to Parliament that three ships from the Royal Navy were engaging in the slave trade rather than protecting shipping and that they were preventing the legitimate traders from buying slaves by offering higher prices to the African slave dealers. Enemy privateering, particularly by the French, hit such record levels in the 1740s that, as we have seen, the losses more or less forced the Bristol merchants to temporarily abandon their participation in the slave trade.

However, the biggest threat to slave ships came from the enslaved rather than from pirates or privateers. As examined earlier, any captain ignoring the risk of a slave revolt was likely to imperil himself and his crew, but an even greater danger came from disease. Crew members often became ill or died from a variety of tropical diseases while waiting for their ship to acquire and load its slaves. The dreadful conditions for the slaves on the Middle Passage then generated health issues which took the lives of not only many of them but also the crew. To give just two examples: the *Bonny*, which sailed from Bristol in 1731, lost 141 of the 260 slaves on board to illness (i.e. 54%) but it lost twenty out of its crew of twenty-seven (i.e. 74%) and the *Britannia* which sailed in 1762 to Jamaica lost 239 of its 300 slaves (80%) and forty out of its crew of forty-four (91%). These losses are particularly high but the figures are not unusual in showing a higher percentage death rate among the sailors than among the slaves. That is not surprising because white sailors were more prone to tropical diseases and were at sea for a much longer period. It is estimated that on average at least 20% of the sailors never returned home to Bristol. Malaria, typhus, yellow fever, dysentery, consumption, scurvy, injuries and wounds, etc, all took their toll.

Beware, beware the Bight of Benin: for few come out though many go in

Old sailor rhyme about the Bight or Bay of Benin, a 400 mile stretch of coastline (now part of Ghana, Togo, Benin and Nigeria) to which about 30% of all enslaved Africans were brought for sale and transportation

---

Many of the captains had to resort to 'crimping' in Bristol in order to recruit a crew for their ship. This involved doing a deal with an inn-keeper (usually one of those in Marsh Street near the quayside) to get men insensibly drunk by lending them money. The drunken men would then be taken on board and, when sober, told they had to work off their debt or face prison. This was the merchant equivalent of the press gang. The activities of the latter in war-time made merchant recruitment even harder. On a corner of Queen Square there is a pub originally known as the *Coach and Horses* but which today is called *The Hole in the Wall*. It has a spy hole in one of its walls that was allegedly created so those drinking could have a look-out able to pre-warn them about the arrival on the dockside of a press gang or other unwelcome visitors, such as customs agents out seeking to capture smugglers. The Royal Navy often resorted to using a press gang to forcibly recruit its sailors and they particularly liked to get experienced sailors from merchant ships. If a sailor was press-ganged there was usually little chance of rescuing him, but there were occasional exceptions if the conscripted person had the right contacts. One example of this was when a press gang in 1769 seized a captain called James Caton, who had become a ship owner and merchant in Bristol. The incident took place in the Corn Exchange and Caton's mercantile associates immediately secured a magistrate's order for his release. This was ignored until the city's M.P. Edmund Burke, intervened with the Admiralty. Caton was then not only released but also paid compensation.

Given that many sailors were more or less conscripted into serving on slave ships it is not surprising that crews often deserted at the first opportunity. This, and the susceptibility of white sailors to tropical diseases, led a few of the captains to begin using some Africans as part of their crew on the Middle Passage. They saw it as an advantage that, if they chose, they could then sell these African sailors alongside the slaves! On occasion crews would rebel. In 1765, for example, a seaman from Bristol called Stephen Porter led two of his friends in a rebellion on a ship called the *William* after its captain, John Westcott, had him beaten with a stick. Porter murdered the captain and the chief mate with an axe and ran the ship aground on the Dutch island of St Jago. A more spectacular case involved one of James Laroche's ships, the *Black Prince*, in 1769. The crew murdered the captain and other officers a few hundred miles off the African coast, renamed the ship *Liberty,* and sailed it towards Brazil until internal arguments led to disaster. Some of the crew were murdered, some were set ashore in various places, and those that were left were eventually shipwrecked off the coast of the island of Hispaniola in the Caribbean.

Bristol's sea captains often came from the various ports of the south-west and usually they had been at sea since the age of fourteen or fifteen. Experience mattered. Research has shown that it was not uncommon for a seaman to have done three or four slave voyages before being promoted to captain and that a number of captains had previously been a first mate or a ship's surgeon. Merchants wanted the most experienced men they could find to captain their newer and larger ships because of the amount of investment wrapped up in them and so normally only existing captains looking for promotion were considered. Occasionally a captain might be recruited from the Royal Navy as was the case with Michael Pascal, the captain who purchased Olaudah Equiano. A Bristol example is James McTaggert who captained the slave-ship *Africa* in 1783. Some captains owed their appointment to the fact they were a relative of the ship's owner. For example, Robert Jones captained the *Wasp* because it was owned by Thomas Jones. By the end of the eighteenth century, some of Bristol's ships had captains who came from the Caribbean. For example, Samuel Phillips, who captained two voyages in 1790-93, came from St Kitts, and Elisha Arundel, who captained three voyages between 1794 and 1799, came from Anguilla.

The captain of a ship had to be physically fit to resist the rigours of the journey and he had to be multi-talented. It fell to him to oversee the fitting of the ship so he had to be knowledgable about ship construction and be capable of ordering and monitoring any necessary repairs or alterations. He had to carry out the slave trader's trading instructions and so he had to be good at establishing working relationships with not only manufacturers and suppliers in Bristol and in the colonies but also with the chiefs and Muslim slave traders in Africa. This meant being able to negotiate at every stage good prices for what was being bought and sold. A captain also had to find ways of keeping his crew fed properly so as to prevent the risk of a mutiny. The main stay for long voyages was dried beef and pork, oatmeal, hard peas, salted fish, butter and cheese, and tough biscuits made from flour and water. Often these provisions became contaminated or ran out. A not untypical description of a ship's spoiled supplies is this one dating from 1717:

> The Beef was tainted and boiled very black, the Pork was rusty and tainted, the Flour green and inclinable to be musty, and… the Butter and Cheese were both decaying.

Wherever possible, a captain would try to acquire fresher and more varied supplies of food and water drawn from the regions he was visiting. It was never easy to maintain fresh water supplies so beer, ale and rum were mostly drunk instead, but a reliance on alcohol generated its own problems. A captain was also responsible for the navigation of the ship, tricky at the best of times and extremely so whenever the ship faced storms. He also had to be strong-willed enough to dominate the crew, and, in the event of a slave rebellion or an attack from pirates or an enemy ship, be skilled at fighting.

The Slave Captains And Their Crews

There is no method of getting money, not even that of robbing for it upon the highway, which has so direct a tendency to efface the moral sense. The real or supposed necessity of treating the negroes with rigour gradually brings a numbness upon the heart and renders those who are engaged in it too indifferent to the sufferings of their fellow creatures

John Newton, hymn writer and ex-slave trader in *Thoughts Upon the African Slave Trade* in 1788

The best captains were truly remarkable men, possessing real strength of will, presence of mind, courage, patience, good humour, and the ability to stay calm in a crisis. But there were many who were less than ideal and the process of buying, transporting, and selling people was not conducive to encouraging finer feelings and kindness. Only a few captains ever expressed remorse about being involved in the slave trade and many captains developed a reputation for brutality towards their crews. Normally crews had no way of seeking address for their treatment but very occasionally a Bristol captain was put on trial. In 1726 John Jayne was hung for 'the atrocious murder of his cabin boy'. In 1733 Rice Harris was hung for murdering one of his crew 'in circumstances of horrible barbarity'. In 1735 James Newton, who was accused of murdering four of his crew, was hung for trampling his wife to death.

Good or bad, few captains did more than three or four slave voyages. Most of them hoped to earn enough to be able to become an investor in the next ship they captained and to eventually become either a merchant or a plantation owner. The basic pay was not generous. A captain was usually paid around £5 a month (the equivalent today of around £7,000 a year). This compared to wages for the rest of the crew that varied between £1-£2 for the sailors (the equivalent of up to £2,500) and £2-4 (the equivalent of up to £5,000) for the more important crew members, such as the ship's carpenter, the surgeon and the first mate. What made the captain's role attractive was that he was given certain 'privileges'. One of these was that he was permitted to take a couple of the slaves for his own use and for subsequent sale. However, the most important 'privilege' was that he received a bonus related to how much profit the voyage ultimately made. Some merchants also offered lesser privileges to the first mate and surgeon. With the right bonuses it was possible for a captain to make enough money to alter his social position and so, understandably, captains were keen to captain large ships rather than small ones in the hope that would bring them a larger profit. Many captains never attained their dream of becoming a merchant not least because at least 25% of them died whilst on a slave voyage. They had a higher death rate than other crew members because they had to spend more time on shore and that made them more vulnerable to catching a disease.

The captain whose change of status is most remembered is Nicholas Pocock. The son of a seaman, he attained the rank of captain at the age of twenty-six in 1766 and he worked for the merchant Richard Champion, who, despite his Quaker origins, was involved in the slave trade. Today Champion is best remembered as the man who pioneered the manufacture of Bristol porcelain. Between 1766 and 1775 Pocock undertook several voyages and he drew ink and wash sketches of ships and coastal scenes for his log books. When the American War of Independence bankrupted Champion, Pocock married and took up residence in Prince Street, having decided to make a career out of painting ships. He submitted his first oil painting to the Royal Academy in London in 1781 and he received encouragement from Joshua Reynolds, then perhaps Britain's most famous painter. Some of Pocock's work was exhibited the following year and this brought him a number of commissions. Producing large-scale paintings of sea battles became one of his specialities and in 1789 he moved to London where he was appointed Marine Painter to King George III. By the time of his death in 1821 he was Britain's most widely respected maritime artist.

The captains had to exercise constant initiative but essentially they were under the orders of the merchants as to where they went. For example, James Rogers often directed his captains on the outward journey to go to ports in or near to Sierra Leone, whereas John Anderson and James Jones had a preference for trading on the Gold Coast. The most common initial destination was the Bight of Biafra. The main slave port was Bonny, but some merchants, like James Laroche, favoured Old Calabar or Elem Kalibari (also known as New Calabar). Relations with the slave providers were sometimes fraught as each side sought to obtain the best deal. For example, in 1787 Joseph Williams, the captain of the *Ruby*, got into trouble when he fell out with 'Bimbe Jack', his main African supplier. Bimbe refused to accept inferior goods to the ones he had been promised and so Williams had him imprisoned on his ship. However, Bimbe Jack's men then attacked and seized control and took the entire crew on shore:

> The Captain was stripped stark naked, and the same [iron] collar was put upon his neck which he had put upon Bimbe Jack's. He was chained… to a tree… [with] the carpenter and the chief mate… several of the natives walking round them with their lances and muskets… [It was eventually agreed] the Captain, on account of his violent behaviour, should give up to

The Slave Captains And Their Crews

Right: Richard Champion by W.T.Davey. Far right: Pocock's ink and wash drawing of his ship the 'Betsy' 1770. Below: pages from his log book 1768 and Nicholas Pocock by E.Scriven c1811. Bottom: 1807 painting of Admiral Nelson's flagships by Pocock, regarded as being one of his best paintings.

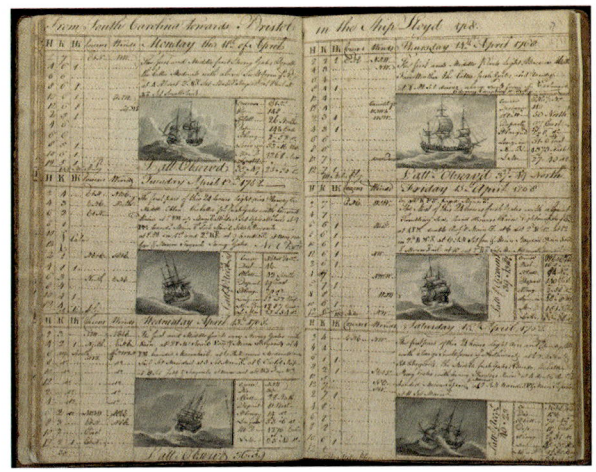

the natives all the articles of trade that then remained in his vessel; that… the slaves that had been released should be forfeited… [and] that every debt then due to the ship should be cancelled.

Another case led to the massacre of three hundred workers belonging to a slave provider in Old Calabar and it will be looked at in a later chapter.

Suffer none of your people to beat or abuse them under any pretence whatsoever
Instructions to Thomas Baker, captain of the *Africa* on leaving Bristol in 1776

As stated in an earlier chapter, most ships were ordered to go from Africa to Jamaica but there were five other relatively common destinations given to captains: Grenada, St Vincent, South Carolina, Dominica, and Demerara. Among the places occasionally visited were Tobago, St Kitts, Barbados, Tortola, Virginia, Antigua, Martinique, Montevideo, St Domingue, and Trinidad. Much depended on how the markets were faring at any one time in these places. It was the norm for a captain's instructions to contain a demand that he should take care of the slaves and so prevent unnecessary 'property' damage. Historians accept that most captains saw the sense of this but also recognise the brutality of the age. The raping of female slaves was commonplace and, as already covered, all slaves were subjected to appalling treatment. The Bristol-born seaman Silas Told, has left us with an account of the brutality that he saw when he worked on slave ships in the late 1720s and early 1730s. Written in old age when he had become a Methodist, Todd recalled with horror the savage behaviour of Timothy Tucker, the captain of the *Loyal George*:

> One of our black slaves, through a violent sickness was worn to a mere skeleton, and as he could not eat his allowance, the savage Tucker invented a scheme to compel the slave to eat, and laid to his charge that he was sulky: however, the poor creature could not, nor did he eat. Upon this the captain called for his black cabin boy, Robin, to bring him his horsewhip; he did so, and Tucker began lashing the poor sick man till I fairly believe from his neck to his ankles there was nothing to be seen but bloody wounds. The poor creature made no kind of resistance, nor spoke one word… [The captain]… ordered two ammunition pistols well loaded with ball… and with a malicious and violent grin, pointing one of the pistols to him, told him he would kill him… The captain applied the mouth of the pistol to the middle of his forehead, and fired. The man instantly clapped his hands to

The Slave Captains And Their Crews

Above: 1790 print of press gang at work; Right: a sailor wearing petticoat breeches 1777 and 'mast-head' punishment. Below right: 'keel-hauling' and the barnacles that the sailors were scraped against, and a cat-o-nine tails. Below: a flogging depicted by G. Cruikshank 1825

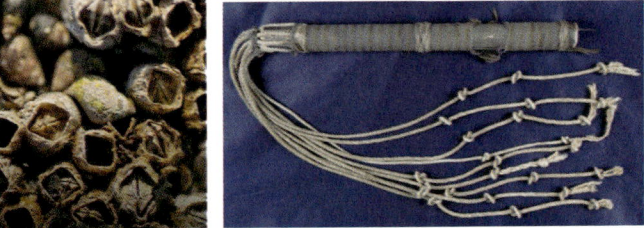

his head… the blood gushing from his forehead like the tapping a cask… Tucker then… clapped another [pistol] to his ear and fired that also.

Todd also records that Tucker enslaved a white woman with a view to selling her to one of the black slave suppliers in Bonny, but that his cruel treatment of her resulted in her death in 'circumstances too shocking to mention'. The ill-treatment of the slaves was matched by ill-treatment of the crew. Todd says of one of the punishments he faced:

Captain Tucker went immediately to the cabin, and brought out with him his large horse-whip, and exercised it about my body in so unmerciful a manner… [until] every sailor on board declared they could see my bones.

Another seaman, Robert Barker, wrote an account of his experience of serving on Bristol ships in the early 1750s and had it published in 1760. Its main focus was the voyage of the *Thetis* and the behaviour of its first mate, Robert Wapshutt, who took control after the ship's captain had died in Africa. Barker alleged that Wapshutt had conspired with the ship's surgeon to poison the captain so they could take over and he described how the two men had then fallen out with each other over their desire to rape the same female slave:

They were determined to cut her in two. Wapshutt to take one half of her, and the doctor the other, though she was not the property of either.

However, the main thrust of Barker's account was not the ill treatment of the slaves but of the crew. For example, he says he was made to work naked and that Wapshutt and the ship's surgeon would 'frequently order the negroe women and girls to haul me backwards and forwards by the privvies'. Fear of public humiliation was one way that a captain could impose his will on a largely conscripted crew.

A natural step on from this was to inflict measures that would terrorise the crew into total submission. Some of the things for which sailors were punished are understandable – a sailor who slept on watch, for example, endangered the lives of all – but not all discipline was related to misbehaviour. It was not uncommon for a sailor to be struck with a whip simply to indicate it was time for him to start working. Most of the punishments for offences were extraordinarily brutal. Sailors could be hung from a rope for long periods or forced to 'mast-head' (i.e. climb the mast and stay there to suffer either from heat or cold). They could be tarred and feathered or made to 'run the gauntlet' (i.e. made to walk past the rest of crew while being beaten with sticks). They could be ducked repeatedly overboard or, even worse, 'keel-hauled' (i.e. dragged by a rope underneath the ship so that their bodies were lacerated). The latter was usually fatal. The commonest punishment was the one described by Silas Todd: flogging. This could be done either with the end of a rope or, far worse, with a cat-o-nine tails, which was designed to slice the skin and cause immense pain. Anyone attempting mutiny would be hung from the ship's yard arm. This involved slowly pulling the seaman's body into the air until he died from strangulation.

Here's padlocks and bolts, and screws for the thumbs,
That squeeze them so lovingly till the blood comes'
                        Lines from an eighteenth-century sea-shanty

Given the barbaric treatment the sailors received, it is not surprising that they treated the captive Africans with even more barbarity whenever left to their own devices. The only thing that restricted their cruelty was that the slaves were a commodity that the captain had eventually to sell. The sailors, of course, had no value and that meant they were 'disposable', especially when they became surplus to requirements. Some captains were prepared to jettison some of their crew once the Middle Passage was over because they did not require as many men for the homeward journey. They simply sailed without them or, even worse, dropped them off on uninhabited islands (hence the marooning mentioned earlier of Alexander Selkirk, the prototype for the character of Robinson Crusoe).

Robert Barker wrote his account of his ill-treatment in enforced retirement through the loss of his eyesight and the Society of Merchant Venturers were incensed by the bad publicity that it gave to the slave trade. As a consequence they claimed the account was untrue and punished Barker by taking away the pension that they had given him. Any whistle-blower was likely to face similar condemnation. In 1789 a surgeon called Matthew Neely, who had worked on the slave ship the *Juba*, lodged a complaint against its captain John Kennedy with the ship's owner, James Rogers. He said that Kennedy had repeatedly and brutally raped the female slaves. He described how on one occasion Kennedy had demanded sex from the sister of one of the slaves he had already raped:

> He beat her unmercifully account she would not submit to sleep with him though [she was] a savage... At last [she] was forced to comply... even in

The brutality of life at sea: insurrection, warfare with pirates and privateers, and ruthless discipline. The 1792 Issac Cruikshank cartoon is of Bristol slave-ship captain John Kimber and his brutal treatment of an enslaved woman.

the middle of the day and on deck. His actions were more like a beast than a man.

Such behaviour obviously broke the traditional request that captains should not engage in needless beating or abuse of the slave 'merchandise', but Rogers' response was to sack Neely as a trouble-maker and rehire Kennedy.

These are the woes of Slaves;
They glare from the abyss;
They cry, from unknown graves,
'We are the Witnesses!'
    Henry Wadsworth Longfellow, American poet in *Poems on Slavery* in 1842

In June 1792 *Felix Farley's Bristol Journal* featured the trial of Captain John Kimber of the *Recovery* for the murder of a fourteen or fifteen year-old female slave. She was one of twenty-seven slaves to die on the crossing. This case arose because of action taken by the abolitionist William Wilberforce. He had heard that her death had resulted from a refusal to jump up and down on deck which was the common method used to make the enslaved exercise. Kimber had decided to make her dance by whipping her. The surgeon on board, Thomas Dowling, said he knew no reason why Kimber had beaten her to the extent he had and described the event:

> She was ordered to be suspended by one hand, and then by another, and then a boy was ordered to pull her legs by a sudden jerk... [The captain] then ordered her to be suspended by the leg, and then by the other, and during the time she was suspended he flogged her... [for] half-an-hour.

The defence argued that Dowling and another witness, Stephen Deveraux, were malcontents with a grudge against Kimber. Their careers were destroyed and the captain was acquitted. The only consolation that abolitionists drew from the case was that it had established a legal precedent that those who killed slaves could be tried for murder.

SLAVERY AND BRISTOL

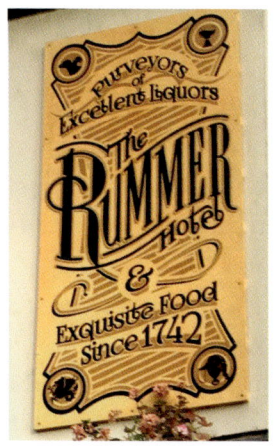

Above: the 'Rummer' near the St Nicholas Market. Right: Sugar cone and sugar axe and sugar tongs. Far right: the ship's figurehead outside 'The Drawbridge' next to the Bristol Hippodrome on St Augustine's Parade. Below left: the 'Christmas Steps' originally called the 'Three Sugar Loaves'. Below right: the Lewins Mead Sugar House (now the Hotel du Vin), the only one of Bristol's sugar houses to have survived.

216

5

THE SLAVE OWNERS

> **The pleasure, glory and grandeur of England has been advanced more by sugar than by any other commodity**
> Sir Dalby Thomas in *Historical Account of the Rise and Growth of the West-India Colonies and of the Great Advantages They Are to England, in Respect to Trade* in 1690

Sugar is not a good foodstuff because it is high in calories and low in nutrients but its sweetness is addictive. It has been described as 'the food nobody needs but everyone craves'. As was indicated in the first section of this book, it was demand for sugar that kickstarted Bristol's interest in the Caribbean and slavery. Sugar had been commercially produced for many centuries but in Europe it was a rare and very expensive spice rather than an everyday condiment until the Portuguese and Spanish began cultivating it in their colonies by utilising slave labour. Richard Aldworth, the first Bristol merchant to import Portuguese sugar, rapidly became the wealthiest in the city. Dutch, French, and British merchants soon saw the value in also engaging in sugar production. The island of Nevis, which forms part of the inner arc of the Leeward Islands chain in the West Indies, provides a classic example of this. Initially just a stop-over point, Nevis was first settled in 1628 and the island's first governor, Sir James Russell, immediately set about acquiring Africans so the British colonists could create and run plantations. This attracted the interests of merchants from Bristol and by the 1670s three of these, John Coombes, Thomas Woodward, and John Knight, were able to bequeath very valuable plantations on Nevis to their families.

> **[My] automatic thought was, 'Why didn't they raise up? Why didn't they overpower? They had the numbers.' But really these people their hope was broken. Their sense of love was broken. Their appreciation for who they were was broken**
> Aldis Hodge, American actor in discussion on TV series *Underground* in 2016

It was John Knight who created the first sugar refinery in Bristol so he could process his own sugar rather than paying someone else to do it. Bristol eventually was to have about twenty sugar houses where the sugar could be further boiled and refined and poured into cone-shaped moulds to crystallise. The resulting 'sugar loafs' were bought by shopkeepers who cut them into pieces for sale to their customers. It was the identification of Bristol as a major producer, importer and refiner of sugar and a major player in the provision of the slaves required for the sugar plantations that attracted many merchants to seek to base their business there. It explains, for example, why Isaac Hobhouse moved to Bristol from Minehead, Thomas Deane from Chard, John Pinney from Okehampton, George Gibbs from Exeter, James Laroche from London, Robert Gordon from Scotland, and John Becher from Ireland. By 1728 there were 513 firms involved in Bristol's sugar trade and the amount of sugar coming into its port constantly increased. The Lewins Mead Sugar House, built in 1728 is the only one of the sugar houses to have survived. It is now the Hotel du Vin. However, there are pubs in Bristol that hark back to the sugar trade as the following three examples indicate. The *Christmas Steps* pub was originally called the *Three Sugar Loaves* because it was near to a sugar refinery. *The Drawbridge* prominently sited next the *Bristol Hippodrome* on St Augustine's Parade sports a replica of a ship's figurehead from the ship *Demerara*, which was named after a Dutch sugar colony that later became a British one. The *Rummer Tavern* near the St Nicholas Market was named after a vessel used for drinking rum and it now boasts that the poets Southey and Coleridge who were opposed to slavery used to meet there.

Those who involved themselves with the sugar industry have usually not been signalled out for condemnation in the way that the slave traders have been, although the plantations relied entirely on slave labour. A good example of this is the American born John Elbridge, whose philanthropic role in Bristol has not been subjected to the criticism levied against Colston, although the two men were near contemporaries. Elbridge's name may not be blazoned across the city, but it cannot be denied that his wealth was undoubtedly born out of the profits of slave labour. Elbridge's parents sent him to school in Bristol and he was apprenticed to his cousins, John and Thomas Moore, who were both customs officials. Elbridge eventually became the Deputy-Controller of Customs. This was a huge responsibility given the extent of Bristol's trading activities. His status was further enhanced by his inheriting the wealth of relatives who were actively involved in the transatlantic trade, notably from a merchant called Robert Aldridge, who had large estates in Jamaica. Elbridge invested in the sugar trade and became increasingly wealthy. He lived first in King Street, then leased the Royal Fort, and, from 1724 onwards, he began lavishly decorating

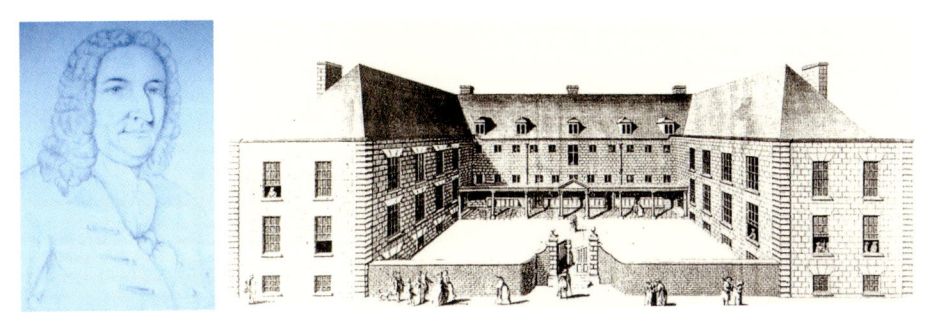

Top: John Elbridge sketched from 1716 painting by M.H.Holmes and Bristol Infirmary as it was in 1742. Above: Elbridge's home, Cote House. Right: a portrait from c 1640 by Gilbert Jackson thought to be of Florence Smyth, showing her with an African servant. This indicates the family's early ties with the African trade. Below: the Smyth family home Ashton Court with its classical façade.

and furnishing Cote House near Westbury-on-Trym.

Like Colston Eldridge was unmarried and so, as he grew older, he began giving away considerable money to philanthropic causes. Also like Colston, one of his main interests lay in encouraging education. He created Eldridge's School (or the 'Blue School' as it was later called) to educate girls from really poor backgrounds. This was a very unusual step because female education at that time was normally restricted only to the daughters of the rich. Equally unusual was Elbridge's decision to promote the creation of the Bristol Infirmary. Plenty of charitable money had found its way into creating almshouses or so-called 'hospitals' designed to help the sick and aged, but the scheme to create the Infirmary was very different because it envisaged a place that would use the latest medical advances to heal people. The funding would come from voluntary subscriptions. Elbridge acted as the scheme's Treasurer and he encouraged a number of merchants involved in the slave trade, such as Nehemiah and Richard Champion and Paul Fisher, to provide financial support. However, it was Elbridge who provided the bulk of the money required. The Infirmary opened in 1737 and he paid for the building of its main ward and for an adjoining apothecary's shop in 1738. The buildings have long been replaced but Elridge's hospital has, of course, developed into the Bristol Royal Infirmary.

When Elbridge died in 1739 he left legacies to both his school and the Bristol Infirmary but most of his estate went to his nephew, Thomas Elbridge, and his niece, Rebecca Woolnough. The latter's share, comprising property in England and Jamaica, became the dowry for her daughter, Elizabeth, when she married John Hugh Smyth, the heir to the Ashton Court estate in 1757. His father, Jarrit Smyth, was a Merchant Venturer and the Smyth family had been investors in the trade with Africa since the 1630s. It was wealth from rum and sugar production that enabled John Hugh Smyth to add a magnificent library extension to Ashton Court and to commence reshaping its parkland to designs by the famed designer Humphrey Repton. After his death successive heirs were able to spend fifty years completing the work on the parkland (albeit amending the original scheme), creating an amazing stable block, and remodelling the house to give it even greater grandeur by creating a 91 metre long classical façade.

If there were no buyers there would be no sellers
Ottobah Cuguano, freed African slave, in Thoughts and Sentiments on the Traffic... of the Human Species in 1787

It is estimated that probably 60% of all the merchants involved in the sugar trade ended up owning West Indian slave plantations. The biggest concentration were in Jamaica but many owned land on more than one island. The Quaker merchant William Reeve, for example, had estates on Nevis, St Kitts, and Grenada. Sometimes the merchants developed their plantations from scratch but sometimes they obtained estates because they accepted land in payment for debts that they were owed. The overwhelming majority of plantation owners chose to be absentee landlords because of the health risks. They ran their estates through agents and each plantation had its appointed overseer. There is plenty of evidence to show that most overseers saw no reason to look after the slaves, judging it cheaper to replace them. Some owners instructed their overseers to be humane but that was not always for humanitarian reasons. For example, William Helyar told his overseers in Jamaica that slaves worked better 'for a master that will treat them a little kindly and with discretion'. It did not take much for all humanitarianism to disappear. A rebellion on Helyar's plantation was ruthlessly dealt with. The rebels had their arms and legs burnt before starving them to death. Owners and overseers alike felt they dared not risk appearing 'weak' because the whites were seriously outnumbered. As early as 1713 there were three times as many Africans as there were whites in Barbados and six times as many in Jamaica. Concern over slave rebellions explains why there were moves to restrict the continued import of more slaves in the second half of the eighteenth century in some places.

Banks were created to help finance the mortgages and other financial agreements required by those wishing to invest in the West Indies. Some banks also held estates in trust for non-trading Bristol families. Links with the Caribbean were strengthened by some merchants occasionally sending out their sons or other family members to check up on what their agents were doing and because some of the agents based in the Caribbean sent their sons to Bristol for their education. Marriage agreements between families in Bristol and families in the Caribbean also helped consolidate business partnerships.

The success of Henry Bright and Richard Meyler provides perhaps the best documented example of how the development of the sugar trade relied on partnerships and on the slave trade. In 1731 the sixteen year-old Henry Bright was apprenticed to Meyler, whose business included sugar production. Once his training was completed, Bright went out to St Kitts so he could personally supervise the Caribbean side of Meyler's business, and, in the early 1740s, Bright created useful trading contacts in Jamaica. By then the two men were trading not just in sugar but also in slaves. In 1746 Bright returned to Bristol and married Meylor's daughter Sarah. The couple set up home in Queen Square. Henry returned to the Caribbean briefly in 1748-51 and found ways to get around the ban which Spain had issued on British ships providing slaves for the Spanish colonies. Two bases were created, one in Kingston and one in Savanna-la-Mar, and these were then run by the brothers of the two merchants, Francis Bright and Jeremiah Meylor, who both acquired slave plantations in Jamaica.

Between 1746 and 1769 Bright and Company organised twenty-one slaving voyages out of Bristol. When Bright fell out with his father-in-law he sent his nephew, Lowbridge Bright, to Jamaica and he forged a new partnership with a West Indian merchant called Nathaniel Milward. Bright spent his last years as very prominent figure in Bristol and he was appointed Mayor in 1771. On his death in 1777, the business was taken over by Lowbridge because Henry's only son, Richard, was dedicating himself to banking and to scientific pursuits. Among Richard's friends were a number of scientific innovators, including Humphrey Davy, the inventor of the miners' safety lamp and a pioneer in electro-chemistry, James Watt, the mechanical engineer renowned for his improvements in steam engine technology, William Smith, the creator of the first nationwide geological map, and Thomas Beddoes, a distinguished chemist who experimented in Bristol with new medical treatments for tuberculosis. Lowbridge entered into a partnership with a former soldier from Scotland, Evan Baillie, who had set up a business centred on the islands of St Kitts and St Vincent. The firm of Bright, Baillie, and Bright developed trade with the Leeward and Windward islands. In later life Baillie was to become an M.P. for Bristol and his eldest son married Elizabeth Pinney, one of the daughters of the sugar merchant John Pinney.

After a lengthy legal battle some of the wealth of the deceased Richard Meyler was inherited by the Bright family and this included not only plantations abroad but Ham Green House at Abbots Leigh on the outskirts of Bristol. In 1790 Richard Bright moved into it and he began creating a stunning garden by bringing over plants and trees from Jamaica. His elder son Henry was to become an M.P. for Bristol and a key opponent of those seeking to end the slave trade but his younger son Richard became an eminent doctor who pioneered new methods of diagnosing and treating various illnesses. He is best remembered today for his work on kidneys and chronic nephritis is commonly named Bright's disease after him. In 1899 Ham Green House was turned into an isolation hospital for any sailors who had returned to Bristol with infectious tropical diseases and, after the Second World War, it became first part of Southmead Hospital and then, in the 1990s, a centre for cancer care run by the Penny Brohn Trust. Thus a building deeply associated with the wealth derived from the slave trade has ended up being a place that saves lives. None of that was envisaged when in the

Above: paintings like this 1790 one of Nevis from St Kitts by Nicholas Pocock were designed to romanticise the sugar trade. Below: Ham Green House and its Gazebo that acted as a scientific laboratory with (left) Richard Bright painted by his son Henry and (right) Dr Richard Bright.

early part of the nineteenth century the family still made the slave trade their business, entering into partnership with George Gibbs & Son, a firm which had been trading in sugar since the seventeenth century. Among that firm's previous partners had been Michael Atkins, the most successful Bristol sugar merchant of the first half of the eighteenth century.

Strange that an article like sugar, so sweet and necessary to human existence, should have occasioned such crimes and bloodshed!
Eric Williams, Prime Minister of Trinidad and Tobago in *Capitalism and Slavery* in 1944

Just how successful a good entrepreneur could become is well illustrated by the case of William Miles, who was the leading importer of sugar by the 1770s. It is said that he arrived in Bristol as young man from Herefordshire with just a couple of coins in his pocket but obtained an apprenticeship and then undertook various roles in the developing trade with Jamaica. Eventually he became a merchant on that island and he earned enough to set himself up as a West India merchant in Bristol. He was able to leave a substantial fortune to his son, Philip John Miles, who became a partner in Miles Bank of Bristol (later to become part of the National Westminster Bank) and who built Leigh Court in Abbot's Leigh in 1814, although his main residence was King's Weston House in Bristol. Because his bank took possession of plantations if their owners defaulted on mortgage payments, Philip John Miles became a very large landowner in the Caribbean. Like many of the other businessmen involved in slavery Philip John Miles was generously philanthropic and also played a political role, first as Mayor of Bristol and then as one of the city's M.P.s. He was therefore, like Colston, seen by contemporaries as being a model citizen: prudent, honest, and liberal. He left an estate of over £1 million, making him the first recorded millionaire of Bristol (in today's values he was worth around £58 million). His son, William, was knighted and made a baronet in 1859. The family subsequently collected one of the most significant art collections in the country. It included works by Michelangelo, Raphael, Titian, Rubens, Poussin, and Van Dyke.

I was shocked at the first appearance of human flesh expos'd for sale. But surely God ordain'd 'em for ye use and benefit of us: otherwise his Divine Will would have been manifest by some particular sign or token
John Pinney Bristol sugar merchant in letter written in March 1765

THE SLAVE OWNERS

Above: Philip John Miles and King's Weston House. Right: the rebuilt Leigh Court as it is today with a view of its central hallway and ceiling and (below) as it was in its heyday set in parkland in 1829 painting by W. Payne.

225

Today the best known of the plantation owners is John Pinney because his house in Great George Street has become the Georgian House Museum. When he was in his twenties Pinney inherited some sugar plantations on Nevis from a cousin. In 1765 he went out to inspect his new property and took up residence on his main estate, which was called Mountravers. He was initially taken aback at witnessing slavery first hand, but he soon adjusted to it. Finding his estate was in a mess, he purchased over sixty new slaves to run it. Pinney was not by temperament a harsh owner. He restricted the hours his slaves were expected to work and he set aside land for them to build little African-style huts of wattle and daub and to grow their own food. He told one of his estate overseers: 'I will not suffer any human being, committed by providence to my care, to be treated with cruelty'. However, there is evidence to show such advice was ignored.

The story of Pero, one of the slaves that Pinney made into a personal servant and later brought to Bristol, is told in a subsequent chapter. Like most slave owners Pinney was keen to be seen as a good man and he wanted people in Bristol to believe that his slaves were well-cared for and better off than if they had stayed in Africa. It was no coincidence that paintings of the Caribbean that the sugar merchants hung in their homes usually portrayed the islands as being idyllic places and, if any slaves were depicted, they were usually portrayed healthy and happy. Some plantation owners created what became known as 'decoy ducks' – these were a few well-dressed slaves that could be shown to any visitor to prove that tales of savage treatment were false. In 1800 Pinney sent special instructions to his overseers when the island was due to be visited by Thomas Wedgwood, the son of the famous porcelain manufacturer and a known abolitionist. Pinney ordered that his overseers should only let Wedgwood see things that would convince him the slaves were well looked after so he would 'leave the island possessed with favourable sentiments'. It was essential that no slave should be punished where Wedgwood might see or hear it happening.

The hypocrisy of Pinney is further shown in his readiness to sell his Mountravers estate to Edward Huggins, a man known for his cruelty. Huggins established his authority by public whippings of those who did not immediately obey him. One eyewitness says he gave five slaves over two hundred lashes each, including a man who received 365 lashes and a woman who received 291. The wealth accumulated by the Pinney family was estimated at £340,000 in 1818 (the equivalent today of around £19 million).

The most wealthy of all the Bristol sugar plantation owners was probably Thomas Daniel, known as 'the King of Bristol' because of his control over the way the city was run. His father (also called Thomas) had established 'Daniel

The Slave Owners

John Pinney by Thomas Maynard 1765 and his wife Jane Weeks from painting lent to Bristol Museums. Left and below: Pinney's six storey townhouse in Great George Street with views of some of its interior rooms. It is now the Georgian House Museum and open to the public.

and Sons' in Barbados, where he acquired a sugar estate of about 364 acres with almost two hundred slaves. He returned to Bristol in 1764 but his son increasingly acquired and developed estates on many other West Indian islands, including Antigua, Nevis, Montserrat, Tobago, Demerara and British Guiana (now Guyana). After the government prohibited involvement in the slave trade in 1807 it was rumoured that Daniel's response was to bring Africans to Hung Road (a section of the River Avon close to Pill) and then have them secretly transferred to ships bound for the West Indies so he could continue to supply labour-starved plantations. Daniel owned so many slaves by the time of the 1833 Abolition of Slavery Act that he received £102,000 in compensation (the equivalent today of around £7 million). Thomas Daniel's wealth did not just mean that he could afford both a fashionable town house in Berkeley Square and a country seat in Henbury. It meant that he was a major political leader of the local Tory Party. It was said that he 'reigned without a rival' as a city councillor for more than fifty years and at various times he served as a master of the Merchant Venturers and as a Mayor and an Alderman. He was also a partner in the Great Western Cotton Factory and one of the owners of the Bristol Prudent Men's Savings Bank. Among his philanthropic activities was acting as treasurer for two of the cities' educational charities, Queen Elizabeth's Hospital and Red Maids.

The blacks are immeasurably better off here than in Africa, morally, physically, and socially. The painful discipline they are undergoing is necessary for their further instruction as a race, and will prepare them, I hope, for better things. How long their subjugation may be necessary is known and ordered by a wise God
Robert E. Lee, who became commander of the Confederate Army, in a letter in 1856

No account of the sugar merchants would be complete without briefly mentioning the London merchant and M.P. William Beckford. 'the uncrowned king of Jamaica' and Britain's 'wealthiest commoner'. The Beckford family had first acquired land there in the 1660s and William had over 20,000 acres of plantations. His immense wealth (calculated at being about £125 million at today's values) passed to his bisexual son, William, now best remembered as the author of the Gothic novel *Vathek*. The son, though hugely talented, was an avid collector and wasted the bulk of his fortune building an extravagant and bizarre Palladian mansion at Fonthill in Wiltshire between 1796 and 1813.

Above: Thomas Daniel, the King of Bristol and William Beckford, father and son. Right: Beckford's Tower with its ornate interior. Below: Fonthill Abbey built by the younger William Beckford in Wiltshire using the profits from the sugar trade.

Designed to shock and amaze, it was a vast maze of curious rooms, deliberately uncomfortable and cold. Thirteen of its eighteen bedrooms, for example, were so small and poorly ventilated as to be unusable, and all eighteen were reached by twisted staircases that made them almost inaccessible. Poor construction led to the collapse of its eighty-five metre tall central tower in 1825 and the virtually bankrupted Beckford then became a recluse in Bath. His home was in Lansdown Crescent and he commissioned the building of a tower to house what was left of the art treasures he had collected in his travels around Europe. The landscaped parkland he created around it (which inspired the creation of Bath's Victoria Park) has gone but the forty-eight metre high Beckford's Tower still stands on its vantage point on the top of Lansdowne Hill looking over Bath, Bristol and the Welsh mountains, one of the strangest buildings created from the profits of slavery.

I fear I shall never be…good for anything in this world, but composing airs, building towers, forming gardens, collecting old Japan, and writing a journey to China or the Moon
William Beckford, novelist and heir to sugar fortune in letter to Lady Hamilton in 1781

Sugar was the country's most valuable import between 1670 and 1820. The resulting profits were the single biggest factor behind Bristol's defence of the slave trade throughout the eighteenth century because the sugar plantation owners were keen to justify their use of slave labour and they formed the backbone of the pro-slavery lobby groups in Parliament. A common claim was that they were an important task force in converting Africans to Christianity, even though evidence now shows that most plantation owners opposed any missionary work because they felt it encouraged the Africans to believe they should be set free.

A decline in the profitability of the sugar trade from the 1780s onwards and an increase in slave rebellions in the 1790s affected the intensity of their defence, but it did not stop it. By the end of the eighteenth century the number of firms involved in the sugar trade in Bristol had fallen to just eighty-five but that was mainly because of mergers and the fact that the more successful merchants had been able to squeeze out weaker competitors. Bristol was dealing with 21,000 hogsheads of sugar per year and Britain's annual per capita consumption of sugar had risen from four pounds in 1700 to eighteen pounds in 1800. This was more than-enough reason, as we shall see in the next section, for the merchants to battle hard against those who wanted to see Britain end its role in the slave trade.

The single refined sugars of Bristol are more esteemed and will get a higher price abroad than those of other places
Edward's New Bristol Guide in 1802.

The focus on slave ownership among sugar producers has overshadowed the use of slavery in tobacco production and that explains why accounts of the Bristol traders who benefitted from the slave trade normally omit reference to the Wills family. However, tobacco production, although initially reliant on white indentured labourers, turned to using slave labour in the eighteenth century. As with sugar, tobacco production was labour intensive. Seedlings had to be hand planted and tended and regularly pruned in order to ensure growth in the broad lower leaves. These were then picked and hung up to dry over a period of four to eight weeks in barns. Those in barns that just relied on natural heat (known as air-curing) developed a flavour that made them particularly suited for cigars. Those in barns that were smoked dry by fires produced leaves more suited to pipe tobacco, chewing tobacco, and snuff. The cured leaves then had to be sorted into different grades and packed in hogsheads very carefully to avoid bruising or tearing them. Taking the barrels to the nearest dock and loading them onto ships was in itself an onerous task.

Bristol became an important processing plant for the imported tobacco leaves. These were processed in three ways. Leaves could be twisted together into a rope or twist (for use in a pipe) or pressed together into a square, brick-like plug (for chewing) or powdered into snuff (for inhaling). The processed tobacco was then sold in Bristol or exported. The slave trader Noblett Ruddock, for example, exported tobacco to Ireland. Today we view tobacco as a health hazard but it was initially sold as a health creator and something that gave 'happy thoughts' as this extract from a 1588 account indicates:

> There is an herb called *uppowoc*, which sows itself. In the West Indies… the Spaniards generally call it tobacco. Its leaves are dried, made into powder, and then smoked by being sucked through clay pipes into the stomach and head. The fumes purge superfluous phlegm and gross humors from the body by opening all the pores and passages. Thus its use not only preserves the body, but if there are any obstructions it breaks them up. By this means the natives keep in excellent health, without many of the grievous diseases

which often afflict us in England.

Not everyone agreed. King James I described smoking as 'a custom loathsome to the eye, hateful to the nose, harmful to the brain, dangerous to the lungs'. As its use became increasingly popular opposition to tobacco use disappeared and profit took over. The main British sources were the colonies of Virginia, Maryland, and North Carolina and so historians have tended to assign the evil of tobacco slavery to the Americans and not the British, but the British tobacco industry was a beneficiary.

> *The Wills' use of slave-produced tobacco allowed the family to become the great philanthropists for which they are now remembered*
> Tayo Lewin-Turner, student at Bristol University on Bristol Museums website

The Wills family's connection with the tobacco industry commenced in 1786 when Henry Overton Wills, the son of a Salisbury watchmaker, set up a tobacco shop in Castle Street with Samuel Watkins. It was one of fourteen in the city. By then tobacco was essentially slave produced. Three years later Watkins retired and Wills entered into partnership with another business man, Peter Lily, who owned a snuff mill at Barrow Guerney. Eventually the business was taken over by Will's two sons, William Day Wills and Henry Overton Wills II, and so the company of W.D. and H.O. Wills was formed in 1830. By then Britain had abandoned its role in the slave trade but had not yet rejected slavery. The company became a major tobacco importer. Tobacco production in America continued to rely on slave labour until 1865 and so it cannot be disputed that the initial wealth of the Wills family undoubtedly came from the work of enslaved labourers. The Wills family's development of cigarettes and promotional cigarette cards hugely expanded tobacco use and, in 1901, their company became part of the Imperial Tobacco Company, the world's fourth-largest cigarette company.

One of the chief benefactors was Bristol University when it was created in 1909. The Wills family gave it an estimated £10.5 million in today's values and, not surprisingly, H.O. Wills III was made the University's first Chancellor. Clearly the Wills family were not slave owners but in 2017 a group of students at Bristol University petitioned that the Wills Memorial Building should be renamed because a university that was proclaiming its commitment to 'diversity and inclusivity' could not continue to honour the name of a family whose wealth came from 'slave-profited money'. The University rejected the petition and it was pointed out that Henry Overton Wills II had supported the abolition of the

THE SLAVE OWNERS

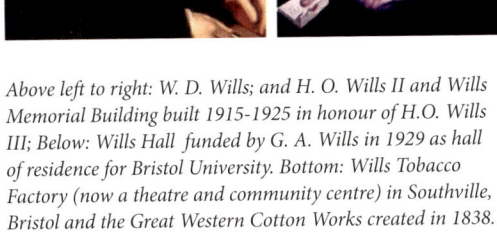

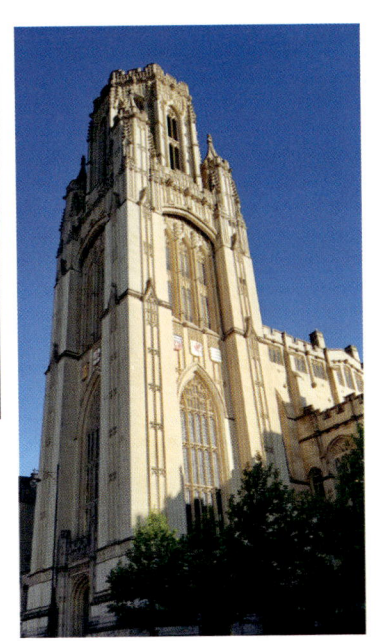

Above left to right: W. D. Wills; and H. O. Wills II and Wills Memorial Building built 1915-1925 in honour of H.O. Wills III; Below: Wills Hall funded by G. A. Wills in 1929 as hall of residence for Bristol University. Bottom: Wills Tobacco Factory (now a theatre and community centre) in Southville, Bristol and the Great Western Cotton Works created in 1838.

slave trade in the 1830s. Nevertheless it could not be denied that his company had owed its early profits to slave-produced tobacco and so, in 2019, Bristol University commissioned Professor Olivette Otele, an expert in the history of colonialism, to carry out a two-year research project on the extent to which the university had benefitted indirectly from the philanthropic support of families who had made money from businesses involved in one way or another with the transatlantic slave trade:

> We cannot alter the past but we can enable reflection upon it and add to knowledge about slavery past and present.

The chocolate manufacturing company, J.S. Fry & Sons, provides another example where there was not slave ownership but there was 'slave-profited money'. England's first chocolate house was opened in London in 1657 by a Frenchman who promised his customers an 'excellent West India drink', but the man who really started the craze for drinking chocolate was Sir Hans Sloane, a governor of Jamaica. He is credited with devising a recipe that involved mixing chocolate with milk. The most fashionable chocolate house was *White's*, which opened in 1693 in St Jame's Street in London. It survives today as a private member's club. Chocolate houses sprang up in Bristol and other cities and chocolate also became a popular drink for the wealthy in their homes, especially among women. It was not uncommon, for example, for their breakfast to consist of drinking chocolate mixed with egg yolks and grated bread. Leading porcelain factories began to produce fashionable tableware just for chocolate drinking. Joseph Fry was a Quaker doctor who became convinced that drinking cocoa was a nutritious alternative to alcohol. He began selling cocoa in Bristol in 1756 and by 1777 he had created a cocoa works on the banks of the River Frome to process the cocoa beans sourced from the slave plantations in the Caribbean. His son, Jospeh Storrs Fry, then transformed cocoa production by using a James Watt steam engine and, in 1822, created the company of J.S. Fry and Sons.

It was 'the sons', Joseph, Francis, and Richard, who then created a method of turning cocoa into chocolate bars in the 1860s and thus revolutionised the entire industry. The Frys are often rightly praised for their role in supporting the abolition of slavery, but that should not make us forget the cocoa business was in its origin reliant on slaves. It is also worth noting that today Fair-Trade continues to publicise the extent to which cocoa farmers are still exploited as if they were slaves because over 60% live below the poverty line. Child labour is also still extensively used. For example, there are over two million children

The Slave Owners

Top: etching of Sir Hans Sloane 1729 and painting by J.B. Charpentier in 1768 showing a wealthy family drinking chocolate. Above: etching of J.S. Fry and the Frys' chocolate factory in the 19th century (then the largest in the world). Above right: the oldest surviving Bristol coffee house in Corn Street. Bottom: the interior of a coffee house c.1700.

working on cocoa farms in Ghana and Côte d'Ivoire. Given the extent to which consumers today are often uninterested in how products are sourced, it should not come as a surprise that most people in the eighteenth-century were equally if wrongly disinterested in how the cocoa for their chocolate was sourced. .

> *Like Noah's ark, every kind of creature in every walk of life frequented coffeehouses*
> Aytoun Ellis, historian in *The Penny Universities: A History of the Coffee Houses* in 1956

Slavery played an important role in the production of many items, not just sugar, tobacco and cocoa. The other three that most spring to mind are rice, coffee and cotton. African familiarity with rice-growing led to the American colonists in South Carolina creating rice plantations. Male slaves took on the task of clearing the mosquito-infested swamps and building canals and the female slaves planted the rice. Once the rice had grown, it was harvested by hand and threshed and pounded for sale. Some was exported to Bristol from 1695 onwards. Far more significant within Bristol was the impact of coffee. Coffee is often not mentioned in books on eighteenth century slavery although it was produced in the West Indies. It is ignored largely because the British colonies mainly grew coffee just for internal consumption and not for export. However, the French and Dutch used significant numbers of slaves to produce coffee and about half of the world's coffee came from French-occupied Saint-Domingue (present day Haiti) in the eighteenth century. It was not until the nineteenth century that coffee production was dominated by Latin America, notably Brazil, where slavery was not made illegal till 1888.

Although the British were not major producers, they were major purchasers. Though long consumed as a drink in Turkey and elsewhere, coffee was originally viewed as a medicinal plant in England until the first coffee house was created in around 1651 in Oxford. It is thought the first coffee house in Bristol may have been the *Elephant* in All Saints' Lane in 1677. Coffeehouses quickly became fashionable and were seen as an alternative meeting place to pubs. They offered a better environment for serious discussion on matters of common interest. They also soon became a venue where the latest newspapers and periodicals could be read and discussed. Some historians argue that coffeehouses helped generate better manners and encouraged more reasoned debates on politics, science, religions, etc. Anyone could enter if they paid a penny for a cup of coffee and by 1739 London had over 550 coffeehouses, more than any other city in the western world. Some were hugely influential in shaping the economy. The London Stock Exchange, for example, had its beginnings in *Jonathan's Coffee House* and the insurers Lloyd's of London in *Lloyds Coffee House.*

Bristol of course followed suit, although until 1808 the coffee beans imported into Bristol had to be taken to London and then brought back because only certain London merchants were authorised to roast coffee beans. The Rev William Goldwin in his *Poetical Description of Bristol in* 1712 wrote about the coffeehouses and 'Turkish lap' as he termed coffee:

> Here wise remarkers on the Church and state
> O'er Turkish lap and smoky Whiffs debate.
> Here half-shut Authors in confusion lye,
> And kindling stuffs for Party Heats supply.

There were many coffee houses in Bristol by the mid-eighteenth century, among them *Little John's Coffee House* in Temple Street, *St Michael's* in Maudlin Street, and the *London Coffee House* (sometimes known as Cooke's after its proprietor, John Cooke) in Corn Street. The last named still operates as a coffee house but it is now called Cafe Revival. The Commercial Rooms built in Corn Street in 1811 were modelled on the *LLoyd's Coffee Room* in London . However, by then the coffee craze was already beginning to end. Tea was to take over from coffee as the preferred drink in the nineteenth century. Coffee has reasserted its role in the last fifty or so years but sadly slave labour is still pretty pervasive in many of today's coffee-producing nations.

An integrated cup of coffee isn't sufficient pay for four hundred years of slave labour
  Malcolm X, African-American civil rights activist in his *The Black Revolution* speech in 1963

Cotton became a viable commercial crop in the 1790s after the creation of the 'cotton-gin', a machine that quickly and easily separated cotton fibres from their seeds. It rapidly became the major wealth producer across all of the United States and it was their biggest export from 1803 to 1937. In nineteenth-century Britain it is estimated 20% of the population were eventually directly or indirectly involved with cotton textiles and 80% of the cotton used came from America. In turn the British textile industry was responsible for 40% of the nation's exports. The southern plantation owner, James Hammond, famously made a speech in

1858 in which he said that the northern states would never dare to go to war with the south over slavery because it would destroy the economies of both America and Britain:

> England would topple headlong and carry the whole civilised world with her… No, you dare not make war on cotton. No power on earth dares to make war upon it. Cotton is king.

Bristol was never a centre for importing cotton – that role fell to Liverpool – but it did involve itself in manufacturing cotton. The Great Western Cotton Factory was opened on a site in Barton Hill in 1838. The cotton it used may have been imported via Liverpool but it was slave-produced. Moreover, the Cotton Factory's creation was in part the result of slave money – some of its investors were using money that they had received from the government as compensation for the loss of their slaves after Britain abolished slavery in 1833.

Sugar may have been king in Bristol but from all the above it is obvious that other slave-produced products played their own role in generating wealth and in shaping the lives of Bristol's inhabitants. This should not be forgotten or ignored.

[From when he rises in the morning] a planter… is attended by half a dozen of the finest young slaves, both male and female, to serve him… [When he dines] nothing is wanting that the world can afford… He passes the night in the arms of one or another of his sable sultanas… Like a petty monarch… he is despotic and despisable. Such absolute power… cannot fail to be particularly delightful to a man who, in all probability, was in his own country… a nothing
>> John Stedman, a colonial soldier, on the character of plantation owners in *The Narrative of a Five Years Expedition against the Revolted Negroes in Surinam* in 1796

6

SLAVES IN BRISTOL

That, I decided, was what it meant to be a slave: your past didn't matter, in the present you were invisible and you had no claim on the future
　　　　　　　　Lawrence Hill, Canadian novelist in *The Book of Negroes* in 2007

Some historians have described the appalling conditions in which the working classes in Britain lived and worked as amounting to a kind of 'white slavery', especially the use of children in factories and mines. Certainly the exploitation of the white working classes meant there was no domestic need to use Africans or African-Americans. A few did become servants in Britain, but that was largely because it became something of a status symbol to have one. They were a kind of exotic ornament to be displayed to visitors. The fact they were called 'servants' rather than 'slaves' did not mean they were free. Society in general saw nothing wrong in a master selling his black servant to another person or, if he no longer required him, sending him back to the colonies to work as a plantation slave. Of course a master or mistress could choose to formally free a black servant and, in that case, they joined the ranks of the white working classes, although their different colour made them still open to different treatment.

I was taught about slavery at school. It was the only thing we were taught about black history, that we were slaves. It made me feel a bit shit
　　　　　　Dizee Rascal, British rapper, song writer and producer in *The Guardian* in December 2006

In the sixteenth and early seventeenth centuries Britain was so little directly involved in the slave trade that to find an African in the country was an exceptionally rare occurrence. The earliest known mention of an African in the Bristol area is in 1560 when a 'blackemore' was used to guard the home of Robert Young. He may have been acquired from one of John Hawkins's slaving expeditions. The first named African is Gylman Ivie, 'a negro of the age of thirty'. His baptism in 1575 is recorded in the parish records of St Peter's Church in Dyrham. The first mention of a black woman occurs in 1612. It is the burial of Katherine 'a blacke negra servante' at the church of Christ Church and the church record says she had worked at the Horsehead Tavern in Christmas Street. In and around Bristol there are a smattering of public houses called *The Black Boy*. The name, like that of *The Saracen's Head,* may simply recall the time when England was fighting 'blackamoors' in the Crusades, but it may indicate that some pub owners used Africans as an attraction because of their rarity.

The number of Africans in Bristol remained small throughout the seventeenth century. There are records of 'blackemores' or 'negroes' being buried in the churchyards of St Philip and St James' Church in 1603, 1610 and 1632 and in the graveyard of the Broadmead Baptist Chapel in 1640. Baptismal records refer to a 'barbarian Moor' called Philip White at the Temple Church and to the baptism of two slaves, Solomon and William, the former in 1631 and the latter, who is described as 'the son of a black', in 1684. The first African to be named who was definitely free is a woman in Almondsbury called Cattellena in 1625. She left a will and it lists her belongings, which included a cow. The first African to be depicted is a black servant who was painted in around 1652 beside the daughter of Thomas Smyth of Ashton Court. He may be one of the two black slaves brought to Bristol by the merchant Robert Yeamans as part of the spoil from a captured Portuguese ship. The most interesting reference to a black person is found in the account of a trial held in 1667. It concerned the legal status of 'a servant' named Dinah Black, who had worked for five years for a woman called Dorothy Smith. She had put Dinah on board a ship to return her to the West Indies and someone had clearly judged this wrong and so asked the court to order her release. The court judged Dinah should be temporarily released and allowed to find alternative work until her case was resolved at the next quarter sessions. Sadly we do not know the final outcome.

The number of black people in Bristol increased once the city became a key player in the slave trade but the historian Madge Dresser could only find fifty-five examples in the period 1700-1750 when she compiled a list of Africans residents in Bristol for her book *Slavery Obscured*. The main sources of information are parish records of baptisms, marriages, and deaths. Among the early baptisms are Ann Jones, a 'blackemore of riper years' at the Temple Church in 1704, Thomason Lawsen, 'black boy' at the Temple Church in 1721, and John Gloucester, 'a negro servant to Captain Edmond Saunders' at St Mary Redcliffe in 1722. Among marriages are those of Mary Columbus and Joseph Thomson, 'a negro' and 'a negress' at St Stephen's Church in 1702, Commodore and Venus at St Michael's Church in 1721, William Rice and Rebecca Neale, 'blacks' at St Augustine the Less in 1728, and John Gloucester to a white woman called Mary Ven at St Leonard's Church in 1746. Among the burials are those of Scipio Africanus at Henbury Church in 1720 and Sabina, 'a negro maid' at St Philip and St James in 1734. Some of the named Africans are very young like Hannah, an eight year old 'negro servant of Mr Richard Lathrop' baptised at the Church of St Thomas the Martyr in 1715, and Noah, a five-year old 'black boy' buried at the Temple Church in 1729, and Black Jonis, a 'little boy' buried at St Andrew's Church in Clifton in 1731, and Elizabeth Cambridge, 'a negro child' baptised at St Augustine's Church in 1744.

We also allow you for your diligence and care of our negroes to the place of sale, seven privilege negroes... We allow your chief mate... two slaves privilege, your second mate... one slave privilege, and your doctor... one slave privilege
Instructions to Thomas Baker, master of the Bristol slave-ship *Africa* in 1776

There are stories circulating Bristol that shiploads of slaves were landed and held in the Redcliffe Caves and that shackles have been found in the cellars of various eighteenth-century houses and that Blackboy Hill (the popular name for the top part of Whiteladies Road in Bristol) was so-named because it was the site of slave sales. However, there is no evidence to support any of this. It is true that about fifty skeletons and the remains of shackles were found in a bricked-up cellar in a warehouse on Welsh Back in the 1970s, but it is almost certain these were the remains of French or Spanish prisoners of war. The truth is that the Africans or African-Americans who arrived in Bristol largely did so only in ones or twos. This was because they arrived either because a plantation owner had decided to bring their personal servants with them or because they were 'privilege negroes', the 'human bonus' given to supplement the wages given to a captain or a first mate or a doctor on a slave-ship. Some captains chose not to sell their 'privilege negroes' but to use them as their servants and so advertise their success. One such 'privilege negro' was William Jones. He was put on trial in 1749 for threatening to kill his master, the ship's captain Matthew Craven.

There were no slave markets in Britain. Any 'sale' was usually done in private but sometimes that sale was advertised in advance in the press as the following four examples illustrate:

- 'Newly landed, a lad of 14' (in *The Bristol Intelligencer* in January 1754);
- 'A negro boy, about ten years old. He has had the smallpox' (in *Felix Farley's Bristol Journal* in August 1760) ;
- 'To be sold, a Black Boy, about 15 years of age, capable of waiting at table' (in *Felix Farley's Bristol Journal* in June 1767);

- 'A healthy negro slave named Prince, 17 years of age, extremely well grown' (in *Felix Farley's Bristol Journal* in January 1768).

Bristol newspapers also acted as the main vehicle for trying to recapture any slave who 'eloped' (i.e. ran away). Usually this took the form of advertisements which offered a reward to anyone helping to recapture the slave. An early example of this from 1746 is one in *Felix Farley's Journal* asking Bristolians to help recapture Lewis Mingo, an English-speaking slave owned by a captain called Thomas Eaton. Mingo was described as having 'a good black complexion' and 'smooth face' that was marred by 'scagged and broken' teeth. The advertisement also said he had a noticeable scar on his right wrist and was wearing when he escaped a black wig, a blue waistcoat and black breeches. At the time of his escape he had been 'in and out' of Bristol with his master for eight years. Eaton said that anyone helping Mingo would do so 'at their peril'. Among other examples are three advertisements in *Felix Farley's Bristol Journal* that appeared between 1757 and 1759. The first was inserted by a publican in Princes Street to recover an African called Starling 'who blows the French horn very well'. The second was placed by a man called McNeal demanding the return of a mulatto boy (i.e of mixed race) and threatening legal proceedings against whoever had him. The third advertisement was entered by a sea captain called Holbrook, promising 'a handsome reward' to anyone who helped him to recover his 'negro man named Thomas'.

An account of the capture of an escaped slave was written in a letter from the social justice campaigner Hannah More to her friend, the former politician Horace Walpole, in 1790:

> I cannot forbear telling you that at my city of Bristol, during church-time, the congregations were surprised last Sunday with the bell of the public crier in the streets… [He was] crying a reward of a guinea to anybody who would produce a poor negro girl who had run away because she would not return to one of those trafficking islands whither her master was resolved to send her. To my great grief and indignation, the poor trembling wretch was dragged out from a hole at the top of a house, where she had hid herself, and forced on board ship. Alas, I did not know until too late, or I would have run the risk of buying her, and made you, and the rest of my humane, I had almost said human, friends help me out if the cost had been considerable.

The two biggest reasons for a slave trying to escape was brutal treatment at the hands of their master or, as in this case, a decision to send them back to the Caribbean or Americas. The latter decision was often taken by captains when they returned to sea. It must have taken a high degree of desperation (as well as immense courage) to try escaping because it was virtually impossible for a black person to hide in a country that was so overwhelmingly made up of whites. Most runaways, if not recaptured, either ended up, if they were male, signing on as sailors in order to get away, or, if they were female, turning to prostitution to survive. Others turned to crime, often making their way to the lawless slums of London where there were enough free Africans to provide them with cover.

Hannah More's story of the recaptured slave may have had a happy ending. The girl managed to escape from the ship on its journey upriver to the sea and the Bristol Quakers took out a warrant for her protection. We do not know if she remained free or not, but the Quakers were well organised and influential so perhaps she won her freedom. In 1796 the Quaker leader Harry Gandy sought the advice of the lawyer Granville Sharp over another case. It concerned a young escaped slave called Harry Harper who had fled from his master in Dominica and stowed away on the ship *Levant* bound for Bristol. Once discovered Harper had willingly worked as a sailor on the understanding from the ship's captain, a man called Alleyne, that he would be a free man once the ship docked. However, on the ship's arrival the captain had consulted the ship's owner, Walter Jacks, and the two men had agreed to have Harper imprisoned in Newgate Prison until a ship could take him back to his former master in the Caribbean. Gandy had protested to the authorities in Bristol that it was against the law to re-enslave a runaway, but Jacks and Alleyne were claiming that they were returning Harper not as a slave but because he had agreed to be an indentured worker. As proof of that Jacks was showing an indentured agreement on which Harper had made his mark (i.e. signed it with a cross because he could not write). Gandy told Sharp that the two men had forced Harper to sign the document and, being unable to read, he knew nothing of its contents. We don't know what Sharp advised or the eventual outcome for Harper, but it is likely the document would have been held as legally binding.

The battles that count aren't the ones for gold medals. The struggles within yourself—the invisible, inevitable battles inside all of us—that's where it's at
  Jesse Owens, the 1936 Olympic gold medal winner and the grandson of a slave

---

The fact that enslaved Africans or African-Americans were sometimes brought over as personal servants by plantation owners has sometimes been used to argue that a genuine affection could exist between master and slave. One example often quoted is that of the relationship between Charles William Howard (commonly called Lord Waldren) and his manservant, Scipio Africanus as evidenced by the impressive gravestones provided for Scipio in the churchyard of St Mary's Church in Henbury. The Howards were a very famous noble family with many branches. They claimed to be descendants of the Saxon hero, Hereward the Wake, and, among Charles William's ancestors were Catherine Howard, the ill-fated wife of Henry VIII, and Charles Howard, the Admiral who had defeated the Spanish Armada. Born in 1693, Charles William was the son of the sixth Earl of Suffolk. In 1715 he married Arabella Astry, who three years earlier had inherited the Astry family home in Henbury known as 'the Great House'. Henbury is now a suburb of Bristol, but it was then a village about five miles north-west of the city. One of Arabella's sisters, Diana, is still remembered today because she compiled a recipe book that drew its contents from what was being served in the homes of the Astry's wide circle of aristocratic friends.

It is not clear when or how Howard acquired the African servant who was named after the Roman general Scipio but it is very likely that the slave belonged to Arabella Astry. Her family owed much of its wealth to the African trade and Arabella's sister, Elizabeth, had married Sir John Smyth of Ashton Court, a family even more involved in the slave trade. It is thought Scipio Africanus was born in 1702 so he would have been around thirteen years old at the time of Arabella's wedding, an ideal age to become Howard's manservant. In 1718 Howard's father died and so he became the seventh Earl of Suffolk. Two years later Scipio died and he was buried in the village with an elaborate painted headstone and footstone. The latter bears the inscription:

> I who was Born a PAGAN and a SLAVE
> Now sweetly sleep a CHRISTIAN in my Grave
> What tho' my hue was dark my SAVIOUR'S sight
> Shall change this darkness into radiant Light
> Such grace to me my Lord on earth has given
> To recommend me to my Lord in heaven
> Whose glorious Second Coming here I wait
> With saints and Angels him to celebrate

It is, of course, possible that it was Arabella who wanted Scipio remembered and not her husband. Either way, the two elaborate tombstones show he had been liked otherwise they would not have been erected. However, the main inscription

Above: The Great House in Henbury drawn by J.Kip in 1722 and an African page boy serves a family in engraving of Bristol by S. & N. Buck 1734. Right: advert for slave in Felix Farley's Bristol Journal 1768. Below: the tombstone memorial to Scipio Africanus in graveyard at St Mary's Church, Henbury (photo: William Avery)

To be Sold,
A healthy NEGRO SLAVE,
Named PRINCE,
Seventeen Years of Age, five Feet ten Inches high, and extremely well grown.
Enquire on JOSHUA SPRINGER, in St. Stephen's-Lane.

I who was Born a PAGAN and a SLAVE
Now Sweetly Sleep a CHRISTIAN in my Grave
What tho' my hue was dark my SAVIORS sight
Shall Change this darkness into radiant light
Such grace to me my Lord on earth has given
To recommend me to my Lord in heaven
Whose glorious second coming here I wait
With saints and Angels Him to celebrate

HERE
Lieth the Body of
SCIPIO AFRICANUS
Negro Servant to y Right
Honourable Charles William
Earl of Suffolk and Bradon
who died y 21 December
1720 A Years

is written in such a patronising tone that it reflects the inherent racism within the relationship. Scipio's dark hue is something to be cast off and his enslavement is justified by the fact it turns him from being a pagan to a Christian. Even Scipio's place in heaven is attributed to his master's recommendation. The Earl and his wife both died childless in 1722 and the Great House in which Scipio served no longer exists.

[Black people] are taught really to despise themselves from the moment their eyes open on the world. This world is white and they are black. White people hold the power, which means that they are superior to blacks… and the world has innumerable ways of making this difference known and felt and feared
James Baldwin African-American novelist in *Letter from a Region in my Mind* in 1962

Some of Bristol's schools contained African students. The Bristol-born poet Robert Southey, described how, when he was a schoolboy in the 1770s, there were a number of black pupils. Some of these were the sons of the leading African slave traders. It was judged beneficial to teach them English and other useful skills, such as book-keeping. The majority were mixed-race mulattoes. Most plantation owners gave little or no special attention to the offspring of African women with whom they had sex, but sometimes a master genuinely fell in love with a particular slave and then he wanted to treat her and their children differently. The best gift a father could give was freedom and that freedom was made securer if it was accompanied by an education. The Bristol merchant Nathaniel Milward, for example, had two of his illegitimate Jamaican sons, Edward and Benjamin, apprenticed at a metal workshop in the Welshback area of Bristol. He may have felt this was appropriate because their mother was a mulatto and so they were more white than black in appearance.

According to Southey the black boys were 'neither better nor worse' than the white boys in terms of their intelligence and were marked out only by their 'stronger national cast of countenance'. However, they did face racial prejudice and not just from their schoolmates. Southey records how his schoolmaster Mr Williams dealt with a boy 'with negro features and a shade of African colour in him' whom he judged to be inherently stupid:

Williams, after flogging him one day, made him pay a halfpenny for the use of the rod, because he required it so much oftener than any other boy in the school.

I now entered on my fifteenth year – a sad epoch in the life of a slave girl. My master began to whisper foul words in my ear. Young as I was, I could not remain ignorant of their import

Harriet Ann Jacobs in autobiography *Incidents in the Life of a Slave Girl* in 1861

Inter-racial sex, sometimes voluntary but usually forced, was common in the colonies where a master had every right to do whatever he wanted with female slaves. It was rarer in Britain, where the raping of maids rather than slaves provided many masters with their sexual gratification. That black men had an attraction to some white women was recognised. *The Bristol Weekly Intelligencer* in 1751 included an advertisement purporting to be from a handsome black man looking for a liaison with one of the ladies of Bristol. This presumably was intended as a joke:

> He is of the age of 32… He is a black man, generally reputed comely; his one inclines to the Roman; his teeth are white and even; his forehead is high; his eyes are full of fire and the hopes of sweetness; and his beard… when fresh shaved, looks blue upon his chin'.

In 1737 Samuel Farley's *Bristol Journal* recorded a very unusual case involving a white woman, Sarah Green, and Richard Cornwell, who is described as 'a Christian negro servant to Captain Day in College Green'. The woman had attempted to extort money from Cornwell by falsely claiming that she had had a child by him. He had asked to see the baby, and, because there was none, she had borrowed a white baby and blacked it up. This had not fooled Cornwell. He had called for a wet napkin and, in the words of the newspaper, 'rubbing the child's face, found it of a fair complexion, quite different to his species'. What is interesting about this case is that the law was prepared to punish the white woman for her deceit because she was imprisoned in Newgate Prison. In the early 1800s there were accounts in the press of white women who did give birth to black babies and who then tried to deny that had anything to do with having had sex with an African. For example, one describes how a lady who gave birth to a black child told her husband it was the result of her love of 'charcoal biscuits' rather than having anything to do with a black sailor. Another tells of a woman who claimed her black baby was the result of walking with friends in Clifton and being unexpectedly shocked when a black footman had crossed their path. In her case the broadsheet suggests the two must have done more than just bump into each other!

In the first half of the eighteenth century the attitude towards mixed marriages was not entirely negative because of Britain's growing trade with India. Until at least the 1770s it was judged acceptable for a white person to marry into a rich Indian family. Indeed one of the interesting features of the period between 1736 and 1770 is the number of novels that feature marriages between Britains and Indians. These books were obviously popular because they were all reprinted at least twice and many three or four times. In one story published in 1744 in a collection entitled *The Lady's Drawing Room*, the heroine Henrietta de Bellgraves defends her wish to marry a black Indian by saying:

> How ridiculous is it… to confine our liking to… [an outward appearance that] is merely owing to the difference in climates?… And what, except a skin, is wanting to render his person as agreeable as any European I have ever seen?

In these novels religion mattered more than colour. For example, in *The Female American* published in 1767 an English landowner marries an Indian princess on one condition: 'My God will be angry if I marry you, unless you will worship him as I do'. Some historians therefore argue that opposition to a white person marrying an African was based originally on their enslaved status and their 'paganism' rather than on their colour. This changed to opposition simply on the grounds of colour in the second half of the eighteenth century as a consequence of the constant claim of the slave traders and slave owners that Africans were inherently savage and inferior. The resulting increase in colour prejudice then impacted on India where mixed marriages also ceased to be acceptable. In the nineteenth century opposition to mixed marriages in America led to the concept of miscegenation – that any kind of relationship between black and white was wrong because it was a mixing of two different species. Laws banning 'race-mixing' were enforced in some U.S. states until 1967 and not entirely removed from all the statute books until 2000.

It did not help that eighteenth-century newspapers helped promote the view that all Africans were stupid and vicious savages. Occasionally a newspaper might report a positive story about how a grateful slave had helped his master or mistress out of a dangerous situation, but normally the focus was on reporting how slaves had rebelled on board ships and in the plantations in order to massacre all the white people, even those who had treated them well. In the

Slaves In Bristol

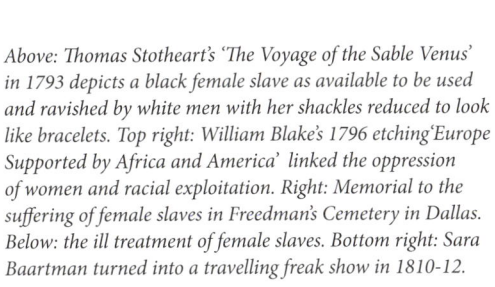

Above: Thomas Stotheart's 'The Voyage of the Sable Venus' in 1793 depicts a black female slave as available to be used and ravished by white men with her shackles reduced to look like bracelets. Top right: William Blake's 1796 etching 'Europe Supported by Africa and America' linked the oppression of women and racial exploitation. Right: Memorial to the suffering of female slaves in Freedman's Cemetery in Dallas. Below: the ill treatment of female slaves. Bottom right: Sara Baartman turned into a travelling freak show in 1810-12.

one year of 1750, for example, Bristol newspapers published articles on how Africans had burnt down much of the town of Port Royal in Jamaica, how slaves had taken over control of the Bristol ship the *King David* killing most of the crew, and how some negro slaves had butchered their white mistress in New York.

Some will always be above others
Attributed to Ralph Waldo Emerson, nineteenth-century American essayist

Occasionally there was a recognition that it was not helpful to behave as if all Africans were the same. A very popular book published in 1749 was *The Royal African*, which purported to be the memoirs of Sessarakoo, a prince of Annamaboe (modern day Ghana). This was produced by the Royal African Company as a way of asserting how good its relations were with the African slave dealers and how the latter had to be nurtured if the slave trade was to flourish and not treated with 'ludicrous contempt'. That year the Company had brought over to London an African 'prince' whom they said had been freed from wrongful enslavement and the book told his story in such a way as to make clear that African leaders could be educated and made to appreciate Western culture. Sessarakoo says at the end of his memoirs: 'It is as of great consequence to be esteemed and to be loved, as to be dreaded or revered'. The book's editor explicitly says that disrespect for all Africans was encouraging seamen to lose all sense of right and wrong:

> [When] they look down upon the poor black people as infinitely beneath them, they really degrade themselves, and, which is much worse, draw a scandal upon their countrymen by their barbarous, iniquitous and profligate behaviour... For whatever some may think, human nature is the same in all countries and under all complexions, and to fancy that superior power or superior knowledge gives one race of people a title to use another race... with haughtiness or contempt is to abuse power and science... and show ourselves worse men than those who have neither.

There was, of course, a vested interest in treating the African chiefs differently and the editor of *The Royal African* is clear that what concerns the Company is what 'can assist or injure us in our trade'. That same self-interest explains why Bristol fêted a French-speaking African prince called 'GongGlass' when he visited the city in April 1759. Such treatment was, of course, a veneer. The real attitude of most of Bristol's captains towards the African slave dealers is best shown in the story of their attack on the slave dealer 'Grandy King George' in Old Calabar in 1767 and the resulting massacre. This event will be examined in the next section of this book.

History has different yardsticks for... a slave-owner who through cunning and violence shackles a slave in chains, and a slave who through cunning or violence breaks the chains
   Leon Trotsky, Russian communist revolutionary in *Their Morals and Ours* in 1938

Those blacks who had the status of being 'free' in Bristol mostly came from a naval or military background. They had earned their freedom either by working as crew members on board ships or by fighting in America for the British Army. The rest had been freed by their masters either as a reward for good service or because they were no longer wanted. Among the free Africans whose names are known are Thomas Quaqua (or Quaco), an ex-slave who served as a sailor (including on slaving ships) in the 1750s, James Martin, who made enough money to warrant leaving a will, the Jamaican-born William Richardson, who was given a home by the Moravians in 1768, Peter Stephens, who lived in Marsh Street in the 1770s, and John Dean, who gave information about the slave trade when this was being sought by the abolitionist Thomas Clarkson in 1788. Perhaps the most unusual named free black is 'Brother Franks' who was made a member of the Bristol Freemasons in 1782. The freemasons made it a rule that any member mentioning his colour would be fined!

I had crossed the line. I was free; but there was no one to welcome me to the land of freedom. I was a stranger in a strange land
   The Incredible Memoirs of Harriet Tubman American abolitionist born into slavery (1868)

Finding onshore employment was often extremely difficult for Africans or African-Americans. Some chose to become entertainers. *Felix Farley's Journal* for 4 June 1752, for example, advertised the forthcoming appearance of 'the African Prince or Surprising Negro' at the Saint James' Fair. It said that among his attributes was the ability to undertake 'several new and astonishing performances on the slack wire'. A few were used as 'freaks'. A 'savage Ethiopian' was put on show at the St James' Fair in 1780 and many Bristolians flocked to see the South African woman, Sara Baartman, displayed as 'the Hottentot Venus' in 1811 so people could look at her large buttocks. A letter written from London to the Bristol slave-trader James Rogers by a former slave called James Harris in 1786 encapsulates the racism that so often prevented a black person finding proper employment:

> I am sir… in the greatest distress imaginable, wanting bread of bread and clothes for the quality in general have such an aversion to black servants so that there is not one in a hundred that will employ or take one into their service.

I have learned that success is to be measured not so much by the position that one has reached in life as by the obstacles which he has had to overcome while trying to succeed
                        Booker T. Washington in his autobiography *Up From Slavery* in 1901

The eighteenth-century slave who has received most attention in Bristol in the modern era is 'Pero' and a new footbridge in Bristol's Harbourside was named after him in 1999. He was one of three Caribbean slaves brought to Bristol by the sugar merchant John Pinney. Born on the Caribbean island of Nevis, Pero and his sisters were bought by Pinney when they were young. Pero was twelve and his sisters, Nancy and Sheba, were aged respectively eight and six. Pinney selected Pero and a ten-year old white boy called Tom Peaden to become his personal servants. Tom had gone to the Caribbean as an indentured worker. Their duties are not known but it is reasonable to assume that Pero and Tom would have helped Pinney dress and undress, waited at table, and undertaken various tasks around the house. One of Pero's later duties was probably to shave his master because he was taught the skills of a barber. In 1772 Pinney selected Pero's sister Nancy to become the personal maid to his new wife, Jane Weekes, and both Pero and Nancy accompanied the couple on their honeymoon to Philadelphia. Between 1773 and 1781 five children were born to the Pinneys and it appears that a mulatto child born to Nancy was permitted to play with them, although Nancy herself was sold. Was Pinney the father of this mulatto child and had his wife insisted on Nancy's removal whilst accepting the illegitimate child had to be accepted as 'family'?

    In July 1783 the Pinneys returned to Britain, taking with them three slaves. Pero, who by then was aged thirty, was still acting as Pinney's personal servant. The other two, Fanny and Kate Coker, were mulattos. Fanny was the personal

Top: a black servant hunting with his master by unknown artist 1765 and a black musician painted by William Hogarth 1746; Above: Pero's Bridge in Bristol Harbour 1999. Right: statue of Boston King in the American Revolution Museum in Yorktown. Below: Kingswood School where King was taught and Derwin Jordan as King in TV series Canada in 2000.

servant and seamstress of Pinney's wife and Kate was the children's servant. After some travelling the Pinneys settled down in Bristol in March 1784. Initially they rented a house in Park Street, but in 1791 they moved into their own home in No 7 Great George Street. This is now open to the public as the Georgian House Museum. Pero lived in the servants' quarters at the top of the house. Obviously, as a slave, he never received a wage, but it appears he was pampered compared to some of Pinney's white servants. Moreover, his training as a barber had given him some dentistry skills and he used these to earn some money from his fellow servants. This was sufficient for him to be able to offer them small loans and so make a little money.

We know nothing of what Pero thought about his life as a slave and little about his life except for a few incidents that are mentioned in Pinney's writings. For example, it appears that for a time Pero was unable to walk after accidentally scalding one of his legs. In December 1793 the Pinneys paid a return visit to the West Indies and Pero accompanied them. While back on the Montravers estate Pero had affairs with two other slaves and both women gave birth to daughters. It is possible that this – plus the status he had temporarily been given on the island – made him resent having to return to Bristol in September 1794. He took to heavy drinking. Pinney wrote that Pero 'became so great a lover of liquor and connected with such abandoned characters, that we could not depend on him a moment'. In the summer of 1795 the abolitionist William Wilberforce stayed at Pinney's house for five weeks but Pero may well have been kept away from him. Had they met one wonders what Wilberforce would have made of Pero's presence and status and whether Pero would have known that his master was hosting one of the leading spokesmen against slavery. By May 1798 Pero was very seriously ill and an upset Pinney affectionately wrote:

> He has waited on my person upward of thirty-two years, and I cannot help feeling much for him, notwithstanding he has not lately conducted himself as well as I could have wished.

Pero died that autumn and Pinney said his end came as 'a great relief to himself and us'. We do not know where he was buried but what little Pero had – his clothes, a watch, and a pair of earrings – were sent off to his family in Nevis. There is a danger that the affection Pinney displayed for Pero has obscured rather than helped people to appreciate the nature of slavery. We should not forget that Pero was never given his freedom, that he was taken away from his birthplace to a foreign land, that he was forced to leave his own children, and that he died as a drunken and broken man.

We do not know what happened to Fanny Coker but Pinney appears to have eventually given Kate Coker her freedom. She died in 1820 and was buried in the Baptist cemetery in Redcross Street. It is possible she may not have ended up any more happy than Pero because former slaves, if old and infirm, often faced destitution.

Money is sacred as everyone knows… So… must be the hunger for it and the means we use to obtain it… [A slave] becomes a flesh and blood form of money, a walking investment. You can do what you like with him, you can work him to death or you can sell him. This cannot be called cruelty or greed because we are seeking only to recover our investment and that is a sacred duty
    Barry Unsworth in his Booker Prize-winning novel *Sacred Hunger* in 1992

It is a pity that Pero's story has eclipsed that of Boston King, who was in Bristol from 1794 to 1796, because we know far more about King than we do about Pero. Indeed King is revered in North America for producing one of the most interesting early memoirs written by a former slave. Born into slavery in South Carolina in around 1759, King suffered at the hands of a cruel master until he fled and joined the British forces at the start of the American War of Independence. He later wrote about that experience: 'I began to feel the happiness, liberty, of which I knew nothing before'. He agreed to serve as a messenger for the army and, after various adventures, ended up in New York. There he discovered that freedom was not always accompanied by fairness. The New Yorkers did not treat black people well. His wages were often withheld or reduced to such a level that he could not afford to keep himself in clothes. Nevertheless, he married and started a family. This did not prevent those colonists who were opposed to British rule arranging for him to be abducted and once more enslaved. By the time he managed to escape from his new owners and return to New York the British forces had been defeated.

All the former slaves in the city faced the prospect of their former masters coming to take them back to captivity. To avoid that the British authorities arranged before they left for King and his wife and hundreds of other African-Americans to be taken to a newly created British settlement in Nova Scotia. The next few years were a fight for survival – so much so that many of the African-Americans ended up selling themselves to merchants, viewing slavery as better than starvation. Boston managed eventually to forge a career as a fisherman on a herring boat in the Gulf of St. Lawrence. His conversion to Christianity led to him becoming in his spare time a Methodist lay preacher. In 1792 Boston and his wife became two of over a thousand of the colonists who decided to relocate to the new British colony in Sierra Leone which had been created as a result of the efforts of Granville Sharp (and which Olaudah Equiano had worked on for a time). King sought permission to begin a Methodist school there. When his wife died from tropical fever, it was agreed that King should be given a proper education in Britain in order to better equip him as a teacher. The London Methodists warmly welcomed him in the spring of 1794 before sending him on to Bristol.

In the former part of my life I had suffered greatly from the cruelty and injustice of the Whites, which induced me to look upon them, in general, as our enemies… [but now I have found] a more cordial love to the White People than I had ever experienced before

Boston King's *Memoirs* in 1798

King later confessed that his experiences in Britain made him realise for the first time that white people could be genuinely kind towards a black person. In August he arrived in Bristol so he could study at the Methodist school at Kingswood. He spent two happy years there and then left in September 1796 to return to Sierra Leone, saying:

> I have great cause to be thankful that I came to England for I am now fully convinced that many of the White People, instead of being enemies and oppressors of us poor Blacks, are our friends, and deliverers from slavery, as far as their ability and circumstances will admit. I have met with the most affectionate treatment from the Methodists of London, Bristol, and other places which I have had an opportunity of visiting. And I must confess, that I did not believe there were upon the face of the earth a people so friendly and humane as I have proved them to be… I pray God to reward them a thousand fold for all the favours they have shown to me in a strange land.

The status given to Boston King by the Methodists was not welcomed by the governor of Sierra Leone, Zachary Macaulay. He had been a plantation owner and he was used to treating black people as inferiors so he felt King had been raised far above his natural station:

> Methodism has so direct a tendency to exalt animal feelings to an undue

empire over the judgement, that with people of weak judgement or little or no knowledge, it may be expected in most cases to produce enthusiasm. This enthusiasm manifests itself among our blacks here, by a proud conceit of their own spiritual gifts… fancying themselves wiser than their teachers.

In 1798 the Methodists published King's account of his experiences as both an enslaved and a free man whilst King continued to serve as a teacher in Sierra Leone. He became effectively the first Methodist missionary in Africa until his death in 1802. He should be better remembered in Bristol, not least because his story provides a rare example of Bristolians treating a former slave not just with respect but truly as an equal.

As I would not be a slave, so I would not be a master
Abraham Lincoln, American president in speech in 1858

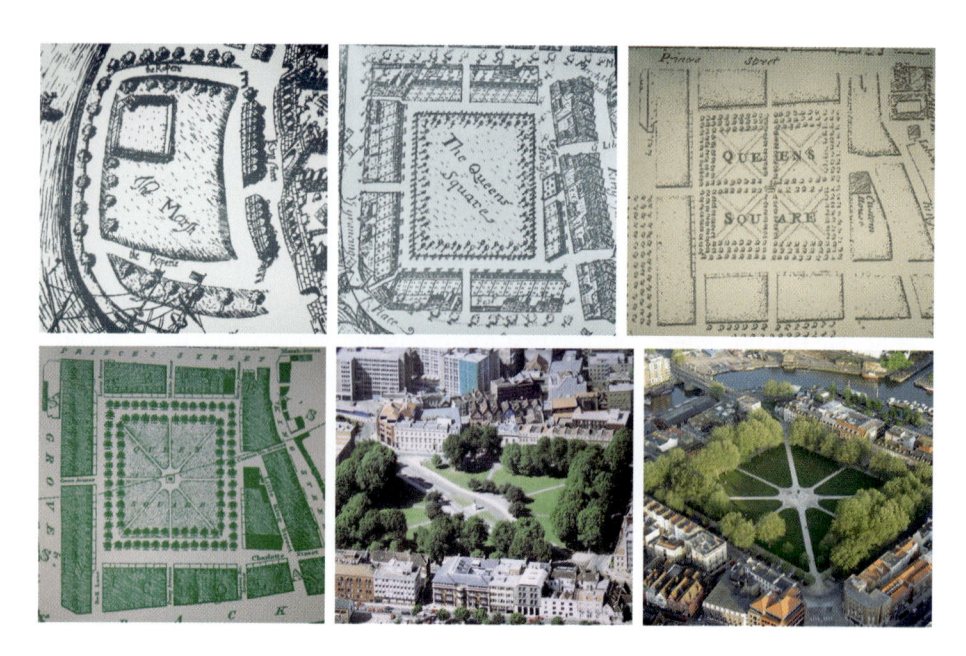

Above: 1670 map showing the Marsh and maps from 1710, 1750 and 1817 showing the changing shape of Queen Square, plus two photos, one of when the Square had a road bisecting it and the other as it is today. Below: Queen Square in 1827 watercolour by T.L.Rowbotham.

7

THE TRANSFORMATION OF BRISTOL

Such finery, paid for at the small cost of human lives and dignity
     Alyssa Cole award-wining author in *An Extraordinary Union* in 2017

In the past the profits that were earned in manufacturing and other industries and from internal or European trade were usually regarded as being unconnected with the profits made from the slave trade. It was therefore argued that slave-produced wealth accounted for only a small percentage of the nation's income and that only between 5% and 10% of the great houses that sprang up in the eighteenth-century were built with slave money. However, over the past twenty years or so more and more historians have challenged this view. They have shown just how much the country's early industrial, commercial, and technological development stemmed from Britain's involvement in the slave trade and from colonial slavery and how money from the slave trade was invested in all kinds of manufacture and trade. They have also pointed out the big regional differences in the background of those responsible for building stately homes and shown what a huge proportion of the buildings in the Bristol area owed their existence to money that came directly or indirectly from slavery. Bristol has the biggest concentration of homes connected to slave money outside of London.

A good example of the connection between a manufacturing industry and slavery is provided by the brass and coal industries, which were such a big source of Bristol's wealth. The African trade was vital to their growth. Nehemiah Champion, who took over control of the Bristol Brass Company in the 1720s, saw the potential profits to be made by selling manufactured brass and copper items, such as kettles, pots, pans, and the like, in Africa. In his case, he also invested in the slave trade and that also helped fund his business' growth. Other families, such as the Goldneys, the Eltons and the Harfords, who were all in one form or another involved with slavery, also invested in the company's growth and so Baptist Mills became the main production centre for brass and copper items in the country. As a consequence the local coal mines around Kingswood flourished because around two thousand cartloads of coal per week were required to fuel the furnaces. To what extent can profits from the expanding brass and coal industries therefore be viewed as 'slave-free'? And the African trade similarly encouraged the expansion of other existing Bristol businesses such as soap-making, glassware production, pottery manufacture, and, of course, shipbuilding, with its associated manufactures, such as rope-making, sail-making, etc.

Slavery was also behind the creation of entirely new manufacturing industries. The importing of new raw materials from the slave-worked colonies, notably sugar, cocoa, tobacco, and later cotton, encouraged diversification into a range of new Bristol enterprises, of which the sugar refineries were the first fruit. Should not the profits from all these be viewed as stemming from slavery? By 1750 large amounts of money from the slave trade and from the slave-worked colonies, alongside profits from other ventures, were being used to invest in scientific investigations and a range of new enterprises, of which the most significant was the creation of a new banking system capable of encouraging greater investment in all kinds of enterprise. Money linked to slavery helped fund new forms of transportation, such as toll roads and canals like the Somerset Coal Canal, built around 1800. Given all this it is easy to see why some now argue that virtually every aspect of Britain's economy was tainted to a greater or lesser extent by slave money.

It has now become common in historical circles to speak of slave-derived wealth and slavery-associated wealth. Researchers at English Heritage and University College, London, agreed in 2013 that a person's wealth could be directly linked to slaving interests if they were engaged in any of the following:

- investing in slave ships;
- earning money from insuring slave-ships;
- investing in shares in companies that were involved in the slave trade (such as the Royal African Company or the South Seas Company);
- providing trade goods to Africa or the slave plantations;
- dealing in slave-produced goods from the plantations;
- owning plantations that operated on the use of slaves (whether that ownership came from purchase, marriage, inheritance or as the default payment on a loan);
- using slaves in other contexts – in homes, on ships, etc.;
- holding colonial office or otherwise being involved in the administration of colonies which contained slaves.

Using this criteria slave-produced wealth was much more central to the wealth of many families than was once thought, especially in Bristol and its surrounding

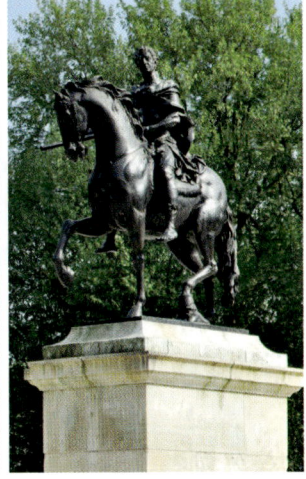

Above left: No 29 the best preserved of the original houses in Queen Square. Above: statue of King William III erected in 1736. Left: images of Prince Street by T. L Rowbotham (1826)and E.Cashin (1825). A picture of the Shakespeare Tavern can be found in the chapter on slave traders. Below: converted warehouses in Farr's Lane.

area. Recent research has shown that many wealthy families covered up their involvement with slavery once Britain took a stand against the practice. Some still do.

> *Until recently, most studies of such properties took a 'connoisseurship' approach, focusing on their architectural features, the glories of their collections and the genealogies of the families who owned them… [Their links with slavery] have often been either studiously ignored or actively repressed*
> Madge Dresser and Andrew Hann in *Slavery and the British Country House* in 2013

Queen's Square, which was built mostly between 1699 and 1710, has become a symbol of the urban transformation of Bristol in the eighteenth century and how that was bound up with the profits drawn from the slave trade. An area of marsh was transformed into a magnificent square of houses named after the reigning Queen Anne and at least ten of the twenty-four developers who took up residence were men engaged in the slave trade. These included Woodes Rogers, Nathaniel Day, Joseph Earle, Lewis Casamajor, Abraham Elton, Isaac Elton, Joseph Jefferis, and Thomas Freke. When it was built it was the largest square of its type in Britain, outclassing the London squares on which it was modelled. Its location made it the perfect place to live if you were a merchant because it made networking easy. It was close to the docks, close to the Merchants Hall, and close to the Back and Quay where numerous alehouses and coffeehouses were located. It was no accident that the Square contained a brand new Customs House as one of its features.

After some final construction work and tree planting in the 1720s, the Square was further enhanced in 1736 by the erection of a statue to William III. Diagonal walks were added in 1750. Other slave merchants moved into the Square in the second half of the eighteenth century, notably Isaac Hobhouse, James Laroche, Henry Bright, and John Anderson. In 1792 number 37 became the first American Consulate in Britain because of Bristol's important role as an importer of slave-produced tobacco. In 1819 gas lamps were added to the Square. Today the Square is still magnificent to look at because of restoration work completed in 1999 but sadly almost all the original buildings have not survived. Two sides were completely destroyed in the Bristol Riots of 1831 and further substantial damage was caused by a decision in the 1930s to knock down some houses to make way for a road and by the German blitz on Bristol during World War II. That's why the historical plaques dotted around it usually contain the words 'in a house on this site'. The best preserved original house is number 29 built for Nathaniel Day and later lived in by another slave trader, Henry Bright. It is now English Heritage's regional headquarters.

The nearby Prince Street, which was built and named after Queen Anne's husband, Prince George of Denmark, was also created in the early 1700s. Its location was not quite as good as Queen Square because it was very close to Marsh Street, which was one of the roughest areas of the quayside, containing thirty-seven public houses. The buildings closest to the water were built as warehouses to store goods ready to go to West Africa and goods brought back from the Caribbean and the Americas. However, the street did contain some grand residential properties built for merchants and it had a tavern and coffee house known as *The African House* where the merchants could meet. In 1755 it also became the location for a new entertainment centre – the Assembly Rooms – and this was funded by a tontine of merchants, each contributing £30 (the equivalent today would be around £3,000). Almost all of its buildings have now been replaced and not very attractively but three merchants' houses dating from 1725 remain, two of them, as mentioned in an earlier chapter, built for the slave traders and owners John Becher and Henry Combe. These were converted into a public house in 1777 and are now the Shakespeare Tavern. Other merchants who lived in Prince Street and were involved in the slave trade included Henry Tonge, Noblett Ruddock, and the copper manufacturer Thomas Coster. One of the streets bisecting Prince Street is Farr's Lane and that is named after Richard and Thomas Farr, the rope manufacturers who organised many slaving voyages and whose family later acquired what is now Blaise Castle Estate.

There is not a brick in the city but what is cemented with the blood of a slave
A Bristol saying

King Street predates Queen Square and Prince Street but it came to house various men connected with the slave trade, including the slave ship captain Henry Webb and the slave ship surgeon, Robert Walls. It was first laid out in 1650 to develop the Town Marsh and it was named after Charles II following the restoration of the monarchy in 1660. It contained the early headquarters of the Society of Merchant Venturers and, although this was destroyed in the Second World War, their Almshouses, built in 1696-9, can still be seen. There are also three pubs remaining which the merchants and sailors used: the *Llandoger Trow*, dating from 1664, the *King William Ale House*, dating from 1670, and the *Old Duke*, dating from 1775. The *Llandoger Trow* is said to be where the writer Daniel Defoe interviewed the marooned sailor Alexander Selkirk before producing his novel *Robinson Crusoe*. It is also claimed that it was the inspiration for the Admiral Benbow pub for pirates in Robert Louis Stevenson's *Treasure Island*. A number of the original houses have also survived. Numbers 33 and 34 date from 1653 and incorporate parts of the old town wall and numbers 6 to 8 and 16 to 17 all date from 1665. The difference the wealth brought in by the slave trade made can be seen in the upgraded frontage of number 6 (erected in 1720), in the subscription Library (now a Chinese restaurant) built in 1738-40, and in the façade created for the Coopers' Hall in 1743-6. The latter was later used as the frontage for the *Theatre Royal*, built in 1766. The theatre was funded by forty-nine financial backers, mostly members of the Society of Merchant Venturers, and at least twelve of these were slave traders and at least another six were plantation owners. Many others would have had some wealth drawn from the sugar trade.

There was also development north of the river. An early street of elegant Georgian houses were built in Orchard Street, not far from Bristol Cathedral, in 1717-18. Among its prominent residents were William Swymmer, John Becher, Mark Davies, and Alexander Neale, who were all linked to the triangular trade. James McTaggart, one of the slave-ship captains, also lived on the street. In 1726 a Huguenot Chapel was built in the street and among those who worshipped there were Louis Casamajor, Stephen Peloquin, and, the greatest of all the slave traders, James Laroche. Other traders lived on nearby College Green. These included Cranfield Becher and James Hillhouse. The Cathedral, which benefitted from the generosity of many merchants, has not only a memorial window to Edward Colston but also a number of memorials to other men engaged either, like Thomas Coster, in the slave trade or, like Thomas Daniel, in the sugar industry. One memorial that evokes particular interest today is to Abraham Cumberbatch, who owned at least seven sugar plantations in Barbados, making him one of Bristol's richest men. He is the great-great-great-great-great-grandfather of the famous actor Benedict Cumberbatch. Interestingly the latter has acted in two films that have focused on the issue of slavery: in 2006 he played the Prime Minister William Pitt the Younger in *Amazing Grace*, a film about the abolition of the slave trade, and in 2013 he played a slave-owner in *Twelve Years A Slave* about the nineteenth-century African-American Solomon Northup.

By the mid-eighteenth century the sugar merchants were operating about twenty refineries in Bristol. Only the one built by the shipbuilder and merchant James Hillhouse in Lewins Mead has survived and it is now converted into a hotel. The merchants were very important contributors to the funding of not just

The Transformation Of Bristol

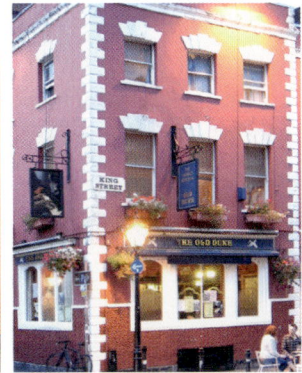

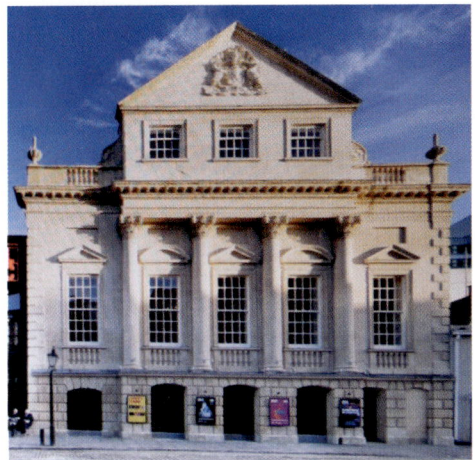

Top: the Llandoger Trow, the King William Ale House, and the Old Duke. Above: the Theatre Royal (now Bristol Old Vic) and its interior auditorium. Below left: the Old Library. Right: Abraham Cumberbatch from painting in Barbados. Below right: Benedict Cumberbatch with Chitwetel Ejiofor in 2013 film 'Twelve Years A Slave'.

the Library and the *Theatre Royal*, but other public buildings, especially those connected with finance and trade. Some of the best remaining examples are in Corn Street, which, with Broad Street, Wine Street and High Street, formed the traditional centre of Bristol. The sixteenth-century uncovered meeting place known as the Merchants' Tolzey was replaced with a new business centre, the Corn Exchange, in 1741-43. This was designed by the famous architect John Wood the Elder and the rich carving below the frieze at the front of the building was designed to represent trade with the four quarters of the world by including images of various products, exotic animals, and, of course, people, including an African slave. Business was also undertaken in the city's coffeehouses and in its many inns and alehouses (there were 850 of these by the 1750s, about one for every fifty inhabitants). In 1750 some of the traders set up one of the first banks outside London in nearby Broad Street and this acquired a more prestigious building in Corn Street in 1798. By then Corn Street had been extended down to the quayside by the demolition of St Leonard's Church in 1771. The Commercial Rooms, were built in 1810-11. Another indicator of the growing wealth and status of the city was the creation of a new Council House in 1824-7.

We have no plans to remove the windows and monuments to those involved in the transatlantic slave trade, but we must contextualise them. We will make a more robust commitment to commemorate the suffering, resistance, and achievements of the victims of slavery and their ancestors…We acknowledge our past failings and we will go on listening and learning as we seek to identify, with others, the ways in which we can honour victims of slavery and those individual and collective stories, which have been too long forgotten
       Statement from Dean and Chapter of Bristol Cathedral in Nov 2017

The importance of trade in the increasing transformation of Bristol was shown in the names given to some of its streets, such as Jamaica Street, Carolina Street, and Guinea Street. It is often said that the latter was named after the Guinea coin. This was a gold coin first issued by Charles II in 1663 and called that because the gold came from the Guinea coast as West Africa was then named. The value of a Guinea coin was fixed at twenty-one shillings (£1.05 in decimal money) in 1717 and guineas were minted by various monarchs until 1816. However, the street was almost certainly named directly after the Guinea trade (i.e. the slave trade) rather than after the coin because several houses on the street were built by the sea captain turned slave trader Edward Saunders. Three of them, built in 1718, have survived and one of them, No 10, has become nationally known

The Transformation Of Bristol

Right: the Corn Exchange and a print from 1882 showing its original courtyard. Bottom right: the Old Bank 32 Corn Street. Below: Commercial Rooms (now a Wetherspoons Pub) and the Council House. Bottom left: two of the bronze tables from 16th/17th century known as the Nails in Corn Street at which merchants made cash on the nail deals.

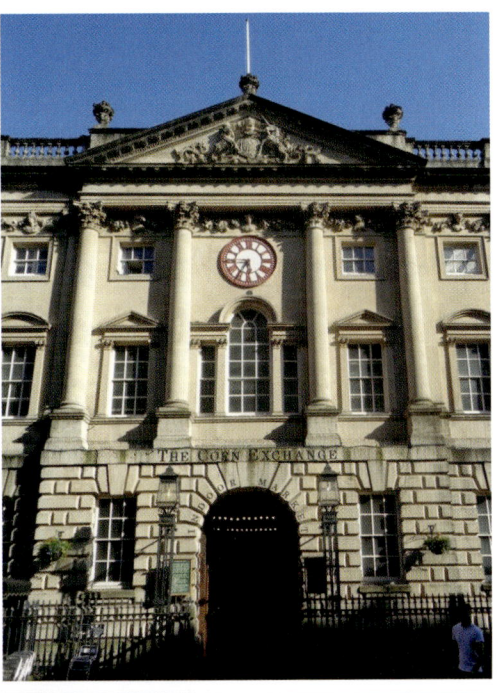

through being featured in the BBC series *A House Through Time* in 2020. Its presenter David Olusaga says Saunders was responsible for enslaving around 12,000 Africans. Saunders lived at No 11 and No 10 was rented to another captain involved in the slave trade, Joseph Smith, and his wide Mary, who came from Minehead. The story of Smith's involvement in a piracy trial was told in an earlier chapter. Among the house's later residents were John Shebbeare, who later became a well-known political writer in London, and another sea captain, Joseph Holbrook, whose wealth was based on the sugar trade and who, as was said in the previous chapter, advertised in the press to seek the capture of his slave Thomas when he ran away. In the 1770s the Methodists built a chapel in Guinea Street and in *A House Through Time* Olusaga and the historian Madge Dresser reflect on how it must have been difficult for Holbrook's widow to know that some of her neighbours were listening to John Wesley's views, given his strong attacks on the mercenary behaviour of Bristol's merchants and his opposition to the slave trade.

[This house was built on money] made through the sale of human beings. Their names don't appear in any of the documents. They are invisible but we cannot tell the history of this house without remembering them
  David Olusaga on No 10 Guinea Street in *A House Through Time* in 2020

It was not just the city centre that benefitted from slave wealth. Gradually Clifton became the fashionable place for the rich to live. For centuries this area had been outside Bristol's city walls and even at the end of the seventeenth century it was essentially still rural apart from the stretch of land that ran directly alongside the River Avon. The Society of Merchant Venturers, which had bought huge tracts of land in Clifton, redeveloped the Hotwell Spring as a fashionable spa in 1696 and then encouraged both bespoke and speculative housing. From the 1720s onwards substantial houses were built in Dowry Square and Dowry Parade for letting to the spa's visitors and this was followed by a handful of merchants building new homes. Thomas Goldney created an eleven-acre garden for the rebuilt Goldney Hall between 1737 and 1760. Among other substantial creations were the Royal Fort (now part of the University of Bristol) built by the banker Thomas Tyndall in 1739, Clifton Court (now the Nuffield Private Hospital) built by the metal manufacturer Nehemiah Champion in 1742, Clifton Hill House (now a university hall of residence) built by the linen draper Paul Fisher between 1746 and 1750, and Beaufort House built by the merchant Thomas Pedlar in 1767. All these men had made some of their money from investing

The Transformation Of Bristol

Top left: No 10, 11 and 12 Guinea Street built by Edward Saunders. Above: Guinea coin first issued by Charles II. Below: Thomas Tyndall and family by T. Beach. Right from top to bottom: the Royal Fort 1739, Clifton Court 1742, Clifton Hill House 1746-50, and Beaufort House 1767.

in the slave trade and sugar production. The area of central Bristol known as Tyndall's Park was once an ornamental park created by the Tyndall family with its gardens landscaped by the designer Humphrey Repton in 1799.

There has been in the city the addition of so many fair streets and stately edifices on every side that at present it is near one third part bigger than it was forty years ago
Sketchley's *Bristol Directory* of 1775

A 1769 map of Clifton listed that the area had nine residents of particular note. Five were slave traders (Henry Hobhouse, Richard Farr, Matthew Brickdale, Jonathan Freeman and Joseph Jefferis) and one was a man with extensive slave holdings in the West Indies (Christopher Bethel Codrington, whose father had been Governor of the Leeward Islands). Nevertheless, Clifton-on-the Hill (as some called it) remained essentially undeveloped until around 1782 when the ever-increasing wealth coming in from the sugar plantations led to an explosion of building activity. It is estimated that by the 1780s the annual value of Bristol's ships and cargoes in the West India trade was about £450,000 (the equivalent of £39 million today) and that the produce imported to Bristol from the Caribbean was worth annually £750,000 (the equivalent of £65 million today). It is not surprising that the historian Madge Dresser has described Clifton as being 'awash with slave-based wealth'.

A spirit of emulation and improvement has pervaded Bristol within these few years, and contributed much to the beauty of its appearance. In that part towards Clifton it bids fair to rival Bath
Julius Ibbetson, a watercolour and landscape painter in *A Picturesque Guide* in 1793

Another factor in Clifton's later growth was that some of the West Indian merchants began choosing to retire to Britain and a number of them, such as the Bayly family from Jamaica, the Alleyne and Cumberbatch families from Barbados, and the Mills family from St Kitts, took up residence in Clifton. Plantation owner families tended to intermarry and this encouraged a shared identity that was strongly in favour of maintaining slavery. A good example of this is the marriages that were arranged in the 1790s for the daughters of Thomas Oliver, a former Governor of Massachusetts who had property in Antigua. Penelope Oliver married the Bristol banker John Cave, who had

The Transformation Of Bristol

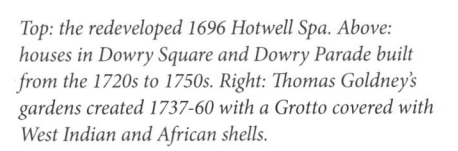

Top: the redeveloped 1696 Hotwell Spa. Above: houses in Dowry Square and Dowry Parade built from the 1720s to 1750s. Right: Thomas Goldney's gardens created 1737-60 with a Grotto covered with West Indian and African shells.

estates in Jamaica, Harriet Oliver married Henry Haynes, whose family had estates in Barbados and Jamaica, Lucy Oliver married Henry Hope Tobin, whose family had estates on Nevis, and Mary Oliver married Charles Anthony Partridge, who was also a slaveowner. Anyone with wealth wanted to have a new fashionable home and so spectacular terraces sprang up in endless succession. That is why, for example, the Baillie family made a home in Rodney House and the Cunningham family in Rodney Place, the Vidal and Hall families in Richmond Terrace, the Johnson, Allwood and Trotman families in York Place, the Daniel family in Berkeley Square, and the Cave family in Caledonia Place. The two greatest building developments, which were started in the 1790s, were Cornwallis Crescent and the Royal York Crescent. The latter was funded by six merchants, most with African or West Indian connections. Building on all projects was stopped by the prolonged war with France between 1793 and 1816 so the Royal York Crescent was not completed till 1820 and Cornwallis Crescent not until 1830 when Clifton was formally made part of Bristol.

Of course the most wealthy did not confine themselves to living in a posh house in the city centre or in Clifton. Many families wanted to join the ranks of the landed aristocracy even though the agricultural sector was not a great wealth generator. Over forty beautiful 'stately homes' were created all around Bristol, sometimes on greenfield sites and sometimes by purchasing and then enlarging existing manor houses. It is worth mentioning just a few examples in addition to the ones, such as Coker Court, Clevedon Court, and Leigh Court, mentioned in earlier chapters. In 1669 Sir Robert Cann, the son of a successful Bristol merchant, bought land at Stoke Bishop just outside Bristol to build himself Stoke House, using money he had acquired from properties in Barbados, Jamaica and North America. It is now Trinity College, a theological college. The Gorges family, who developed Wraxell Court, were involved in setting up the colonies of Virginia and Bermuda in the first half of the seventeenth century and were early investors in sugar refineries and the sugar trade in the eighteenth. Wraxell Court was further extended in 1720 by Elizabeth Gorges's husband, John Codrington, whose family wealth stemmed largely from Barbados, Antigua and Barbuda. Charles Bragge, who married into the Bathurst family, extended and re-cased Cleve Hill House at Downend with a beautiful new Georgian exterior in the 1740s. Norborne Berkeley, who became the governor of the colony of Virginia, remodelled the family home and gardens at Stoke Park in the 1740s and 1750s. Many compared what he had created to Windsor Castle. When he went bankrupt the house passed to his sister, the Dowager Duchess of Beaufort, and it became known as the Dower House.

The Transformation Of Bristol

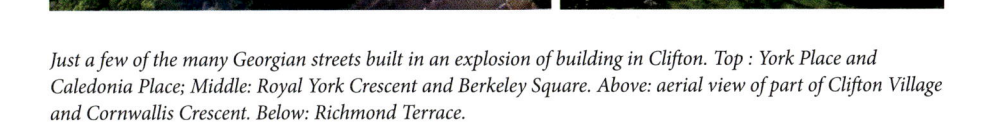

Just a few of the many Georgian streets built in an explosion of building in Clifton. Top: York Place and Caledonia Place; Middle: Royal York Crescent and Berkeley Square. Above: aerial view of part of Clifton Village and Cornwallis Crescent. Below: Richmond Terrace.

> *My house was built but for a show,*
> *My lady's empty pockets know:*
> *And now she will not have a shilling*
> *To raise the stairs or build the ceiling*
> *Some South-Sea broker from the City,*
> *Will purchase me, the more's the pity,*
> *Lay all my fine plantations waste,*
> *To fit them to his vulgar taste*
>
> Jonathan Swift, satirist, poet and novelist in A Pastoral Dialogue in 1727

William Champion built Warmley House in 1750 and created very ornate gardens for it over the next twenty years. Although best known as a metal manufacturer, he was a part-owner of a slave ship and his cousin Joseph was a key member of the Company of Merchants Trading to Africa. The merchant and slaver Lewis Casamajor bought Tockington Court and enlarged it in 1753 and it was subsequently sold to another slave-ship owner, Samuel Peach, in the 1780s. The Quaker merchant William Reeve used the family's wealth, much of it acquired from investment in the triangular trade, to build Arnos Court (now the Arnos Manor Hotel) in 1760. Before that Reeve also built a folly called the Black Castle (now a pub) which was made from pre-cast black copper-slag blocks and pieces from Bristol's demolished medieval city gateways. The sugar merchant Thomas Farr, whose family were deeply involved in the slave trade, purchased the state of Henbury Manor and built the folly known as Blaise Castle on it in 1766. When he went bankrupt during the American War of Independence, the estate was sold and a subsequent owner, the banker John Scandret Harford (sometimes spelled Hartford), pulled down the manor and built Blaise Castle House in 1796-8 and Blaise Hamlet in 1810-12. The Harford Bank had been formed by John's father and four others, of whom at least two are known to have owed their wealth to sugar. In 1808 Tracey Park was built near Wick by the son of the Bristol pewter, brasier and brass founder Robert Bush, who had derived much of his wealth from supplying goods for slave ships and the Virginia trade.

It was not just the Bristol merchants who chose to build in the area. Others who had money from London's colonial trade sometimes spent their money in and around Bristol. In 1682 Henry Somerset, later the first Duke of Beaufort, married the heiress Rebecca Child, the daughter of the Director of the East India Company and a founder member of the Royal African Company. Money from the Caribbean slave trade thus helped him fund major developments at

The Transformation Of Bristol

Top: Stoke House as painted by J. Turner and old print of Cleve Hill House, Downend. Above: Stoke Park (the Dower House) and Wraxall Court. Right: Arnos Court. Below: Warmley House and Blaise Castle. Bottom: Blaise Castle House.

Badminton House. Their son, Henry Somerset became a major figure in the Bahamas and South Carolina, a colony built on the use of enslaved Africans. That enabled him to to complete the transformation of Badminton. It was no coincidence that Badminton's gardens became noted for their plants from Virginia because the family's links with that colony became ever stronger as the century progressed. Not far from Badminton another property was developed. William Blathwayt, a Secretary of State for both James II and William III, acquired through marriage a Tudor manor house near the village of Dyrham and used his wealth from his involvement in encouraging participation in the slave trade in America and the West Indies to build Dyrham Park between 1692 and 1704.

The son of one of Blathwayt's friends, Edward Southwell, whose father had purchased an Elizabethan house at Kingsweston near Bristol from a Bristol merchant called Humphrey Hooke, had a new house built between 1712 and 1719 to designs by the leading architect Sir John Vanbrugh, the man responsible for designing Blenheim Palace. Southwell was actively involved in the government's administration of the colonies in the West Indies as had been his father. The London merchant John Cossins, who had traded in the West Indies purchased an Elizabethan house called Redland Court in the 1730s, which had previously been owned by the brother and son of John Yeamans and then by the Meyricks, another Bristol family with estates in Barbados. Cossins' wealth, most of it gained from slave-produced sugar, enabled him to create an iconic Palladian mansion. It is currently being turned into prestigious new homes after having been used to house Redland High School for Girls for 130 years. The Codrington family, who had purchased an Elizabethan house at Dodington, owed their wealth to sugar plantations in Barbados. In 1764 Sir William Codrington hired the famous landscaper, Capability Brown, to transform three hundred acres into a beautiful parkland setting for his home. His successor Christopher Bethel Codrington hired the architect James Wyatt to build a new grand mansion in the Roman classical style between 1798 and 1816. In an earlier chapter the lavish expenditure of William Beckford on first Fonthill Abbey between 1796 and 1813 and then Beckford's Tower in Bath in 1826-7 was mentioned.

In the same way as some merchants brought their wealth to the area around Bristol so some Bristol merchants took their profits from slavery and spent it at least in part elsewhere. Somerset and Gloucestershire were natural choices. For example, the Dickinson family purchased King Weston House near Street and the Combe family ended up with Earnshill, a Palladian mansion in the Somerset village of Hambridge, while the Clutterbuck family made Gloucestershire their

The Transformation Of Bristol

Wealthy families brought their wealth into Bristol area. Top: Dyrham Park (1692-1704). Right: Map shows Bristol has highest number (181) of slave owners' properties outside London. Below: William Blathwayt by M.Dyall c1690, Edward Southwell by G. Kneller 1701 and William Codrington by N.Dance-Holland c.1790 . Bottom:Dodington Park. (1798-1816)

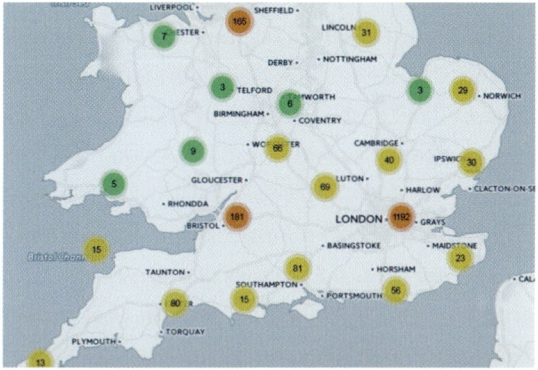

home, building Frampton Court and having connections with Newark Park and Ozleworth Park. Some moved further away. For example, the Pinney family built two homes in Dorset: Bettiscombe Manor and Racedown House. The latter was famously rented out for a time to the poet William Wordsworth.

The Brickdales are an example of a family who tried to keep both a fine house in Bristol and a second home in Devon and who ended up over-stretching themselves. The wooden draper John Brickdale diversified into trade at the start of the eighteenth century and, in 1714, married the daughter of one of Bristol's leading slave traders, Philip Freke, who was also part owner of a sugar house. Brickdale began investing in the slave trade and, as a member of the Society of Merchant Venturers, regularly lobbied in favour of it until his death in 1765. His son Matthew took on that mantle, becoming an M.P. for Bristol so he could defend the slave trade from its detractors. The Brickdale fortune eventually collapsed because of some bad business decisions and because of the huge sums spent on their second home in Devon.

The British country house in all its opulence and refinement seems worlds away from the fetid horrors of a slave ship… [but] enslaved Africans and slave-produced goods fuelled the wealth that funded the creation of many 17th-to-19th-century British stately homes

Madge Dresser in lecture *Hidden Connections* in 2018

The main focus of all the above has been on residential buildings but the lifestyle enjoyed within these buildings should not be forgotten. Bristol was known as 'the Opulent City' because of the lavish expenditure of the sugar merchants on fitting out their houses with the latest fashionable furniture and fittings. The wealthy lived an ostentatious lifestyle, organising sumptuous banquets, drinking only the finest of wines and spirits, and organising a multiplicity of entertainments. This sustained a host of businesses and it promoted the work of writers, artists, sculptors, landscapers, musicians, furniture makers, etc. Between them the merchants, the industrialists and the investors in Bristol were responsible for creating most of the city's public buildings in the eighteenth century and, through their philanthropy, they also largely funded the city's almshouses, schools, churches, and hospitals. Some historians have argued that the economic impact of slavery on Britain was limited because so much of the profits were spent on extravagant living but that ignores how much money found its way into funding industrial and commercial projects and scientific research. The money-making ventures of those who drew wealth from the enslaved became increasingly diverse and included things like undertaking contracts for the Royal Navy, promoting new engineering projects, and lending money to the government.

Although the main impact of all this was felt in the eighteenth and early years of the nineteenth centuries, the wealth inherited by later generations continued to play a significant role for much longer than that. Members of the Society of Merchant Venturers, for example, helped establish the Great Western Railway in 1833 and fund the Clifton Suspension Bridge, which was completed in 1864. The truth is that the business networks which the slave trade and the plantations had developed remained influential even when British involvement in the slave trade had long ceased. For example, the great Victorian mansion, Tyntesfield House, was originally thought to be somewhere that had no link with slavery because it was built by William Gibbs on profits made from selling bird guano for fertiliser. However, recent research has shown that as young man William worked in a West Indian trading house owned in part by his uncle, George Gibbs, who was married to the daughter of Richard Farr, a leading slave trader. George worked in partnership with Bristol traders like Richard Bright who had slave plantations. The guano business grew out of the connections that all this gave William Gibbs.

Given all the development that took place it is not surprising that the period 1698-1793 is often described as Bristol's 'golden age'. For a time it was the second biggest city in the country, totally eclipsing Norwich, which had traditionally held that role. The wealth from the slave trade and sugar industry also spilled over into the nearby city of Bath, which also experienced its golden age as it was transformed into a leisure centre for the wealthy. The Methodist preacher John Wesley, one of the strongest of the early anti-slavery voices and a strong opponent of the huge divide between rich and poor, chose to describe Bristol's merchants as 'man-stealers' and to describe Bath as 'Satan's throne', but his was a rare condemnation. Most saw nothing wrong in a golden age built on the exploitation of the working classes and of black slaves. Those, like Wesley, who opposed slavery on moral grounds were to find they faced an uphill task to persuade people it was wrong.

Disguise thyself as thou wilt, still, Slavery! still thou art a bitter draught; and though thousands in all ages have been made to drink of thee, thou art no less bitter on that account
Laurence Sterne, clergyman and novelist in *A Sentimental Journey Through France and Italy* in 1768

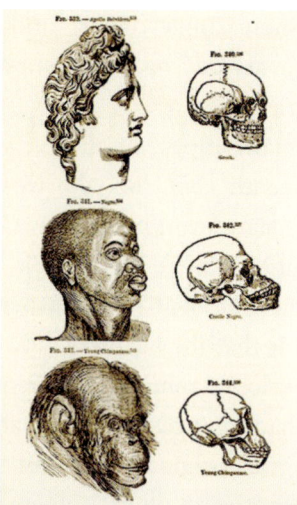

Left: Edward Long in 1780 watercolour and his three species still in print in Types of Mankind 1854. Below: 1777 painting that depicts sixteen mixed race groupings at different social levels.

SECTION FOUR

THE ANTI-SLAVERY MOVEMENT AND ITS IMPACT

I believe in God who made of one blood all races that dwell on earth. I believe that all men, black and brown and white, are brothers, varying through time and opportunity in form and gift and feature, but differing in no essential particular, and alike in soul and in the possibility of infinite development
William Du Bois American civil rights activist in his *Credo* in 1904

Those in Bristol who invested in the slave trade or in the slave plantations did so within a society in which hardly anyone spoke out against either practice. When voices in favour of abolition began to appear those involved in the slave trade justified its continuation by using various arguments as this section will show. However, fundamental to the defence of slavery was the argument that the Africans were an inferior species. Initially based on the view that they were a race cursed by God to be enslaved, the myth sought a new basis following the scientific revolution that took place in the seventeenth century. In 'an age of enlightenment' when many traditional Christian beliefs came under challenge, it became fashionable to claim that science justified slavery. The slave traders and slave owners began claiming that the Bible was wrong in depicting a common ancestry for all human races in the person of Adam. They asserted that medical experiments were showing that Africans had a different type of skin, blood, brains, and even sperm from whites. Out of this arose an even more potent belief in white supremacy. As this section will show, even some of the abolitionists thought that whites were superior. They just wanted a fairer treatment of Africans.

The Scottish philosopher David Hume wrote in his book *Of National Characters* in 1753 that negroes were 'naturally inferior to the whites' and any that appeared to be educated were just behaving 'like a parrot':

> There never was a civilised nation of any other complexion than white, nor even any [black] individual eminent either in action or speculation. No ingenious manufactures amongst them, no arts, no sciences... Such a uniform and constant difference could not happen, in so many countries and ages, if nature had not made an original distinction betwixt these breeds of men. Not to mention our colonies, there are negro slaves dispersed all over Europe, of which none ever discovered any symptom of ingenuity.

That same year a French doctor called Pierre Barrère published *Anatomical Observations*. The stated that blackness 'was derived from a dark bile that tainted the skin and blood alike'. The inferiority of all enslaved races, not just Africans, was subsequently expressed in a book on native Americans written in 1768 by the Dutch geographer Cornelius de Pauw:

> The timidity of his soul, the weakness of his intellect, the necessity of providing for his subsistence, the power of superstition, the influences of climate, all lead him far wide of the possibility of improvement;... his happiness is not to think... and to be concerned about nothing but the means of procuring food when hunger torments him... .In his understanding there is no gradation so he continues an infant to the last hour of his life.

The belief in white supremacy was to find its most extreme eighteenth-century expression in *The History of Jamaica*, written in 1774 by a sugar plantation owner called Edward Long. He had become increasingly concerned that Jamaica was becoming full of people of mixed race because of the raping of the slaves by their masters:

> [This is] a place where by custom so little restraint is laid on the passions... [that] men, of every rank, quality, and degree here... would much rather riot in their goatish embraces, than share the pure and lawful bliss derived from matrimonial, mutual love. Modesty, in this respect, has but little footing here. He who should presume to show any displeasure against such a thing as simple fornication, would for his pains be accounted a simple blockhead; since not one in twenty can be persuaded that there is either sin; or shame in cohabiting with his slave.

Long saw mixed race people as being a real danger to white supremacy and he argued the threat was being ignored because of a false belief that you could 'mend' the black race by breeding it to gradually become white. The breeding issue was very evident in Jamaica because a whole new terminology had been created to mark a progression towards whiteness. The child produced by a white and a black was called a *mulatto,* a word based on the Spanish and Portuguese word *mulato,* which may have come from the Portuguese word for a mule, the hybrid offspring of a horse and a donkey. Any child produced by a white and a mulatto was known as a *quadroon.* Any child produced by a white and a quadroon was known as an *octoroon.* Any child of a white and an octoroon was known as a *mustee.* Any child of a white and a mustee was judged finally to have become a white. Of course some ignored this and just applied the word mulatto or the French word *créole* to all those of mixed race. The latter word was derived from the Portuguese word *crioulo,* meaning a person raised in one's house.

The Spanish also used the word *zambo* (possibly drawn from the African word *nzambu,* meaning monkey) to identify anyone who was of mixed African and Amerindian blood, and in the nineteenth century the Americans turned zambo into *sambo* and began applying it as a derogatory word for African Americans. It was popularised in 1899 by the publication of a children's book called *The Story of Little Black Sambo.* Sambo was a patronising way of addressing a black African-American. It implied that he was a kind of perpetual child who was not capable of living independently and it was often applied to those who were judged 'to know their place'. The female equivalent of a sambo was a *mammy.* The Americans also coined an entirely new word for African-Americans in the nineteenth century. This was the word *coon* and it arose out of the minstrel shows which made African-Americans into good-for-nothing figures of fun. The Jim Crow Museum of Racist Memorabilia in America, which is dedicated to fighting intolerance, says:

> The coon caricature is one of the most insulting of all anti-black caricatures. The name itself, an abbreviation of raccoon, is dehumanising… Coons were increasingly identified with young, urban blacks who disrespected whites. Stated differently, the coon was a sambo gone bad… [They were] no-account niggers… unreliable, crazy, lazy, subhuman creatures… Unlike Mammy and Sambo, Coon did not know his place. He thought he was as smart as white people… [not recognising] that blacks were inherently less intelligent… His leisure was spent strutting, styling, fighting, avoiding real work, eating watermelons, and making a fool of himself. If he was married,

his wife dominated him. If he was single, he sought to please the flesh without entanglements.

All this can be traced back to the racial superiority of whites proclaimed by those who supported slavery. Long said that no amount of interbreeding could not get rid of black blood – even the passing of thirty generations would not be sufficient to discharge the 'stain'. He argued that skin colour was not, as some alleged, just nature's response to living in a hot country because, however long white people lived in hot climates, they would never, to use his words, 'exchange hair for wool or a white cuticle for a black'. Skin colour was something far more sinister:

> The White and the Negro had not one common origin… I think there are extremely potent reasons for believing that the White and the Negro are two distinct species.

Long argued that science had proved there were three types of 'human': the white, the negro, and the orangutan. Orangutans were humans with no intellectual capacity, negroes were humans with a significantly reduced intellectual capacity, and whites were humans with a full intellectual capacity. Historians have noted with interest that Long uses the word 'negro' and not the word 'black' and they have surmised that he wanted to focus on the enslaved Africans so as not to offend the indigenous inhabitants of Jamaica because their support was required in the event of any slave insurrection. According to Long it was the Africans who were 'the most to be feared' and he argued that any apparent intelligence shown by an African was no more than a parrot-like copying of white intelligence.

Looking to the world at no very distant date, what an endless number of the lower races will have been eliminated by the higher civilised races throughout the world
Charles Darwin, naturalist and proponent of evolution in letter to W. Graham in July 1881

Some historians say that Long's book was so ridiculous that no one took it seriously. It is true that many of his contemporaries found it totally detestable (or at least said so in public) and it also true that opponents of slavery quoted it to show the irrational racism that slave ownership had generated. However, the false science it represented did not go away and Long's erroneous idea about three species was still appearing in some books up to a century after his book was published. The myth of white supremacy led in the nineteenth century first to a paternalistic approach, which saw the white man's role as being to control and civilise those of a different colour, and then to a politicised version of Darwin's theories on evolution. Life was about 'the survival of the fittest' and the white man was the fittest. The fundamentalist rejection of evolution stemmed largely from some Christians in America seeking to reject such a pernicious worldview of human relationships. The myth of white supremacy continued to flourish in the twentieth century where it found legal expression in things like the Jim Crow laws in the United States, the various Nazi 'master race' decrees in Germany, and apartheid in South Africa. Sadly even in the twenty-first century there are still white people who like to assert their racial superiority, even though we now know humans of all races share 99.9% of their DNA. The racism that slavery engendered thus still bedevils the modern world.

This section begins with a chapter on why from the outset slavery posed a particular problem for the British because of their belief in a person's right to freedom. It then has two chapters on the early voices that opposed slavery and how that brought the morality of slavery increasingly into question in Bristol and elsewhere. The chapters focus particularly on the Quakers and the Methodists and the legal challenges created by Granville Sharp, all culminating in John Wesley's *Thoughts Upon Slavery*. The next two chapters cover the role played by Thomas Clarkson, William Wilberforce, and others in the Society for Effecting the Abolition of the Slave Trade and how Bristol merchants and plantation owners opposed the abolitionists. The final chapter covers the battle to secure the abolition of slavery and how Bristol's mercantile community was reluctantly forced to accede to it. Much of this book has depressingly shown just how badly humans can behave towards each other but in this section there is also evidence that it is possible for right-minded and good-hearted individuals to make a difference to the world in which they live.

My story is not about condemning white people but about rejecting the assumption – sometimes spoken, sometimes not – that white is right: closer to God, holy, chosen, the epitome of being… The ideology that whiteness is supreme, better, best, permeates the air we breathe – in our schools, in our offices and in our country's common life. White supremacy is a tradition that must be named and a religion that must be renounced

Austin Channing Brown, African-American writer and speaker in I'm still here: Black dignity in a World made for Whiteness in 2018

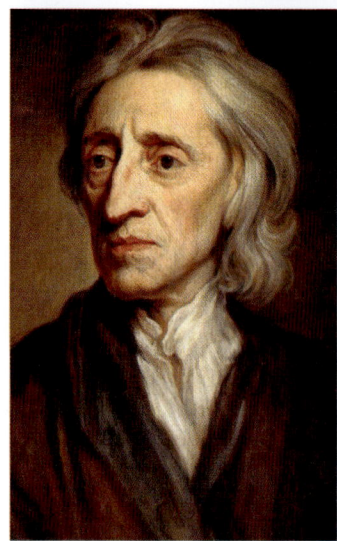

Top: Richard Baxter by R. White 1670, Quakers with their slaves in Barbados in 1726, and engraving of George Fox. Above: Oronooko as depicted in early edition of book and Aphra Behn by P. Lely 1670. Far left: John Locke by G. Kneller 1697. Left: Sir John Holt by Van Bleeck 1700.

1

SLAVERY AND THE RIGHT TO BE FREE

Slavery is so vile and miserable... that 'tis hardly to be conceived, that an Englishman, much less a gentleman, should plead for it
John Locke, British philosopher in *Two Treatises of Government* in 1689

As looked at earlier, England's role in the slave trade was tiny prior to 1660 and part of the reason for that lay in the belief that a country which was dedicated to 'freedom' could not really embrace slavery. Whereas Portugal, Spain, France, the United Provinces, and other nations were happy to pass laws legalising slavery, England was not. To acquire slaves for use within the country was viewed as unnecessary and undesirable and it had been ruled in 1569 that a slave brought in by a foreigner was no longer legally a slave because England had 'too pure an air for slaves to breathe in'. The English Civil War had further heightened the perspective that to be patriotic meant upholding and defending human rights against unwarranted power. However, Parliament's victory had resulted in the two sons of the defeated Charles I spending their formative years in exile in France and there they had seen the wealth that slavery could generate and absorbed a different perspective on its legality. The restoration of the monarchy in 1660 thus opened the way to significant change. Charles II strongly promoted that it was perfectly acceptable, indeed desirable, for England to engage in the African trade, and James II, when he inherited the crown from his brother in 1685, was even more pro-slavery, not least because witnessing the total power wielded by the French monarch had made him hostile to the English emphasis on individual rights.

The way in which merchants, particularly those involved in the sugar trade, responded to the royal promotion of slavery has already been covered. The lack of any outcry was largely due to two factors. First, most people had no concept whatsoever of what was happening to the Africans either during the Middle Passage or in the colonies and merchants were quick to say that the enslaved were much better off under white care than living in their native country. Second, churches of all denominations largely accepted that God had created Africans to be slaves so few Christians chose to challenge what was going on. The most outspoken voice was that of Richard Baxter, a puritan operating outside the religious establishment. In 1673 he published a tract aimed at slave owners:

> Understand well how far your power over your slaves extends, and what limits God has set thereto... [Recognise that] they are reasonable creatures as well as you, and born to as much natural liberty; that they have immortal souls, and are equally capable of salvation with yourselves. Remember that God is their absolute owner, and that you have none but a derived and limited property in them;... [and that] God is their tender Father, and if they be as good, does love them as well as you, and that the greater your power is over them, the greater your charge is of them, and your duty for them.

Baxter said no one should be able to own slaves unless they first agreed to provide them with a Christian education and that any slave owners who maltreated their slaves were 'incarnate devils'. These view were not welcomed by the authorities because they thought any talk of 'rights' or converting slaves into Christians undermined the acceptability of slavery.

If this should be the condition of you and yours, you would think it hard measure, yea, and very great bondage and cruelty. And therefore consider seriously of this, and do you for and to them, as you would willingly have them or any other to do unto you...were you in the like slavish condition
George Fox, founder of the Quaker movement in Gospel Family Order in 1676

George Fox, the instigator of the Society of Friends or, as they were more commonly nicknamed, the Quakers, also urged good treatment because he saw at first hand this was not happening when he visited Barbados in 1671. Many Quaker families had fled there to escape religious persecution and become slave-owners. Fox reminded them that all people were equal in the eyes of God. He ordered them to cease separating families when they bought slaves and he instructed them to commence sharing worship with the Africans with a view to setting them free after ten years of service. His comments carried no weight in England because the Quakers were a heavily persecuted minority with no political influence whatsoever. In 1674 one of the men who had accompanied Fox on his visit, William Edmundson, returned to Barbados and was appalled to discover that Fox's advice was also being totally ignored by the island's Quakers. Unlike Fox, Edmundson also saw at first hand the conditions on board a slave ship. He was utterly horrified and he immediately told the Barbadian authorities that slavery should be made unlawful just as it was unlawful in England. Their response was to say he was 'nothing but a bundle of ignorance' and they imposed restrictions on any Quakers who showed signs of agreeing with him.

In 1677 Charles II pressurised judges into saying that those who were aliens (i.e. anyone not English) had no rights under the law, and therefore they could be considered as property. Effectively this legalised the enslavement of Africans in not just the colonies but within England. The further promotion of slavery by James II meant that the tax revenue from customs duties on sugar and tobacco kept on rising until it amounted to a third of the Crown's income. This made the economic value of slavery indisputable. The start of an anti-slavery movement built on moral opposition is usually linked to 'the Germantown petition' of 1688 in Philadelphia in the Quaker-created colony of Pennsylvania. Three German Quakers petitioned the English Quakers to reject slavery on the grounds it was not compatible with the 'golden rule' of Christianity that people should love each other. The petition demanded that liberty should be extended to all, regardless of their colour or race, and it laid down the simple principle that no one should do to someone else what they would not want done to themselves.

We have men-stealers for ministers, women-whippers for missionaries, and cradle-plunderers for church members. The man who wields the blood-clotted cowskin during the week fills the pulpit on Sunday, and claims to be a minister of the meek and lowly Jesus ... The slave auctioneer's bell and the church-going bell chime in with each other, and the bitter cries of the heart-broken slave are drowned in the religious shouts of his pious master. Revivals of religion and revivals in the slave-trade go hand in hand together. The slave prison and the church stand near each other. The clanking of fetters and the rattling of chains in the prison, and the pious psalm and solemn prayer in the church, may be heard at the same time. The dealers in the bodies of men erect their stand in the presence of the pulpit, and they mutually help each other. The dealer gives his blood-stained gold to support the pulpit, and the pulpit, in return, covers his infernal business with the garb of Christianity

Narrative of the Life of Frederick Douglass, an American slave in 1845

The problem with identifying the Germantown petition as the start of a movement to oppose slavery is that the petition was totally rejected by the English Quakers. About half of them, including the founder of the colony, William Penn, were slave owners and they had no intention of changing. Quaker organisation centred around local meeting groups and over the next ten years only four out of hundreds of such groups decided to oppose slavery. In England Quaker merchants remained very happy to engage in the growing sugar and slave trade and, in 1701 they republished what their founder George Fox had written on the subject to show that all that was morally required was humane treatment. An anti-slavery movement did arise in 1688 but it was among the establishment and it arose because of James II's obsession with asserting his royal power. Fear that he was seeking to enslave people and force the nation to return to Catholicism did not just lead to his dethronement in the so-called 'Glorious Revolution' of 1688. It also led some to question the political desirability of Britain accepting any kind of enslavement.

This mood found its most powerful expression in a popular novel entitled *Oroonoko or the Royal Slave*. It was written by Aphra Behn, the first woman to make a professional career out of writing. Her husband was involved in the slave trade and she claimed her book was based on the true story of an African 'prince'. In the novel Oroonoko is captured and enslaved and taken to Surinam, one of the English colonies in the West Indies. From the outset Behn makes clear that black people are just as attractive, intelligent, and brave as whites and not, in any sense, inferior. Here is an extract from her description of the African prince:

> He came into the room, and addressed himself to me... with the best grace in the world. He was pretty tall... [and] the most famous statuary could not form the figure of a man more admirably turned from head to foot... Barring his colour, there could be nothing in nature more beautiful, agreeable and handsome... Nor did the perfections of his mind come short... for his discourse was admirable upon almost any subject... He was as capable of ... governing as wisely... as any Prince civilised in the most refined schools of humanity and learning.

To his surprise Oroonoko discovers that the woman he loves, Imoinda, has also been enslaved on Surinam. Behn describes Imoinda in equally glowing terms, making much of her beauty, modesty, wit and courage. The couple are renamed Caesar and Clemene and both serve their master well until Imoinda becomes pregnant. Oroonoko cannot bear the thought of his child being born into slavery and so he leads a slave revolt in the hope that he and Imoinda can return home:

> He made a harangue to them of the miseries and ignominies of slavery... [a condition] fitter for beasts, than men, senseless brutes than human souls...

> [In accepting slavery] they suffered... like dogs that loved the whip and bell, and fawned the more they were beaten... [and] had lost the divine quality of men... 'And why', said he... 'should we be slaves to an unknown people?... Shall we render obedience to a degenerate race, who have no human virtue left?'.

As narrator Behn makes clear that it is legitimate to oppose slavery by any means and her sympathies are with the enslaved and not the enslavers when the rebellion is crushed. She contrasts the nobility of Oroonoko with the brutal savagery of the white slave owners, who determine to make an example of him. The pregnant Imoinda is imprisoned and Oroonoko is brutally whipped and, says Behn, his wounds are rubbed with pepper 'to complete their cruelty'. Oroonoko manages to escape and he rescues Imoinda. Rather than see her suffer after his inevitable recapture, Oroonoko slays her and then tries to commit suicide by slicing his throat and ripping his belly open. He is prevented from dying but only so the slave owners can publicly execute him. They slice off his genitals, cut off his ears and nose, and then hack off his arms. The body is cut into four and the pieces are hung up as a warning on four plantations. Behn ends by saying 'thus died this great man, worthy of a better fate.'

We want to live by each other's happiness, not by each other's misery... [but] greed has poisoned men's souls, has barricaded the world with hate, has goose-stepped us into misery and bloodshed... Our knowledge has made us cynical; our cleverness, hard and unkind... More than cleverness, we need kindness and gentleness... Without these qualities all will be lost
       Charlie Chaplin, film comedian in *The Great Dictator* in 1940

Opposition to slavery also found philosophical expression in 1689 in the publication of John Locke's *Two Treatises on Government*. What made this particularly unusual was that Locke had been involved in promoting slavery in the 1670s. Born in 1632 Locke was brought up as a child in Pensford, about seven miles south of Bristol. The son of an attorney, he went to Westminster School in London and then to Oxford University, where he studied medicine. In 1667 he became the personal physician of Lord Ashley, a prominent politician and one of the founders of the Whig party (later to become known in the nineteenth century as the Liberal Party). Ashley had been a prominent figure in helping restore the monarchy and so Charles II had appointed him as his Chancellor of the Exchequer. In 1669 he sought Locke's assistance to draft the constitution of the new 'province of Carolina', named after the King. This included most of the American coast between Virginia and the Spanish colony of Florida and the resulting constitution stated that 'every freeman of Carolina shall have absolute power and authority over his negro slaves'. After this Locke was made Secretary of the Council of Trade and Plantations and he became a recipient of the profits from the slave trade by holding shares in the Royal African Company.

In 1672 Charles II further rewarded Ashley by making him the first Earl of Shaftesbury. However, both the Earl and Locke then began voicing concern at the increasing emphasis of the King on his right to absolute power. The Earl fell from royal favour and Locke had to flee to France in 1675. It is thought his *Two Treatises on Government* with their emphasis on human rights, were mostly written in the four years he spent in exile, although it was not possible to publish them as long as Charles II and then James II ruled. Locke returned to London when the Earl's fortunes temporarily rose again, but then had to flee again in 1683, this time to Holland, to escape charges of treason. It was 'the Glorious Revolution' of 1688 that permitted his return and his book's publication because it created a more constitutional monarchy. The Catholic James II was deposed and the throne was given to his Protestant daughter, Mary, and her Dutch husband, William of Orange. Locke's book was a reassertion of the British belief in freedom and the opening sentence in his *First Treatise* made clear that belief was incompatible with slavery:

> Slavery is so vile and miserable an estate of man, and so directly opposite to the generous temper and courage of our nation; that it is hardly to be conceived, that an *Englishman,* much less a gentleman, should plead for it.

The Treatises were rather overshadowed at the time of their publication by Locke's most famous book, *An Essay Concerning Human Understanding,* but they were to play a major role in encouraging the Americans to assert their 'rights' and claim their independence in the eighteenth century. Locke's role was not confined to words. The new King and Queen appointed him as Commissar of a new Board of Trade, effectively giving him a prominent role in determining what should happen in the colonies. They also removed all the judges appointed by James II and that resulted in a new Court ruling in 1696 that reaffirmed that in England no man could own another. Locke was to hold his post until his retirement through ill-health in 1700 but historians disagree on whether he seriously sought to undermine African slavery. Some point out that little was actually achieved and that in his writing Locke often seems to qualify his opposition to slavery when it comes to Africans. For example, he wrote that Africans had forfeited their natural human rights by engaging in constant tribal wars and he also said that becoming a Christian did not change 'their condition or state of life'. Others point to his production of a forty page plan for law reform in Virginia in which Locke suggested that all the Africans and American Indians should be 'baptised, catechised, and bred Christians' so that they could take an oath of loyalty to the English Crown and become subjects of the King. Under English law a King's subject could not be enslaved so, if it had been implemented, slavery would have become illegal in the colony.

The world has never had a good definition of slavery… We all declare for liberty, but in using the word we do not mean the same thing… The word may mean for some men to do as they please with other men
　　Abraham Lincoln, American President in speech made in Baltimore in 1864

That slavery was unacceptable within England was reiterated in 1706 when the Lord Chief Justice Sir John Holt resurrected the 1569 ruling and judged that any slave brought into the country should be automatically freed. In 1707 England and Scotland united and thus created 'Great Britain'. Alexander Pope, then arguably the country's greatest poet, wrote that the role of the new nation should be to promote world peace and to end all slavery:

> Oh stretch thy Reign, fair Peace! from Shore to shore,
> Till Conquest cease, and Slav'ry be no more.

However, the succeeding lines in Pope's poem mention freeing Indians, Peruvians, and Mexicans (i.e. those enslaved by other nations) rather than freeing the Africans enslaved by the British. There were political and economic reasons for that. The accession of Queen Anne, James II's younger daughter, in 1702 and the fall from power of the Whig Party had opened the way to a more reactionary approach and it was felt Britain should not turn its back on the wealth to be had from the African trade. In 1711 the government created the South Sea Company to encourage private investors to trade 'in the south seas' and South America. Alexander Pope was one of the many who invested in it and the monarch's blessing was evident because Queen Anne held 20% of the stock. The Company was set up in anticipation that British military success in the War of the Spanish Succession would result in acquiring the monopoly over the *asiento* or slave trade between Africa and Spanish America.

The Peace of Utrecht effectively initiated the maritime, commercial and financial supremacy of Great Britain and, as stated in an earlier chapter, this triggered the country in general and Bristol in particular into taking over as the leading slave-trading nation in Europe. One of Daniel Defoe's novels, *Colonel Jack,* written in 1722, is all about why an Englishman who values his freedom can condone the enslavement of Africans providing the slaves are treated humanely. Jack is a white man who is enslaved as an indentured worker and who is expected to supervise enslaved Africans. Defoe portrays how Jack initially resists inflicting punishments on them and finds that only leads to them not working properly:

> Now I began to see that the Cruelty so much talked of, used in Virginia and Barbados and other colonies, in whipping the Negro slaves was… owing to the brutality and obstinate temper of the negroes, who cannot be managed by kindness and courtesy, but must be ruled with a rod of iron.

However, Jack then discovers that the threat of appalling punishments is sufficient providing it is accompanied by a readiness to show mercy because this generates a gratitude and loyalty that transforms the master-slave relationship:

> The gentle usage and leniency with which they had been treated had a thousand times more influence upon them, to make them diligent, than all the blows and kicks, whippings, and other tortures could have, which they had been used to… It appeared Negroes were to be reasoned into things as well as other people… If possible posterity might be persuaded to try gentler methods with these miserable creatures, and to use them with humanity… the Negroes would do their work faithfully and cheerfully. They would not find any of that refractoriness and sullenness in their temper that they pretend now to complain of, but they would be the same as their Christian servants, except that they would be the more thankful and humble and laborious of the two.

The ever-escalating profits from the slave trade and from the sugar industry enabled the merchants to pressurise for a review of the law as it related to slaves brought into Britain. In 1729 Sir Philip Yorke, the Attorney-General and Solicitor General of England, said it was his opinion that no slave had the right to automatic freedom either on entering the country or on being baptised and that a master had every right to return a slave to the plantations. Some judges

Slavery And The Right To Be Free

Above: Alexander Pope by G.Kneller 1719. Below: etching of Jacobus Capitein 1742. Bottom left: Sir Philip Yorke by W.Hoare 1763. Right: Francis Williams by unknown artist c.1740 and Benjamin Lay by W. Williams 1750.

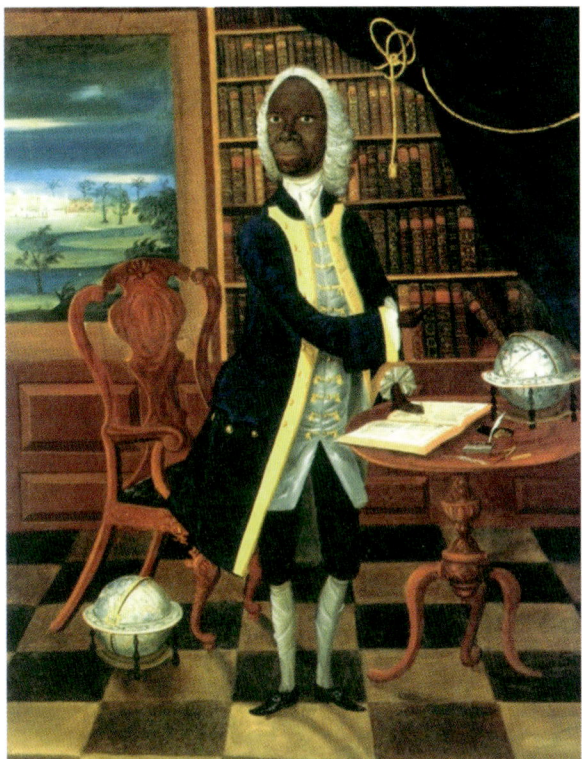

remained unsure about the legality of Yorke's opinion in a country which boasted of its freedom, but Yorke's view held sway. The desire to profit from slavery had swept away all other considerations. In the colonies Jamaica introduced new laws in 1730 that not only upheld the legality of slavery but also reduced the rights of those Africans who had been freed. In 1731 a black Jamaican lawyer called Francis Williams lodged an appeal in London, urging that these new laws should be judged illegal.

Williams' father was a freed slave who had created his own business in Jamaica and he had sent Francis to school in London and paid for him to be trained as a lawyer at Lincoln's Inn. On his return to Jamaica Francis had been made most unwelcome because he was so obviously well-spoken and well-qualified that he posed a challenge to the concept of white superiority. A dispute between Williams and one of the white colonists had triggered the Jamaican colonial authorities into passing legislation designed to reduce his status and to render, in their words, 'free negroes more serviceable to the island'. The new laws obliged freed blacks to wear 'badges of distinction' and laid down that their word carried no weight in any legal case, thus rendering them open to any abuse, including enslavement. Williams always carried a sword and pistol with him for protection and so one law placed a ban on any black person carrying a weapon of any description. Williams' appeal effectively asked the question: was this legislation compatible with British freedom? In the new market-driven environment his legal appeal was rejected and not long afterwards Williams died at the young age of thirty. The Jamaican Act soon became the model for other colonial legal codes.

Throughout the West Indies no black man's testimony is admitted, on any occasion, against any white person whatever

Olaudah Equiano in his autobiography in 1796

The case of Jacobus Capitein shows that not all educated Africans were prepared to challenge slavery issues in the way that Williams attempted. Captured at the age of about seven or eight Capitein was sold to a Dutch merchant who gave him away to a friend as a present. The friend more or less adopted Capitein as a son. He went to school in the Netherlands and was baptised as a member of the Dutch Reformed Church. In 1735 when he was eighteen he asked to be trained so he could go as a Christian missionary to Africa. To facilitate that he was sent to study theology and further his knowledge of Greek, Latin, and Hebrew at the University of Leiden. For his dissertation he chose to write a study defending slavery. He said being a slave did not conflict with the liberty that came from being a Christian and that baptised Africans had no legal right to demand their freedom. This was published and became a bestseller. It has to be remembered that Capitein, had hardly any real experience of what it was like to be a slave because he had been freed by his master and given a far better lifestyle than most white men enjoyed.

His skin is black but his soul is white. With him the Africans once whitened will always honour the Lamb.
Dedicatory prayer on the ordination of Jacobus Capitein, the first black African Protestant minister in 1742

Capitein's story did not end well. The first black African to be ordained as a Protestant minister, he was sent to the fort of Elmina, then the hub of the Dutch slave trade along the Gold Coast. He is credited with being the first person to translate the Lord's Prayer and the Ten Commandments into Fante, one of the African languages. However, he did not have a happy time as a missionary because the white slave traders did not like having a black minister and the Africans did not like the fact he was so Dutch in his dress and behaviour. In a sense he belonged to neither culture. When he tried to marry a local girl the Church refused permission for him to marry 'a heathen'. Instead it decided to provide him with a Dutch wife, but that did not help his position. The slave traders demanded his dismissal and Capitein was forced to abandon his role as a minister. He started creating a school but died an embittered man in 1747, aged just thirty. The Dutch Reformed Church viewed his ordination as a mistake that it would not repeat.

Within the British colonies one Quaker openly challenged what was going on. This was an idiosyncratic dwarf called Benjamin Lay. He had worked as a sailor and in Barbados and so he had seen at first hand the horrors of the slave trade. One incident in particular convinced him that slavery had to be stopped. He saw a slave commit suicide rather than face further beatings from his master. Lay began proclaiming in the 1730s that anyone who enslaved a human being was acting for the Devil and that all such people should be cast out of any group that called itself Christian. Slave keeping was 'gross', 'filthy', 'heinous'. In 1737 he published an anti-slavery pamphlet and he followed it up with staging a protest at his local Quaker meeting house in 1738. He took a bible and hollowed it out so he could insert into it a pig's bladder filled with bright red juice. At the meeting he declared that God would shed the blood of slaveowners and, raising his bible above his head, plunged his sword through it, sending what appeared to be blood splattering everywhere. The Quakers' belief that all were equal in the eyes of God did not prevent them judging Lay to be a madman. They expelled him from membership.

If you have any true tenderness of the Love of God in you... quit yourselves of slaves... [Slavery] is as directly opposite to our holy principles as light is to darkness... This practice be the greatest sin in the world... Oh! my soul mourns in contemplating their miserable, forlorn, wretched State
Benjamin Lay, a Quaker in *All Slave-Keepers that keep the innocent in bondage: Apostates* in 1738

It is doubtful that the Quaker merchants in Bristol even got to hear of Lay's protests. Their focus, like that of Colston, Cary and other merchants belonging to the Church of England, was not on the morality or otherwise of slavery but on charitable work among the poor. Wealth obtained from participation in the slave trade was a significant factor in enabling them to build their first meeting house, Quakers Friars, in Broadmead, in 1747. Madge Dresser in her book *Slavery Obscured* has shown that eight of the twenty largest financial contributors to that project were still active slave traders as late as 1755. In a subsequent chapter it will be shown that it was not until 1758 that the Quaker movement finally instructed all its members to cease their involvement.

The growing conflict between Britain and Spain in the Caribbean in the 1730s led some people to once more question whether it was right for a 'free' Britain to engage in the slave trade because stories began to circulate about Spanish privateers treating the crews of English slave ships as if they were no different from the African slaves they carried. In 1739 war was declared and that spurred James Thompson and Thomas Arne to write the words and music for *Rule Britannia* in 1740:

> When Britain first, at Heaven's command
> Arose from out the azure main;
> This was the charter of the land,
> And guardian angels sang this strain:
> 'Rule, Britannia! rule the waves:
> Britons never will be slaves.

The poet Richard Savage, who spent the last five years of his life largely living in

Bristol, saw the inherent hypocrisy in free Britons enslaving others and wrote in one of his verses:

> Why must I Afric's sable children see
> Vended for slaves, though form'd by Nature free,
> The nameless tortures and cruel mind invent
> These to subject, whom Nature equal meant?

Compassion becomes real when we recognise our shared humanity
Pema Chodrun, American Tibetan Buddhist in *The Places that Scare You* in 2007

One of Savage's friends was Samuel Johnson who later found fame as the producer of the first English dictionary. He was to become an increasingly outspoken critic of slavery in the second half of the eighteenth century. The idea that the British love of liberty should overrule all other considerations and make participation in the slave trade impossible was perhaps best voiced in 1746 in an anonymous tract entitled *An Essay Concerning Slavery*:

> That the Frenchman, a slave himself, should think it no great matter to make others so, is not at all surprising.; that the Dutchman should sacrifice everything to gain is not to be wondered at; but that the generous free Briton, who knows the value of liberty, who prizes it above life, and loves it the more that he enjoys it, that he should for vile lucre make Traffick of Liberty, that he should be instrument in depriving others of a blessing he would not part with … that he should [en]slave , this does surprise me.

However, by then any chance of getting Britain to abandon its role in the slave trade had long been lost. In 1745 the French-had supported an attempt by Bonnie Prince Charlie to regain the throne lost by his grandfather James II. In the wake of this national threat what mattered most was to secure Britain's safety against its enemies. The merchants and manufacturers involved in the slave trade had no difficulty persuading the government that ending the nation's role in the slave trade would simply guarantee Britain's destruction. It would cause financial ruin and hand over a commercial opportunity to France and Spain that would make them unbeatable. Suddenly sustaining the liberty so dear to British hearts seemed to require not the ending but the promotion of slavery.

Money speaks sense in a language all nations understand
    Aphra Behn, writer and dramatist in her play *The Rover* in 1677

2.
How The Idea Of Abolition Came To Bristol

It is impossible for us to suppose these creatures to be men, because, allowing them to be men, a suspicion would follow that we ourselves are not Christians
Baron de Montesquieu, French philosopher in *The Spirit of the Laws* in 1748

The Protestant group that first voiced its unequivocal dislike of slavery most clearly in Bristol was probably the Methodists rather than the Quakers. The Methodists were in origin not a separate denomination but a revival movement within the Church of England that encouraged people to follow a lifestyle based on the ideas of two clergymen, John and Charles Wesley. Born in Lincolnshire but educated at prestigious schools in London and at Oxford University, the brothers, prior to their ordination, had started a religious society which was designed to encourage university students to live a more Christian lifestyle. John had fixed regular times for its members to pray and study the Bible study, to worship and take holy communion, to meet together for mutual encouragement, and to do voluntary work in the local community. Other students at Oxford had jokingly called this society 'the Holy Club' and they called its members 'Methodists' because of their methodical approach to how a Christian should live. After their ordination, the Wesleys left Oxford and, in 1736, went as Church missionaries to the American colony of Georgia. The leadership of their society was temporarily taken over by one of their protégés, George Whitefield, a student who came from Gloucester but whose family had strong links with Bristol.

Born in 1714, Whitefield knew Bristol very well because his sister lived in Wine Street and he had spent part of his youth in the city. In 1737 he agreed to go as a missionary to Georgia to replace Charles Wesley, who had been forced to return to Britain through ill-health. Before leaving Whitefield preached in Bristol to great acclaim. In the winter of 1738 he chose to briefly return to Britain in order that he might be fully ordained by the Bishop of Gloucester and because he wanted to raise money to build an orphanage in Georgia. The death rate among the colonists was very high. In February 1739 he chose to ignore Church rules by preaching not just in churches but also in the open-air, first in Kingswood and then in Bristol. This attracted immense crowds and his frequent references to his days as an 'Oxford Methodist' led people to describe as Methodists any who responded to his preaching. Committed to returning to America, Whitefield invited the Wesleys to take over his open-air preaching. John by that time was also back in Britain. John commenced preaching in Bristol in April 1739 and Charles in November 1739. Methodism as a revival movement rather than a university society was thus born. Within a few weeks of John's arrival in Bristol he was organising the development of 'the New Room' as a base for the work of two of Bristol's religious societies in the city centre and the building of a preaching house at Kingswood.

The prime aim of the three leaders of Methodism was 'saving' as many people as possible by 'awakening' them to a deeper reliance on God, but all three had strong social consciences and they constantly stressed that it was the duty of Christians to help others. George Whitefield, for example, promised to help build a school for the colliers at Kingswood, and John Wesley built the New Room in the city centre. It became the base to organise food banks for the starving, to run schools for the children of the poor, to offer free medical advice and treatment for the sick, and to organise visits to help those in prison and those dying. Not surprisingly, the three men expressed their unhappiness about enslavement. Although relatively young (George was 25, Charles was 31, and John was 36), they had what most clergy lacked – a first-hand experience of colonial slavery. Whitefield during his time in America had travelled widely across all the colonies preaching to both the free and in January 1740 he penned a public letter to the inhabitants of Maryland, Virginia, and North and South Carolina expressing his loathing for the slavery he had encountered:

> As I lately passed through your provinces in my way hither, I was sensibly touched with a fellow-feeling for the miseries of the poor negroes. Whether it be lawful for Christians to buy slaves, and thereby encourage the nations, from whom they are bought, to be at perpetual war with each other, I shall not take upon me to determine. Sure I am, it is sinful, when they have bought them to use them as… [if] they were brutes… for your slaves, I believe, work as hard, if not harder, than the horses whereon you ride… Your dogs are caressed and fondled at your table, but your slaves, who are frequently styled dogs or beasts, have not an equal privilege [because] they are scarce permitted to pick up the crumbs which fall from their master's table; not to mention what numbers have been given up to the inhuman usage of cruel taskmasters, who, by their unrelenting scourges have ploughed their backs

Above left: Quakers Friars in Broadmead (now a restaurant). Above right: engraving of Richard Savage. Below left: Charles Wesley by T. Hudson 1749. Below right: John Wesley by N. Hone 1766. Bottom: The interior of Wesley's New Room as it is today.

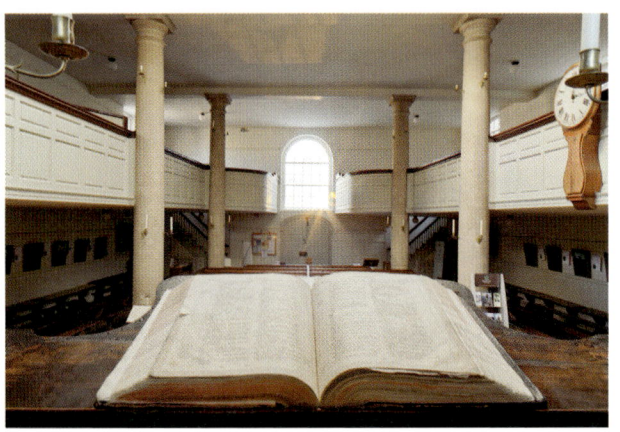

and made long furrows, and at length brought them even unto death…
[When] I have viewed your plantations cleared and cultivated, many
spacious houses built and the owners of them faring sumptuously every day,
my blood has frequently almost run cold within me, to consider how many
of your slaves had neither convenient food to eat, nor proper raiment to put
on… God does not reject the prayer of the poor and destitute, nor disregard
the cry of the meanest Negroes! The blood of them spilt for these many
years in your respective Provinces, will ascend into Heaven against you.

It's hard to imagine that the man who wrote this was silent on the subject in Bristol when it was the most important centre of the slave trade.

To subjugate another is to subjugate yourself
Elbert Hubbard: a nineteenth-century American philosopher in *Selected Writings* in 1923

Charles Wesley's experience of slavery was less wide but he had spent weeks in Charleston waiting for a ship to take him home and there he saw just how horrible it could be:

I observed much, and heard more, of the cruelty of masters towards their
negroes… Mr. Hill, a dancing-master in Charlestown, whipped a she-slave
so long that she fell at his feet for dead. When, by the help of a physician, she
was so far recovered as to show signs of life, he repeated the whipping with
equal rigour; and concluded with dropping hot sealing-wax upon her flesh.
Her crime was over filling a tea-cup.

It shocked Charles that there was no means of addressing such cruelty. There was a penalty of just £7 if a slave was actually killed but nobody bothered to collect such fines. He decided that the moral mindset of the slaveowners had been corrupted by the fact they knew no other world. Too many of them had owned slaves from a very early age:

The giving a child a slave of its own age to tyrannise over, to beat and
abuse out of sport, was, I myself saw, a common practice. Nor is it strange,
being thus trained up in cruelty, they should afterwards arrive at so great
a perfection in it… [It explains why] Mr Star, a gentleman I often met…
[could boast how he would] first nail up a negro by the ears, then order him

to be whipped in the severest manner, and then have scalding water thrown over him, so that the poor creature could not stir for four months after. Another much applauded punishment is drawing their slaves' teeth. One Colonel Lynch is universally known to have cut off a poor negro's legs, and to kill several of them every year by his barbarities.

Charles' experiences were doubtless relayed to his brother. John made himself very unpopular among the colonists in Georgia by refusing to support their demand that they should be allowed to own slaves. He was as upset as his Charles had been when he also spent some time in Charleston. After holding conversations with a number of slaves he questioned how anyone who claimed to be a Christian could treat Africans in this way. Each one of them was just as much a child of God as any white man. In his *Journal* he wrote:

Alas for those whose lives were here vilely cast away, through oppression, through divers plagues and troubles! O earth! How long wilt thou hide blood? How long wilt thou cover thy slain?

His *Journal* also records that he spent time on his voyage back to Britain 'instructing a negro lad in the principles of Christianity'. This would either have been a black sailor or a slave on board the ship.

Many years later John confided to the abolitionist Granville Sharp that he had detested 'the horrid slave trade' even before he went to America. The most likely source of John's early information on slavery would have been James Edward Oglethorpe, a former British soldier who had become an M.P. and a Director of the Royal African Company. Oglethorpe was a friend of John's father, Samuel Wesley, and the main founder of the colony of Georgia. That's why John chose to go there and asked Charles to accompany him. Prior to them taking that decision John and Oglethorpe may well have discussed the issue of slavery, and possibly in the company of a slave. In 1733 Oglethorpe had received reports from a planter in Maryland about an amazingly well-educated slave that he had recently acquired. The slave's African name was Ayuba Suleiman Diallo but his owner had renamed him Job Ben Solomon. Intrigued, Oglethorpe made arrangements for the slave to be brought to London. It turned out that Solomon was a Muslim who had grown up within the circle of a Senegalese prince. His obvious learning quickly brought him celebrity status in London, so much so that he was given an audience with the royal family and he had his portrait painted by the fashionable painter William Hoare of Bath. Merchants clamoured to welcome him to their houses and clergyman lined up to invite him to their churches. If Oglethorpe did introduce the Wesleys to Solomon it might explain why from very early on John believed that those of a different skin colour were not in any way inferior to Europeans.

Laundry is the only thing that should be separated by colour

Author unknown

That was not, of course, the conclusion of most people. They saw Solomon's intelligence as more freakish than representative. It was agreed that Solomon should be freed and repatriated home so he could resume his proper rank, but the motive for that was probably economic rather than humanitarian. It was recognised that Solomon would be a useful contact to help British traders capture the trade of Senegal from the French. One of those responsible for securing his freedom was the Duke of Montagu and, as covered in an earlier chapter, his response was to test out how intelligent Africans might be by educating a family slave named Ignatius Sancho. That only led to Sancho eventually becoming famous as 'the extraordinary negro'. Like Solomon, his case was not viewed as typical. It is worth recounting in this context a similar experiment in Germany because it completely confounded the view that Africans lacked intelligence. In 1707 an enslaved Ghanian called Amo was gifted at the age of four to the Duke of Brunswick. The Duke named him Anton Wilhelm Amo and provided him with an education at a prestigious grammar school in Wolfenbuttel and at the University of Helmstedt. In 1727 Amo graduated and he then commenced studying law at the University of Halle.

The university Rector attached the following note to one of Amo's papers:

> We proclaim Africa and its region of Guinea… the mother not only of many good things and treasures of nature but also of the most auspicious minds… You have excellently proved the felicity and superiority of your genius, the solidity and refinement of your learning and teaching, in countless examples up to now and… in your present dissertation.

The praise was justified because by this time Amo had mastered six languages and, as well as studying law, he went on to take a doctorate in philosophy and then a degree in medicine and science at the University of Wittenberg. In 1734 he returned to the University of Halle and became first a lecturer and then a professor and in 1740 he took up a post in philosophy at the University of Jena.

Unfortunately by then his patron had died and, without the Duke's support, Amo faced mounting racial prejudice. All his philosophical work was ignored and he took the decision to return to Africa to search out his family. It is not clear exactly what happened but an educated African was not welcomed by the slave traders and Amo ended up dying imprisoned in a slave fort.

> ***Stay in your calling at all costs, for it is Providence that has made you 'servants of men', Give up the thought of seeking freedom from your masters… Serve Him [i.e. God] in serving them***
> Anonymous author of *A Letter to the Negroes lately converted to Christ in America* in 1743

There was one way in which John Wesley's anger over slavery stood out from that of George Whitefield. Wesley wanted slavery abolished but Whitefield just wanted to see a radical improvement in the way Africans were treated and he wanted them to be given a proper education. Like many churchmen of his generation Whitefield thought slavery was an institution ordained by God. That's why, when he successfully created his orphanage in Georgia, he saw nothing wrong in seeking permission to use slaves to run it. It has been suggested that Whitefield was the author of the anonymous 1743 tract *A Letter to the Negroes lately converted to Christ in America* which opposed slave rebellions by suggesting that it was the slaves' duty to accept the status God had given them. In 1748 Whitefield petitioned the trustees of Georgia to remove their ban on slavery, saying 'Georgia can never be a flourishing province unless negroes are employed'. Clearly in his eyes slavery was not just acceptable but desirable providing the enslaved were treated humanely.

Charles Wesley probably initially agreed with Whitefield but there is no doubt that he became an advocate for abolition. The difference of opinion between the Wesleys and George Whitefield mattered because it meant Methodism could not speak with one voice on the subject. The main aristocratic supporter of early Methodism was the Countess of Huntingdon, Selina Hastings, and some of her wealth came from estates in the Caribbean. She naturally supported Whitefield's view. It did not help that the Methodist movement was theologically divided because that generated tensions between Whitefield and the Wesleys. He was a Calvinist (i.e. he believed only a few people were predestined to be saved) but John and Charles Wesley believed that God offered salvation to everyone. In the 1740s there was an exchange of views with Whitefield and presumably the Countess on what should be done about slavery but John Wesley could not persuade them to campaign for abolition.

It is likely that John Wesley also held discussions with Bristol's Quakers on the subject because these two groups had a natural reason for co-operating. They were both facing persecution and they both believed in the importance of caring for others and in fighting for social justice. Sarah Perrin, the New Room's first housekeeper, was a Quaker and so too was George Tully, the builder chosen by John Wesley to rebuild the New Room in 1748. At the time Tully had just finishing his work on building Quaker Friars in Broadmead and he built the New Room to a design that was remarkably similar. By 1744 John Wesley was writing publicly of the 'blood and guilt' of those in Bristol who involved themselves in the slave trade. No Quaker leader in Bristol or London was as yet so outspoken. In his 1965 book *Methodism and Slavery* the historian Donald Matthews summarised John's influence in the following way:

> Although Wesley never proposed a plan for getting rid of slavery, he did provide the Methodists with an incipient antislavery sentiment as well as the moral urgency to enforce it.

I am apt to suspect the negroes to be naturally inferior to the whites. There scarcely ever was a civilised nation of that complexion, nor even any individual, eminent either in action or speculation. No ingenious manufactures among them, no arts, no sciences
    David Hume philosopher and scientist in *Of National Characters* in 1753

As was stated in the introduction to this section the 1740s and 1750s was a time when those in favour of continuing the slave trade largely ceased using the Bible to support their actions and instead began using a pseudo-science to justify what they were doing. In Britain the most significant support for the inherent inferiority of the African came from the philosopher David Hume in his book *Of National Characters*, published in 1753. One of John Wesley's hobbies was medical science and he totally rejected this new justification. In 1755 he published a massive commentary on the New Testament in conjunction with Charles and he used the opportunity to reinforce that the gospel message was more important than any other consideration and that it did not support slavery. He referred to slavers in the book as 'man-stealers' (a phrase that the Quaker Benjamin Lay had used) and he described those involved in the slave trade as 'the worst of all thieves, in comparison of whom highwaymen and house-breakers are innocent!'

Top left: Job Ben Solomon by W. Hoare 1734. Above right: African couple statues erected at Halle University in 1965 to honour Anton Wilhem Ano. Above left: Selina Hastings, Countess of Huntingdon by unknown painter c.1770. Bottom from left to right: George Whitefield by J. Wollaston 1742, and etchings of John Hippisley 1801 and Thomas Chatterton 1797.

His and his brother Charles' total distaste for slavery had almost certainly been enhanced by their continued links with America and by their work in both Bristol and London. Neither city had a large black slave presence but there were enough Africans to act as a permanent reminder of the slave trade. Although there is no written evidence of the brothers engaging with black slaves in Bristol there is evidence that John held meetings with three slaves in London in 1758. These were house servants brought over from Antigua by the clergyman Nathaniel Gilbert, who had estates out there. John baptised two of them.

To consider mankind other than brethren...plainly supposes a darkness of understanding

John Woolman, eighteenth century Quaker merchant in *Some Considerations on the Keeping of Negroes* in 1754

In America the anti-slavery voice among the Quaker community became much stronger, boosted by the campaigning of the Pennsylvanian merchant John Woolman and the publication of his book *Some Considerations on the Keeping of Negroes* in 1754. Woolman, like Wesley, urged putting the gospel before what society judged normal:

> Customs generally approved and opinions received… become like the natural produce of a soil, especially when they are suited to favourite inclinations… But it would be the highest wisdom to forego custom and popular opinions and try the treasures of the soul by the infallible standard: Truth.

This change in the American attitude did not go unnoticed among the Quaker merchant community in Britain because there were so many family and trading connections. In 1756 it was agreed that two London Quakers, Christopher Wilson and John Hunt, would go out to investigate what slave conditions were actually like in New York, Maryland, Virginia and Pennsylvania. They returned in the spring of 1758 and their damning reports led the annual policy-making meeting of the Society of Friends in London to agree that Quakers everywhere should 'keep their hands clear' of the slave trade because it was 'a most unnatural traffic' and 'repugnant to our Christian profession'. Quaker meetings all around the world from Edinburgh to New York began one by one to declare their members should cease importing or owning slaves. The more cynical have wrongly implied that this only happened because the Seven Years War had made the profitability of the slave trade plummet. In fact it was first and foremost a genuine moral response. The War did have an influence on the decision but that was because the Quakers viewed it as God's punishment on the nation for its immorality. The London meeting commented in 1759:

> A Day of Adversity teaches us to consider our ways and in a humbling sense of our own unworthiness to say… '[it] was good for me that I was afflicted, for before I was afflicted I went astray'.

The Quakers in Philadelphia petitioned London to make non-involvement in slavery a condition of membership and in 1761 London responded. The annual meeting announced that in future any Quaker who continued to engage in the slave trade should be expelled from membership. This meant that any Quaker merchant who persisted in slave trading would lose not just his religious place of worship but access to the Quaker community's administrative and monetary services. Bristol's Quaker merchants ceased slave trading. They knew they had lost the argument that merchants treated slaves benignly with the publication in 1760 of Robert Barker's account of the appalling ill treatment of both sailors and slaves on board a Bristol slave ship (as detailed in an earlier chapter). However, this did not mean that henceforth Bristol's Quakers were squeaky-clean. Some Quaker manufacturers, like William Champion who was involved in the brass industry, continued to supply goods for the African trade. Many others continued trading in goods that were slave-produced and it took till 1775 for the Bristol meeting to expel William Reeve, the one Quaker merchant who remained an active slave trader.

Man is born free and everywhere he is in chains… To assert that the son of a slave is born a slave is to assert that he is not born a man
Jean-Jacques Rousseau, French philosopher in *The Social Contract or Principles of Political Right* in 1762

The Methodists were not able to match the Quakers in obtaining unity of opinion over how to deal with slavery because of the continued split between the Wesleyan Methodists and the Calvinistic Methodists. Fortunately the deep friendship between Charles Wesley and George Whitefield meant there was more co-operation than conflict. The Wesleyans had the edge over the Calvinistic Methodists in Bristol for two reasons.First, Whitefield did not want to set himself up as the head of a separate organisation and was almost continuously engaged in preaching tours, either across the whole of Britain or in America. Secondly, Charles reduced his itinerary after his marriage in 1749 and made Bristol his main home. The New Room was one of the three main centres of Wesleyan Methodism in the country – the other two being in London and Newcastle – so the most visible expression of the split in the Bristol area was in Kingswood where the Wesleyans ran Kingswood House and Kingswood School and the Calvinistic Methodists ran Whitefield's Tabernacle.

Both the Quakers and the Methodists were viewed as undesirable anti-establishment radicals and so their political influence was negligible in most parts of the country. Laws to impose religious uniformity imposed after the restoration of the monarchy had exposed to persecution all those who did not conform to what the Church of England authorities judged appropriate. The Quakers had been particularly singled out in the first instance and around 15,000 were imprisoned between 1660 and 1685. After the Glorious Revolution of 1688 they were more tolerated but they were still denied the right to hold any public office. The Methodists, even though they were a movement within the Church, had been judged 'enthusiasts' (i.e. fanatics) and both the Wesleyan Methodists and the Calvinistic Methodists faced appalling mob attacks organised by the clergy and local gentry in the 1740s and early 1750s. Many churches denied access to Methodists and the Church authorities blocked them from seeking ordination. The Bristol Methodists were not immune from this persecution and there were some attacks on the New Room, but, in general, the city had a reputation for being much more open to nonconformity. This meant that both the Quakers and the Wesleyan Methodists had far more influence in Bristol than was the norm in most other places.

Historians often point out that the Quakers had a strong presence within Bristol's mercantile community but they tend to ignore that the Methodists had a strong presence in the city's printing and publishing community. The publishing of John's prolific writings and of Charles' many hymnbooks in the course of the century turned Bristol into the biggest publishing centre outside London. From the outset Methodism grasped the importance of the press and John Wesley established a very important working relationship with two Bristol printers, first Felix Farley and then William Pine, both of whom ran newspapers. Farley abandoned his Quaker roots to join the Methodists and he looked on John and Charles Wesley as his 'honoured and much-esteemed friends and pastors'. This meant his newspapers, *Felix Farley's Bristol Advertiser* and its successor *Felix Farley's Bristol Journal*, were from the outset supportive rather than hostile to Methodism. This was so evident that there were attempts by the opponents of Methodism in the 1740s to fund the creation of newspapers in Bristol that would condemn the movement's ideas. After Felix's death in 1753, his widow Elizabeth was equally supportive because she was a committed Methodist. William Pine started his career working for her and married a Methodist, Elizabeth Owen. When Elizabeth Farley retired *Felix Farley's Bristol Journal* fell into the less sympathetic hands of Thomas Cocking and Pine took over as the main Methodist publisher in the 1760s and 1770s. His creation of the *Bristol Gazette* meant Methodism continued to get a relatively good press until he fell out with John Wesley over their different responses to the American War of Independence.

The Methodists also had access to higher social levels than the Quakers. In the 1750s and 1760s Charles Wesley was welcomed into the homes of many influential families in Bristol because he and his wife Sarah, were almost regarded as a son and daughter-in-law by the Countess of Huntingdon, Selina Hastings, who frequently took up residence in Clifton to be near them. She was one of the leading aristocrats in the country and moved in royal circles. On occasion she used both Charles Wesley and George Whitefield as her personal chaplain and she often arranged for them to preach to the nobility in London. Indeed Whitefield's preaching was so effective that at one stage it was rumoured the Prince of Wales was going to 'turn Methodist'. The Countess was not keen on John Wesley mainly for theological reasons but also because their strong personalities clashed too much. However, he too received invitations from the wealthy of Bristol. An indicator of the difference the Countess could make is that she used her patronage to unblock the opposition that had prevented James Rouquet, a chief master at Kingswood School and a Methodist lay preacher, from becoming a clergyman. Rouquet married into the aristocracy and became one of Bristol's leading Church figures, noted in particular for his work in prison reform.

What neither the Quakers nor the Methodists could do was reduce the grip of the Merchant Venturers over the city and so the public voice of Bristol remained rock-solidly in favour of slavery. What really challenged that position was not what the Wesleyan Methodists or Quakers were saying but the fact it became fashionable among the educated to read and discuss the books of the French philosophers. Neither the Quakers nor the Methodists approved of their anti-religious stance but John Wesley, who was a voracious reader, welcomed some of their views, especially their opposition to slavery. It may have been his suggestion that led Elizabeth Farley to publish Voltaire's *A Remarkable Account of a White Moor Brought From Africa to Paris* in 1760. It was a satire on the concept of racial superiority. Voltaire's most famous novel *Candide*, first published in 1759, was to particularly satirise the plantation owners' claims that they were looking after the best interests of the Africans:

> As they drew near to the city, they came across a negro stretched out on the ground, with no more than half of his clothes left… [and] the poor man had no left leg and no right hand. 'Good God!' said Candide to him… 'What are you doing there, my friend, in such a deplorable state?' 'I am waiting for my master, Monsieur Vanderdendur, the well-known merchant,' answered the negro. 'And was it Monsieur Vanderdendur', said Candide, 'who treated you like this?' 'Yes, Monsieur,' said the negro, 'it is the custom… this is our only clothing. When we work in the sugar-mills and get a finger caught in the machinery, they cut off the hand; but if we try to run away, they cut off a leg: I have found myself in both situations. It is the price we pay for the sugar you eat in Europe… Dogs, monkeys and parrots are a thousand times less miserable than we are; the… [preachers] tell me every Sunday that we are all children of Adam, whites and blacks alike. I am no genealogist; but if these preachers are telling the truth… you must admit that no one could treat his relatives more horribly than this.

I have averted my eyes from that sordid sight with loathing, horror and pity; and seeing one fourth of my fellow men changed into beasts for the service of others, I have grieved to be a man
Jeans-Jacques Rousseau, French philosopher in his novel *Le Nouvelle Heloise* in 1761

John Hippisley, Bristol's theatre impresario, cashed in on the interest being shown in the morality of slavery by staging the play *Oroonoko* on no less than five occasions between 1760 and 1766. It was an adaptation by an Irish dramatist called Thomas Southerne of the 1695 novel written by Aphra Behn. The climax of the stage version was the African prince and Imoinda choosing suicide over enslavement. The final performances of this play in 1766 would have coincided with the more widely read among the audience having just looked at the following outright condemnation of slavery contained in the French philosopher Denis Diderot's *Encyclopédie*:

> This purchase of negroes to reduce them into slavery is a negotiation that violates all religion, morals, natural law, and human rights… If a trade of this

kind can be justified by a moral principle, then there is absolutely no crime, however atrocious, that cannot be legitimised… Nobody has the right to buy these subjects or to call himself their master. Men and their freedom are not objects of commerce; they can be neither sold, nor purchased, nor bought at any price. Thus, a man must blame only himself if his slave escapes. He paid money for illicit merchandise, even though all laws of humanity and equity forbid him to do so… Each of those unfortunates who are wrongly called slaves has the right to be declared free since he never lost his freedom and never could. Furthermore, neither his prince, nor his father, nor anybody else in the world has the ability to own this freedom. Accordingly, the purchase of it is worthless: this Negro does not, nor could he ever, deprive himself of his natural right. He carries it everywhere, and can demand that he be allowed to enjoy it wherever he goes. It is thus an obvious inhumanity that, in the free country to which the Negro is transported, judges do not immediately decide to liberate him by declaring that he is free, as he is the judges' fellow man and has a soul like theirs.

The impossibility of doing without slaves in the West-Indies will always prevent this traffick being dropped. The necessity, the absolute necessity… of carrying it on must… be its excuse
                                  John Hippisley in *On the Populousness of Africa* in 1764

Hippisley's son, also called John, had spent some time in Africa working for the Company of Merchants Trading to Africa, and he was clearly unhappy about the play's message. In 1764 he published a defence of slavery, arguing that it might be inhumane at times but it was economically essential. The solution to any criticism lay not in abolition but in the better treatment of slaves:

> We do hope… it will be remembered that the traffic is in human creatures… [and that] negroes… are not totally devoid of… [feelings]… and that bodily feeling at least is the portion of everything that has life. Shall we then forget that many of these poor creatures… have been torn from the woman, the child, or the parent they loved? Circumstances of so piteous a nature… instead of inspiring wanton cruelty, or cold neglect, should teach the white possessors to soften the misery of their condition by every safe and reasonable indulgence that their humanity can suggest, and that the nature of the case will admit.

This approach appears to have been welcomed by not just the Anglicans in Bristol but also the Baptists. Most of their leaders took the view that 'politics' should be kept out of religion and that the economic benefits of slavery were too great to be lost. However, Hippisley's economic defence did nothing to appease the antislavery stance of the Wesleyan Methodists and Quakers. John Wesley might have become more outspoken on the slavery issue had not his authority within the Methodist movement been under threat throughout the 1760s. However, his strong anti-slavery views were to take centre stage in the 1770s.

One new voice in Bristol against slavery was the young poet Thomas Chatterton, even though he was a supporter of colonisation and had no time for the Methodists. In 1770 he wrote his *African Eclogues*. Today the poems are often seen as being racist because of their depiction of Africans as savages, but Chatterton's intention was to present them as savages who were noble and who possessed an inherent morality that made them far superior to greedy Europeans, the 'pale children of the feeble sun'. He may well have been influenced by Afra Behn's depiction of Oroonoko as a noble savage. Like her, Chatterton made clear that rebellion was a legitimate response to such injustice:

> Now judge… have I cause for rage?
> Should aught the thunder of my arm assuage?
> In ever-reeking blood this jav'lin dy'd
> With vengeance shall be never satisfied;
> I'll strew the beaches with the mighty dead
> And tinge the lily of their features red.

Actual slave rebellion was to be another nail in the coffin of the slave trade as the century progressed and, as will be shown later, it was a Quaker who had to cope with an insurrection, Harry Gandy, that later became one of the main voices in Bristol against slavery in the 1770s and 1780s.

Let every voice be thunder, let every heart beat strong
Until all tyrants perish our work shall not be done
Let not our memories fail us the lost year shall be found
Let slavery's chains be broken the whole wide world around
>> Peter, Paul and Mary, American folk group in song *Because All Men Are Brothers* in 1965

3.

How The Right To Be Free Was Legally Tested

As soon as a man sets foot on English ground he is free: a negro may maintain an action against his master for ill usage, and may have a Habeas Corpus if restrained of his liberty
  Robert Henley, Lord High Chancellor giving his legal view on slavery in 1762

In 1760 an Edinburgh lawyer called George Wallace called on judges to uphold that there was no law in Britain legitimising slavery and to declare that any slave brought into Britain was automatically freed:

> If this trade admits of a moral or rational justification, every crime, even the most atrocious, may he justified… No man has a right to acquire or to purchase them; men and their liberty are not 'in commercio'; they are not either saleable or purchasable… There is such a thing as justice, to which the most sacred regard is due. It ought to be inviolably observed.

The plea was ignored but between 1767 and 1774 the issue of slavery came to the forefront of many educated people's attention because of the legal cases initiated by a government civil servant called Granville Sharp. Born in Durham in 1735, Sharp was the son of the archdeacon of Northumberland and the grandson of John Sharp, the chaplain of James II and later the Archbishop of York. Having decided that a career in the Church was not for him, Sharp apprenticed himself to a Quaker linen draper in London and he subsequently obtained a post as a clerk in the Ordnance Office of the Tower of London. Though he had no legal training he instigated three very important court cases in London, all designed to reopen the question of whether it was legal to own slaves in England given the fact there was no British law legalising it.

Some histories of slavery give the impression that abolition was achieved almost solely by the efforts of groups who were outside the religious establishment. This is not the case. Sharp's family moved very much within a circle of Anglicans who were opposed to slavery. Perhaps the most notable member of that circle was the distinguished writer Samuel Johnson, who had a black servant called Francis Barber. Johnson was a very outspoken critic of slavery and Barber was not only paid for his work but treated as a friend. In fact on his death Johnson was to leave Barber his estate, providing him with an income of £8,000 a year (around £700,000 in modern values). Being twenty-six years older than Sharp, Johnson was probably something of a mentor to him.

I hate a fellow whom pride or cowardice or laziness drives into a corner, and who does nothing when he is there but sit and growl. Let him come out as I do, and BARK
Samuel Johnson as quoted in Mrs Piozzi's *Anecdotes of the late Samuel Johnson* in 1786

Thomas Clarkson and William Wilberforce, the two men most responsible for turning the abolitionist demands into a political movement at the end of the eighteenth century, were both fervent members of the Church of England. It should also be remembered that the Wesleys saw themselves as being staunch Anglicans even though Methodism was not viewed in that light by the Church authorities. Within the Bristol area there were important other Anglican clergy voicing opposition to slavery from quite early on. Two obvious examples are William Warburton, the Bishop of Gloucester, who condemned the 'sacrifice' of Africans to the colonial 'God of Gain', and Josiah Tucker, the Dean of Gloucester Cathedral, of whom more will be said later.

The first case in which Sharp was involved arose because he was living with his brother who was a surgeon in Wapping. William Sharp ran a surgery for the poor once a week and one night he had to deal with a badly-beaten eighteen-year old black slave called Jonathan Strong. Strong's master was a London lawyer named David Lisle and he had flung Strong onto the streets, assuming he would die. William and Granville paid for four months hospital care for the injured man and then persuaded a Quaker friend to employ him, although the African was still very frail. Two years later, in 1767, Lisle discovered his former slave was still alive and he arranged for Strong to be seized so he could sell him. Granville Sharp immediately took the case to court, arguing that this amounted to kidnapping. In 1768 the Lord Mayor of London authorised Strong's release and so the African was restored to freedom, although sadly he died not long afterwards because of complications from the beating he had received. Heartened by this legal victory, Sharp took up the case of an escaped slave called Thomas Lewis, who had been recaptured by his former owner and

How The Right To Be Free Was Legally Tested

Above left: Granville Sharp by G.Dance 1794. Above right:Lord Mansfield by J.Singleton 1782-3. Below:Dido with her cousin Lady Elizabeth Murray by D.Martin 1778.

put on board a ship bound for Jamaica. Again Sharp was successful because he managed to persuade a jury to have Lewis released before the ship could sail, although the reason for their decision was that Lewis' owner had not provided proof of ownership rather than that it was wrong to send an African back to the Caribbean for sale.

A toleration of slavery is, in effect, a toleration of inhumanity… The plea of private property in a negro, as in a horse or a dog, is very insufficient and defective…[This] cannot be justified, unless they shall be able to prove that a negro slave is neither man, woman, or child
    Granville Sharp, abolitionist in *A Representation of the Injustice …of Tolerating Slavery* in 1769

In 1769 Sharp published *A Representation of the Injustice and Dangerous Tendency of Tolerating Slavery* in which he argued that slavery was 'an innovation' that ran counter to British law. He determined to prove that 'as soon as any slave sets foot upon England he shall be deemed free'. In 1771 he took up the case of a slave called James Somerset who had arrived from Virginia. Sharp argued that Virginian law had no authority in England and so, by bringing him to London, his owner had effectively set him free. The Somerset case seriously worried all those who owned slaves and it is not surprising that it fell to the Lord Chief Justice to decide the case. John Wesley took a serious interest in the trial and so did his brother Charles because the Lord Chief Justice at the time was William Murray, the Earl of Mansfield, and he was one of Charles' close friends. They had been at school together. Lord Mansfield was particularly fond of Charles because Charles had rescued him from being bullied and the two men regularly went for walks together whenever Charles was in London.

We have no slaves at home – Then why abroad?
Slaves cannot breathe in England; if their lungs
receive our air, that moment they are free.
They touch our country, and their shackles fall
    William Cowper, poet and hymn-writer in his poem *The Task* in 1785

Mansfield clearly struggled over what he should do. He did not wish to undermine the property rights of all slaveowners yet at the same time he was no fan of slavery. His friendship with Charles Wesley may well have been a factor in that, but there was also a personal reason for his dislike. Mansfield had more or less adopted a young black girl, Elizabeth Belle, nicknaming her 'Dido' after the famous queen of Carthage. She was the illegitimate daughter of one of his nephews. Her slave mother had been brought to England and had died shortly after giving her birth in 1763. Mansfield had taken the unusual step of having the child treated almost exactly the same as her white half-cousin, Lady Elizabeth Murray. Mansfield had no children of his own and he seems to have looked on both girls as his daughters. One aristocratic visitor to his house reflected the views of most when he commented that it might not be 'criminal' but it was certainly undesirable to have to attend a meal in which Dido sat at the same table and to watch her link arms with other ladies as if she was a white woman. In 2018 the famous portrait of Dido with her cousin was the subject of a BBC investigation which discovered it was probably painted by the distinguished Scottish artist David Martin.

At the time of the trial Dido was still technically a slave. Lord Mansfield was to later give her her freedom as a twenty-first birthday present. In the Somerset case he sat on the fence. He was very careful not to say that any slave arriving in England was automatically free, but he said slavery was 'odious' and he ordered Somerset's release on the grounds that no foreigner could be put into prison on the authority of 'any law existing in another country'. The decision effectively meant that, although the law would not automatically free a slave brought into the country, it would not support the re-enslavement of any slave who escaped. Unfortunately this decision was to have two undesirable consequences. The first was that some owners sought to repatriate their slaves to the West Indies or to America rather than risk their loss and this meant those slaves suffered greatly. The second was that some owners decided to just get rid of the slaves they had in Britain and they were released without anywhere for them to go and without any hope of them finding employment. As most of them only spoke a variant of Caribbean patois rather than English, they were soon reduced to turning either to prostitution or crime. This served only to reinforce negative attitudes towards black people.

True justice makes no respect of persons and can never deny to any one that blessing to which all mankind have an undoubted right, their natural liberty
    Granville Sharp in *An Argument Against Property in Slaves* in 1772

In *Felix Farley's Bristol Journal* Mansfield's decision was published alongside an article on the punishment given to slaves who had murdered a plantation owner. The account of the burning alive of the ringleader could be seen as implying that a black person was immune to normal feelings:

> Sam a mulatto man was staked to iron bars and burnt. The fire being set at a small distance and continued till it came to his feet. He bore it with such savage sullenness and brutal ferocity as if he was deprived of inward and outward feelings.

His accomplices were given lesser punishments: one was flogged, two were transported, and three had their noses cut off. Madge Dresser in her book *Slavery Obscured* has suggested the juxtaposition of the two stories was not a coincidence:

> Did not this story… attempt to undermine the confidence that readers might otherwise have felt in the wisdom of the Mansfield judgement? Was it not a way of warning its readers that the Mansfield judgement might open the way to the freeing of such brutal beings as Sam the mulatto?

In the aftermath of the Somerset case Sharp developed strong connections with both the Methodists and the Quakers because of their support for his actions. In July 1772 Sharp told the Archbishop of York that 'the Methodists are highly offended at the scandalous toleration of slavery in our colonies' and that John Wesley totally endorsed the Lord Chief Justice's decision. Through Wesley Sharp was brought into contact with Anthony Benezet, a Quaker who had been campaigning in America for the abolition of slavery for almost twenty years on the grounds that all Africans deserved to be treated as equals:

> I can with truth and sincerity declare, that I have found amongst the negroes as great a variety of talents as amongst a like number of whites; and I am bold to assert, that the notion entertained by some, that the blacks are inferior in their capacities, is a vulgar prejudice, founded on the pride of ignorance of their lordly masters, who have kept their slaves at such a distance, as to be unable to form a right judgment of them.

In 1767 Benezet had written a book on the slave trade called *Some Historical Account of Guinea* and its graphic account of the treatment of slaves on the Middle Passage and in the plantations had shocked Wesley to the core. Never before had he read anything that showed so overwhelmingly just how barbarous the slave trade was. He had entered into correspondence with Benezet and the

Above: Anthony Benezet by B. Rush, engraving of Phillis Wheatley, and Charles Wesley by J. Russell 1771. Left: letter from Acona Robin to Charles Wesley 1774. Bottom left: English ships and African canoes in Old Calabar from Illustrated London News 1850. Below: John Wesley's Thoughts Upon Slavery 1774.

two men had become friends.

Wesley knew that the American's book was too long for most people to read and that something shorter and punchier was required and he and Benezet suggested to Sharp that what was required was 'some weekly publication… on the origin, nature, and dreadful effects of the slave trade'. This would generate more widespread awareness of the evils of slavery and this in turn would lead to an ability to lobby both the King and Parliament about the need for changes in the law. Sharp's reply to their suggestions is interesting. He told them he had already started encouraging the production of short anti-slavery tracts and lobbying influential figures in the Church. As a consequence the Archbishop of York had agreed to become proactive in encouraging the clergy to oppose the slave trade. Lobbying Parliament to end the slave trade was necessary but lobbying it to end slavery might be counter-productive because the colonies were already obsessed with asserting their right to decide their own laws. They would resent any imposed abolition. Lobbying the colonial administrations to reject slavery was therefore a safer procedure.

Liberty… is one of the most precious gifts which heaven has bestowed… and… captivity is the greatest of all evils that can befall one
　　　　　　　　　　　Miguel de Cervantes, Spanish novelist in *Don Quixote* in 1612

In 1772 Wesley was given an opportunity to hear first hand evidence from slaves about what was going on through a case taken up by his brother Charles. In Bristol a captain called Thomas Jones had asked for Charles' help to rescue two Africans named Little Ephraim Robin John and Ancona Robin Robin John, who were in prison in the city prior to being returned to Virginia for sale. Jones told Charles Wesley that the escaped slaves were 'princes' from Old Calabar. This port, now part of Nigeria, was one of the main bases used by the Bristol merchants to acquire slaves and the two Africans were members of the ruling Efrik tribe. Little Ephraim was the brother and Ancona Robin the nephew of Robin John, better known as 'Grandy King George', the main Muslim slave dealer in Old Calabar. Charles met the Africans and they told him how they had been enslaved five years earlier following a massacre instigated by the Bristol sea captain James Bevan. Annoyed at the prices being asked for slaves, he and four other captains had done a deal with a rival African slave trader and ambushed Grandy King George on board Bevan's ship, killing about three hundred of his men. Although Grandy King George had managed to escape, some of his family had not. His brother was decapitated and Bevan enslaved Little Ephraim and

Ancona Robin, selling them to a doctor who worked on the French island of Dominica.

The 'princes' went on to say how they had used their ability to speak English to try and persuade someone to return them home. A merchant from Virginia called John Mitchell had helped them escape but had then betrayed them by selling them as slaves in Virginia. There they had suffered at the hands of a brutal master called John Thomson. Fortunately his sudden death had given them another opportunity to escape. A merchant called Terence O'Neil had agreed to take them on his ship to Bristol, saying from there they would be able to find a ship back to Africa. However, once in Bristol, they had fallen into the hands of the Bristol merchant, William Jones, a trading partner of John Mitchell, the man who had sold them as slaves in Virginia. Jones had arranged for them to be imprisoned until he could return them for re-sale.

__Now I've been free, I know what a dreadful condition slavery is. I have seen hundreds of escaped slaves, but I never saw one who was willing to go back and be a slave__

The Incredible Memoirs of Harriet Tubman: the female Moses – a former slave who helped many others to escape to freedom in America in the 1850s

---

The sea-captains and merchants in Bristol were constantly claiming that they always acted responsibly and Charles knew what he was being told showed otherwise. He asked Lord Mansfield to secure the release of the 'princes' until their status and story could be checked. The resulting court case, which centred on the claim that they had been wrongfully enslaved, was held in London in 1773. By then Mansfield had exchanged correspondence with Grandy King George. The slave trader pleaded for the release of his relatives and said he would provide replacement slaves if that was required. The prosecution tried to reduce sympathy for the two Africans by making out that Little Ephraim and Ancona Robin were little better than pirates. Once again Mansfield was placed in a difficult position. If he said they had been wrongfully enslaved then it opened the floodgates to any slave claiming he or she had also been wrongfully enslaved, and that would have effectively presented a massive legal challenge for all those involved in the slave trade whether as traders or owners. His solution was to order the release of the two Africans but without clarifying their status. The princes returned to Bristol, where they stayed with Thomas Jones, who set about improving their education by having them taught to read.

> *In every human Breast, God has implanted a Principle, which we call Love of Freedom; it is impatient of Oppression, and pants for Deliverance*
>   Phillis Wheatley black poet in letter to Samson Occam in Feb 1774

That same year the Countess of Huntingdon inadvertently showed that the arguments about black inferiority were false by taking an interest in Phillis Wheatley, a twenty-year old slave who belonged to a wealthy visiting merchant from Boston called John Wheatley. Phillis had been born in West Africa (probably in either Gambia or Senegal) and sold into slavery at the age of seven or eight. She had been bought by Wheatley as a servant for his wife but the family had been amazed by her intelligence and so taken the unusual step of giving her a good education. This even included her learning Greek and Latin. Hearing that Phillis wrote poetry, the Countess helped arrange for some of her verses to be printed in a book entitled *Poems on Subjects Religious and Moral*. Phillis thus became the first African-American female to be published. Her most famous poem addressed ideas of liberty, religion and racial equality:

> Twas mercy brought me from my pagan land,
> taught my benighted soul to understand
> that there's a God, that there's a Saviour too:
> once I redemption neither sought nor knew.
> Some view our sable race with scornful eye,
> 'Their colour is a diabolic dye'.
> Remember Christians, negroes, black as Cain,
> may be refin'd, and join th' angelic train.

Phillis Wheatley became a celebrity in America when the poems were also published there and Wheatley gave Phillis her freedom in 1778. Sadly a combination of racism and sexism then forced her into hard domestic labour which soon killed her. She died in 1784 aged just 31.

> *Brethren in our Creator's eyes,*
> *I dare not injure or despise*
> *the workmanship of God.*
>   Charles Wesley in *The Master's Hymn* published in Bristol in 1767

How much time Charles Wesley spent with Little Ephraim and Ancona Robin after their release is not known but their subsequent correspondence with him shows they got to know him and his family and really appreciated his support. Little Ephraim and Ancona Robin became Christians. Whether this was a genuine conversion or something they did out of gratitude or to further advance their cause is not clear. Charles baptised both of them at the New Room in January 1774. He wrote: 'They received both the outward visible sign and the inward spiritual grace in a wonderful manner and measure'. Shortly afterwards arrangements were made for the two freed men to board a ship called the *Maria* so they could return home to Old Calabar. Charles provided them with some books as a farewell gift. Unfortunately the ship on which they sailed was captained by a heavy drinker called William Floyd. His drunkenness led to the ship being wrecked off one of the Cape Verde Islands in May. The crew and the ship's passengers managed to escape in an open boat, but they suffered considerably from lack of any supplies until a Bristol-bound ship chanced to rescue them.

Little Ephraim and Ancona Robin thus arrived back in Bristol in June 1774 'dressed in borrowed rags'. Once again the two Africans looked to the Methodists for help. Charles Wesley was not in Bristol at the time of their return but Elizabeth Johnson, a Methodist known for her kindness, provided them with temporary accommodation in her house near Portland Square for about eight or nine weeks, and the two men became regular worshippers at the New Room. That year the annual Methodist Conference was held in Bristol and John Wesley spent time with them. Little Ephraim wrote to Charles, who was absent in London:

> Your brother has been so kind as to talk to us and has given us the sacrament thrice. I find him so good as to show me when I do wrong. I feel in my heart great trouble and see [a] great deal more of my own faults and the faults of my countrymen which I hope the Lord will permit me to tell them when I come home.

There was talk of Ancona Robin writing down their experiences so people would know how bad the slave trade was. Elizabeth Johnson wrote to Charles:

> Ephraim is greatly altered, more thoughtful and humbled. He often speaks of feeling in his heart… You would be pleased to see how they see the idleness and stupidity of their past lives… Ancona reads exceeding well [and] it comes easy to him [to] pronounce proper. They both understand

every word preached better... Some of our preachers felt great union with them, talked with them, and prayed for them.

After the Conference Captain Jones arranged once more for the two Africans to board a ship for home. Little Ephraim appears to have been worried about the prospect of facing another voyage but Ancona Robin was 'as easy as a bird without care'. In October 1774 the latter left behind a letter to Charles, thanking him and the Bristol Methodists for their many kindnesses:

We can never thank you enough for your love to us... You know how kind our Bristol friends have been to us... We had a very blessed time. Last night [John] Wesley offered us up in a very solemn manner to God and we humbly hope his prayer will be heard.

Little Ephraim also wrote a thank you letter, adding 'I hope if we shall do well we shall hear from one another again'. A letter from Charles to a friend in November refers to his delight that 'my two African children got safe home'.

Little Ephraim and Ancona Robin appear to have promised the Wesleys that they would abandon their involvement in the slave trade and help convert their people to Christianity. However, what scarce evidence we have suggests that they soon resumed their role as slave traders and reverted back to being Muslims. There is a letter from Little Ephraim to a Liverpool slave trader written in December 1775 which says he wants two guns for every slave he sells. It is also apparent that Thomas Jones made commercial gain out of his action in helping secure their freedom because he traded successfully with the Old Calabar slave traders in 1777 and indeed helped them attack New Calabar, the base of their rivals.

Not all attempts to help escaped slaves were successful. As covered in an earlier chapter, Olaudah Equiano was unable to save his friend John Annis from being returned to slavery in 1774. The truth was that the opposition to slavery was too uncoordinated. What was needed was something to bring the issue into national focus and it was John Wesley who provided that in the shape of a tract entitled *Thoughts Upon Slavery*.

4.
JOHN WESLEY'S 'THOUGHTS UPON SLAVERY'

One principal sin of our nation is the blood that we have shed in Asia, Africa, and America... The African trade is iniquitous from first to last. It is the price of blood! It is a trade of blood, and has stained our land with blood!
John Wesley in *Thoughts Upon Slavery* in 1774

It was probably no coincidence that John Wesley's *Thoughts Upon Slavery* was written while the Calabar princes were in Bristol, although they did not feature in it. John instead made special use of the anti-slavery evidence contained in the book which Anthony Benezet had written. He condensed its contents so that people would more easily grasp the evil ways in which slaves were acquired and treated:

> Banished from their country, from their friends and relations for ever, from every comfort of life, they are reduced to a state scarce anyway preferable to that of beasts of burden... Their sleep is very short, their labour continual, and frequently above their strength.

He included a graphic account of their transportation aboard the slave ships and their subsequent enslavement, describing their inadequate diet and clothing and the constant and often brutal punishments they faced:

> They frequently geld them, or chop off half a foot... Some drop melted wax upon their skin; others cut off their ears, and constrain them to broil and eat them.

And he posed the question: 'Did the Creator intend that the noblest creatures in the visible world should live such a life as this?':

> Notwithstanding ten thousand laws, right is right, and wrong is wrong still. There must still remain an essential difference between justice and injustice,

cruelty and mercy… Who can reconcile this treatment of the negroes… with either mercy or justice?

Briefly Wesley tackled all the arguments that had been given in favour of slavery. That it had always existed did not mean it was sacrosanct. Was there to be no moral progress? That the Africans were an inferior species did not stand up to scrutiny. They were neither 'stupid, senseless, brutish, lazy barbarians' nor 'fierce, cruel, perfidious savages' but a 'remarkably sensible' race, considering their lack of educational opportunity. If anyone lacked humanity and behaved like animals it was their white masters. That slaves were a product of tribal warfare did not make it lawful. No one was born a slave and neither capture nor contract justified making a person a slave. That God had preordained the Africans should be slaves ran counter to the gospel of a God of love as proclaimed by Christ. Those who engaged in the slave trade and in slave ownership were opposing what God wanted not fulfilling his will:

> The great God will deal with you as you have dealt with them, and require all their blood at your hands… You act the villain to enslave them… Give liberty to whom liberty is due, that is, to every child of man, to every partaker of human nature… Away with all whips, all chains, all compulsion!… Do with everyone else as you would he should do to you.

Against the economic arguments used to defend slavery, Wesley argued that the colonies could function equally well without it. Although people claimed it was necessary for 'the trade and wealth and glory of our nation', what a country needed most was not wealth born of greed but 'wisdom, virtue, justice, mercy, generosity, public spirit [and] love of our country'. He added that, even if he was wrong and slavery made economic sense, it was still unjustifiable. Economic necessity could never justify the atrocious ill-treatment:

> What, to whip them for every petty offence, till they are all in gore blood? To take that opportunity of rubbing pepper and salt into their raw flesh? To drop burning sealing-wax upon their skin? To castrate them? To cut off half their foot with an axe? To hang them on gibbets, that they might die by inches with heat and hunger and thirst? To pin them to the ground and then burn them by degrees?…When did a Turk or Heathen find it necessary to use a fellow-creature thus?'

Better no trade than trade procured by villainy… Better is honest poverty, than all the riches bought by the tears, and sweat, and blood of our fellow creatures.
John Wesley in *Thoughts Upon Slavery* in 1774

It was the emotional appeals scattered throughout the tract that made *Thoughts on Slavery* so memorable. He literally begged the sea captains, merchants, and planters to put their conscience before their pocket. Surprisingly *Thoughts Upon Slavery* has not received the historical recognition it deserves, probably because it was only briefly mentioned in the first history of the abolitionist movement written by Thomas Clarkson in 1839. All he says in his book is that Wesley was a heart-felt opponent of slavery and that the Methodists were 'friends to the oppressed Africans' and helped promote 'a softness of feeling towards them'. Clarkson also says George Whitefield was 'a firm friend to the poor Africans' who never lost 'an opportunity of serving them' and who interested 'many thousands of his followers in their favour'. It seems strange that he puts Whitefield, even though he was not an abolitionist, almost on the same par as Wesley. It is, of course, possible that Clarkson was such a devout Anglican that he looked upon the Wesleyan Methodists (who by then had separated from the Church of England) with disfavour.

At the time of its publication those opposed to slavery were very appreciative of Wesley's *Thoughts Upon Slavery*. Granville Sharp said it summed up the entire anti-slavery argument 'into a small compass, which infinitely increases the power and effect of it, like Light collected in a Focus'. It immediately received favourable reviews in two of London's most important magazines. The September issue of *The Monthly Review* praised its 'pertinent observations' and said it did honour to Wesley's 'humanity' and *The Gentlemen's Magazine* made similar observations in March 1775. By then it had already gone through three editions and it was shortly to have a fourth. Benezet did not mind that Wesley had plagiarised sections of his book to provide some of the factual content. He told Wesley that *Thoughts on Slavery* afforded him such satisfaction that he was going to ensure its publication in America. It went through thirteen editions there and its heart-felt appeal to empathise with the plight of slaves won over many readers to the anti-slavery cause. It was still being reprinted in America right up to the time of the American Civil War and its use of emotional questioning was to be copied in Harriet Beecher Stowe's *Uncle Tom's Cabin*.

In the letter in which Benezet thanked Wesley for producing *Thoughts Upon Slavery* he gave some examples of the dehumanising impact of slavery on white people. This included the text of an advertisement which offered £20 to anyone bringing back the severed heads of runaway slaves. In reply John wrote about the Bristol captains massacring Africans in Old Calabar and Benezet said it was a story that deserved more publicity. The historian Irv Brendlinger has described the co-operation between Sharp, Wesley and Benezet as creating 'an effective triumvirate in the antislavery movement':

> [They] provided genuine support and encouragement to each other. Their correspondence reveals how they valued each other… and how they welcomed each other to what they considered to be the most significant moral challenge of their world.

The co-operation was helped by the arrival in Britain in 1774 of one of Benezet's star pupils and followers, a Quaker merchant called William Dillwyn, because he was a great networker. It meant that the London Quakers became far more involved in what Sharp was doing. Dillwyn was to act as a tutor to Thomas Clarkson, the man most historians regard as central to the success of the abolitionist cause.

Is that which can bend and turn, and descend and ascend, to fit every crooked phase of selfish, worldly society, religion? Is that religion which is less scrupulous, less generous, less just, less considerate… No! When I look for religion, I must look for something above me, and not something beneath
Harriet Beecher Stowe, abolitionist in Uncle Tom's Cabin in 1852

Wesley did not confine his attack on slavery to just words. In 1770 he had decided, after George Whitefield's death, to send out Methodist lay preachers to continue the evangelical work in the colonies, especially as Methodist immigrants were swelling the ranks of the Methodists in America. In 1774 he instructed one of the preachers, Thomas Rankin, to do all he could to turn the talk of human rights in America into a demand for the abolition of slavery. Wesley felt the colonists were being hypocritical in demanding greater political and economic liberty for whites whist continuing to uphold the enslavement of black Africans. It is worth noting that many American historians judge that Whitefield had been critically important to the development of the colonists' demands. He was the first person to traverse all the colonies and so connect them together. He was also the first person in America to grasp how the media could be used to promote interest in a subject – so much so that his name was virtually a household word. And he consistently spoke of the importance of freedom. When the American War of

Independence broke out soldiers raided the crypt where Whitefield was buried so they could snip bits of his jacket and wear them as talismans of liberty as they went into battle.

Thomas Rankin contacted antislavery activists and he lobbied the first Continental Congress organised by the colonists when it met in September 1774. Unfortunately the Americans were by this stage well down the road towards declaring their independence from Britain and, although they had acquired an astonishingly gifted set of leaders in George Washington, Thomas Jefferson, Benjamin Franklin, Thomas Adams, and James Madison, abolishing slavery was not on their agenda as a priority.

I wake up every morning in a house that was built by slaves
　　Michele Obama, wife of American President in a speech to the Democratic Convention in 2016

Bristol's many trade connections with the colonies made it look favourably on the colonists' demands for fairer treatment, but, as the prospect of a war for independence increased, trade began to haemorrhage, causing massive unemployment. Until this stage John Wesley had generally supported the colonists, saying they had genuine grievances, but he now chose to argue that those who embraced slavery had no right to demand freedom. In a leaflet entitled *A Calm Address to Our American Colonies* he said very few British people had the vote so there was no reason for the colonists to use their lack of voting rights as an excuse for seeking independence. This was a hugely unpopular tract in Bristol because the merchants were still very supportive of the Americans. They wanted the government to make concessions. One consequence was that Wesley lost his main publisher, William Pine. In May Thomas Rankin held a meeting of the Methodist preachers from the different circuits in Philadelphia and they resolved 'to follow the advice that Mr Wesley and his brother had given us' and view the preparations for war as God's punishment for 'the dreadful sin of buying and selling the poor Africans'. Simultaneously Benezet created the first-ever anti-slavery society in Philadelphia. He called it 'the Society for the Relief of Free Negroes Unlawfully Held in Bondage'.

The revolution in public opinion which this cause requires, is not to be expected in a day, or perhaps in an age
　　Thomas Jefferson, American President on the abolition of slavery in a letter written in 1826

On 20 July 1775 Thomas Rankin gave the first recorded sermon by a Methodist preacher in America on the unacceptable immorality of slavery at Forks Chapel in Maryland. Whitefield, of course, had never taken such a strong line. That autumn Wesley produced another leaflet, *A Seasonable Address*, describing himself as 'a lover of Peace' and he re-iterated that a war would be God's punishment on both sides for engaging in enslavement. All this did not go down well with the American leadership. George Washington told one of Wesley's lay preachers, Martin Rodda, that the Methodists should stick to religion and not enter the political arena:

> Mr Wesley I know; I respect Mr Wesley; but Mr Wesley, I presume, never sent you to America to interfere with political matters. Mr Wesley sent you to America to preach the gospel to the people. Now you go and mind your proper work: preach the gospel and leave politics to me and my brethren.

In the midst of all these events the son of a Bristol ironmonger, William Combe, published *The Philosopher in Bristol*, a book which was designed to cash-in on the slavery debate. Born in 1741, Combe had inherited quite a lot of wealth, but then squandered it. After working as a soldier, a waiter, a teacher and a cook, he had resorted to using his pen to earn a living. In essence the book contained imagined conversations with three slave-traders in which each rationalised what he was doing. One trader defends slavery on economic grounds:

> If any substitutes could be found… I would willingly forego a commerce which is so dishonourable to the human species. But while it continues there cannot be any good reason why I may not receive those profits, which, if I were to relinquish them, would be eagerly pursued and gladly obtained by another.

The second trader says that 'the trade itself is deservedly stigmatised' but that he always treats his slaves with 'the utmost humanity'. The third trader just asserts his delight at the wealth that slavery has brought him:

> 'You may say what you please… that it is contrary to religion and humanity and all that, but this I know… that I have got this full of money by it'.

Combe's take on all this is that it is fine to be a slave trader like the first two. You just must not be boorish and crude like the third man. The book was a far cry

Top left: W. Hogarth's 'A Committee of the House of Commons' depicts the parliamentary relationship between white and black. Top right: Edmund Burke. Left: Burke's statue in Bristol. Middle left to right: Thomas Rankin and William Coombe. Above: Francis Asbury and Thomas Coke, the architects of Methodism in the United States.

from the pleas of Quakers and Methodists for people to show love to all.

Do all the good you can. By all the means you can. In all the ways you can. In all the places you can. At all the times you can. To all the people you can. As long as ever you can

Ascribed to John Wesley

On 4 July 1776 the American colonists formally produced their Declaration of Independence, declaring their faith in equal rights and their inalienable right to life, liberty, and the pursuit of happiness. Both John and Charles Wesley condemned the demand for independence and their chief agent in America, Thomas Rankin, declared it was 'a farce' for any Americans 'to contend for liberty when they themselves keep some hundreds of thousands of poor blacks in most cruel bondage'. The Wesleys urged all American Methodists not to fight and all but one of the British lay preachers returned to England. The one who stayed, Francis Asbury, had volunteered to go out there whilst attending a meeting at the New Room in Bristol. He backed the Wesleys' stand against slavery but made clear his readiness to work within an independent United States should that be the outcome of the conflict.

Is life so dear, or peace so sweet, as to be purchased at the price of chains and slavery? Forbid it, Almighty God! I know not what course others may take; but as for me, give me liberty or give me death!
Patrick Henry, a founding father of the United States speaking at Virginia Convention in 1775

All the debate about rights and freedom in the build up to the American War of Independence inevitably encouraged discussion in Britain about slavery. It is interesting that the books most borrowed from Bristol's chief circulating library between 1774 and 1784 were all philosophical ones written by French writers. The most popular choice was Abbé Raynal's *A Philosophical and Political History of the Settlements and Trade of the Europeans* which was highly critical of slavery. It was a sign of the changing attitudes that Edmund Burke, one of Bristol's M.P.s between 1774 and 1780, judged it prudent to start drafting 'a Negro Code' to define the rights of slaves and restrict the punishments inflicted upon them.

Burke is the only one of Bristol's M.P.s to be given a statue and it is interesting that this has not been more challenged. Just as Colston was revered in the nineteenth century, so also was Burke. He was seen as the man who defended

Britain against the worst excesses of the French Revolution in the 1790s. The statue was erected in 1894 by the Wills family. Born in Dublin in 1729, Burke abandoned a potential career in law to become first a philosophical writer and then a politician, serving as an M.P. from 1765 to his death in 1797. He was an immensely gifted orator. The Prime Minister William Pitt the Elder described Burke's maiden speech as being 'spoken in such a manner as to stop the mouths of all Europe'. He made a name for himself by arguing the benefits of having a constitutional monarchy and the importance of having political parties so that a government's actions were always subjected to the scrutiny of an opposition. He joined a circle of leading intellectuals and celebrities that included the multi-talented Samuel Johnson, the writer Oliver Goldsmith, the actor David Garrick and the artist Joshua Reynolds. It was his support for the grievances being expressed by the American colonists that made him an attractive candidate for Bristol.

Burke still has his advocates today but many historians view him as essentially a defender of the rights of the rich and a defender of the exploitation of the masses. Burke's writings are full of praises for the wealthy landed aristocracy and the need for the general populace to recognise 'the principles of natural subordination' and their lower place in the social order. He condemned offering any help to the poor because that meant giving them what God in his wisdom had denied them. He disapproved of elections, judging that it created M.P.s who were 'flatterers rather than legislator, the instruments not the guides of the people', and he was fairly dismissive about democracy in general, saying that electing a head of state was almost always destructive to the unity and peace of the nation. The reason he gave for not seeking re-election as Bristol's M.P. in 1780 was that he had no desire to be 'a bidder at an auction of popularity'. He knew his re-election was in serious doubt because those who held power in Bristol disliked his support for free trade with Ireland and for an end to discrimination against Catholics. He secured his return to parliament by becoming an M.P. for a 'pocket borough' (i.e. a place were there was no real electorate and so the seat was in the hands of a local nobleman). That had been how he had entered Parliament in the first place.

For Burke commerce was God-approved and he saw nothing wrong in exploiting other nations. Slavery was justified by economic considerations and by the need to civilise superstitious savages. It was an inescapable fact of life, 'a weed that grows on every soil'. This is description of how slaves should be treated:

> I am far from contending in favour of an effeminate indulgence to these people. I know that they are stubborn and intractable for the most part, and that they must be ruled with a rod of iron.

Like Daniel Defoe sixty years earlier he argued humanity was required but largely because it encouraged slaves to better serve their masters and because it reduced the danger of rebellions. Christianity should be taught so that slaves would learn the value of 'humility, submission and honesty'. According to the *Parliamentary History* in June 1777 Burke spoke in Parliament 'against revising the state of the trade to Africa… for fear of doing more harm than good'. He is reported as having said:

> Africa, time out of mind, had been in a state of slavery, therefore the inhabitants only changed one species of slavery for another.

The Code, on which his reputation as an opposer of slavery largely rests, was never completed. He presented a sketch of it for consideration to a leading government figure, Henry Dundas, in 1792, but that was only because he felt it might counter the demand for immediate abolition. He told Dundas

> The people like short methods, the consequences of which they sometimes have reason to repent of. It is not that my plan does not lead to the extinction of the slave trade; but it is through very slow progress… We must precede the donation of freedom by disposing the minds of the objects to a disposition to receive it without danger to themselves or us… [Until the Africans are civilised] I am fully convinced that the cause of humanity would be far more benefitted by the continuance of the trade and servitude, regulated and reformed.

The sketched rights he offered slaves were not wonderful. For example, one was the right to purchase their freedom but Burke must have known that only a few slaves had roles that enabled them to earn money. Another was the right to lodge a legal complaint if a slave was being cruelly and inhumanly treated, but the chances of that being fairly heard would have been very remote. The historian David Brion Davis argues in his *The Problem of Slavery in Western Culture* that Burke's sole contribution to the slavery question was to prolong the traffic in human beings. It should also be noted that Burke's racism extended to more than just the African. He was, for example, strongly anti-Jewish and

John Wesley's 'Thoughts Upon Slavery'

Three examples of the many pictures used to portray the infamous 1781 Zong massacre and .the underwater sculpture 'Vicissitudes' by Jason de Caires Taylor in the underwater sculpture park off coast of Grenada 2006. Though not designed as such, this is now viewed by many as a fitting symbol of the enslaved Africans who ended up on the Caribbean seabed because of the chains the sculptor uses to hold the figures together.

339

he was particularly derogatory about the American Indians. The words on the pedestal under Burke's statue are his own: 'I wish to be an M.P. to have my share of doing good and resisting evil'. His definition of good and evil leaves a lot to be desired.

> *Canst thou, and honour'd with a Christian name*
> *Buy what is woman-born, and feel no shame?*
> *Trade in the blood of innocence, and plead*
> *Expedience as a warrant for the deed*
> William Cowper, hymnwriter and poet in *Charity* in 1782

During the War of American Independence there took place an event that is now often seen as a turning point in Britain's attitude towards slavery. This was 'the *Zong* atrocity'. The *Zong* was a slave ship purchased by a syndicate of Liverpool merchants in 1781. Its captain Luke Collingwood loaded it with 442 slaves – more than twice the number it could safely transport. The ship was supposed to carry its slaves to Jamaica but navigational errors meant it lost its way. By the time this was realised several of the crew and sixty-two of the Africans had already died from overcrowding, disease and, because the ship was inadequately provisioned, malnutrition. It was then appreciated that the ship had just a few days' water left and they were many days from land. Because the captain was ill, it fell to the first mate, James Kelsall, to handle the situation and he sought the advice of a former ship's captain who was on board, Robert Stubbs. According to Kelsall's later account they faced pressure from the crew to throw some of the slaves overboard and so reduce the demand on the water supply before all on the ship perished. On 29 November fifty-four women and children were thrown through cabin windows into the sea. On 1 December forty-two males were thrown overboard, and thirty-six more followed in the next few days. Another ten of the Africans, in a display of defiance at the inhumanity of the slavers, committed suicide by jumping into the sea. The remaining 208 slaves were landed in Jamaica on 22 December and sold.

The ship's owners then made an insurance claim. A dead or a sick slave who died shortly after landing had no value, but any slaves jettisoned to save the rest of 'the cargo' could be claimed for on the ship's insurance at up to £30 per head – the equivalent today of around £2,500. The ship's owners put in a claim to their insurers for around £350,000 in today's values. The insurance company accused the ship's crew of having committed unnecessary murder just in order to obtain the insurance money. This led to a court case in 1783 but John Lee, the Solicitor

General, said he saw nothing wrong in the actions of the crew and compared the slaves to dead wood:

> What is this claim that human people have been thrown overboard? This is a case of chattels or goods. Blacks are goods and property; it is madness to accuse these well-deserving honourable men of murder. They acted out of necessity and in the most appropriate manner for the cause… The case is the same as if wood had been thrown overboard.

---

they ask for water we give them sea
they ask for bread we give them sea
they ask for life we give them only the sea
                                            M. NourbeSe Philip, Caribbean writer in *Zong!* in 2006

The insurance company lodged an appeal because it saw grave anomalies in Kelsall's account of events. The most obvious was that the ship had not been short of water when it eventually docked in Jamaica. Kellsall argued that was because it had rained after the killings and the ship's water butts had refilled, but the insurance company was able to produce evidence from others that the rain had taken place in-between the killings and not afterwards. Olaudah Equiano brought the case to the attention of Granville Sharp, who campaigned to raise awareness of what had happened, writing letters to the press and to various bishops and politicians. William Murray as Lord Chief Justice had to hear the appeal and he overruled the Solicitor General. He judged that the insurers were not liable for losses resulting from errors committed by the *Zong*'s crew in relation to the navigation and provisioning of the ship. By then, of course, what had happened on the *Zong* had become far more than an insurance case. The killings undoubtedly disproved the slavers' traditional argument that they looked after their slaves and the cruel inhumanity of the Solicitor General's words encouraged many people to join the ranks of those who thought Britain should have nothing more to do with the trade. The first petition to the House of Commons from a municipality to abolish Britain's involvement in the slave trade took place within a year of the American war ending. It came from the town of Bridgewater.

In Bristol most of the merchants continued to uphold the trade but their position had not just been morally weakened. The War had seriously disrupted trade to the extent that a number of traders and manufacturers were facing bankruptcy. The story of the *Zong* has continued to stir the conscience of later generations. It has been depicted by various artists, most famously William Turner, and, within the last twenty years alone, become the basis for a novel, a play, a collection of poems, and a television programme. In March 2007, a sailing ship representing the *Zong* was sailed to Tower Bridge in London to commemorate the 200th anniversary of the Act for the Abolition of the Slave Trade. That same year a memorial stone to the enslaved who died was erected in Jamaica.

> ***Let justice, humanity, advocates for freedom, and the sacred name of Christians cease to be the boast of American rulers***
> David Cooper, American Quaker abolitionist in *A Serious Address* in 1783

Throughout the American war Quakers and Methodists continued to lobby against any continuation of slavery. On the Quaker side the dying Benezet was replaced by David Cooper, a farmer from New Jersey, as the leading abolitionist voice. In 1783 Cooper produced a tract that was printed on both sides of the Atlantic. Its very long title more or less summarised its content: *A Serious Address to the Rulers of America on the Inconsistency of their Conduct respecting Slavery, forming a Contrast between the Encroachments of England on American Liberty and American Injustice in tolerating Slavery.* A short extract will indicate Cooper's sense of outrage at the hypocrisy of the colonists in demanding freedom for themselves whilst upholding slavery:

> I am not ashamed to declare myself an advocate for the rights of that highly injured and abused people… Must not every generous foreigner feel a secret indignation rise in his breast, when he hears the language of Americans upon any of their own rights as freemen being in the least infringed, and reflects that these very people are holding thousands and tens of thousands of their innocent fellow men in the most debasing and abject slavery, deprived of every right of freemen, except light and air?… If they imitate our example, and offer by force to assert their native freedom, they are condemned as traitors, and a hasty gibbet strikes terror on their survivors, and rivets their chains more secure… Why ought a negro be less free than… a white face in America?

The Methodists were no less active. At a Methodist meeting held in Baltimore in April 1780 it was agreed that no Methodist preacher should buy slaves:

> Slave-keeping is contrary to the laws of God, man, and nature; and hurtful to society, contrary to the dictates of conscience and pure religion, and doing that which we would not another should do to us and ours.

In 1783 it was further ruled that Methodist preachers should free any slave they possessed. In that year the rebels achieved victory and the United States of America was officially created. The separation was not just political. It was also religious because the Church of England had no desire to look after the welfare of the rebellious Americans. To fill the gap Asbury and another of Wesley's preachers, Thomas Coke, created the Methodist Episcopal Church in America. The new Church's Book of Discipline laid down that all Methodists should cease engaging in the slave trade and free all their slaves:

> The buying and selling the souls and bodies of men...is totally opposite to the whole spirit of the gospel.

Unfortunately enforcing this ruling proved impossible to enforce. It did not help that most American Methodists did not see why they should continue to obey John Wesley. American Methodists increasingly turned their back on his anti-slavery views, judging the issue to be too divisive for a young Church to handle. After John's death in 1791 the Methodist Episcopal Church declared it would have no policy on slavery. Instead it would leave the matter entirely to the individual conscience of each person. It was thus left to the Quakers in America to became the real holders of the torch for black freedom, campaigning within each state for the abolition of slavery.

Those who deny freedom to others, deserve it not for themselves
        Abraham Lincoln, American President, in a letter written in April 1859

Within Bristol there was a flurry of anti-slavery articles published in the Bristol press, much of it as result of Quaker initiatives. By this stage they had acquired a key spokesman against slavery in Harry Gandy. Born in Bristol in 1722, Gandy knew all about what went on in the slave trade from personal experience. As a young man he had served on slave-ships in the Caribbean and helped defeat a slave insurrection and by the 1750s he had risen to the rank of captain. On two occasions he had acted as the captain of a slave-ship – in 1752 and 1767 – and he deeply regretted having done so. He knew that the conditions on slave ships were such that no captain, however well-meaning, was able to treat the enslaved in a humane fashion. This had made him turn to Quakerism, although there is some evidence to suggest he also flirted with becoming a Swedenborgian. This new church group, which had originated in Sweden, laid great emphasis on Christians expressing their faith through active love and charity towards others and it was sending out missionaries to Africa and proclaiming that the abolition of slavery was essential because the Africans were 'in greater enlightenment than others on this earth, since they… think more 'interiorly', and so receive truths and acknowledge them'.

On his return to Bristol Gandy became a conveyancer and he was eventually to become the city's Notary Public, a role which involved authenticating legal documents. From the outset he commenced campaigning for the abolition of the slave trade. In 1785 he encouraged the Bristol Men's Meeting of Quakers, which had around fifty members, to distribute three hundred free copies of *Caution against the Slave Trade to Great Britain*, a work that Benezet had written in 1766, and to undertake a survey to see if any Quakers were still participating in the slave trade, despite being prohibited from doing so. The resulting report stated:

> We find Friends are generally clear; not one person being engaged therein, or holding any one in slavery. Some few in the course of business furnish goods to merchants in that trade and only one family, who from principle have retired from the West Indies to this city and have not yet been able to withdraw their property, hold a mortgage on an estate whereon slaves are employed.

The American war, as mentioned in an earlier chapter, radically increased the number of free black people entering Britain because the government felt duty-bound to prevent the re-enslavement of black Americans who had fought on their side. Most went to London but it is highly likely that some found their way to Bristol. There is a reference in John Wesley's journal to him baptising 'a young negro' at the New Room on 3 March 1786 and the congregation being 'deeply affected'. Given the strong links that the New Room had with American Methodism, it is quite possible that this was one of those black African-Americans seeking refuge.

Mr Wesley had this great cause much at heart
Thomas Clarkson, leading abolitionist reflecting on how victory was obtained in The History of the Rise, Progress and Accomplishment of the Abolition of the Slave Trade *in 1839*

5.

THE SOCIETY FOR EFFECTING THE ABOLITION OF THE SLAVE TRADE

A half-starved negro, may, for breaking a single cane, which probably he himself has planted, be hacked to pieces with a cutlass
James Ramsey, clergyman on St Kitts in *An Essay on the Treatment and Conversion of African Slaves in the British Sugar Colonies* in 1784

Fresh impetus to those who opposed slavery came from Thomas Clarkson. Born in 1760, the son of a Norfolk clergyman, he had begun reading about slavery whilst he was a student at Cambridge University in order to produce a dissertation. Like John Wesley before him, Clarkson was heavily affected by reading the work of Anthony Benezet on the inhumane conditions and barbaric treatment to which the enslaved were subjected. The result was a life-long commitment to ending such injustice. He commenced studying all the anti-slavery literature that was available, including the relevant section in William Paley's *Moral Philosophy*, a highly academic study based on lectures given in Cambridge, and *An Essay on the Treatment and Conversion of African Slaves in the British Sugar Colonies,* written by James Ramsay, a former ship's surgeon. Ramsay had been so horrified by seeing slaves lying bound in a mixture of blood, vomit and excreta on a slave ship that he had opted to seek ordination so he could serve as a missionary. He had worked on the island of St Kitts for nineteen years, facing ever-increasing hostility from the plantation owners because of his attempts to help the enslaved.

Ramsay's book was to inspire not just Clarkson but many others of his generation to oppose slavery. and it is seen as the biggest single influence behind the creation of an organised abolition movement. The fact it was written by a clergyman on what he had seen first-hand made it a difficult book to argue against, although that did not stop the pro-slavery press labelling it as 'unpardonable, indecent, unjust, ungenerous'. What gave the book its impact was the sheer level of detail it contained about daily life in the Caribbean and the grinding down of the slaves by a relentless sixteen-hour working day and a culture that relied on brutal punishments. This was a world in which it was the norm that every so often the mill machinery would 'grind off a hand, or an arm, of those drowsy worn down creatures who feed it', in which young girls were regularly 'sacrificed to the lust of white men; in some instances their own fathers', in which new mothers had to take their babies into the fields and leave them in furrows exposed to the elements, and in which the cart whip that 'cuts out flakes of skin and flesh with every strike' was just one of many ways of enforcing control. Clarkson said he sometimes could not close his eyelids for grief after reading sections of Ramsey's book.

It is in the master's power to render his slaves' lives miserable every hour by a thousand nameless stratagems
> James Ramsey, clergyman on St Kitts in *An Essay on the Treatment and Conversion of African Slaves in the British Sugar Colonies* in 1784

Clark's dissertation was published in 1786 under the title *An Essay on the Slavery and Commerce of the Human Species, particularly to Africans*. It made a big impact. One of the men it particularly affected was the M.P. William Smith, a radical politician who belonged to an organisation for social and political reform called the Society for Constitutional Information. Granville Sharp was also a member of it and so was the pottery manufacturer Josiah Wedgwood, the human rights campaigner John Horne Tooke, and the publisher and newspaper owner Joseph Gales. All these men felt that Clark's book provided a case for abolition that was both unanswerable and irresistible. The book also won accolades from William Dillwyn and other Quakers and Clarkson began to work with them and Olaudah Equiano in support of Granville Sharp's Sierra Leone scheme to create a colony for freed Africans.

After the collapse of the initial scheme a second attempt successfully created Freetown. The colony's governor from 1794 to 1799 was Zachary Macaulay and he was well-known in Bristol because he had married a Quaker, Selina Mills, the daughter of one of the city's printers. The Baptists agreed to send out three missionaries to Sierra Leone from their College. Its principal, John Ryland, commissioned Jacob Grigg, James Rodway, and John Garvin with the words:

> Show that you would account it greater gain to rescue one sable brother from idolatry and sin than to return to Europe with thousands of pieces of gold and silver.

The emphasis on conversion should be noted because Ryland did not approve

THE SOCIETY FOR EFFECTING ABOLITION

Top left: Thomas Clarkson by C. von Breda 1788; Top right: James Ramsay by C. von Breda 1789. Above: William Dillwyn by C. Leslie 1815. Left: William Wilberforce by K. Anton Hickel 1793. Below: bust of Zachary Macaulay in Westminster Abbey.

when the three men began complaining that Macaulay was behaving in a racist fashion towards the African-Americans. As noted in an earlier chapter, the governor's attitude towards the Methodist-educated Boston King shows he did not welcome Africans being treated as equals or in them receiving too much education. Macaulay asked Ryland to recall Grigg, Rodway, and Garvin because they had, in his words, 'gone native'. John Garvin, who was the most outspoken critic of Macaulay, was so incensed by Ryland's agreement to this that he left the Baptists and joined the Methodists. Today Macaulay's belief in white superiority is usually skated over and he is praised for making the new colony a success and for his later roles in helping found the Society for the Mitigation and Gradual Abolition of Slavery in 1823 and becoming the editor of the *AntiSlavery Reporter*. His son, the famous historian, politician, and poet Thomas Babington Macaulay, also acted as a prominent campaigner for the abolition of slavery, but he too was at heart a racist, believing that natives benefitted from firm British control.

I know that it would be not only a wicked but a shortsighted policy, to aim at making a nation like this great and prosperous by violating the laws of justice
Thomas Babington Macaulay, historian in a parliamentary speech against accepting products made with slave labour in 1845

Historians now view the Sierra Leone project as being very significant not so much for what it achieved but because it encouraged collective action and political lobbying and brought the issue of slavery right to the top of the agenda because of the press coverage it received. It was also the first occasion on which the white abolitionists worked alongside black abolitionists. Equiano's role has already been covered, but it is worth saying something about Cugoano, whose role is often ignored. He was born in 1757 in Ajumako in what is now the central region of Ghana and kidnapped and enslaved when he was thirteen. He was sold to work on a plantation in Grenada but was purchased not long afterwards by an English merchant, Alexander Campbell, who brought him to Britain in 1772. Campbell gave him the name 'John Stuart' and treated him as if he were a free man. He gave him a good education and ensured he was converted and then baptised. In 1784 Cugoano found employment as a servant, working for a leading portrait painter, Richard Cosway, and his multi-talented wife, Maria Hadfield. She was an accomplished artist and musician and a gifted society hostess. Through her Cugoano was introduced to many leading figures, including the poet William Blake and the politician Edmund Burke.

> *Slavery is an evil of the first magnitude... and contrary to all the genuine principles of Christianity*
>
> Ottobah Cugoano, black abolitionist in Thoughts and Sentiments in 1787

As one of the Sons of Africa Cugoano's major contribution was writing *Thoughts and Sentiments on the Evil and Wicked Traffic of the Slavery and Commerce of the Human Species* in 1787. Much of it was extensively borrowed both in content and style from the earlier writings of white abolitionists like Wesley, Benezet, Sharp, Ramsey, and Clarkson but it made him the first English-speaking African historian and there were points in the text when his personal experience of slavery was recorded. For example, he gave a quite detailed account of his own kidnapping and enslavement at the beginning of the book and then commented on how that still emotionally impacted on him:

> Death was more preferable than life... [and] the grievous thoughts which I then felt, still pant in my heart; though my fears and tears have long since subsided... It is still grievous to think that thousands more have suffered in similar and greater distress... and that many even now are suffering in all the extreme bitterness of grief and woe, that no language can describe.

He also included in the books some examples of things he had personally witnessed, such as slaves having their teeth pulled out to prevent them eating any of the sugar cane and one of his fellow-slaves being given twenty-four lashes for being seen at a church on a Sunday when he should have been working in the fields. At one point he states 'Vice to be hated needs to be seen'.

The book was a call to all Europeans to live up to their professed Christian faith and to their professed belief in freedom. For Cugobano a person's colour made no difference:

> External blackness... is as innocent and natural as spots in leopards... The difference of colour and complexion, which it has pleased God to appoint among men, are no more unbecoming unto either of them, than the different shades of the rainbow are unseemly to the whole.

It is interesting that in the modern era Desmond Tutu and Nelson Mandela chose to refer to South Africa as it emerged from apartheid as 'the rainbow nation'.

Cugobano was aware that many people were saying the white working classes were just as badly off as the slaves and he took issue with that:

> It may be true… that some of them suffer greater hardships than many of the slaves; but, bad as it is, the poorest in England would not change their situation for that of slaves… For the slaves, like animals, are bought and sold, and dealt with as their capricious owners may think fit.

Many bookshops refused to stock his book because it made a number of radical proposals. For example, Cugoano urged that all existing colonial officials should be replaced, that all slave ships should be stopped by a naval blockade, and that slave owners should be punished. He also made clear he thought it was the duty of every slave to resist and hinted that the alternative to abolition might be a slave rebellion on a massive scale:

> To some what I have said may appear as the rattling leaves of autumn, that may soon be blown away and whirled in a vortex where few can hear and know… [but] the voice of our complaint implies a vengeance, because of the great iniquity that you have done, and because of the cruel injustice done unto us Africans; and it ought to sound in your ears as the rolling waves around your circumambient shores; and if it is not hearkened unto, it may yet arise with a louder voice, as the rolling thunder, and it may increase in the force of its volubility, not only to shake the leaves of the most stout in heart, but to rend the mountains before them, and to cleave in pieces the rocks under them, and to go on with fury to smite the stoutest oaks in the forest; and even to make that which is strong… become as stubble.

Everyone seemed to execrate it, though no one thought of its abolition
Thomas Clarkson abolitionist in The History of the Rise, Progress, and Accomplishment of the Abolition of the Slave Trade *in 1839*

Clarkson's involvement with the Sierra Leone scheme led him to abandon his planned ordination within the Church so he could continue working alongside Sharp and others. He felt God was calling him to organise a political campaign that would not just demand the creation of a colony for free blacks but which would demand an end to slavery. Clarkson had a gift of encouraging people to believe they could make a difference and he reached out to others who were just beginning to appreciate the immorality of enslavement. Among these was a twenty-seven year-old evangelical Christian from Kingston upon Hull named William Wilberforce, who had been an M.P. for almost seven years and who came from a mercantile background. The two men were to become close colleagues for the next fifty years.

Wilberforce's father had died in 1768 when William was just nine years old and so he had moved to London to live with an uncle and aunt. The latter was a great admirer of John Wesley and had many contacts with Methodists. Wilberforce's mother became so fearful that her son was going to turn Methodist that she had him moved to an Anglican boarding school when he was thirteen. His education at Pocklington School and then at Cambridge University and his subsequent decision to enter Parliament did not entirely erase his evangelical leanings. In 1784 he resolved to cease living a life devoted to pleasure and to commit himself to serving God. He contemplated becoming a clergyman and discussed that option with a leading evangelical, John Newton. Newton told him he could serve God better by staying in Parliament and campaigning for the abolition of the slave trade and other social reforms. Newton was a former slave trader and he is best remembered now for the famous hymn *Amazing Grace*, written to mark his gratitude that God was prepared to forgive him for being involved in such a wicked activity:

> Amazing Grace, how sweet the sound
> That saved a wretch like me.
> I once was lost but now am found,
> Was blind, but now I see.

Wilberforce had been made well aware of the immorality of slavery by his discussions on the subject with a group known as the Testonites. These were a group of wealthy Anglicans who held regular meetings at Barham Court in Teston (hence the name), the home of the M.P. Charles Middleton, a former admiral. At the heart of these discussions was the personal testimony of the Vicar of Teston, who was James Ramsay, the author of *An Essay on the Treatment and Conversion of African Slaves in the British Sugar Colonies*. He had taken up the post there after returning from the Caribbean and it was Middleton who had encouraged him to write his book. Like Clarkson, Wilberforce was deeply moved and shocked by what Ramsay had to say.

> ***Women, like our negroes in our western plantations, are born slaves, and live prisoners all their lives***
> Judith Drake, English intellectual in *An Essay in Defence of the Female Sex* in 1696

One of the Testonites was Hannah More, a famous female playwright and social campaigner from Bristol and a friend of John Newton. Born in 1745, Hannah was the fourth of five daughters of Jacob More, a schoolmaster at Fishponds, a village just north of Bristol. He started a boarding school in Trinity Street in Bristol and Hannah and her sisters were educated at it. In 1767 she accepted a proposal of marriage from a man twenty years her senior but he allegedly jilted her at the altar and then kept postponing their wedding until she broke off their engagement in 1773. Presumably he felt guilty because he gave her an annuity that left her financially independent. She commenced regularly visiting London and made a name for herself as a poet and dramatist. Her first play, *The Inflexible Captive*, was performed at the *Theatre Royal* in Bath in 1775. Today she is best remembered not for her poetry or plays but for her promotion of women's education, her contribution to the Sunday school movement and her production of cheap tracts for the poor as part of her commitment to lifelong learning. It was probably fighting for women's rights that led her into also campaigning for the rights of the enslaved.

Wilberforce decided to work with Hannah More to create Sunday schools for the poor. His former interest in Methodism was aroused when he heard that one of Hannah's sisters was friendly with the wife of Charles Wesley and he asked Hannah to arrange for him to meet Charles. The two men got on together extremely well despite the huge gap in their ages and, through Charles, Wilberforce went on to meet John Wesley. It is reasonable to assume that one of the issues discussed was slavery. This was the situation when Clarkson made his first contact with Wilberforce in the early spring of 1787. Wilberforce's understanding of the slavery issue was as yet relatively superficial, but no one doubted that acquiring his support would be valuable. Physically he was short of stature and very slender and that gave him a kind of elf-like quality, but he was amiable and witty and a very gifted speaker. More importantly, he had powerful connections in Parliament because he had become a close friend of William Pitt the Younger, the Prime Minister. Clarkson began meeting up with Wilberforce weekly, bringing to his attention all the evidence he could muster about slavery.

The obvious choice to head an anti-slavery lobby group in Parliament was

THE SOCIETY FOR EFFECTING ABOLITION

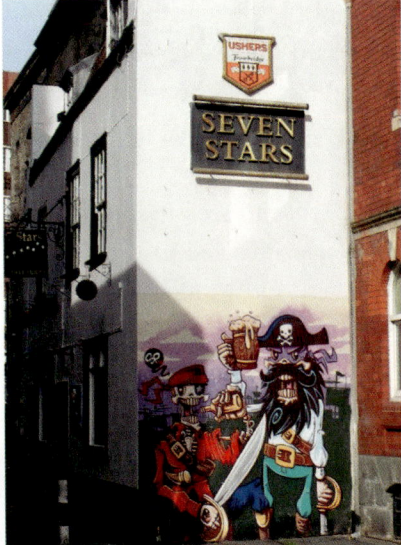

Top: the commemorative plaque of Clarkson's 1787 visit to Bristol and the Seven Stars pub today. Above left: Hannah More by J.Opie 1786. Above Wilberforce meeting John Wesley. Far left: engraving of Josiah Tucker, Dean of Gloucester. Left: Josiah Wedgwood by G.Stubbs 1780.

Charles Middleton, the leader of the Testonites, but he said that Wilberforce possessed far greater oratorical skills. On 13 March Wilberforce tentatively agreed he would become the chief advocate in Parliament for the abolition of slavery 'provided that no person more proper could be found'. He told Clarkson that it would be too big a step to persuade Parliament to abolish slavery so it made sense to seek first just the abolition of the slave trade. Once Britain was no longer involved in the trade, it would be easier to seek the total abolition of slavery. On 12 May Wilberforce held a meeting with Pitt and another of his parliamentary friends, William Grenville, under a large oak tree in the grounds of Holwood House in Kent to discuss the issue of how parliament might be persuaded to end Britain's role in the slave trade. Pitt had read Ramsay's book and it had convinced him that parliamentary action was required. The outcome was a decision that Wilberforce would present a motion to that effect and that Clarkson would create a society dedicated to bringing pressure on Parliament so that M.Ps would support it.

If you are neutral in situations of injustice, you have chosen the side of the oppressor
Desmond Tutu, South African activist and Bishop cited in *Unexpected News* in 1984

Ten days later Clarkson organised the first meeting of a Committee to organise 'The Society for Effecting the Abolition of the Slave Trade'. He took on the role of Secretary, Granville Sharp agreed to become its Chairman, and a Quaker called Samuel Hoare accepted the role of Treasurer. The Committee was predominantly made up of Quakers because, in addition to Hoare, there were eight others, one of them being William Dillwyn. It is easy to see why the Quakers were so keen. Since 1783 they had been looking at ways of creating a political lobbying group but they had been hampered by their legal position. They and other dissenting groups were forbidden by law from holding any public office and so no Quaker could enter Parliament. They therefore warmly welcomed the opportunity to belong to a non-sectarian organisation that could have a political impact. Granville Sharp took issue with the aim being just to abolish the slave trade rather than slavery, but he was outvoted. The committee was soon joined by Josiah Wedgwood, the pottery manufacture.

Winning over M.P.s would rely on producing irrefutable proof of the evils of the slave trade so in June Clarkson set off on a fact-finding tour first to Bristol and then to Liverpool. Harry Gandy agreed to act as his host in Bristol. The

Wesleys were not directly involved because Charles was very ill in London (he was to die in March 1788) and John had commitments elsewhere. Knowing the city's pro-slavery merchants constituted a strong lobbying group in Parliament, Clarkson feared what opposition he might face in the city:

> I anticipated much persecution… and questioned whether I should even get out of it alive… [but] I entered it with an undaunted spirit, determined that no labour should make me shrink, no danger, nor even persecution, deter me from my pursuit.

The ship owners and the captains of slave ships refused to see him 'as if he had been a mad dog' but Gandy introduced him to the seven Quaker families best placed to assist him and, with their guidance, Clarkson was able to speak with those in Bristol who opposed the continuation of the slave trade. The latter comprised a far larger group than he had been led to expect. This made his time in Bristol a very different experience from what subsequently happened to him in Liverpool, where very few people were opposed to slavery and where he felt he was lucky not to be killed. The fact that far more people were prepared to question the morality of slavery in Bristol than in Liverpool is often attributed to the fact that Liverpool had overtaken it as the main port involved in the slave trade. However, Bristol was still very actively involved and its sugar merchants and plantation owners were still a powerful force in favour of slavery. Some of the difference between the two cities must therefore be attributable to the different religious climate within the two cities.

We, I say, the boasted patrons of liberty and the professed advocates of the natural rights of mankind, engage deeper in this murderous traffic than any other nation whatever
  Josiah Tucker, Dean of Gloucester in *A Series of Answers to Certain Popular Objections* in 1776

For thirty years the Quakers in Bristol had been loudly voicing their condemnation of slavery but in Liverpool the Quaker movement was tiny and its leaders were reluctant to be too outspoken. The difference at the Methodist level was even greater. John and Charles Wesley had very little direct contact with Liverpool but Bristol was one of the three great centres of their work. After almost fifty years John had become so famous that he was viewed with respect even by his opponents and Charles was particularly highly regarded in

Bristol because he had made the city his home from 1748 to 1771 and after that remained a very frequent visitor. It is also fair to say that two of the Anglican clergy based in Bristol were far more vocal and long-standing opponents of slavery than any of their counterparts in Liverpool. These were John Camplin, Vicar of All Saints, and Josiah Tucker, Rector first of All Saints' Church and then of St Stephen's Church and, from 1758, Dean of Gloucester Cathedral. Tucker in particular was a very prominent figure. Passionately interested in politics and economics, he had developed a formidable understanding of trade and he thought the economic arguments being made for the continuation of the slave trade were a nonsense:

> We make slaves of these poor wretches contrary to every principle, not only of humanity and of justice, but also of national profit and advantage.

Like the Wesleys, Tucker was prepared to be outspoken because he did not fear unpopularity. The only downside to Tucker's role was his hatred of anyone who challenged his view of the Church. He would not, for example, have anything to do with the Wesleys and he encouraged Hannah More to avoid them.

Gandy arranged for Clarkson to meet not only Tucker, Camplin, and More but also the Moravian minister Henry Sulgar, who was also opposed to slavery. Some historians have been critical that Tucker, Camplin, and More enjoyed very friendly relationships with the Bristolians who were still making money from the slave trade, but that ignores how much the slave trade had inextricably linked itself with so much of the wealth in the city. Even John Wesley had found himself in the unenviable position of having to recommend that those Methodists who were entitled to vote in the 1784 Bristol election should do so for Matthew Brickdale, a known supporter of the slave trade but less hard-line than the other candidates.

Clarkson's investigation in Bristol really took off after Gandy introduced him to William Thompson, the landlord of the *Seven Stars* , a pub which boarded discharged sailors until they could find fresh employment. Thompson was known to be hostile to the slave trade because he was refusing to recruit sailors for slave ships. He disguised Clarkson as a collier and guided him so he could venture into the rough taverns and alehouses behind Broad Quay and talk direct with sailors. Today Bristol's Radical History group point out that the pub's name stems from the seven stars which form the constellation known as the Plough and this was used as a navigational tool to identify the North Star. They say it makes for an interesting coincidence that in nineteenth-century America one of the slave songs that gave coded directions on how to escape to freedom in the north was sometimes called the *Seven Stars* and the North Star was known as the Freedom Star.

Those who deny freedom to others deserve it not for themselves
    Abraham Lincoln, U.S. President in letter to Henry Pierce in April 1859

Clarkson made nineteen visits to the dockside. The sailors spoke to him about the terrible conditions suffered by the slaves but what struck him most was the appalling treatment they had also endured on the slave ships. A ship called the *Brothers* was still in port because its captain had acquired such a bad name for cruelty that no sailors could be found to man it. On its last voyage thirty-two sailors had died. Clarkson spoke to a black sailor called John Dean who had survived the voyage. Dean told him the captain had punished him for something minor by fastening him to the deck, pouring hot pitch onto his back, and cutting out bits of his flesh with hot tongs. Clarkson asked the Deputy Town Clerk about the cruelty being shown toward the sailors and he was told there was only one captain 'who did not deserve to be hanged'. Tucker used his influence to enable Clarkson to have access to the records in the Customs House. These unquestionably proved that, far from being a source of recruiting sailors, the slave trade was a cause of their loss. The mortality rate was extraordinarily high. Clarkson saw the potential to explode the myth that the captains were humane men and that the slave trade was a valuable source for training sailors.

More harrowing tales of brutality emerged, especially about life on board a ship called the *Alexander*. The ship's surgeon, Alexander Falconbridge, said he was prepared to speak publicly about what he had seen if required and the surgeon's mate, James Arnold, promised to keep a journal on his next voyage so he could provide Clarkson with more detailed evidence. Of all the cases he heard, Clarkson was drawn to one in particular. He met three sailors who were all recovering from a voyage on the slave ship the *Thomas*. They asked him to investigate the murder of one of its crew, Willian Lines, by the ship's chief mate. He met the mother of Lines and four other members of the crew, who all said they were willing to testify to the murder. Clarkson decided that he could not let such a crime go unpunished and so, before leaving Bristol, he had the mate arrested and imprisoned whilst he could arrange for him to be tried in London at the Admiralty Court. He took this step even though he had been warned that the merchants would ensure the collapse of the case. That was what happened. The case was dismissed because none of Clarkson's four witnesses made it to

London. Two of the sailors were bribed away to sea and the other two were taken away to work in a Welsh colliery. By the time Clarkson found them it was too late. However, what the anti-abolitionists could not do was dispute the documentary evidence that Clarkson had acquired on the heavy mortality rate among the sailors.

The Society for effecting the Abolition of the Slave Trade was officially launched in the summer of 1787. Each member of the Committee was asked to circulate twelve copies of a letter announcing its formation to friends. Because of the membership of the Committee most letters were sent to Quakers around the country but Sharp, Clarkson, and Wilberforce did what they could to draw in Anglicans. On receipt of his letter John Wesley immediately voiced his support in a letter to Samuel Hoare, the Society's Treasurer:

> I have long wished for the rolling away of this… reproach not only from religion, but to humanity itself… Mr Clarkson's design strikes at the root of it. And if it can be put into execution will be a lasting honour to the British nation… With men this is impossible; but we know all things are possible to God! What little I can do to promote this excellent work I shall do with pleasure.

He also wrote to Clarkson and, although that letter has been lost, we have Clarkson's summary of it. Wesley accepted that it made sense to seek the abolition of the slave trade as a first step towards the abolition of slavery. He warned him that they must expect to face intense opposition from those profiting from slavery and that some of that opposition would be duplicitous and underhand. He promised to reprint a new edition of his own *Thoughts Upon Slavery* and he asked for God's blessing on all their endeavours.

Another recipient, Thomas Cooper, wrote four letters to the *Manchester Chronicle* praising the efforts of Sharp, Clarkson, Wesley and others and incorporated within them the best evidence and the best arguments of all those who had written in favour of an end to slavery. He singled out for particular praise the Quakers, encouraged all Methodists to follow the excellent example set by their leader, and urged those who belonged to the Church of England to become proactive supporters of the new Society. The letters were edited and published nationally.

The idea that some lives matter less is the root of all that is wrong with the world
Paul Farmer, American physician and anthropologist in *The Company of the Poor* in 2013

The Society benefitted most from having the input of Josiah Wedgwood. Today he is best remembered as the great pottery entrepreneur who founded the Wedgwood Company, but he was also a great innovator in the field of marketing. He pioneered, among other things, self-service, direct mail, illustrated catalogues, money-back guarantees, buy-one-get-one-free, and travelling salesmen armed with display boxes. He had already marketed Methodism by creating the first bust of John Wesley and other Wesleyana. He offered to produce an emblem for the new Society. It used to be thought that Wedgwood asked the sculptor Henry Webber to design something based on the cameo gemstones of the classical world and that Webber then came up with the idea of a kneeling slave with his hands in chains, an image that was noble but not threatening. However, there is now a suggestion that Wedgwood may have asked Webber to base his design on an engraving of a slave made by the Northumbrian artist Thomas Beswick. Either way, Wedgwood's modeller, William Hackwood, took Webber's design and carved the figure in black jasper against a white background. Above it was written a direct challenge to view the black man as an equal: 'Am I not a man and a brother?' Wedgwood undertook the cost of its mass production and distribution.

It rapidly established itself as the emblem of the anti-slavery movement, becoming the forerunner of all today's badges, printed T-shirts, mugs, etc that are used to advertise a product or a cause. Men and women acquired the Wedgwood cameos for display on hair pins, pendants, snuff box lids, bracelets, and even shoe buckles. Copies were sent to America and became equally fashionable there. A version with a female slave and the words 'Am I not a woman and sister?' appeared there in 1832 and it was turned into a glass embossing seal by the American Anti-Slavery Society. Some people today criticise the cameo's design, saying it provided no focus on the barbarities being inflicted on slaves and that it was wrong to portray an African begging for his freedom rather than being prepared to fight for it. They have a point, especially as in the nineteenth the image was often made to look even more 'humble', but this still seems a rather negative response given the huge boost the cameo gave to the cause of setting Africans free. Wedgwood's emblem is still much in evidence and in 2010

Left: use of kneeling African in Beswick's engraving and Wedgwood's cameo 1787. Above: The chained African, one of a pair of candle stands at Dyrham Park. Below: the image used in a plaque, a coin, and a painting.

The Society for Effecting Abolition

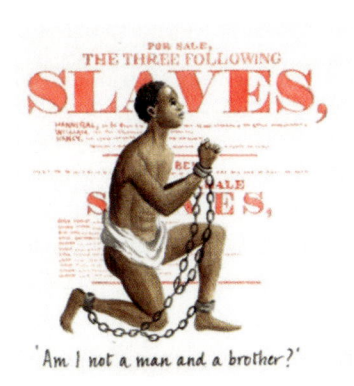

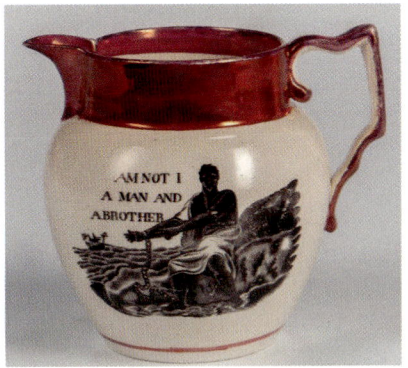

The emblem adapted for a first-day cover, a tee-shirt, a jug and an egg cup. A 19th-century print emphasises the humble begging which is why the emblem has become unpopular with some black people. Right: the female version on poster and in 1832 seal, and 2010 updated version about modern human trafficking.

361

an updated version of the female version was produced by the modern-day abolitionist Ken King to try and encourage people to tackle human trafficking. On its reverse side was cited a quote from Proverbs 31 v 8-9:

> Speak up for those who cannot speak for themselves, for the rights of all those who are destitute. Speak up and judge fairly; defend the rights of the poor and needy.

Clarkson recognised that part of the strength of the Quaker and Methodist organisations lay in their regional and local networks and so he suggested the Society should not be just a body in London but a nationwide organisation with regional committees whose members could lobby local M.P.s. Bristol was the first city to create a committee and it held its first meeting on 28 January 1788 at the Guildhall. It had twenty members. They were a mix of merchants, manufacturers, city officials, doctors and clergy, and most denominations were represented. Among its members were three Anglican clergy (Dean Tucker, John Camplin and Dr John Hallam, who was the Dean of Bristol), four prominent Quakers (Harry Gandy, Thomas Rutter, Matthew Wright, and Joseph Beck), two Baptists (Caleb Evans and John Harris, the minister and dean at Broadmead Baptist Church), and a Presbyterian (John Prior Estlin, the minister at Lewin's Mead). The surprise names among these are Caleb Evans, because there is no prior record of him opposing slavery, and John Prior Estlin, because some prominent slave-trading families worshipped at Lewins' Mead. Estlin may have decided to become more of a radical because he was influenced by Unitarian thinking. The one notable gap was the absence of a Methodist minister. That was because John Wesley was not resident in Bristol, although Tucker would not have wanted to work alongside him if he had been. There is reference to one member, Thomas Wright, being 'a dissenting minister' and he may have been a Methodist leader, although as yet Methodism had not broken away from the Church of England. Both in Britain and America there are references to a Methodist preacher named Thomas Wright, although the name is a common one.

The present alarming crisis respecting the abolition of the African trade, operates so strongly on my mind that I am resolved to contract... all my concerns in the West Indies

Bristol sugar merchant John Pinney in letter to his agent in Feb 1788

The first task of the regional committees was to produce signed petitions that could be sent to Parliament and the Bristol branch agreed to do that immediately. It was this that prompted the sugar producer John Pinney to panic and write to his agent in Nevis:

> The present alarming crisis, respecting the abolition of the African Trade, operates so strongly on my mind, that I am resolved to contract, with the utmost expedition all my concerns in the West Indies. Never again, upon my own private account, will I enter into a new engagement in that part of the world.

Petitions were successfully produced in ninety-three places and some sent in more than one. This was a remarkable achievement, although producing the petitions took up to a year in some places and they varied in how they were drawn up. Most were just signed by those judged locally to be significant citizens but twenty-four towns did succeed in sending in petitions that had been signed by the public. Most of these were in the north where a strong artisan and working-class culture had developed because of the Industrial Revolution. Bristol's petition had eight hundred signatures. The petitions produced across the country varied in what they requested. Some asked for the abolition of slavery, some for the abolition of the slave trade, and some just for better regulation of the trade. The suggested timescale for reform also differed with some asking for immediate action and others wanting a gradual process of change. All this made the Society appreciate it would have to clarify exactly what it did want to see happen.

Slavery is the bane of man and the abomination of heaven
James Tallmadge, American lawyer and politician in debate in U.S. House of Representatives in 1819

Parliament felt obliged to respond to the obvious growing public interest even before the bulk of the petitions arrived. In February 1788 it agreed to set up a committee to investigate the slave trade. Wilberforce supported the move but this did not go down well with some of the other abolitionists who saw it simply as a delaying device by those who opposed abolition. In March the Society of Merchant Venturers lobbied Parliament not to harm the African trade. John Wesley travelled to Bristol and announced that he would preach against the slave trade from the pulpit of the New Room. For the 85 year old to preach in public on the topic at this heated juncture was a brave step. He wrote in his journal that the chapel at the New Room was 'filled from end to end with high and low, rich and poor' for the occasion, but the meeting was at times chaotic, probably because of the impact of a hostile mob:

> About the middle of the discourse, while there was on every side attention still as night, a vehement noise arose, none could tell why and shot like lightning through the whole congregation. The terror and confusion was inexpressible. You might have imagined a city taken by storm. The people rushed upon each other with the utmost violence; the benches were broken in pieces, and nine-tenths of the congregation appeared to be struck with the same panic. In about six minutes the storm ceased, almost as suddenly as it rose. And all being calm, I went on without the least interruption. It was the strangest incident of the kind I ever remember and believe none can account for it without supposing some preternatural influence. Satan fought lest his kingdom be delivered up.

By this stage John Wesley's age and national stature had made him a celebrity and so Bristol's mayor invited him to preach before the aldermen of the city in the Mayor's Chapel of St Mark in College Green on Sunday 16 March. The dignitaries may have got more than they expected because Wesley had no problem choosing his text – he preached on the story of Dives and Lazarus and condemned those who put their faith in worldly wealth. At this time Hannah More was beginning to argue for a boycott on slave-produced sugar and, not long after Wesley's sermon was given, the *Bristol Gazette* published verse written by William Cowper, one of her friends:

> I own I am shock'd at the purchase of slaves
> And fear those who buy them and sell them are knaves;
> What I hear of their hardships, their tortures, and groans,
> Is almost enough to drive pity from stones.
> I pity them greatly, but I must be mum,
> For how could we do without sugar and rum?
> Especially sugar, so needful we see;
> What, give up our dessert, our coffee and tea?

The Society For Effecting Abolition

Above from left to right: William Pitt the Younger by J. Hoppner c1806, Ann Yearsley in 1814 print and Mary Darby Robinson by T. Gainsborough 1781. Right: Matthew Brickdale by H.Singleton 1812 and Henry Cruger by G.Stuart 1781. Below: John Wesley addressing the Mayor and Corporation of Bristol by H. Holt Yates Titcomb 1918.

> **Talk of the abuses of slavery! Humbug! The thing itself is the essence of all abuse!**
>
> Harriet Beecher Stowe, American abolitionist and novelist in *Uncle Tom's Cabin* in 1852

The Committee of the Society for effecting the Abolition of the Slave Trade encouraged the publication of anti-slavery pamphlets and books to arouse 'the general moral feeling of the nation'. Hannah More played her part by publishing a number of poems on slavery, some written by her and some by her female friends. For example, one of her proteges, Ann Yearsley, wrote *A Poem on the Inhumanity of the Slave Trade*, which attacked the moral hypocrisy of punishing those who committed theft whilst letting those who stole men go free:

> I scorn the cry of avarice, or the trade that drains
> a fellow creatures' blood…
> Laws, with prudence, hang the meagre thief
> that from his neighbour steals a slender sum,
> though famine drives him on…
> Say, doth this law, that dooms the thief, protect
> the wretch who makes another's life his prey,
> by hellish force to take it at his will?

There was criticism in Bristol of women getting involved in the debate and, because Yearsley was a farmer's daughter, her opponents mockingly referred to her as the milkmaid poet 'Lactilla'. The right of women to express their views was staunchly defended in a letter published in *Bonner and Middleton's Bristol Journal* and simply signed' Amelia'. It is thought the author may have been another of Hannah More's pupils, the Bristol born actress Mary Darby Robinson. She later wrote a number of a number of anti-slavery poems, of which the most popular were *The Negro Girl* and *The African*. The *Negro Girl* portrayed black and white as sharing a common humanity: 'whate'er their tints may be, their souls are still the same'. *The African* depicted the slave traders and slave owners as sexual predators – 'the wan tyrant whose licentious touch seals the dark fate of the slave's despair'.

In the late summer of 1788 the M.P. for Oxford University, Sir William Dolben, put forward a private member's bill to restrict the number of slaves that a ship could legally carry, based on the ship's tonnage. The defenders of slavery argued the restriction would make slave voyages unprofitable, but even with the new regulations a slave had only half the space allocated to any white convicted criminal being transported overseas as a punishment. The leading abolitionists did not like Dolben's bill because they feared lessening the evil would weaken the argument for total abolition. Ramsay's comment was 'Regulate murder as much as you please, it still remains murder'. The bill was passed so all the abolitionists could then do was take comfort in the fact that the inhumanity of the slave trade had been marginally reduced.

How can we hesitate a moment to abolish this commerce in human flesh which has for too long disgraced our country and which our example would no doubt contribute to abolish in every corner of the globe?
William Pitt the Younger, Prime Minister speaking to Parliament in 1791

William Pitt the Younger agreed to give a free vote on a private member's bill to abolish the slave trade in 1789. Inevitably those opposed to abolition sought to rally their adherents across the country by creating their own regional committees to produce pro-slavery petitions prior to that free vote. An anti-abolition alliance was formed that included not just commercial interests but members of the royal family, most of the admirals, and many landowners. The group set up in Bristol to defend the slave trade had forty-seven members and was under the control of the Society of Merchant Venturers. Matthew Brickdale and Henry Cruger, the two M.P.s for Bristol, agreed to voice the commercial arguments in favour of retaining Bristol's involvement in the slave trade and to present to Parliament any pro-slavery petitions that could be produced by Bristol Corporation and the city's merchants and manufacturers. The Merchant Venturers had largely funded the creation of the *Theatre Royal* and so they got its management to stage a comic opera called *Inkle and Yarico* in the hope this would reinforce racial stereotypes.

To counter the pro-slavery backlash the abolitionists came up with something as effective as Wedgwood's emblem. William Elford, a partner in a banking firm in Plymouth and an amateur artist, created a print that portrayed tight-packing on a Liverpool slave ship called the *Brookes*. In Clarkson's words, it 'seemed to make an instantaneous impression of horror upon all who saw it'. It is still the illustration that most books on slavery include. Prior to the Parliamentary debate the Privy Council produced a remarkably detailed two-volume report on the slave trade based on evidence produced by Clarkson and others. On 12 May 1789 Wilberforce opened the debate in Parliament on his bill to abolish the slave trade with a three-and-a-half hour long speech that summarised the evidence. William Pitt then spoke on behalf of the bill and he was strongly seconded by Edmund Burke. Both men gave brilliant speeches. However, Parliament had been flooded with pro-slavery petitions, among them one from Bristol.

The Bristol petition had been produced by a committee chaired by the sugar merchant William Miles and it stated that the commerce and revenue of the nation relied on the trade with the West Indies and that it constituted 'at least three fifth of the commerce of the port of Bristol'. If the slave trade were to be abolished, it would result in the city's commercial collapse and thus lead to 'the ruin of thousands'. One of the city's M.P.s, Matthew Brickdale, was ill so it fell solely to Henry Cruger to speak in Parliament on behalf of Bristol. He said to end the slave trade would destroy the viability of all the British-owned plantations because the plantation owners from other nations would continue to benefit from the use of slaves. Britain would lose all its colonies and it would cease to be a world power. Why should the nation commit economic suicide when most slaves were well cared for and indeed better off than most of the workers in Britain? The slavers in Liverpool and London were even more vociferous in declaring abolition would create chaos and they were strongly backed by the cities of Birmingham, Manchester, and Liverpool, all of whose manufacturing wealth was closely linked to the transatlantic trade. The bill to end Britain's role in the slave trade was defeated on the grounds that the Privy Council report was insufficient and a special parliamentary enquiry was required before any major change could be considered.

Where we have (mostly) condemned slavery, we have refused to condemn its defenders, choosing to view their actions not as villainous but historical anomalies. We allow them the excuse of being 'products of their time', as if they had no hand in shaping the political and social dynamics of that time. We give them the cover of states' rights', as though that has not always meant further tyranny visited upon black people
Mychel Denzel Smith in *Historical Amnesia About Slavery Is A Tool of White Supremacy* in 2017

If the battle had been lost, the war was not over. The publication of Olaudah Equiano's autobiography created a wave of fresh support for the abolitionist cause and in January 1790 Wilberforce managed to persuade Parliament to set up a select committee to deliver its special parliamentary enquiry into the slave trade. This was about the speediest method possible. By this stage John Wesley's health was breaking down, but he told one of his friends in March:

> I would do anything that is in my power toward the extirpation of that trade which is a scandal not only to Christianity, but humanity.

The same level of determination drove on Clarkson, Wilberforce, Sharp, and all the other abolitionist leaders. Clarkson, for example, visited 320 ships in various ports and travelled 7,000 miles in the course of 1790 collecting more information. The creation of what is known as 'the Clapham Sect' to promote a revival in the Church and to generate a more moral society helped co-ordinate the efforts of Clarkson, Wilberforce and Sharp with other key Anglican supporters, such as Hannah More, the M.P. William Smith and the merchant banker and politician Henry Thornton. Whenever they could its members worshipped at Holy Trinity Church on Clapham Common (hence the name). In 1792 it acquired as its rector John Venn, the son of Henry Venn, a clergyman who had been friendly with George Whitefield and a number of the clergy linked to the Methodist movement.

Delay of justice is injustice
       Walter Savage Landor, English poet in *Imaginary Conversations* in 1824

Poor whites and their children were often subjected to working conditions that were little better than slavery. The pictures on this page illustrate a few examples: children carry clay in a brickyard; child labour in a factory; child and adult workers in coal mines; a family found dead from starvation; a child turning the wheel for a potter making sugar loaf moulds. Bottom right: William Hogarth's famous portrayal of how the poor turned to gin to drown their sorrows.

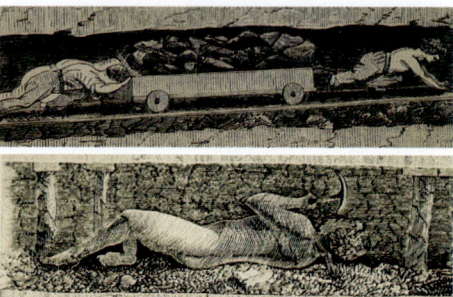

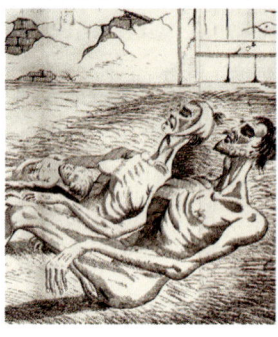

6.

THE BATTLE TO END THE SLAVE TRADE

The slave breeders and slave traders are a small, odious and detested class among you; and yet in politics they dictate the course of you all, and are as completely your masters as you are the master of your own negroes
Abraham Lincoln, American President in letter to J.Speed in 1855

Many of the abolitionists supported the French Revolution at its outset in 1789 because they also wanted to see radical political and social reform at home. One obvious example is provided by the paintings and poetry of Willam Blake. He presented the slavery issue as just one of a catalogue of issues requiring action. Among the topics covered in his work are the impact of senseless wars, the hypocrisy of conventional religion, the treatment of women, and the appalling social effects of the Industrial Revolution. Within this context slavery had to be ended primarily because it was an abuse of power and a denial of human equality. In Blake's 1789 poem *The Little Black Boy* a black boy speaks of how a white boy grows up with an unearned sense of superiority whilst a black boy grows up with an undeserved sense of inferiority. Society makes it impossible for the black boy to portray the 'whiteness' of his heart. Only in heaven is skin colour unable to obscure the essential brotherhood of black and white:

> I am black, but O! my soul is white;
> White as an angel is the English child:
> but I am black, as if bereaved of light…
> When I from black and he from white cloud free
> and round the tent of God like lambs we joy…
> I'll stand and stroke his silver hair ,
> And be like him, and he will then love me.

It has been suggested that the inspiration for Blake's little black boy may have been Peter Panah, a young African rescued from slavery in the spring of 1788 by one of Harry Gandy's friends, a Swede called Carl Bernhard Wadstrom, who spotted him in London's dockyards. If Blake's black boy was Panah, the story does not have a happy ending. Panah was sent to a school in Croydon to be educated but died of consumption in 1790 when he was about eighteen years old. In a subsequent poem, *Visions of the Daughters of Albion*, published in 1792, Blake produced a remarkable condemnation of the prejudices directed at both women and slaves. In it he describes a female slave being raped by a slave driver and how the man she loves then blames her and not the rapist because he cannot believe that a black woman has any inherent purity.

Another bill to abolish the slave trade was introduced into Parliament in November 1790 following the completion of the new investigative report and a general election in the summer. However, Parliament did not get round to debating the bill until March 1791. In the interim the abolitionists tried to encourage more of the public to join their cause. Wesley, for example, published anti-slavery articles in his *Arminian Magazine*. One of the items he printed was a 1788 poem called *The Negro's Complaint* written by William Cowper:

> Forced from home and all its pleasures,
> Afric's coast I left forlorn;
> to increase a stranger's treasures,
> o'er the raging billows borne.
> Men from England bought and sold me,
> paid my price in paltry gold;
> but though their hearts have enrolled me,
> minds are never to be sold.
>
> Still in thought as free as ever,
> What are England's rights, I ask,
> me from my delights to sever,
> me to torture, me to task?
> Fleecy locks and black complexion
> cannot forfeit nature's claim:
> skins may differ, but affection
> dwells in black and white the same…
>
> Is there, as ye sometimes tell us,
> is there one who reigns on high?
> Has he bid you buy and sell us?
> speaking from his throne – the sky?
> Ask him, if your knotted scourges,
> fetters, blood-extorting screws,

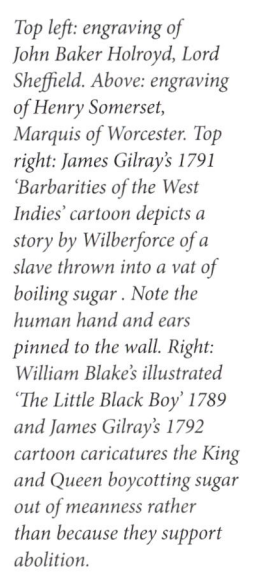

Top left: engraving of John Baker Holroyd, Lord Sheffield. Above: engraving of Henry Somerset, Marquis of Worcester. Top right: James Gilray's 1791 'Barbarities of the West Indies' cartoon depicts a story by Wilberforce of a slave thrown into a vat of boiling sugar . Note the human hand and ears pinned to the wall. Right: William Blake's illustrated 'The Little Black Boy' 1789 and James Gilray's 1792 cartoon caricatures the King and Queen boycotting sugar out of meanness rather than because they support abolition.

are the means which duty urges,
agents of his will to use?…

Deem our nations brutes no longer,
till some reason ye shall find,
worthier of regard and stronger,
than the colours of your kind;
slaves of gold, whose sordid dealings
tarnish all your boasted powers,
prove that ye have human feelings
ere ye proudly question ours.

The pro-slavery lobbyists recognised that the tide had turned in terms of the public perception of the slave trade and that arguments about the commercial necessity of the trade only made them look morally adrift. What was required was a moral argument in favour of retaining the trade and they came up with one. They claimed the slaves were not ready to receive their freedom and it would be morally wrong to act speedily. In Bristol the election had produced two new M.P.s because Matthew Brickdale was replaced by Henry Somerset, Marquis of Worcester and Henry Cruger by John Baker Holroyd, Lord Sheffield. It was the latter who effectively became Bristol's voice in Parliament. He reiterated why the slave trade was commercially essential and made clear those who upheld the trade were not averse to accepting reforms that would ensure humanitarian treatment of both slaves and sailors. Then he moved onto the moral argument saying there was a need for a paternalistic approach because any rapid emancipation would be disastrous for the Africans. They simply would not survive if they were removed from their white masters. All his views were subsequently published in a substantial pamphlet. The bill to abolish the slave trade was defeated by 163 votes to 88 and the news of this was celebrated in Bristol by the ringing of church bells, the firing of cannon on Brandon Hill, a firework display, and the granting of a half-day holiday to workmen and sailors.

As an abstract question, freedom must be held preferable to slavery, but I very much doubt whether, if the Negroes in the West Indies were to have their freedom granted them, they would be nearly as happy as that are now?
James Tobin, sugar trader speaking to the committee set up by Parliament in 1790

A dying Wesley wrote a final letter to Wilberforce, encouraging him to continue campaigning. He told him that if he tried to act alone he would never achieve success because 'the opposition of men and devils' would overcome him. However, he could not fail if he had God on his side:

> If God be for you, who can be against you? Are all of them stronger than God? O be not weary in well-doing! Go on, in the name of God and in the power of his might, till even American slavery (the vilest that ever saw sun) shall vanish away before it.

He added that his reading of Equiano's autobiography had made him realise even more the sheer unjustness of a law that meant 'a man who has a black skin, being wronged or outraged by a white man, can have no redress… [because] the oath of a black against a white goes for nothing'. He ended his letter by praying that God would continue to strengthen Wilberforce 'in this and all things'. There is no doubt that the letter meant much to Wilberforce and helped sustain him in what was to prove a long and drawn out war of attrition.

How can you carry on the slave trade moderately? How can a country be pillaged and destroyed in moderation? We cannot modify injustice
    Charles James Fox leading Whig politician in speech to Parliament in April 1792

The frustration felt among the abolitionists found expression in a campaign that was not initiated by the Society. Hannah More and many others began advocating that people should boycott buying sugar. The key tract to encourage a boycott was written by a Baptist bookseller in London called William Fox. It was called *An Address to the People of Great Britain on the Propriety of Abstaining from West Indian Sugar and Rum*. It said that a boycott was the only way of undermining the wealthy slave lobby because Parliament was 'not only unwilling but perhaps unable to apply a remedy.' Fox argued that anyone who bought sugar was complicit in the suffering of the slaves who had produced it and he memorably suggested that to eat a pound of sugar was to consume two ounces of human flesh. Some ridiculed this approach. For example, a spoof letter allegedly written by a six year old boy appeared in *Felix Farley's Bristol Journal*:

> I cannot think… how anybody… can handle gold or silver or find themselves with silver spoons or forks, for, if eating sugar is eating negroe's flesh, sure

every time anybody puts a fork or spoon in their mouth, it is putting a dead negro's finger or toe there.

The defenders of the slave trade dubbed those who agreed to boycott sugar as 'anti-saccharites' and attacked their stance as being based on an ill-informed and over-emotional response to slavery. Typical of the kind of nonsense put out to counter the boycott was a 1791 poem written by James Boswell, a writer now best remembered for his biography of Samuel Johnson:

> Lo then, in yonder fragrant isle
> Where Nature ever seems to smile,
> The cheerful gang!--the negroes see
> Perform the task of industry:
> Ev'n at their labour hear them sing,
> While time flies quick on downy wing;
> Finish'd the bus'ness of the day,
> No human beings are more gay:
> Of food, clothes, cleanly lodging sure,
> Each has his property secure;
> Their wives and children are protected,
> In sickness they are not neglected;
> And when old age brings a release,
> Their grateful days they end in peace.

They could not stem the tide. 70,000 copies of William Fox's tract were circulated and other writers also produced tracts on the subject. By the end of 1791 Clarkson estimated from his travels around the country that 25,000 families had given up purchasing sugar. This significantly impacted on the government's sugar revenue. In a sense the boycott provided individuals, especially the disenfranchised, with a way of feeling they could achieve abolition despite what Parliament had done. The Committee of the Society for Effecting the Abolition of the Slave Trade declared:

> The luxuries of Rum and Sugar can only be obtained by tearing asunder those ties of affection which unite our species and exalt our nature.

Wilberforce asked the first Methodist Conference that met after Wesley's death to help him produce an anti-slavery petition that would more than match the petitions of the supporters of the slave trade. The response was overwhelming because Samuel Bradburn, who was one of the movement's key leaders, issued thousands of copies of a tract entitled *An Address to the People called Methodists; concerning the criminality of encouraging slavery*. The Methodists managed to obtain 229,426 signatures and a further 122,978 signatures came from other nonconformist groups. In total 519 petitions against the slave trade were sent to Parliament in 1792 prior to Wilberforce introducing another abolition bill.

> *Africa, Africa. Your sufferings have been the theme that has arrested and engages my heart. Your sufferings no tongue can express, no language impart*
> William Wilberforce in speech to Parliament in April 1792

The parliamentary debate was given massive coverage in Bristol, not least because Wilberforce signalled out the bad behaviour of some of the city's slave traders. This included speaking out against three ships that had been involved in bombarding New Calabar and, as recounted earlier, accusing John Kimber, the captain of the Bristol ship the *Recovery*, of assaulting and killing a fifteen year-old African girl who had refused to dance naked for him. William Pitt, as Tory Prime Minister, delivered arguably the greatest speech of his distinguished career in favour of passing the abolition bill, saying it was time to restore Africans 'to the rank of human beings'. Charles James Fox, the leader of the Whig opposition and a formidable political debater, gave an equally brilliant speech. Unfortunately the bill was successfully amended by William Pitt's friend, Henry Dundas, Treasurer of the Navy and the leading politician on the board of the East India Company. In essence Dundas argued that overnight abolition was too destabilising and that what was required was a series of steps that would gradually lead to abolition. It was, in the words of the historian Hugh Thomas, 'a ruse for indefinite postponement' but the amended bill for the.gradual abolition of the slave trade was passed by 230 votes to 85.

> *Since all Europe is in a state of confusion, it would be highly imprudent to adopt any untried expedient*
> Edmund Lechmere, M.P. for Worcester in speech to Parliament in1794

A provisional date was set for achieving abolition by 1796 but no one thought that timescale would be met and events in France guaranteed that. The fact that many of the abolitionists had supported the French Revolution at its outset now put them in a bad light because in 1792 the Jacobin government in Paris commenced what soon became known as 'the Terror', a series of executions and massacres that deeply shocked Britain. From the moment the French government executed Louis XVI in January 1793 support for abolition markedly began to fall. The following month Britain went to war with France and the pro-slavery lobby group was able to accuse the abolitionists of undermining the political stability of the country. Despite this, Clarkson and Wilberforce continued to press for abolition and to present bills to Parliament but there was no chance of success, especially as Pitt's focus had to be the war effort not abolishing the slave trade.

I see my country still given up without remorse to the unbridled career of slave trading speculators. The monster, instead of being cut off, as the first burst of honest indignation promised, has been more fondly nourished than before, and fattened with fuller means of misery and murder

James Stephen, brother-in-law of Wilberforce, in 1804 anti-slavery tract

---

Far from declining, the slave trade flourished as never before. The decision of the French government to end its role in the slave trade and to abolish slavery opened up opportunities for British expansion. In addition a whole new market opened up in the Spanish colony of Cuba and there was a boom in slave-produced cotton following the invention in America of the cotton gin. The growth in the slave trade was matched by a massive reduction in sympathy towards Africans. That stemmed in part from the French use of black soldiers in the war against Britain in the Caribbean. The hostility can be seen in the ill treatment given to enemy prisoners in October 1796 after the French garrison on St Lucia surrendered. Of the male prisoners 2,080 were black (and therefore almost certainly former slaves) and only 333 were white. All the Africans were imprisoned in cold and damp cells in Portchester Castle and it took lobbying from the Royal Naval surgeon Dr James Johnson to persuade the government to move them into less barbaric conditions on board two prison ships.

It was the traders in Liverpool and in America rather than those in Bristol that took the lead in the resurgence of the slave trade but plenty of Bristol's merchants and manufacturers had very strong interests in the Caribbean trade and hoped to see their share in the slave trade ultimately revive. The historian Madge Dresser has analysed the theatre shows being presented in Bristol in the 1790s and she has shown how the popular shows either did not mention slavery or presented Africans in a bad light. A good example was the play *Obi or*

Three-Fingered Jack which was billed as being based on a true story and which portrayed the terrifying exploits of a black robber who was prepared to practice black magic against the Christian whites in Jamaica. Slaveowners in the city became more comfortable about reasserting their right to recapture escaped slaves. Hence the instances to try and challenge that examined in an earlier chapter, involving Hannah More and Harry Gandy.

> *Ye came as helpless infants to the world;*
> *Ye feel alike the infirmities of nature;*
> *And at last moulder into common clay.*
> *Why then these vain distinctions?*
>
> Robert Southey, poet in *Watt Tyler*, a play written in his youth and eventually published in 1817

It was left to an egotistical but well-meaning Bristol bookseller, Joseph Cottle, to be the voice for abolition. Between 1791 and 1799 he published books of poems that contained anti-slavery verse and in the process he encouraged the career of three great poets: Robert Southey, Samuel Taylor Coleridge, and William Wordsworth. Born in 1770, Joseph had been educated for a couple of years in a school in Hanham run by a Methodist, Richard Henderson, and that had strongly influenced him. His family knew the Wesleys well because Charles Wesley's daughter was very friendly with Joseph's sisters, who attended the school created in Park Street by Hannah More. His interest in the abolition movement also stemmed from his family's membership of the Baptist Church and his elder brother Amos' membership of the evangelical Clapham Sect. Both Amos and Joseph had been supporters of Granville Sharp's Sierra Leone scheme. They opened a bookshop on the corner of High Street and Corn Street in 1791. Joseph's anti-slavery verse has not always been well-regarded because he was careful to condemn not just British involvement in slavery but also the black slavers who provided the bulk of the slaves:

> The white men, and the black, pre-eminent,
> Each in his way… lured by gold

Mentioning the role of black people in enslaving Africans is usually not appreciated by those who prefer to focus entirely on the role of the white Europeans.

He is best remembered for the poetry of others that he published. This included the anti-slavery verse of Ann Yearsley, the milkmaid poetess, and of Robert Lovell, the son of a wealthy Quaker merchant in Bristol. In one of his poems Lovell summed up the slave trade in just two lines:

> Their motive avarice, and trade their plea,
> Their means oppression, and their commerce man.

Did Jesus teach the abolition of it? No! He taught those principles of which the necessary effect was to abolish all slavery. He prepared the mind for the reception before he poured the blessing. You ask me what the friend of universal equality should do. I answer: 'Talk not politics. Preach the Gospel!'
Samuel Taylor Coleridge, poet in letter to his brother November 1794

Lovell introduced Cottle first to Robert Southey and then, in 1794, to Samuel Taylor Coleridge, who had come to Bristol because of his friendship with Southey. The two men were at that stage courting two sisters who lived in Bristol and whom they eventually married. Joseph was captivated by both men and introduced them to a wide circle of his friends, including Hannah More. By 1795 he was organising them to give public lectures and Coleridge chose to speak on 'political and moral subjects'. Slavery was an obvious topic. Coleridge said no one taking the name 'Christian' could uphold slavery:

> They who believe in God, believe him to be the loving parent of all men. And is it possible that those who really believe and fear the Father should fearlessly authorise the oppression of his own children? The slavery and tortures and the most horrible murders of tens of thousands of his children.

Cottle provided the financial support that enabled Coleridge and his friend, William Wordsworth, to devote time to writing their poetry. Also in the group was Charles Lamb, later to win fame not as a poet but as the author of *The Essays of Elia* and *Tales from Shakespeare*. Southey, Coleridge, Wordsworth and Lamb had all had one or two poems printed, but it was Cottle who gave their work far greater exposure, particularly by publishing the poetry of Coleridge and Wordsworth in *Lyrical Ballads* in 1798. This was produced just a year before his bookshop, which had already had to move to less good premises in Wine Street, went bankrupt. It included Coleridge's *The Rime of the Ancient Mariner* which contained an attack on slavery:

THE BATTLE TO END THE SLAVE TRADE

Top from left to right: Robert Southey and Samuel Taylor Coleridge by P. Vandyke 1795, and Joseph Cottle by R. Hancock 1800. Left: Leonard Parkinson, leader of a slave revolt in Jamaica. The gun was later changed to a spear to make him look more primitive. Below: Haitian Revolution by M. De Norvins 1839.

… … … … ..From east to west
a groan of accusation pierces Heaven!
The wretched plead against us; multitudes
countless and vehement, the sons of God,
our brethren! Like a cloud that travels on,
steamed up from Cairo's swamps of pestilence,
even so, my countrymen! have we gone forth
and borne to distant tribes slavery and pangs,
and, deadlier far, our vices, whose deep taint
with slow perdition murders the whole man,
his body and his soul!

An orang-outang husband would by no means disgrace a negro woman
  Edward Long Jamaican plantation owner speaking in Parliament in 1804

Coleridge opposed the nonsensical arguments of men like Edward Long who were promoting white supremacy. He believed that Africans were not just intellectually equal to Europeans but morally superior because they were not enslaving people simply to provide themselves with unnecessary luxuries. Southey devoted a whole section of a 1797 volume of his poetry to the slave trade but his most effective anti-slavery poem was *The Sailor who had served in the Slave Trade*, which was published in the same year as *Lyrical Ballads*. The poem was based on a Bristol sailor's account of how a captain had forced him to flog an enslaved woman to death because she had refused to eat:

> The Captain made me tie her up
> and flog while he stood by,
> and then he curs'd me if I stayed
> my hand to hear her cry.
>
> She groan'd, she shriek'd – I could not spare
> for the Captain he stood by -
> Dear God! that I might rest one night
> from that poor woman's cry!
>
> She twisted from the blows – her blood,
> her mangled flesh I see -
> and still the Captain would not spare -

Oh he was worse than me!

She could not be more glad than I
when she was taken down,
a blessed minute – 'twas the last
that I have ever known!

I did not close my eyes all night,
thinking what I had done;
I heard her groans and they grew faint
about the rising sun.

She groan'd and groan'd, but her groans grew
fainter at morning tide,
fainter and fainter still they came
till at the noon she died.

They flung her overboard – poor wretch
she rested from her pain –
but when – O Christ! O blessed God!
shall I have rest again!

I saw the sea close over her,
yet she was still in sight;
I see her twisting everywhere;
I see her day and night.

Go where I will, do what I can,
the wicked one I see -
Dear Christ have mercy on my soul,
O God deliver me!

This poem is sometimes criticised for focusing more on the remorse of the sailor than on the suffering of the slave, but the very fact that the poem was written from the viewpoint of the sailor made it more effective than some of the other anti-slavery poems.

Cottle, Southey, and Coleridge did not let the horrors of the French Revolution put them off also demanding wider social change. Cottle's poetry is often criticised for not being focused enough on the suffering of the enslaved Africans and African-Americans but that was because he wanted to attack all forms of enslavement, including the appalling working conditions in Britain. That's also why Southey constantly described the British worker as 'a white slave'. Influenced by the radical politician, Thomas Paine, Coleridge was even more outspoken. He argued that both the white working classes and the black enslaved had a right to rebel. This was hugely controversial because there were mounting numbers of slave rebellions occurring in Jamaica, Dominica, Saint Lucia, Grenada, the St Vincent islands, and many other places in the 1790s. These were all inspired by the success of a revolution in the French colony of Saint Domingue led by an ex-slave, Touissaint Louverture. The latter created the largest slave revolt since Spartacus' rebellion against the Roman Republic and eventually he forced the French in 1804 to accept Saint-Domingue's independence as the black state of Haiti.

> **Deep rooted prejudices entertained by the whites; ten thousand recollections, by the blacks, of the injuries they have sustained; new provocations; the real distinctions which nature has made...will divide us into parties, and produce convulsions which will probably never end but in the extermination of the one or the other race**
>
> Thomas Jefferson, American President in *Notes on the State of Virginia* in 1782

The reaction of one of Bristol's abolitionists, Anna Maria Falconbridge, to the black revolts was not untypical. She announced that she had been mistaken in supporting abolition and that slavery was totally justifiable as long as Africans were subject to 'innate prejudices, ignorance, superstition and savageness'. However, some abolitionists tried to remind the public of the injustice that lay behind the rebellions. For example in 1796 the radical orator and writer John Thelwall wrote in his *The Rights of Nature*:

> I deplore... the robberies and murders of these poor wretches... but I cannot forget that slavery itself is robbery and murder; and that the master who falls by the bondsman's hand, is the victim of his own barbarity.

British ships were still carrying around 50,000 slaves to the Americas every year and this was fully supported by Horatio Nelson, the Commander of the Royal Navy and the nation's greatest hero in the war against France:

> I was bred as you know in the good old school, and taught to appreciate the value of our West Indian possessions; and neither in the field, nor in the state, shall their just rights be infringed, while I have an arm to fight in their defence or a tongue to launch my voice against the damnable doctrine of Wilberforce and his hypocritical allies.

It is estimated that between 1790 and 1806 there was a 25% increase in the number of slaves in the British Empire.

It is remarkable therefore that Wilberforce and his key supporters did not surrender to despair, especially after the strain of constant political lobbying led to the physical collapse of Thomas Clarkson. What kept most of the abolitionists going was their religious faith, their recognition that the opponents of abolition were no longer trying to defend slavery as an institution, and their appreciation that the profitability of the slave trade had markedly decreased as a consequence of war and the restrictions placed on the number of slaves that a ship could carry. The one success they had in the war years was in 1799 and it was to further restrict the number of slaves a ship could carry from an average of one slave to every five or so square feet to an average of eight feet.

The possibility of rekindling the abolitionist cause arose when the Revolutionary War ended and it was rapidly followed by war in 1803 with France's new Emperor, Napoleon. One of Napoleon's first acts as Emperor was to reintroduce slavery into the French Empire. This meant the abolitionists could argue that if Britain ended its role in the slave trade it would show that it was more civilised and progressive than its enemy. It was a sign of the change in mood that in 1804 Wilberforce managed to pass a bill through the House of Commons to abolish as soon as was practicable Britain's role in the slave trade, even though the House of Lords then blocked it. Evan Baillie, one of the two Bristol M.P.s, wrote to his son that it was only a matter of time before the ports that still were involved in the slave trade would have to cease their role because the Lords would not be able to continue blocking what the Commons passed. He feared that considerable problems for the plantation owners would then occur:

> The frenzy that has seized all parties on this subject is most unaccountable. I confess it alarms me most seriously; and it will induce me to think of abridging my West India businesses within very limited bounds… [The abolition of the slave trade] must prove a most fatal stab to West India credit as it renders all security on Estates highly precarious.

However, the real focus for the attention of Bristol's merchants at this stage was not defending the slave trade, in which the city was no longer the major player, but seeking to remedy the reason for the decline in Bristol's role as a major port by creating a new and much needed floating harbour for the city. This was to eventually be completed in 1809.

The Prime Minister William Pitt announced he was going to put a timetable to the gradual abolition of the slave trade. He was able to do that because some key opponents had gone. Lord Nelson had been killed at the Battle of Trafalgar. Henry Dundas, the chief opponent in the government to abolition, was facing impeachment for alleged misappropriation of public money. Lord Thurlow, a key figure in the House of Lords, was seriously ill and shortly to die. Pitt said it was the government's intention to impose a ban on the import of slaves from Africa from 1 January 1807 and that he was setting up a slave register so that the ban could be enforced. Pitt unexpectedly died in January 1806 but his cousin, William Grenville, took on running the government, creating a coalition known as 'the Ministry of all the Talents'. One of its first actions was to ban the supply of slaves to conquered territories and foreign colonies. This was the real growth area and so a very significant blow to the slave traders. Building on that, Grenville reversed the usual order in which bills were passed. He used his influence in the House of Lords so that it passed a bill approving the ending of Britain's role in the slave trade 'with all practicable expedition' by 100 votes to 34 and then he presented the passed bill to the House of Commons in February1807. The bill stated that the slave trade was 'contrary to the principles of justice, humanity and sound policy'.

The pro-slavery lobby in the Commons knew that they had lost and the bill was passed by an amazing majority of 283 to 16. Bristol's Tory M.P. Charles Bragge, who was a member of the Bathurst family, voted no, but the Whig M.P. Evan Bailie merely abstained. Wilberforce received a standing ovation. On 25 March, King George III gave the bill his royal assent. A month prior to that Bristol sent out its last slave ship and the *Alert* delivered 240 slaves to Jamaica in November 1807. The Act banning the slave trade came into force from 1 January 1708. Under its terms any British captain found transporting slaves would be fined £100 (about £4,500 in modern terms) for every slave on board. A handful of British traders ignored the ban and so Wilberforce persuaded Parliament in 1711 to increase the punishment to transportation to Australia for fourteen years. This was virtually a death sentence and it had the desired effect in making virtually all British slave shipping cease.

The Battle To End The Slave Trade

Above: James Gillray's '1796 cartoon Philanthropic consolations after the loss of the Slave Bill' pokes fun at Wilberforce and the pro-abolition Bishop of Rochester by showing them drinking, smoking and receiving sexual favours from black servants.
Right: William Grenville by J.Hoppner 1800. Below left: Bronze slave trade abolished tokens were issued to mark the end of the slave trade. This one is from Sierra Leone in 1808. Below right is coin issued to mark bicentenary in 2007.

> ***Wilberforce's achievement is one of the most remarkable examples of the triumph of an individual statesman on a major philanthropic issue, and at the same time one more reminder that individuals can make history***
>
> Hugh Thomas, historian, in *The Slave Trade* in 1997

By a remarkable coincidence the American government also banned further involvement of its merchants in the slave trade from 1 January 1808. After years of ambiguity, Thomas Jefferson had decided as President to back his conscience rather than commerce. The decision resulted in some of the slave owning states setting up breeding farms. In Britain the question posed was what should now happen to existing slaves in its Empire? Even Britain's most radical political speaker Thomas Paine, who had long denounced the slave trade, was quite conservative on this issue:

> What should be done with those who are enslaved already? To turn the old and infirm free, would be injustice and cruelty; they who enjoyed the labours of their better days should keep, and treat them humanely. As to the rest, let prudent men, with the assistance of legislatures, determine what is practicable for masters, and best for them. Perhaps some could give them lands upon reasonable rent, some, employing them in their labour still, might give them some reasonable allowances for it; so as all may have some property, and fruits of their labours at their own disposal, and be encouraged to industry; the family may live together, and enjoy the natural satisfaction of exercising relative affections and duties, with civil protection, and other advantages, like fellow men. Perhaps they might sometime form useful barrier settlements on the frontiers. Thus they may become interested in the public welfare, and assist in promoting it; instead of being dangerous, as now they are, should any enemy promise them a better condition.

> ***One of the worst results of being a slave and being forced to do things is that when there is no one to force you any more you find you have almost lost the power of forcing yourself***
>
> C.S. Lewis, writer and novelist in a Narnia book *The Horse And His Boy* in 1954

Thomas Clarkson, Grenville Sharp, and a few others, such as James Cropper, a Quaker merchant based in Liverpool, argued that it was essential to immediately begin campaigning for the abolition of slavery altogether. They argued that not just for moral reasons but also for a practical one. They felt as long as slavery existed an illegal trade in slaves would continue, whatever the law said about abolishing it. In this they were correct because there is evidence to support that a few British ships did continue to carry slaves and that some captains simply jettisoned the slaves by throwing them overboard to drown if they risked being caught. However, Wilberforce thought it was vital to delay the abolition of slavery because he thought the existing slaves were not educated enough to handle freedom:

> It would be wrong to emancipate. To grant freedom to them immediately, would be to insure not only their masters' ruin, but their own. They must [first] be trained and educated for freedom.

One of the criticisms levied against Wilberforce is that, unlike Sharp and Clarkson, he was not comfortable working alongside Africans or women and he therefore tended to see abolition as something that white men would have to deliver and control. This was a view shared by many. Wilberforce's view won the day and the Society for effecting the abolition of the slave trade was not given a new target. Instead it was disbanded and in its place was created 'the African Institution' to introduce 'the blessings of civilisation'. Wilberforce hoped to use the upsurge in evangelical Christianity within Britain to send out missionaries who would convert the enslaved to Christianity and provide them with an education that would instil Christian values, thus preparing them for their eventual freedom.

If women want rights more than they got, why don't they just take them and not be talking about it?
Narrative of Sojourner Truth, escaped slave and women's rights activist in 1850

The racism underpinning slavery. Robert Cruikshank portrays a thick-lipped African as a devil playing the fiddle (possibly an allusion to a black entertainer called Billy Waters) in 1820. Below: a cartoon of 1819 and some details from it drawn by George Cruikshank. It portrays Wilberforce and his supporters enmeshed with grotesque blacks who are savage, superstitious, drunk, and promiscuous.

7

THE VICTORY OF 1833

People need to remember about slavery. It pains the ancestors when we forget
Grandson of a slave in South Carolina in 1990 cited in International Slavery Museum in Liverpool

It is easy to see why most of the campaigners for the abolition of the slave trade accepted that the time was not right to campaign for the end of slavery. It was not just that the spate of slave rebellions had led some abolitionists to believe the plantation owners' propaganda that it would be wise to 'civilise' the enslaved before taking the final step of freeing them all. Many wrongly assumed that abolishing the slave trade would in itself prove sufficient to end slavery. They thought that slave owners would have to begin to treat their slaves more humanely because they could no longer rely on acquiring cheap replacements and that, as a consequence,. slave labour would become not radically different from other forms of labour. Almost all the abolitionists, whatever their view, accepted that winning a victory against France was an essential first priority. And this was not just for patriotic reasons. They believed a victory would place Britain in a uniquely powerful position to extend its Empire and pressurise other countries into abolishing or restricting their role in the slave trade.

Although the abolition of slavery was put on the back burner , it resurfaced in Bristol as an issue in the 1812 parliamentary election because a radical reformer named Henry Hunt, tried to end the merchants' electoral control over who became the city's M.P.s. Born in Upavon in Wiltshire in 1773, 'Orator' Hunt (as he came to be called) fought a campaign on the slogan that there was no life without liberty. This encouraged a debate on the issue of slavery, especially as another candidate in the election was Sir Samuel Romilly, who had campaigned for its abolition. All this was an anathema to the two Caribbean merchants whose candidature had the support of the Society of Merchant Venturers. They were Richard Hart Davis, who was a traditional Tory, and Edward Protheroe, who was a traditional Whig. Their supporters used every dirty trick they could. They offered bribes to attract votes and threats to prevent votes going to the opposition. Anyone thinking of voting for Hunt or Romilly was told it would result in financial ruin because he would have his shop blacklisted or have his job taken away or have his charitable grant removed. Davis saw Romilly as a more serious threat than Hunt and so created a fighting force to attack anyone who proposed to vote for him. He had churches draped with blue banners and clothed a mob in blue jackets and white trousers, arming each man with a blue bludgeon. Not to be outdone Protheroe had cannon brought in and pointed at Romilly's headquarters, although this was later described as just 'a prank'. Hunt and Romilly were both defeated.

Victory against the French was not finally achieved until 1815 but the outcome was that Britain acquired massive colonial gains in the Caribbean and elsewhere. In the peace negotiations the government tried to persuade other countries to follow its lead in abolishing the trade in slaves. The greatest pressure was applied on the defeated French and Wilberforce managed to organise that massive petitions signed by around three-quarters of a million people were sent to Louis XVIII, France's restored monarch. The French government reluctantly agreed it would do what it could to collaborate with Britain on ending the slave trade. The British Foreign Secretary, Lord Castlereagh, also managed to obtain a general recognition from Spain, Portugal, Austria, Prussia, Russia, and Sweden that the slave trade was 'repugnant to the principles of humanity and universal morality' and that they would work towards abolishing it. All this was worthless because virtually nothing concrete happened afterwards. A few Latin American countries, keen to develop a positive relationship with Britain. abandoned their role in the slave trade but Portuguese, Spanish, French, and American ships operating under the Spanish flag continued to operate. Many British plantation owners were prepared to access fresh slaves via these sources. Fear that Britain might one day use its Navy to block all slave ships served only to increase the demand for slaves as some sought to 'stockpile'. It should also not be forgotten that Islamic traders were continuing to operate the slave trade they had run for centuries and African chiefs were continuing to enslave for their own purposes. One French traveller in Africa commented in 1820 that it was the dream of any poor African to own ten to fifteen slaves.

An ageing Wilberforce increasingly stormed at the hypocrisy of governments but racism was still endemic in Britain. Some of the political cartoons of the period were particularly offensive in their presentation of Africans. In 1822 Wilberforce decided it was to step down from politics and inevitably this led to a re-evaluation of what line the abolitionists should be taking next. The abolitionist James Cropper suggested that a new society dedicated to abolishing slavery was the only way that progress would ever be made. He was immediately supported by Thomas Clarkson. Thus was born the Society for the Mitigation and Gradual Abolition of Slavery throughout the British Dominion. However, the title indicates that even the most committed abolitionists had bought into the concept that slavery could not be introduced overnight. There were other issues within the country also needing to be addressed and abolition would require careful planning if the slave owners were to be also treated fairly. Out of the 519 people who immediately became members of the new Society only six were from Bristol. They comprised three Quakers (the chocolate manufacturer Joseph Storrs Fry and the timber merchants Joseph and James Wright), two Anglicans (the evangelical incumbent of St Jame's Church, Thomas Biddulph, and the seed merchant Thomas Sanders) and one Baptist (the land surveyor George Ashmead).

> Oh when I think of my long-suffering race
> For weary centuries despised, oppressed,
> Enslaved and lynched, denied a human place...
> My heart grows sick with hate, becomes as lead...
> Then from the dark depths of my soul I cry
> To the avenging angel to consume
> The white man's world of wonders utterly
>
> Claude McKay, Jamaican poet in *Enslaved* in 1921

Wilberforce agreed to become the Vice-President of the new Society, but its voice in Parliament was the M.P. Thomas Fowell Buxton, the M.P. for Weymouth. He had earned a reputation as a skilful campaigner through his effective work in promoting prison reform. Buxton immediately introduced a bill committing Britain to the gradual abolition of slavery and he forcibly reminded Parliament of the inherent immorality involved in such an institution:

> The slave sees the mother of his children stripped naked and flogged unmercifully; he sees his children sent to market, to be sold at the best price they will fetch; he sees in himself not a man, but a thing – an implement of husbandry, a machine to produce sugar, a beast of burden!

The Bill was passed but with the proviso that the interests of the planters would be taken into account in the process of moving towards abolition. The Society decided the best role it could play was to continue producing evidence of the immorality of slavery and to find evidence that the sugar and other plantation industries could function without using slave labour.

In October 1823 Clarkson returned to Bristol to address a meeting at the Savings Bank so those who were interested could hear about the aims of the Society. He hoped to be able to revive the regional committee that had existed in the city. That there was still a continued moral antipathy towards slavery in the city was evident. For example, it is visible in some of the paintings undertaken by the artist Samuel Colman (or Coleman). In a painting called *St John preaching in the Wilderness* he included a negro posed like the one on the medallion that Wedgwood had produced, and in his *St James's Fair* he chose to depict a Quaker bookseller pointing to a sign that referred to one of Hannah More's anti-slavery poems. Some think his painting of a burning Westminster Abbey in *The Edge of Doom* was his way of condemning the failure of the Church of England to wholeheartedly condemn slavery.

However, only thirty-nine Bristolians joined the Society. It is never easy to evoke enthusiasm by talking of doing something gradually and the West India Association had successfully persuaded many that the country's commercial wealth was dependent on maintaining the status quo. It was claimed that over 60% of Bristol's wealth was dependent on the West Indian trade. Historians have found it difficult to assess whether that percentage figure was actually true but they accept the percentage would have been a very substantial one. When the West India Association agreed to fund its campaigning by dividing the expense on a pro rata basis to the four main ports benefitting from the West Indian trade (London, Glasgow, Liverpool, and Bristol), it judged Bristol to be benefitting from just under 18% of the entire trade.

The whole history of mankind… has been a history of class struggles, contests between exploiting and exploited, ruling and oppressed classes
Friedrich Engels, one of the founders of Communism in his introduction to The Communist Manifesto in 1888

Many liberals felt the abolitionists were overstating their case and that the focus on slavery was preventing the country from tackling the far worse working and living conditions within Britain. William Cobbett, now viewed as the greatest liberal political journalist of the early nineteenth century, railed against Wilberforce and the abolitionists for that reason:

> There is not a man who knows anything of the real situation of the Blacks, who will not declare you to be totally ignorant of the subject on which you are writing… the labours, the lodging, the food, the drink, the state

The Victory Of 1833

Left: Illustration from 'Black Man's Lament' 1826 shows petitioning to emancipate the enslaved. Below left: sections from Samuel Coleman's 'St James' Fair' showing a Quaker selling anti-slavery literature and 'St John preaching in the wilderness' showing slave in right hand bottom corner in pose of the Wedgwood medallion. Below right: Thomas Fowell Buxton, Elizabeth Heyrick and Mary Wollstonecraft.

of health… and the nature and quantity of the labour in the West Indies… Have you ever done anything to mitigate the laws which exist in this country with regard to… free British labourers?

Cobbett asked why were the abolitionists condemning the working conditions of slaves when the masses in Britain faced far worse in factories and mines? Did they not know, for example, that cotton workers in factories worked 'fourteen hours in each day, locked up, winter and summer in a heat of from eighty to eighty-four degrees… gaping for air [and] swallowing cotton-fuz'? This was 'a bondage as complete as that of the negro'. If the abolitionists condemned the flogging to death of a slave why did they not condemn the deaths of soldiers or sailors who were flogged to death without anyone being called to account? They were condemning the living conditions of slaves but ignoring the far worse living conditions within Britain:

> British labourers, these poor, mocked, degraded wretches would be happy to lick the dishes and bowls out of which the Black slaves have breakfasted, dined or supped… No black slave ever suffered for want of food… but a very large part of … [the white working classes] exist in a state of almost incessant hunger… Look at their perishing and emaciated frames, then look at your fat and laughing and singing and dancing negroes and negresses.

Cobbett's especial grievance was that Wilberforce and the abolitionists kept comparing black slavery with white freedom even though, in his opinion, the white working classes were not really free. He pointed out that in Britain it was unlawful for any workers to band together to negotiate what they should be paid or to hold public protests and anyone infringing that could be imprisoned without trial or, as had happened in the 'Peterloo Massacre' in Manchester in 1819, killed. He said Wilberforce and his associates were therefore spouting 'a great deal of canting trash, a great deal of lying', and he accused the Quakers of 'cool impudent falsehood' and the Methodists of 'aiding and abetting all the worst things that have been done in the last twenty years':

> I feel for the care-worn, the ragged, the hard-pinched, the ill-treated, and beaten down and trampled upon labouring classes of England, Scotland, and Ireland, to whom… you do all the mischief that it is in your power to do because you describe their condition as being good, and because you… draw the public attention from their sufferings.

The uphill task facing the new anti-slavery society is very evident if one looks at the speeches made by religious leaders at a public meeting held in Bristol in 1826. The Congregationalist minister Robert Thorpe suggested all that was required in the first instance was for the nation to hold a day of general fasting to show its penitence. The Baptist minister Thomas Roberts said the most important task was simply to ensure that all negroes were 'managed without cruelty'. The Unitarian minister Lant Carpenter said Bristol's plantation owners and merchants were all men of 'high character and respectability' so it was essential to look at protecting their commercial interests whilst seeking to improve the lot of the slaves. The Moravian Church prohibited its clergy from engaging in political meetings so its minister, Christian Ramftler, did not attend. However, it was known he preferred not to alienate the planters because they were the funders of Moravian settlements. The Methodist voice on the issue of slavery had virtually been silenced in Bristol by the internal convulsions that had followed the death of Wesley. This had eventually led to the movement leaving the Anglican Church and becoming a non-conformist separate church. The opposition within the New Room to that change had led the newly created Methodist Church to deliberately engineer the closure of the building and its sale in 1808 to Welsh-speaking Calvinists. Over the next half-century Methodism was bedevilled by break-away groups.

The general feeling at the meeting was best summed up by William Peter Lunell, the man who had acted as the treasurer for the old Society for the Abolition of the Slave Trade and who had agreed to take on that role for the new Society:

> Sudden emancipation would be cruel as well as absurd, nothing qualifies a man of low birth for the confidence, comfort and employments of civil life more than property saved from industry by prudence… I think slaves might be allowed to purchase their freedom, and when able to do it, they might on the whole be considered as qualified for it.

How the enslaved were to raise the money when they were essentially unpaid was not discussed. The sole achievement of the Bristol branch of the between 1826 and 1830 was to produce four petitions reminding the government that slavery was a bad thing and that steps should be being made towards eventually ending it. What those steps should be was not clear.

> *It is a dangerous thing to teach slaves Christianity; you cannot teach Christianity without the Bible... [and in the Bible] they can read texts calling men to liberty, announcing deliverance to the captive, binding up the broken-hearted*
>
> Speaker at meeting held in the Guildhall in Bristol in February 1826

The concept that the African slaves had to prove their worthiness before acquiring their freedom had its counterpart in the arguments then going on in Britain about how the vote could only be given to people with a certain amount of property and a certain level of education. The beginnings of a national educational system were only initiated in 1833 so what kind of education was appropriate for negroes was understandably even less a priority. Many planters refused to permit schools of any kind. Others reluctantly accepted mission schools because they felt they could hardly object to places that promoted Christianity, but they had grave concerns about how their slaves might be influenced by the Bible's messages of brotherhood and for that reason they usually refused to permit the teaching of reading. Any other type of school, such as the one which the Bristol merchant Charles Pinney and his sister Mary Ames founded on the family plantations in Nevis, was usually rooted in teaching obedience, a sense of duty, and a respect for public order and was just a sop to those who disliked slavery. It is thought Charles Pinney probably only created his school on Nevis because at the time he was courting Wilberforce's daughter and he hoped to win his favour. If so, he failed. Wilberforce rejected having Pinney as a possible son-in-law as soon as he discovered he was providing financial loans to plantation owners and thus helping to perpetuate the slave system.

> *The laws respecting woman... make an absurd unit of a man and his wife... [By] considering him as responsible, she is reduced to a mere cypher... Is one half of the human species, like the poor African slaves, to be subject to prejudices that brutalise them... only to sweeten the cup of men*
>
> Mary Wollstonecraft compares the lot of women to the lot of slaves in *A Vindication of the Rights of Women* in 1792

Membership of the Society for the Mitigation and Gradual Abolition of Slavery throughout the British Dominion remained very low in Bristol. It rose only to eighty-four members. The more dynamic voice for action against slavery was the Bristol and Clifton Female Anti-Slavery Society, formed in 1827. It was smaller because it had sixty-six members but among these were a number of liberally minded aristocrats so it carried more weight. Its stated purpose was 'to spread before the footstool of mercy, the cause of our oppressed and degraded African Brethren', but behind that lay a determination to assert all human rights, including that of women. There is no doubt that their lack of rights gave women a natural affinity with the enslaved Africans. Hannah More and another writer, Mary Anne Schimmelpenninck, were among the key leaders of the new Society. Schimmelpennick was a member of the Unitarian congregation at Lewins Mead but came from a Quaker background. Born in Birmingham, she had married Lambert Schimmelpennick, a member of a Dutch family engaged in the shipping trade in Bristol. It was because her husband's business had run into financial problems that she had turned to writing as a means of acquiring money.

The Bristol and Clifton Female Anti-Slavery Society was part of a movement across the country to create female anti-slavery organisations. The initial inspiration for this had come from the work of the widow of a Methodist lawyer from Leicester called Elizabeth Heyrick, who became a Quaker. In 1825 she had published a pamphlet called *Immediate not Gradual Abolition*, which said it was wrong to put the protection of the interests of the planters before the rights of the enslaved and that the the 'slow, cautious, accommodating measures' of the abolitionist leaders were a disgrace:

> Men may propose only gradually to abolish the worst of crimes and only mitigate the most cruel bondage, but why should we countenance such enormities?... We must not talk of gradually abolishing murder, licentiousness, cruelty, tyranny... Too much time has already been lost in declamation and argument, in petitions and remonstrances against British slavery. The cause of emancipation calls for something more decisive, more efficient than words. It calls upon the real friends of the poor degraded and oppressed African to bind themselves by a solemn engagement, an irrevocable vow, to participate no longer in the crime of keeping him in bondage...The perpetuation of slavery in our West India colonies is not an abstract question, to be settled between the government and the planters; it is one in which we are all implicated, we are all guilty of supporting and perpetuating slavery.

In response Lucy Townsend, the wife of an evangelical clergyman in West Bromwich, founded the Ladies Society for the Relief of Negro Slaves, the first anti-slavery society specifically for women. Until then women had only been permitted to attend public meetings, usually from galleries so they were kept apart. They were not expected to directly participate except by donating money. Not only were they not permitted to speak, they were not even permitted to sign petitions. The Ladies Society organised in Birmingham the first ever female petition against slavery and two thousand women signed it. Wilberforce objected to what Heyrick and Townsend were doing because he thought politics was best left to men:

> For ladies to meet, to publish, to go from house to house stirring up petitions – these appear to me proceedings unsuited to the female character as delineated in Scripture. I fear its tendency would be to mix them in all the multiform warfare of political life.

Both European women and African men were excluded (except for exceptional cases) from the power and prestige of public life. Both were seen as unwelcome outsiders
Londa Schiebinger, historian in The Anatomy of Diffference: Race and Sex in Eighteenth Century Science in 1990

The Society for the Mitigation and Gradual Abolition of Slavery took a different view from Wilberforce when it saw female anti-slavery organisations springing up in seventy-two places. It welcomed them and, as a gesture of its desire to work with them, printed copies of Elizabeth Heyrick's next pamphlet, which was entitled *Appeal to the Hearts and Consciences of British Women*. The Bristol and Clifton Female Anti-Slavery Society initially focused on raising money to help fund specific charitable projects, such as helping a particular negro whose case had been given to them and setting up schools in Jamaica. However, in 1829 its members responded to the urging of Elizabeth Heyrick that the sugar boycott of 1791-92 should be revived and they paid for the printing and distribution of a pamphlet entitled *Consumers of West Indian Sugar, the Supporters of West Indian Slavery*. This recommended that people should either stop using sugar or only buy their sugar from Bengal where it was not produced by slaves.

The West Indian Association was quick to denounce this pamphlet as ill-informed nonsense and it claimed Indian sugar was also produced by slave labour. This was a deliberate misrepresentation of the situation. Slaves did produce the sugar cane grown on the Malabar coast, but the sugar produced in Bengal was not produced by slaves, even if working conditions there amounted to virtual slavery. The 'use only free-grown sugar' campaign met with increasing

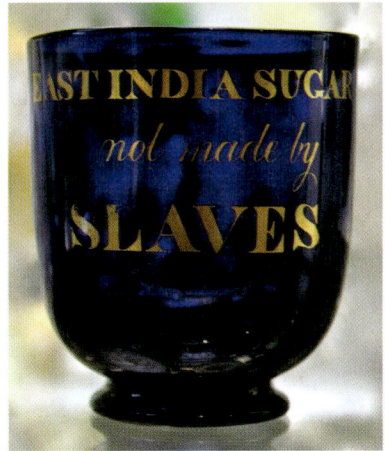

Above left to right: Henry Hunt; Richard Hart Davis and Charles Pinney. Left: sugar bowl with ethical logo c1828-30. Above: Mary Anne Schimmelpennick and Christopher Claxton, Below:1831 riot in Queen Square.

success across the entire country. The message went out that one less slave was required in the Caribbean for every six families who swopped to using East Indian sugar. It soon became fashionable among the rich to have a sugar bowl inscribed with the image of a kneeling slave and the words 'East India sugar, not made by slaves'. Caribbean sales plummeted and sales of East Indian sugar rose tenfold.

I will not purchase sugar till I can procure it through channels less contaminated, more unconnected with slavery, less polluted with human blood
James Wright, Quaker shopkeeper in announcement to his local newspaper in March 1792

In 1830 Heyrick suggested that women could influence the Society for the Mitigation and Gradual Abolition of Slavery to abandon its emphasis on gradual abolition by refusing to contribute towards funding it until it did. This was a serious threat because it is estimated that about ten per cent of the organisation's financial supporters were women and some regional committees were heavily reliant on women subscribers. There is no figure for Bristol but we know in Manchester women provided 25% of the money. Heyrick's call came at a propitious moment because male abolitionists were also questioning whether it was right to continue supporting a gradual process when for over twenty years there had been no practical moves made to prepare the enslaved Africans for freedom. The situation was no different in 1830 than it had been in 1807. In May 1830 it was agreed that the Society would be known henceforth as 'the Anti-Slavery Society' and that its aim would be the immediate abolition of slavery. The impact of that decision was quickly felt in Bristol. On 9 June an Anglican clergyman, William Marsh, delivered a lecture in Clifton calling upon the electorate to insist that their M.P.s should vote for the speedy end of slavery.

On 26 June 1830 King George IV died, parliament was dissolved, and a general election was called. In Bristol as elsewhere the dominant electoral issue was the need for parliamentary reform, but the issue of slavery featured sufficiently prominently in Bristol for it to become known as 'the slavery election'. On the Tory side no one questioned that the party should seek the re-election of Richard Hart Davis, who had been one of the city's M.P.s since 1820, but Henry Bright, the sitting Whig M.P., did not want to stand for re-election. The Whig party split over who should represent their interests. The majority wanted James Evan Baillie, who had substantial banking and mercantile interests in Bristol and whose take on abolition was that it should be gradual. However, a minority backed a candidate who was prepared to back immediate abolition. This was Edward Davis Protheroe and his opponents quickly nicknamed him 'Negro Ned'. Protheroe's position was highly unexpected because he came from a mercantile family and his father had been a staunch defender of slavery as one of the city's M.P.s from 1812 to 1820. Charges of hypocrisy were soon directed at him:

> Tell him that it is to the WEST INDIES and the West Indies ALONE that he owes his every shilling!!! His father and grandfather amasses ALL their wealth as West Indian merchants, and consequently his money is the produce of slave labour. Tell him then, if he wishes to act in accordance to his avowed principles, he should first resign ALL wealth derived from such a source.

The white man's happiness cannot be purchased by the black man's misery
Narrative of the life of Frederick Douglass, an American Slave in 1845

There was an element of hypocrisy in Protheroe's position but not because he was not renouncing his family wealth. Wilberforce's successor, Thomas Foxwell Buxton, had begun suggesting that it would be appropriate for the government to compensate slaveowners if slavery was abolished. Protheroe saw the potential for the plantation owners to obtain large sums of money for the loss of their 'property'. Better to seize that opportunity while it was on the table than persevere with an opposition that was ultimately doomed to fail. If his motivation was questionable, his message was at least crystal clear:

> The word GRADUAL will cover a period of 500 years… Depend upon it, fellow citizens, SLAVE-HOLDERS NEVER WILL EXTINGUISH SLAVERY. The Imperial Parliament must take this matter into their one hands, and enact measure that shall lead directly to the *Speedy Extinction* of SLAVERY.

To win greater support, Protheroe linked emancipation with the need to 'free' white workers from working conditions that amounted to servitude. He promised to support numerous reforms at home, including a major overhaul of parliamentary constituencies and the voting system, lesser taxation, cheaper food and drink, etc.:

> YOU ARE FREEMEN! Teach them a lesson! Convince them that however

they may rule with despotic sway in the West Indies – they shall not Lord it over you! [Tell them] that you will not be their slaves, their vassals or their tools!

Protheroe's stance attracted considerable support from the Methodists, Quakers, Baptists, and Moravians. All these groups had to varying degrees suffered vilification from plantation owners for seeking to educate negroes. His campaign also won the support of many women, notably of course the members of the Bristol and Clifton Female Anti-Slavery Society. Marianne Schimmelpennick wrote:

May you and all of us females lift up our hands in continual prayer whilst our champions are engaged in the conflict and never let us forget that to us appointed by God as their helpers especially belongs the honourable privilege to strengthen, to cheer, and to refresh them in the labours of their day.

Her acceptance that women should play a supportive rather than active role was matched by the patronising tone of some of Protheroe's election material. *The Negro Mother's Petition to the Ladies of Bristol*, written in an English version of West Indian patois, was clearly designed to flatter white women but it did so by making out that badly educated Africans were totally reliant on the goodwill of the white race:

'Missey, missy, tink on we,
Toder side de big blue sea –
How we flogg'd, and how we cry -
How we sometimes wish to die…
How we poor heart t'rob and ache!
How we cry! Dey almost break!
How we head swim round and round!
How we wish we underground!…
Missey, pray her Massa dear
Wipe away de Neger tear…
Massa PROTHEROE – he good man!
Send him Missey – SURE YOU CAN!
Den you fill poor Neger eye
Wid d tear brimful of joy…. .

Den Neger for dear Missey pray,
For Massa too, de lib-long day -
For Fader, Broder, ebery Friend -
For every blessing widget end!

Given Protheroe's electioneering ability, one cannot help wonder if a famous incident in the campaign was deliberately staged to enact out the famous logo produced decades earlier for the Society for the Abolition of the Slave Trade. A black beggar was seized and carried above the heads of Protheroe's supporters for presentation to Protheroe in his carriage. He then grasped the kneeling black man's hand 'in token of his being a man and a brother' .

Bristol owes all her prosperity, nay, I had almost said, her existence to her commerce with the West Indies. Without it she must sink to rise no more. Picture to your imagination, her now crowded streets, grass-grown and desolate – her glittering shops deserted, and the doors shut in her streets!
Poster in 1830 election by those opposed to emancipation of the enslaved

---

In retaliation Evan Baillie's supporters quickly turned to intimidation techniques. They said anyone voting for Protheroe would soon find their businesses boycotted or their employment ended. Violence was also used. Protheroe's headquarters were attacked and he was on one occasion struck on the head and rendered unconscious. Central to encouraging this aggressive response was the main agent working for Evan Baillie's election, Christopher Claxton, the son of the wealthy West India merchant, Robert Claxton, and the brother-in-law of Bristol's mayor. Ironically the Claxton and the Protheroe families had worked together as traders until 1809. Claxton conceded that 'heartless cruelty' towards slaves was wrong but added that electors should remember just how bad the Africans were. It was no wonder that owners sometimes lost their temper when faced with their slaves' reluctance to work and with their stupidity and outlandish attachment to pagan rites and fetishes. He told the electorate that they should not be misled by the 'humbug' of Protheroe about the necessity for an immediate end to slavery because it was a God-ordained institution. Setting slaves free would only result in ruin because 'the negro race... [was] barbarian in grain'.

Claxton knew how to catch headlines. He therefore challenged John Hare, the agent working for Protheroe, to a duel for misleading the public. He also knew how to manipulate people's emotions. Knowing that many of those who supported abolition were also campaigners for animal rights, he deliberately spread tales about how it was common for disaffected Africans to maltreat animals by placing nails in the hooves of horses and by cutting the lips off the mouths of mules so they would starve to death. He also alleged that slaves often sought to secretly poison their masters. It says much about Claxton's racist approach that he accused Protheroe of being the illegitimate son of a Jew – a 'circumcised pencil or orange boy from Change Alley', foisted on the unsuspecting public by the Quakers. The latter charge was made because the man funding Protheroe's campaign was a Quaker banker named Samuel Waring. Claxton claimed Waring was a total hypocrite because he had large shares in Brazilian mining, which used not just workers but many slaves. Waring's response was to immediately dispose of his shares, saying he had not been aware of that.

In the end Hart Davis obtained 5,012 votes, Baillie 3,378 and Protheroe 2,843 so Protheroe's bid to become an M.P. failed. However, the small margin of his defeat encouraged his supporters and they held a public meeting in October 1830 at the Guildhall to discuss creating a petition to Parliament for the immediate abolition of slavery. Claxton urged the supporters of slavery to attend it and make their opposition known:

> The friends of the trade of Bristol – of order – of all sacred institutions – of the laws of the church -of the state – and of practical as well as theoretical emancipation [should all] attend the public meeting.

As was his intention, the meeting became an unseemly brawl. Another public meeting was held in the Assembly Room in November. This time the abolitionists made clear in advance that they wanted owners to be properly compensated. The result, in the words of one local newspaper, was that the meeting was 'one of the most numerously attended which we ever witnessed in this city'.

Nationally the Tories won the election overall and in the new Parliament Hart Davis spoke forcibly against any attempt to introduce abolition quickly, arguing that it was essential first to establish a proper educational system for slaves and to work out a detailed plan for compensating their owners. However, the Tory Party only had a tiny minority and its leader, the Duke of Wellington, was forced to resign as Prime Minister after a vote of no confidence in November 1830 over his refusal to contemplate any reform of the parliamentary system. The result was another election in 1831 and it was generally felt that the mood for political reform in the country would result in a Whig victory. Baillie and Protheroe agreed to bury their differences in order that the Whig party might

To the Independent Electors of the City of Bristol.

Be not deceived by the **Shufflings** of Mr. Baillie's friends. Why did they object to Mr. Protheroe, after having promised him their support? Because he declared himself a **Friend** to the poor oppressed Negroes in the West Indies. Why do now they support Mr. Baillie in opposition to him? Because they know Mr. Baillie is an **Enemy** to the comfort, religious instruction, and freedom of the West Indian Slaves.

> "Man finds his fellow guilty of a skin
> Not coloured like his own; and, having power,
> Chains him, and tasks him, and exacts his sweat
> With stripes, that Mercy with a bleeding heart
> Weeps when she sees inflicted on a **Beast!!!**"

And he must continue to do so, said Mr. Baillie's friends when they first addressed you, or the Trade of the City will be ruined. But now they alter their tone, and wish you to believe he is as great a friend to the Negroes as Mr. Protheroe!!! Yes, THEY KNOW THAT YOU WILL NOT ELECT AN ADVOCATE OF CRUELTY. But ask them, If the sentiments of the two Gentlemen be the same, why they deserted the one, and put the other in opposition to him? They will be silent, and stand convicted by their own consciences that they are now endeavouring to deceive you by SHUFFLING.

The Chairman of Mr. Baillie's Committee, with that part of the Mercantile Interest who support Mr. Baillie, say they do so because he is **hostile** to the glorious cause of emancipation.

The other part of the Committee *whisper* that the sentiments of Mr. Baillie, upon that point are **in unison with Mr. Protheroe's**!!! Which are the people to credit? Let Mr. Baillie publicly avow his sentiments, as Mr. Protheroe has done; and then the Public will know whether the statement of the Chairman and his friends or the whispers of the other part of the Committee, be the truth. If they make any pretensions to honour let them not blow both Hot and Cold.

Protheroe
FOR EVER.

One of Edward Protheroe's 1830 election handbills (Bristol Central Reference Library) take both the Bristol seats. It helped that Claxton was absent in the Caribbean. The cooperation worked and both Baillie and Protheroe were elected. For the first time in over fifty years Bristol had no Tory M.P.

Because the focus of the election was on the question of parliamentary reform the issue of slavery received far less attention in the 1831 election. As a consequence those favouring immediate emancipation decided to launch a campaign that would refocus people's attention onto slavery again by saying it was 'criminal before God' to engage in it. When Claxton returned to Bristol in August he took up the cause of defending the owners' rights to compensation if slavery was abolished. He said no compensation would constitute 'an act of injustice' and lead to social disorder because 'the sacred barrier of private rights' would have been breached.

Nationally the Whigs swept into power with a large majority. The House of Commons approved a long overdue Parliamentary Reform Bill to change constituency boundaries and increase the number of people who could vote. The former was needed because the existing constituencies paid no attention to how much the nation had been reshaped by agricultural and industrial development. At the extremes there were some villages which had ceased to exist and yet the landowner was sending an M.P. and there were major new cities either not represented or underrepresented. Voting rights depended on how much wealth a person had. In Bristol 6,000 out of the 104,000 inhabitants of the city had the vote and that was a high percentage compared to most other places. When the Tory-dominated House of Lords rejected the Reform Bill passed by the House of Commons in November 1831, there were national protests and rioting in many pro-reform cities, including Bristol.

Bristol's riot began because it was reported that a local magistrate, Sir Charles Wetherell, had wrongly told Parliament that Bristol was opposed to reform. A large mob tried to attack him in the Mansion House in Queen Square. Wetherell escaped – one report says by fleeing over the rooftops – but the Mayor, who was Charles Pinney, and various officials found themselves besieged. Police constables were summoned and they made a number of arrests but the authorities did not respond firmly enough. The next day a mob of around five or six hundred gathered at 6.00 a.m. armed with sticks, iron railings and whatever other weapons they could devise. Some went to Bridewell Prison and freed those arrested, while the rest renewed their assault first on the Mansion House and then on surrounding buildings. The Customs House was torched and some of the mob began breaking into and looting the homes of the merchants, among them that belonging to Christopher Claxton. He was absent in the Caribbean at the time of the attack and ironically it is said it was a black servant who defended his house. Afterwards Pinney wrote to Claxton:

> The careless use of the terms Liberty and Slavery… have engendered a spirit in Bristol… [hostile] to the leading interests in Bristol, and a notion… among the lower orders that the great merchants, to whom they were wont to look up to with respect, were drawing their resources from human blood.

With two sides of Queen Square ablaze, some rioters headed off to release those imprisoned in the New Gaol and the Gloucester County Gaol at Lawford's Gate. They used sledgehammers to force their way in. Rioters also commenced attacking the Bishop's Palace on Lower College Green because it was known that he opposed reform. The Palace was gutted and razed to the ground.

Pinney requested military help and a troop of the 3rd Dragoon Guards and a squadron of the 14th Light Dragoons were sent, but a lack of good leadership prevented them and the hundreds enrolled as special constables being used to best effect. It eventually took a cavalry charge with drawn swords to make the mob disperse and even then order was not fully restored until the next day. The official reports say that four rioters were killed and eighty-six were wounded but most historians think the casualties were far higher because many of the drunken rioters perished in the fires. The commander of the Dragoons, Colonel Brereton, was put on trial for incompetence, but he committed suicide before the case was heard. Many of the surviving rioters were imprisoned and 114 of them were eventually put on trial and thirty-one of these were sentenced to death, although mass petitioning against this led to only four of them being hung. The scale of the damage in Queen Square, Prince Street and King Street was enormous and among the civic buildings destroyed were the Mansion House, the Excise Office, the Custom House, and the Toll Houses. Rioting on this scale has many causes and so it would be wrong to attribute what happened to just the parliamentary issue. Some historians, for example, believe the riot was primarily the result of pent-up unhappiness with the way the city was being run. However, the news of the riot shocked the nation and it was seen as proof that parliamentary and other reforms had to take place if the country was not to descend into anarchy.

In March 1832 the House of Commons passed an amended Reform Bill introduced by the new Prime Minister, Lord Grey, and, after weeks of attempted amendments, the Lords surrendered to both popular and parliamentary pressure and reluctantly gave their approval. The resulting Reform Act introduced a system of voter registration and made clear the minimum amount of property a person had to have to qualify to vote. Nationally the number of people entitled to vote rose from around 400,000 to 650,000, but Bristol had already possessed an unusually large electorate and so its electorate only marginally increased. The Act abolished 143 seats that had become unnecessary and which had been in the control of just a few people and it created 130 new seats, giving some towns their first M.P. and many larger towns and cities additional M.P.s. because of the size of their population. This change was a huge blow to those who supported slavery because many of the seats lost had been in the control of the West Indies interest.

The moment the slave resolves that he will no longer be a slave, his fetters fall. He frees himself and shows the way to others. Freedom and slavery are mental states
Mahatma Gandhi, Indian anti-colonialist in *Non-Violence in Peace and War* in 1949

The Reform Act, though in some respects very modest, is usually credited with launching modern democracy and it certainly created a parliament that was more progressive and prone to introduce change. How was a reformed House of Commons going to view the slavery issue? Up until 1832 the case for rapid abolition had still not been generally accepted, largely because there were still many people who were prepared to accept the statements of plantation owners that their slaves were well-looked after and happy. In 1831 a former naval surgeon called William Porter, who had retired to Bristol as a doctor, had published a novel that exemplified that belief. Called *Sir Edward Seward's narrative of his shipwreck and consequent discovery of certain islands in the Caribbean Sea*, it narrated the experiences of a couple purchasing slaves and creating an idyllic home on a Caribbean island:

> Nothing but happy faces met us… The women crowd round my wife, kissing her hand. Indeed she smiled so sweetly on them, and had already done so many kind things to them, they could not but love her… We felt as our first parents would have felt had they been permitted to return to Paradise after their expulsion… [All those creating our plantation] were cheerful and greeted us cordially when we came among them… [and we enjoyed] finishing the day in witnessing the hilarity and mirth of our settlers, round the great tree, in dance and song, enjoying their coffee and

cigars … [We dedicated the Sabbath] to the more especial observance of moral and religious duties; permitting every one to indulge themselves in innocent amusement after duly performing the duties of the day… We were much pleased with the improved devotion of all our people… [and with] the great progress many of them had made in reading words of one and two syllables, in sentences conveying sense and meaning… [When some new slaves arrived my wife told them] 'We will love you and show you all kindness'… and I took the opportunity of stating to them that… I should treat them as the white indentured servants in Jamaica were treated.

However, the nonsense that slaves were happy and cared for had been shattered just after the Bristol riots. On Christmas Day 1831, perhaps as many as 60,000 of the 300,000 slaves in Jamaica rebelled. The rebellion was brutally crushed in eleven days but not before fourteen whites and about five hundred slaves had been killed. Afterwards perhaps up to 340 slaves were executed after rather arbitrary trials and many more were punished in very brutal ways. The planters and their allies tried to attribute the rebellion to the unsettling impact of the abolitionist movement:

[They have] occasioned a very feverish and dangerous excitement in the minds of slaves, and have produced a very extensive and deep rooted insubordination and resistance to authority.

The Jamaican authorities claimed their slaves had been comfortable and contented until they had been encouraged to think beyond their station by the foolish activities of Methodist, Baptist and Moravian missionaries. They showed their displeasure by executing Samuel Shape, a black Baptist preacher, whom they judged to have inspired the revolt, and by punishing three white preachers. One was tarred and feathered and two were imprisoned. Nine Baptist and six Methodist chapels were burnt down.

This was of particular significance to Bristol because two of the arrested missionaries, Thomas Burchell and William Knibb, were from Bristol. Burchell had been a student at the Baptist College and Knibb, who had come to Bristol as a teenager to be apprenticed as a printer, had belonged to the Baptist Broadmead congregation and worked in the city's slums before going to Jamaica with his wife in 1824. These men knew that the talk of happy and contented slaves was a myth. Knibb's journal reveals how much he had been shocked by seeing at first hand the brutalising impact of slavery not just on the slaves but on their masters. For example, he recounts how one owner would insist on his female slaves working naked as a way of preparing them for the time when he would rape them. That Knibb was not entirely immune from the racist attitudes of the day can be seen in the fact he was not prepared to let his white children have a black wet-nurse, but his behaviour towards the slaves was so radically different to that of the plantation owners and overseers that it brought him persecution. His and Burchell's unceasing efforts to create schools for the black community explains why the planters arrested them.

I believe in Liberty for all men: the space to stretch their arms and their souls… uncursed by colour; thinking, dreaming, working as they will
William Du Bois, American civil rights activist in newspaper article in 1904

At first the burning of churches and the ill-treatment meted out to missionaries did not receive much coverage *Felix Farley's Bristol Journal*, for example, did not report what had happened to the missionaries or the churches. Instead it provided accounts of how the rebel slaves had butchered white families. However, that all changed when Knibb returned to Bristol after he was acquitted of the charges brought against him. He commenced telling what he had seen and what the authorities had done and he began campaigning not just in Bristol but nationally in favour of slave emancipation:

> The cursed blast of slavery has, like a pestilence, withered almost every moral bloom. I know not how any person can feel a union with such a monster, such a child of hell. I feel a burning hatred against it and look upon it as one of the most odious monsters that ever disgraced the earth. The iron hand of oppression daily endeavours to keep the slaves in the ignorance to which it has reduced them.

The heated response of the Baptists and Methodists to the treatment of their missionaries helped radicalise Bristol's Anti-Slavery Society.

All this did not immediately impinge on the first election for the reformed parliament in the summer of 1832. Parliamentary reform had cost the pro-slavery group many seats but the West Indian merchants and plantation owners still controlled a large number – including Bristol's two seats. The only change was that Bristol reverted back to electing one Whig and one Tory. Evan Baillie was re-elected but Protheroe, largely because of internal Whig in-fighting, lost his seat to the Tory candidate, Sir Richard Vyvyan, a former M.P for Okehampton.

The Victory Of 1833

Above: Destruction in Jamaica 1831 by Adolphe Duperly and recent banknote displaying Samuel Sharpe. Right: lithograph of William Knibb 1838. Below: Joseph Sturge with negro child by A. Rippingille and medal struck to celebrate the end of slavery in 1834. It quotes a psalm: 'This is the Lord's doing; it is marvellous in our eyes.'

The West India Association put large amounts of money into encouraging M.P.s to vote against a government backed bill for the emancipation of the slaves in the British colonies when it went before the new Parliament in 1833. The abolitionists hoped most M.P.s would not be swayed by this and would be guided instead by reading the outcome of parliamentary enquires into the Jamaican revolt. They organised once again massive petitions. One of those sent from Bristol was signed by 179,000 women. It was left to a former Bristol mayor, Henry Bright to put the pro-slavery view in a printed pamphlet

> We have noticed none of the schemes for emancipation because we look at them all as perfectly chimerical. Continuous labour... is necessary to the agriculture and manufactures of the colonies...We have humanely... administered a system approved and enjoined upon us by our country; and we shall demand from the people of England, who became rich by the profits and participated in the guilt (if guilt there be), a full, fair, and immediate compensation for our slaves, and the most ample pecuniary security and political protection for our lands, should they compel us to adopt any alterations in the system injurious to our property.

The issue of compensation was now central and the government felt it had been elected with a mandate for widespread reform. Once it became clear that the government was prepared to offer compensation if slavery was abolished, there was a massive change of attitude among the plantation owners. Both Baillie and Vyvyan, like many other pro-slavery M.P.s, lost interest in further defending slavery. Vyvyan also admitted later that he found representing Bristol 'irksome'.

The bill was passed by the House of Commons on 26 July 1833 just three days before William Wilberforce died. It went through the Lords and received royal assent, becoming law on 28 August, although it did not come into effect until 1 August 1834. The press in Bristol were varied in their response to the abolition of slavery according to their political bias. The *Bristol Gazette* welcomed the emancipation but the *Bristol Journal* complained at the speed with which the legislation had been rushed through parliament and said it left all the colonists facing 'great anxiety for the future'. The more progressive *Bristol Mercury* focussed in on the fact the Act was a phased emancipation and described it as 'a Bill for continuing slavery in the British colonies for a period of seven years'. This was because only slaves aged below six were immediately freed. All other slaves were designated as 'apprentices' who would be eventually freed. Until then they had to continue working without payment and they had no protection against savage punishments.

It was left to a Quaker called Joseph Sturge to publicise the appalling way in which the emancipated 'apprentices' were subsequently treated. Born in Elberton in Gloucestershire and educated first at a school in Thornbury and then at Sidcot School in Somerset, Sturge had become a grain merchant in Birmingham. As a consequence of his revelations, which followed a visit to Jamaica, the government agreed to end some of the apprenticeships in August 1838 and the remainder in August 1840. An exception was made for slaves belonging to the territories belonging to the East India Company and the two islands of Ceylon (now Sri-Lanka) and St Helena and those slaves were not freed until 1843. Sturge went on to found the British and Foreign Anti-Slavery Society in 1839 and to organise the first international anti-slavery convention in 1840.

There is no king who has not had a slave among his ancestors, and no slave who has not had a king among his
                    Helen Keller a deaf-blind activist in *The Story of My Life* in 1903

The Abolition of Slavery Act provided that compensation of twenty million pounds would be paid not to the enslaved but to the enslavers. In modern terms that is around three billion pounds so the compensation paid to the slave owners was immense. Half was paid to slave-owning families in the Caribbean and Africa and the other half to absentee owners living in Britain. The *Bristol Gazette* welcomed this as showing 'the undoubted rights of property on the one hand and the undoubted mass of public feeling on the other', but the *Bristol Mercury* was less sympathetic to the slave owners and it said the amount of compensation was a ridiculously huge burden for the country to carry. A £15 million loan was taken out to help pay the compensation and that money was not entirely repaid until 2015. The biggest beneficiary in Bristol was the planter Thomas Daniel, the 'King of Bristol', who was awarded £102,000 (around £7 million in today's values) for 3,400 slaves in Barbados, Antigua, Tobago and British Guiana. The Baillie family received £62,000 (just over £4 million) for its slaves in Trinidad and British Guiana, while the Pinney family got just over £36,000 (approaching £2.5 million) for its slaves, mostly on Nevis. A record of the many other beneficiaries can be found in Peter Marshall's 1975 publication, *Bristol and the Abolition of Slavery*.

Much of this compensation money found its way into industrial projects. Christopher Claxton, for example, used his money to become a pioneer of the transatlantic steamship and he is now best remembered for his business partnership with his friend Isambard Kingdom Brunel and the creation of the *S.S. Great Britain*. Many others put their money into the Great Western Railway and, in the words of one historian, were happy 'to replace slaves with sleepers'.

SECTION FIVE

THE SURVIVAL OF SLAVERY AND RACIST ATTITUDES INTO THE MODERN ERA

I too live in the time of slavery, by which I mean I am living in the future created by it
  Saidiya Hartman, American academic in *Lose Your Mother: A Journey Along the Atlantic Slave Route* in 2008

The British often assume that their actions are more important than those of any other nation and some accounts of its decision to abolish slavery give the impression that the world immediately changed as a consequence. It did not. Slavery was far too well established globally to disappear simply because Britain had finally decided to turn its back on slavery. The trade in enslaved Africans continued to flourish until the 1850s and the last known slave ship sailed to Cuba in 1866.

In fairness to Britain it certainly tried to encourage other countries to abolish slavery after it had defeated Napoleon and the first ever World Anti-Slavery Convention was held in London in 1840. In the first instance France was probably the country most affected by Britain's decision to emancipate its slaves because of the intermixing of French and British colonies in the Caribbean. It ended slavery in its colonies in 1848. The Netherlands and Portugal did not abolish all forms of slavery until 1863 and 1869 respectively and Spain only abolished slavery in its colonies in the 1870s and 1880s. In the United States of America the northern states had mostly abandoned slavery even before Britain's decision, but there were still 'indentured servants' or 'perpetual apprentices' in some places till as late as 1860. The seven slave-holding southern states (South Carolina, Mississippi, Florida, Alabama, Georgia, Louisiana, and Texas) refused to abandon slavery. One of the most powerful indictments of the continuation of slavery in America came in 1852 from a fugitive slave, Frederick Douglas, who gave an address on the Fourth of July, the day that Americans traditionally celebrated their acquisition of 'freedom' from Britain:

> This Fourth of July is *yours*, not *mine*. *You* may rejoice, *I* must mourn… What, to the American slave, is your Fourth of July? I answer: a day that reveals to him, more than all other days in the year, the gross injustice and cruelty to which he is the constant victim. To him, your celebration is a sham; your boasted liberty, an unholy license; your national greatness, swelling vanity; your sounds of rejoicing are empty and heartless; your denunciations of tyrants, brass-fronted impudence; your shouts of liberty and equality, hollow mockery; your prayers and hymns, your sermons and thanksgivings, with all your religious parade, and solemnity, are, to him, mere bombast, fraud, deception, impiety, and hypocrisy – a thin veil to cover up crimes which would disgrace a nation of savages. There is not a nation on the earth guilty of practices, more shocking and bloody, than are the people of these United States, at this very hour… The existence of slavery in this country brands your republicanism as a sham, your humanity as a base pretense, and your Christianity as a lie… It fetters your progress; it is the enemy of improvement, the deadly foe of education; it fosters pride; it breeds insolence; it promotes vice; it shelters crime; it is a curse to the earth that supports it; and yet, you cling to it, as if it were the sheet anchor of all your hopes.

It was the law that if a white man was caught trying to educate a Negro slave, he was liable to prosecution entailing a fine of fifty dollars and a jail sentence. . .Our ignorance was the greatest hold the South had on us. We knew we could run away, but what then?
John W. Fields a former slave in Layfayette, Indiana, recording his experiences in *Born In Slavery* in 1936

In 1858 James Henry Hammond, a politician and planter in South Carolina, made his famous 'Cotton is King' speech comparing slavery in the southern states to the alleged 'freedom' of the African Americans in the northern states. It reflected just how strongly the pro-slavery lobbyists were still using the old eighteenth-century arguments about black people being better off under white control and white people being safer because of the suppression of black savagery:

The Survival of Slavery and Racist Attitudes

Above: the first World Anti-Slavery Conference in 1840. Participants had to be male so the few women are there as observers. Right; Josiah Henson, the former slave on whom Harriet Beecher Stowe is said to have based her benign 'Uncle Tom'. Below: a 1865 cartoon depicts the negro as a murderer not a brother and a photograph of black soldiers in the Union army in 1863 fighting for the freedom of all African-Americans in the American Civil War.

The difference between us is, that our slaves are hired for life and well compensated; there is no starvation, no begging, no want of employment among our people, and not too much employment either. Yours are hired by the day, not cared for, and scantily compensated… You meet more beggars in one day in any single street of the city of New York than you would meet in a lifetime in the whole South… .Our slaves are black, of another and inferior race. The status in which we have placed them is an elevation. They are elevated from the condition in which God first created them, by being made our slaves. None of that race on the whole face of the globe can be compared with the slaves of the South. They are happy, content, unaspiring, and utterly incapable, from intellectual weakness, ever to give us any trouble by their aspirations… [Free the slave and] there will be an eternal war of races, desolating the land with blood, and utterly wasting and destroying all the resources of the country.

By then opposition to slavery had significantly mounted in the northern states, helped by vociferous demands for its abolition by the Quakers and by new branches of Methodism that had returned to Wesley's position, rejecting the neutrality that the Methodist Episcopal Church had long sustained. This was an important change because Methodism was the largest Christian denomination in the United States. Nevertheless, it took the American Civil War of 1861 to 1865 to end slavery in the southern states and, even after that, the south remained a centre for racial segregation and racist behaviour of the worst kind.

We all lonesome for our home
Cudjoe Lewis, last surviving male slave trade victim in America in 1932

It is a sobering thought that the last slave ship known to enter US waters was the *Clotilda* the year before the Civil War commenced and that the last male and last two female survivors of its human cargo of 116 slaves died within the living memory of people alive today. The man was called Oluale and he was from the Yoruba people in Benin. He was taken captive at the age of nineteen during a raid of his village. Once in America he was sold and renamed Cudjoe Lewis. He worked as a deckhand on a steamer on the Mississippi. After the Civil War he was freed but he was unable to return home and so he joined others in creating Africatown as a self-contained independent black community which offered a safe haven from racism. He died in 1935. The two women, also from

Benin, were Redoshi Smith, who died in 1937, and Matilda McCrear, who died in 1940. Redoshi was abducted from her home at the age of twelve. She was bought by a plantation owner from Alabama and he renamed her Sally Smith and forced her to immediately marry one of his other slaves. This was a man from another tribe and neither spoke the language of the other. She stayed on the same plantation for the rest of her life, first as a slave, and then, after the American Civil War had produced emancipation, as a sharecropper. Matilda was enslaved at at the age of two along with her mother and three older sisters. We do not know her African name. She was bought with her mother and one of her sisters by a plantation owner called Memorable Creagh and he called her Matilda Creagh. They never saw the other two sisters again. After emancipation Matilda changed her surname to McCrear and became the life-long partner of a white German, thus crossing the traditional race boundaries at a time when this was exceptionally rare.

Racism is not first and foremost a skin problem. It is a sin problem. See, when you believe that racism is a skin problem, you can take three hundred years of slavery, court decisions, marches, and the federal government involvement and still not get it fixed right
  Tony Evans, American radio broadcaster of *The Urban Alternative* in 2019

In Central and South America it took decades for slavery to be officially abolished. The first countries to take action were Chile in 1823 and Mexico in 1824, although it was many years before their decision was enforced. Most of the other countries ceased their participation in the slave trade in the 1840s and 1850s but it took them much longer to abolish slavery: Paraguay in 1842, Ecuador and New Granada (modern day Columbia and Panama) in 1851, Argentina, Peru and Venezuela in 1854, Puerto Rica in 1873, Cuba in 1886, and Brazil in 1888. This book has not focused on the slave trade to Brazil because that was not where Bristol's merchants sold their slaves, but it should be remembered that it is estimated around 45% of all enslaved Africans were taken there. Today there are more than 75 million people of African descent living in Brazil – the second largest black population in the world.

White slavery in Eastern Europe was equally slow to end: Austria ended serfdom in 1848, Moldavia in 1855, Wallachia in 1856, Poland in 1860, and Russia in 1861. Many European countries signed an international agreement to suppress the remaining white slave traffic in 1903.

In Africa multiple forms of slavery continued to flourish. This eventually became an excuse for the European powers to conquer and colonise it in the second half of the nineteenth century. Gradually this led to emancipation occurring in name in most African countries between 1874 and 1936, but that did not mean the practice was actually stamped out. Today there are still an estimated nine million slaves in Africa. What made abolition particularly difficult was the long standing Arab slave trade in West Africa, North Africa and Southeast Africa. Britain in particular worked hard to persuade Muslim countries to abolish slavery but there was huge resistance. British pressure forced the Ottoman Empire to cease officially supporting the slave trade in 1847 but Turkey did not abolish slavery until 1924. Iran followed suit in 1929, Ethiopia in 1935, and Kuwait in 1949 but some states delayed until well after the Second World War. For example, Saudi Arabia and Yemen only abolished slavery in 1962, Oman in 1970, and Mauritania in 1982. Enforcement of abolition has been more noted by its absence than its presence.

In Asia it has been a similar story. Britain secured the ending of the indenture system in India in 1860, but it was replaced by a system that still basically maintained slavery. Today there are an estimated eight million slaves in India. Cambodia abolished slavery in 1884, Korea in 1894, Taiwan in 1895, Siam (now Thailand) in 1912, New Granada (now Malaysia) in 1915, and Nepal and Burma in 1926 but there was little official enforcement in all these countries and so much illegal slavery continues. In Japan there was an accepted use of sex slaves (the so-called 'comfort women') that survived until at least 1945. China never enforced the ban on slavery that it introduced in 1910. and today it is estimated there are still 3.6 million slaves in that country. Across the Asian-Pacific region as a whole there are thought to be over 30 million slaves.

Slavery didn't end… It just evolved
    Bryan Stevenson African-American lawyer in interview on CNN in 2018

All this seems miles away from nations having signed the 1948 United Nations Universal Declaration of Human Rights, which says 'all human beings are born free and equal in dignity and rights' and that, 'whatever your race or colour or sex or language or status or origins and whatever your political or other opinions, you are entitled to all the rights and freedoms'. The truth is that over seventy years after passed since that declaration was made and yet most experts judge there are still between forty and forty-six million slaves in the world.

Anti-Slavery International has produced the following criteria to judge whether someone is enslaved:

The Survival of Slavery and Racist Attitudes

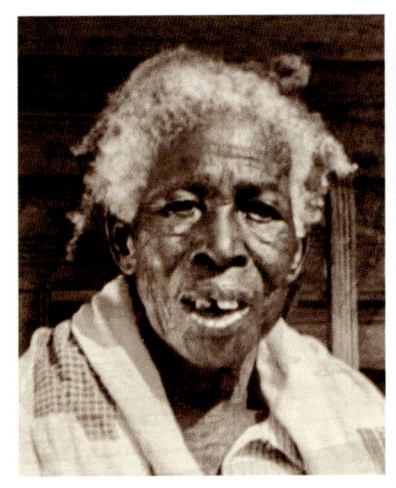

The last survivors of those enslaved and brought to the United States. Above: Redoshi Smith. Right: Cudjoe Lewis and Matilda McCrear and what is thought to be the remains of the slave ship the 'Clotilda' recently discovered in 2019. Below: Frederick Douglas, the fugitive slave who wrote the most famous of all the slave autobiographies.

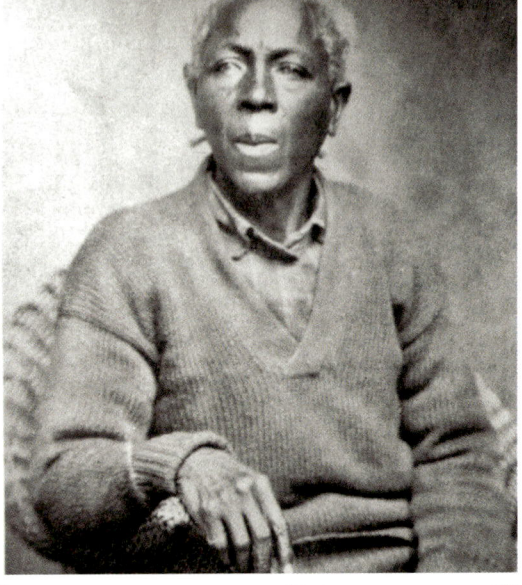

- they are forced to work through coercion by mental or physical threat;
- they are trapped and controlled by an 'employer', through mental or physical abuse or the threat of abuse;
- they are dehumanised, treated as a commodity, or bought and sold as 'property';
- they are physically constrained or have restrictions placed on their freedom of movement.

By those criteria it judges there are thirty million enslaved adults and ten million enslaved children in the world and it judges that about 10% of the enslaved are exploited by governments so it is not just a question of slavery surviving through the bad behaviour of illicit dealers and owners. The most common forms of modern slavery are:

- forced labour (i..e where people are compelled to work against their will under threat of punishment);
- bonded labour (i.e. where people are made to work to pay off debts that never are actually paid);
- human trafficking (i.e. where people are recruited and transported to other places or countries and then exploited and treated violently);
- forced marriage;
- child slavery. This is not to be confused with child labour because it includes things like child trafficking, child marriage, and forcing children to become soldiers.

There is no form of slavery, past or present, that isn't horrific; however, today's slavery is one of the most diabolical strains to emerge in the thousands of years in which humans have been enslaving their fellows

Kevin Bales and Ron Soodalter, American writers in *The Slave Next Door* in 2010

People become slaves in the same way as they always have – by being born into slavery or by being enslaved. And no country is slave-free. For example, here is one set of estimates for slave numbers in some of the countries in which the inhabitants mostly think there is no slavery:

- Australia: 15,000
- Canada: 17,000
- Japan: 37,000

- France: 129,000
- Italy: 145,000
- Germany: 167,000
- Brazil: 369,000
- United States: 420,000
- Russia: 794,000

The estimated figure for enslaved people in Great Britain varies enormously from 13,000 to 136,000. The most common forms of enslavement here are sexual exploitation and forced labour in industries such as agriculture, construction, manufacturing, and hospitality services. It is not just happening in nail bars and car washes!

Over the past decade or so various charitable organisations in Britain have tried to bring the slavery issue to the forefront of people's minds again and, like the abolitionists of the eighteenth century, they have lobbied parliament to introduce legislative measures. One of their successes has been the 2015 Modern Slavery Act. Among other things this made prosecuting traffickers easier, increased sentences for slavery offences, enabled the seizure of the assets of those involved in enslaving, and made some provision (though not enough) for the protection of victims. It also has resulted in the appointment of an Independent Anti-Slavery Commissioner. At the time of its passing James Brokenshire, the Parliamentary Under Secretary for Crime and Security, said:

> [This Act will] send the strongest possible message to criminals that if you are involved in this disgusting trade in human beings, you will be arrested, you will be prosecuted and you will be locked up.

However, currently only a minority of cases are referred to the police. The figure is around 5,000 a year. This is partly because many victims are fearful of going to the police because they believe they are more likely to be punished than their exploiters. This fear is not without foundation. The conviction rate for slavery-related crimes is only around 2% and those trafficked from abroad face the prospect of being forced by the authorities to leave Britain. Recently released statistics show that Avon and Somerset Police had to deal with 40 cases of slavery in 2018 and the Modern Slavery Helpline reported dealing with 78 cases of potential slavery in Avon and Somerset involving 350 victims. It is generally accepted these cases represent just a tiny minority of the slavery that exists in the Bristol area. All this makes rather a mockery of the 2015 Modern

Slavery and Bristol

All over the world there are memorials to remind people of slavery and racism directed at black people. Below left: old statues often portray the African as totally reliant on the white man for his freedom as in these statues to the French abolitionist Victor Schoelcher and to the American President Abraham Lincoln. Below right and opposite page: Modern memorials tend to focus just on the slaves, often depicting their suffering. On this page are examples from Haiti, Amsterdam, and Martinique. On opposite page are examples from North Carolina, Zanzibar, Barbados, Louisiana, and Alabama. Why has Bristol yet to produce a memorial?

The Survival of Slavery and Racist Attitudes

Slavery Act and sadly Brexit may make matters even worse if it damages Britain's collaboration with the police forces of other European countries. Defeating traffickers relies on networking to share information and criminal databases.

Only 1% of victims of slavery have a chance to see their exploiter brought to justice
>Kevin Hymand, UK Independent Anti-Slavery Commissioner in 2018

The survival of slavery is only the tip of the iceberg because the legacy of racism generated by the slave trade affects many more millions today. The justification for black slavery was always that black people were inferior to white people and that mistaken belief was not killed by emancipation. Racism directed against blacks has remained a feature of many societies. In Hitler's Germany it was not just the Jews who were targeted. The Nazis introduced a programme of sterilisation to prevent black people breeding. In South Africa, belief in white supremacy generated a ruthless apartheid system that lasted from 1948 to the early 1990s. In the United States it bred the white supremacy hate group, the Ku Klux Klan, and created 'Jim Crow' laws which enforced racial segregation in the southern states and hindered black people from gaining a good education or employment or having the comforts enjoyed by the whites. Marriage between a white person and a black person was illegal in parts of America until 1967.

The whole concept of racism as we understand it has its roots in slavery. The way it demeaned the black man as less of a human being is where the concept of inferiority of black-skinned people came from
>Paul Stephenson, civil rights activist in Bristol cited in *The Independent* in May 2006

The extent of racial prejudice still prevalent among certain sectors of American society, especially the police, was dramatically highlighted on 25 May 2020 by the murder of George Floyd by a policeman in Minneapolis. It is worth saying in this context that policing in the southern states largely originated in slave patrols that were first set up in the eighteenth century. These were white volunteers who were empowered to use vigilante tactics against any African-American judged to have 'over-stepped the mark' by violating a rule or attempting to escape. When police forces were created in the nineteenth century they were almost entirely recruited from whites and they were empowered to use whatever force was necessary to control the 'dangerous underclass'. That phrase included immigrants but it mainly referred to African-Americans. For over eighty years one of the primary tasks of the police force was to enforce the 'Jim Crow' laws that treated African-Americans as second-class citizens. The courts did not punish policemen for any action they took against an African-American, however brutal, and they never condemned the police for failing to arrest anyone involved in lynching black people. Over the past fifty years the American federal government has been trying to undo this terrible legacy by forbidding states from maintaining racist regulations, but many police forces remain hugely racist in the way they operate. George Floyd's tragic murder in Minneapolis by the policeman Derek Chauvin may have hit the headlines, especially as it was caught on camera, but it is not an isolated incident: hence the massive outcry it evoked across the United States and other countries.

If you don't dominate your city and your state, they're going to walk away with you
Donald Trump, President of the United States on the opposition to the murder of George Floyd in speech in June 2020

The Black Lives Matter response in Bristol and elsewhere in Britain to Floyd's murder indicates that there are still many black people in this country who feel very strongly that they are also racially targeted. Britain may not have engaged in such excesses as sterilisation or legal segregation or public lynchings but racial discrimination was and remains a major feature of life in this country for many non-whites. Discrimination in housing and employment was rampant throughout the twentieth century and there was an insidious acceptance of stereotypes right up to the 1980s that forced many black people and those of mixed race to feel they were profoundly unwelcome. Recalling his childhood the broadcaster and film-maker David Olusoga wrote recently:

> I imbibed enough of the background racial tensions of the late 1970s and 1980s to feel profoundly unwelcome in Britain… Secretly, I harboured fears that as part of the group identified by chanting neo-Nazis, hostile neighbours and even television comedians as "them" we might be sent "back". This, in our case, presumably meant "back" to Nigeria, a country of which I had only infant memories and a land upon which my youngest siblings had never set foot… I was eight years old when the BBC finally cancelled *The Black and White Minstrel Show*. I have memories of my mother rushing across our living room to change television channels (in the days before remote

controls) to avoid her mixed-race children being confronted by grotesque caricatures of themselves on prime-time television… I grew up in a Britain in which there were pictures of golliwogs on jam jars… [and] it is difficult to regard a word [like 'golliwog' or 'wog'] as benign when it has been scrawled on to a note, wrapped around a brick and thrown through one's living-room window in the dead of night… In the face of such hostility, many black people… slipped into a siege mentality, a state of mind from which it has been difficult to entirely escape.

Racism is still a major issue. A report by the Equality and Human Rights Commission in 2016 showed that black graduates in Britain were paid an average 23.1% less than similarly qualified white workers and it reported that between 2010 and 2016 there had been a 49% increase in the number of ethnic minority 16- to 24-year-olds who were long-term unemployed compared to 2% fall for white people. A Guardian/ ICM survey in 2018 reported that those from a minority ethnic background are twice as likely as white people to have encountered rudeness or abuse, to be overlooked for promotion at work, and to be accused of a crime. Other European countries have the same problem. A study in 2018 called *Being Black in the EU* concluded that across the European Union people of African descent are facing 'widespread and entrenched prejudice and exclusion'.

Although slavery may have been abolished, the crippling poison of racism still persists, and the struggle still continues
Ascribed to Harry Belafonte, Jamaican singer and songwriter

Throughout the nineteenth and early twentieth centuries there were relatively few black people living in Bristol and those that did live in it seem to have been reasonably well integrated. However, racism certainly became very prevalent in the city after the Second World War. The two events that usually spring to people's mind in this context are the black-led Bristol Bus boycott in 1963 and the St Paul's riot in 1980 and its aftermath. These two events both stemmed from the racial hatred directed against the so-called 'Windrush generation'. The name comes from the ship the *Windrush*, which brought workers from Jamaica, Trinidad and Tobago and other islands, as a response to post-war labour shortages in Britain. About 3,000 of these African-Caribbean migrants chose to come to Bristol in the 1950s. Far from being welcomed, they were met with racial hatred and they found it very difficult to find employment. Gangs of white youths would lash out at them with bicycle chains. Most of the African-Caribbean immigrants ended up in the St Paul's district because it had suffered badly in the Bristol Blitz and so housing was cheaper there. Roy Hackett, who arrived in Britain in 1952 from Jamaica, recalls his experience of moving to Bristol after working in some other places:

> Great Britain was not great to its Commonwealth people because we were of different colour… Boarding houses displayed signs saying 'No gypsies, no dogs, no Irish and no coloured… There was no rule about discrimination and they thought they could do anything and get away with it… I felt extremely degraded and I thought, 'What am I doing here?' You couldn't go into pubs in Bristol on your own, not if you were black. You'd get a hiding. You had to go in two or three at a time. There were shops that wouldn't serve us. Ninety per cent of us, if we had been able to go back we would have.

What history had I inherited that left me an alien in my place of birth?
Reni Eddo-Lodge, British journalist from Nigerian background, writing in 2018

In 1962 Hackett and three other Jamaicans, Owen Henry, Audley Evan, and Clifford Drummond, set up the Commonwealth Co-ordinated Committee to try and unite the Caribbean community and it met in Drummond's cafe. A black support teacher from Essex called Paul Stephenson soon became its President and he urged radical action should be taken against the Bristol Omnibus Company, which was refusing to employ any black person as either a bus driver or a bus conductor. This was in line with a resolution passed in 1955 by the Passenger Group section of the Transport and General Workers' Union that no 'coloured workers' should be employed in those capacities. This justification given for this ban was that busmen were so badly paid they had to work overtime to survive and, if 'coloured workers' were employed, the overtime would vanish. Knowing that he spoke with an Essex accent and would not therefore be recognised as black, Stephenson telephoned the bus company in April 1963 saying he wanted to arrange an interview for a school friend who was keen to fill an advertised vacancy for a driver. The 'friend' was a black despatch clerk called Guy Bailey. Bailey turned up for the arranged interview looking exceptionally smart but he was turned away as soon as it was seen he was not a white applicant. Stephenson released the story to the local press and the bus company's manager defended its policy by saying that black workers were too unskilled for front-line jobs. He also added that it was not reasonable to expect white conductresses to have to work with black male drivers.

As you grow older, you'll see white men cheat black men every day of your life, but let me tell you something and don't you forget it—whenever a white man does that to a black man, no matter who he is, how rich he is, or how fine a family he comes from, that white man is trash
Harper Lee, American novelist in *To Kill A Mockngbird* in 1960

Armed with such blatant racist remarks, Stephenson called on all people in Bristol to boycott using the buses. This action was opposed by the Labour-run Council who chose to support the policy of the Transport and General Workers' Union. However, the Bristol Labour M.P. Tony Benn supported the boycott. Marches were organised and the bus depot was picketed and students from Bristol University swelled the ranks of the protestors. It was not long before the boycott attracted national and international attention. Various well-known figures supported it, including the famous ex-West Indies cricketer, Sir Learie Constantine, who was then serving as Trinidad's High Commissioner, and the future Labour Prime Minister, Harold Wilson. Stephenson was a gifted spokesman and Bailey had a quiet dignity that made him a perfect figurehead. In the face of mounting adverse publicity the bus company surrendered on 28 August and agreed to begin employing black drivers.

The timing could not have been better from the black perspective because on that same day in Washington the African-American civil rights' activist Martin Luther King made his famous speech about his hope for a less racist world:

Even though we face the difficulties of today and tomorrow, I still have a dream… I have a dream that one day this nation will rise up and live out the true meaning of its creed: 'We hold these truths to be self-evident, that all men are created equal'. I have a dream that one day on the red hills of Georgia, the sons of former slaves and the sons of former slave owners will be able to sit down together at the table of brotherhood. I have a dream that one day even the state of Mississippi, a state sweltering with the heat of injustice, sweltering with the heat of oppression, will be transformed into an oasis of freedom and justice. I have a dream that my four little children will one day live in a nation where they will not be judged by the colour of their skin but by the content of their character. I have a dream… that little black boys and black girls will be able to join hands with little white boys

The Survival of Slavery and Racist Attitudes

Top: the 1963 Bristol Bus Boycott with pictures of Stephenson, Bailey and Hackett and Evening post headline. Above: Guy Bailey and Roy Hackett today. Right: Paul Stephenson with his O.B.E. Below: the plaque in Bristol Bus Station of the five leaders of the boycott plus Raghbir Singh, the first non-white bus conductor.

and white girls as sisters and brothers… I have a dream that one day every valley shall be exalted, every hill and mountain shall be made low, the rough places will be made plain, and the crooked places will be made straight, and the glory of the Lord shall be revealed, and all flesh shall see it together. This is our hope… we will be able to hew out of the mountain of despair a stone of hope… Let freedom ring from every village and every hamlet, from every state and every city… Speed up that day when all of God's children, black men and white men, Jews and Gentiles, Protestants and Catholics, will be able to join hands and sing in the words of the old Negro spiritual: 'Free at last. Free at last. Thank God almighty, we are free at last.'

By September Bristol had its first non-white bus conductor, an Indian-born Sikh called Raghbir Singh. It was not Bailey because he wanted to get out of the limelight and he was uncomfortable with going to work for an organisation which had only changed its policy under duress. That the bus company was reluctant to change is born out by evidence that suggests it may have operated a secret quota system to restrict how many black staff it employed. However, even if that is true, it does not detract from the importance of the boycott's success. It boosted black morale and it made other companies look at their recruitment policies. Even more importantly, it was a significant factor in making the government decide that Britain required a Race Relations Act to make discrimination illegal. Roy Hackett continued to be a leading figure in promoting better community relationships in Bristol, serving on the Bristol Race Equality Council from 1965 to 2005. He also remained a key figure on the Commonwealth Coordinated Committee, which set up and ran the St Paul's Festival from 1968 to 1979 (after which time it was taken-over by others who developed it into the St Paul's Carnival), and he then was key figure in the C.C.C.'s successor organisation, W.I.P.F.A. (the Bristol West Indian Parents and Friends Association). Paul Stephenson played a prominent role in other parts of the country before returning to Bristol in 1992. He became a founder member of the Black Archives Project to 'protect and promote the history of the Afro-Caribbean people'. He was presented with the One Person Can Make A Difference Award in 2006, given the Freedom of the City in 2007 (the first black person to be so honoured), and honoured (alongside Hackett and Bailey) with an O.B.E in 2009 for his work in improving community relations. In 2017 he was also given a Pride of Britain Award for Lifetime Achievement. The judge's citation read:

The Survival of Slavery and Racist Attitudes

Thanks to Paul's courage, principles and determination, Britain is a more open and tolerant place today. He has changed the way we all live for the better, and his story reminds us that the battle for civil rights was not confined to America.

The slave industry shaped the Britain we know, for better and for worse. Some remnants of slavery are despicable – the continuing strain of white supremacy in formal politics. Some are tragic, for example the continuing fragility of black family life. But other legacies, principally those of struggle, are uplifting – the resilience of black church life, the tradition of black popular music and the fierce streak of dissent in British politics are all wholly or partly products of war against the transatlantic slave trade

Trevor Phillips, former Chairman of the Commission for Racial Equality in *The Guardian* in December 2006

The Race Relations Acts of 1965 and 1968 did not end racial discrimination. In Bristol there was extreme unhappiness when more waves of immigrants arrived in the 1970s – first Ugandans and Kenyans and then Bangladeshis. The political and racist campaigning of the National Front party heightened tensions and it did not help that the St Paul's area became even more run-down after it was cut off from the neighbouring area of Easton by the building of the M32 motorway. Relationships with the police force were severely damaged by its use of the 1824 'sus' law which gave it the right to stop and search and/or arrest any suspected person (hence the word 'sus'). It was felt the police were targeting black people. On the afternoon of 2 April 1980 twenty police raided the Black and White Cafe on Grosvenor Road in the heart of the St Paul's district looking for drugs. A riot lasting several hours ensued. The exact event that precipitated the violence is disputed. It is usually said that a customer had his trousers ripped and, when the police refused to pay compensation, they were prevented from leaving by a crowd that had gathered outside. Estimates on how many people were involved range from a couple of hundred to around two thousand.

By around 7.30 p.m. the police were in so much danger from the violence of those attacking them that they were forced to withdraw. Groups set cars on fire and attacked and looted shops before also setting flame to them. A bank, a post office, a warehouse, and an entire row of shops were set ablaze. The fire brigade came under attack when it arrived to deal with the fires and order was only re-established when two hundred policemen, many of them drawn from neighbouring counties, were brought in to deal with the rioters at 11.00 p.m. 134

people were arrested (88 black and 46 white) and 90 of them were subsequently charged. The rioting shocked Bristol and the nation by its level of violence. In the course of the rioting thirty-three people had sustained significant injuries, twenty-one of them policemen and three of them firemen. Some commentators argued the riot stemmed from inadequate parental control among black families but most accepted that deprivation and poverty were the obvious factors behind the riot. This explained the involvement of white Irish as well as blacks in the rioting and the subsequent copycat rioting which broke out not long afterwards in a white working-class housing estate in Southmead.

Racial prejudice had, of course, played a large part in creating the poverty and deprivation in St Paul's and the civil rights campaigner Paul Stephenson, who had played such a prominent role in the 1963 bus boycott, was very clear on what he saw as the main cause of the rioting:

> The riots were ignited by racist and insensitive policing. It was about young blacks who were born in this country saying that they weren't prepared to be treated as second-class citizens any longer.

The black inhabitants of St Paul's wanted to defend the Black and White Cafe (so named because it was run by a black and white husband and wife team) because, as one investigator expressed it, 'they had no where else to go', It was the only black cafe that had not been forced out of business for contravening local authority health or other regulations, and even it had seen its license to sell alcohol removed. The police viewed the cafe as a seedy den where illicit drinking and drug-taking was taking place but for a significant number of the African Caribbeans it was, again to quote the investigator, 'the only bit of territory they had left and they were prepared to fight for the right to do what they liked there'. A not untypical response to the riot among the black community in Britain was to see the riots as a long overdue uprising. Dianne Abbot, later to become a Labour M.P and a Shadow Home Secretary, wrote in the radical magazine *The Leveller* about how community workers and other well-doers had failed to grasp the severity of the situation in St Paul's and how a more assertive and confrontational approach was both justified and required:

> Social workers, vicars, race relations officers, local councillors – in other words the whole structure of social control – wrung its collective hands and wailed 'How could this have happened in Bristol, it had such good community relations?' Someone ought to tell them that… they could try

The Survival of Slavery and Racist Attitudes

Above: the 1980 riot in the St Paul's District.
Below right: the Black and White Cafe.
Below: the procession, one of the highlights of the St Paul's Carnival.

asking black people from St. Pauls. They are scathing about 'community leaders' who are unknown to the community, black social workers who are primarily concerned with holding down their jobs and the local Community Relations Council… The riots have had interesting reverberations within the black community as a whole. My mother is a black working class lady nearing sixty. Eminently respectable and conservative-minded, she was pleased and excited by the ITN film of policemen running away from black youth and said firmly: 'It shows they can't push us around any more'. The riots politicised my mother and others like her.

That kind of 'politicised' response to the rioting is often credited with causing the 1981 black-led riots in Brixton, Birmingham, Manchester, Leeds, and Liverpool. They were also undoubtedly encouraged by the fact most of the Bristol rioters were not prosecuted and a jury did not convict the few who were put on trial. In Brixton, for example, some of the rioters shouted 'Remember Bristol!' whilst charging police lines. It has also to be remembered that, at the time of these 'uprisings' many young black people were well aware of what was going on in America. The non-violent approach of Martin Luther King had been challenged by the more assertive Black Power movement and in particular by the Black Panther Party, which was very active between 1966 and 1982. It had international branches in Britain and in the Caribbean. The 'What We Want Now' demands of the Black Panther Party was attractive to many black people because they included things like decent housing, full employment, an end to police intimidation, and 'an education that teaches us our true history and our role in the present day society'. They were therefore prepared to respond to its claims that violent resistance was the only way of realising black hopes of equal treatment. This encouraged what might be termed 'street toughness' and the importance of defending your community against 'police interlopers'.

It was a place and a time in which 'black' meant 'other' and 'black' was unquestionably the opposite of 'British'. The phrase 'black British', with which we are so familiar today, was little heard in those years. In the minds of some it spoke of an impossible duality… The racism of the 1970s and 1980s and the insecurities it bred in the minds of black people are difficult to imagine or relate to. But they are powerful memories for my generation
    David Olusoga in *Black and `British: A Forgotten History* in 2016

There was no public inquiry after the Bristol riot and so the lessons about what had caused the rioting and about what needed to change to prevent it happening again were not learned. The tensions arising from the fatal mix of prejudice, unemployment and poverty did not go away and the response in Bristol was essentially just to police the St Paul's area less prominently. Unfortunately the reduced police presence served only to enable rival drug gangs to increasingly turn the St Paul's area into a battleground where no one felt safe. The Black and White Cafe became the scene of so many stabbings, shootings, and robberies that it was dubbed by *The Guardian* as 'Britain's most dangerous hard drug den'. However, it is fair to say that during the 1990s significant inroads were made into the racism within Britain and that generated hope in what had seemed a hopeless situation. In Bristol this led to a more determined effort to improve the situation in St Paul's. One way of doing that was to get rid of the chief drug gangs . In 2004 the police acquired a closure order on the Black and White Cafe and the following year it was demolished to make way for housing. Since then police and local community groups have worked very hard to improve matters and the St Paul's district has noticeably become a better and safer place to live, even though racial tensions can still occasionally flare up. Nationally what has become very noticeable is the extent to which West Indians have integrated with the white community through acquiring white partners. According to a report in *The Economist* in 2016 a child under ten who has a Caribbean parent is more than twice as likely to have a white parent as not.

Do you look at me and see a native Bristolian that was born here? Or, do you see another black woman who you don't want to engage with?
Michele Curtis, artist of the Seven Saints of St Pauls murals speaking in 2019

One of the most significant things that people can do to counter the ingrained sense of inferiority that society had imposed on anyone with a black skin is to study history. One of the first to recognise this was the African-American historian Carter Woodson, who founded the Association for the Study of African American Life and History in 1915 and *The Journal of Negro History* in 1916. He created 'Negro History Week' in 1926 as a mechanism to promote a better understanding of the African role in history, saying:

> If a race has no history, it has no worthwhile tradition, it becomes a negligible factor in the thought of the world, and it stands in danger of being exterminated. The American Indian left no continuous record. He did not appreciate the value of tradition; and where is he today? The Hebrew keenly

appreciated the value of tradition, as is attested by the Bible itself. In spite of worldwide persecution, therefore, he is a great factor in our civilisation.

One of Woodson's aims in setting this up was to lobby for changes in what was being taught in American schools. In 1970 when civil rights was at the forefront of American thinking Negro History Week was relaunched as 'Black History Month'. Britain was slow to respond to this initiative but it commenced also recognising this in 1987. The result has been a significant change in historical studies and attitudes. Across the country research was and is being undertaken not just by historians in universities but by hundreds of local amateur volunteers so that the full role played by black people in British history can be appreciated in everything from the world wars to show business. Of course the concept of having a Black History Month is not without its critics. Some have said it is wrong to confine the black issue to one month out of twelve and others have said focusing on black history simply encourages a racist attitude towards whites. However, there is no doubt that the rising interest in the history of Africans has helped put racism into the limelight and it is no longer so easy for whites to glory in Britain's colonial past if they read about the exploitation that accompanied it. Symbolic of this change was the decision in 2012 to bring a replica of the *Windrush* into the London Olympic Stadium.

One of the most remarkable of recent developments designed to celebrate black history is the creation between 2015 and 2019 of seven murals in the St Paul's district. These not only celebrate greater acceptance and inclusion but also reinforce why the black community can feel pride in what it has achieved. Designed by the black artist Michele Curtis working in collaboration with a highly skilled group of mural artists known as the Paintsmiths, each mural focuses on a black person who has contributed hugely to the local community. That prejudice still exists was shown by the initial opposition shown by those in Bristol who did not welcome having 'big black faces' on walls. However, there is now a trail that can be followed to visit the murals and see the seven 'saints'. Four of these are the men who created the Commonwealth Co-ordinated Committee and who devoted so much of their lives to community engagement. On City Road is Owen Henry, on Byron Street is Roy Hackett, on Norrisville Road is Audley Evans, and on a house opposite St Agnes Park is Clifford Drummond. The other three 'saints' are women who have played significant roles. On Morgan Street is depicted Carmen Beckford for her work as the city council's first community development officer and for helping to create and develop the St Paul's carnival. On Ferne Street is Barbara Dettering for her work as a teacher

THE SURVIVAL OF SLAVERY AND RACIST ATTITUDES

The Seven Saints of St Paul's murals completed in 2019: Roy Hackett, Dolores Campbell, Clifford Drummond, Audley Evans, Barbara Dettering, Audley Evans, and Carmen Beckford.

441

influencing young people to overcome social preconceptions and achieve their goals, and on Campbell Street is Dolores Campbell for her work with fostered children and for helping to create and develop the St Paul's Carnival. Each of the seven saints has now been celebrated in verse by Bristol poet laureate, Miles Chambers.

People think racism is about calling people names. And I have had my share of that. But it's also fundamentally about power and access to political and economic opportunities… Getting more people from different backgrounds into positions of power is key
Marvin Rees, Europe's first black elected mayor in *Conversations about Racism in Britain* in 2018

A wave of immigration over the past two decades has been used by some to rekindle racist attitudes. The British African population doubled between 2000 and 2010 largely thanks to the arrival of immigrants from Nigeria, Ghana, Zimbabwe, Somalia, and the Sudan. In Bristol's case its black population was most noticeably affected by the arrival of thousands of refugees and economic migrants from Somalia. As a result Somali is now the third most commonly spoken language in the city. It is much to Bristol's credit that it opted in 2010 to become 'a city of sanctuary', part of a network across the country of places that have said they are committed to being 'inclusive and welcoming'. Unfortunately the financial crisis of 2009 has increasingly led in the last ten years to a widening gap between rich and poor and that, plus a fear of being 'swamped', has encouraged not only a national desire to curb immigration, but also a surge in racist attacks. In this context it is worth quoting recent comments in the press made by Fozia Ismail, who hosts African-inspired supper clubs at her home in Bishopston. She was born in Kuwait to a Somali mother and arrived as a refugee:

> I feel sad that I feel very unwelcome and that comes from Brexit and anti-immigration rhetoric. There have been times where after a terrorist attack, if I'm in a headscarf, buses won't stop for me… If you are black or Muslim, it's so obvious that racism exists… [and] it's unacceptable [for white people] to say 'this does not affect me, so I'm not going to change it'.–

There are, of course, many people in Bristol and elsewhere who continue to campaign for an end to racism in all its forms and not everything is 'doom and gloom', but the statistics cited earlier about current levels of discrimination show that much work still has to be done to free us from inherited racism. There is plenty of talk in the press and elsewhere about the need for Bristol to apologise more fulsomely for its role in the slave trade, but perhaps not yet enough emphasis on modern Bristolians tackling racism and slavery in the city today. It is obvious, for example, that within Bristol the black, Asian and minority ethnic groups (BAME) are still under-represented across the city's major businesses and institutions. In 2109 black and ethnic workers declared there was a 'culture of institutional racism' at the City Council and, after an investigation, it was conceded that a systematic review of HR policies was required. The Council's spokesman commented:

> Historically equality and diversity hasn't been anywhere near where it should be at the council This means, despite recent strides to create an inclusive organisation, attitudes and cultures take longer than desired to change.

The race issue is still affecting the young in all kinds of ways. For example, in December 2019 the officers at the Bristol Students' Union issued an open letter expressing concern about the inaction of the university in dealing with rising cases of racial aggression on campus, in classes, and in student halls.

There are thousands who are in opinion opposed to slavery ... [but they] sit down with their hands in their pockets, and say that they know not what to do, and do nothing
    Henry David Thoreau, American philosopher in *Civil Disobedience and other Essays* in 1849

As far as tackling modern slavery is concerned, there is plenty of advice on what we should all be looking out for. It may be that a person is enslaved if we see someone who
- shows signs of physical or psychological abuse;
- appears frightened and/or looks as if he/she is under the control of someone;
- appears withdrawn and/or is reluctant to talk or interact with other;
- wears the same clothes every day or clothes that are unsuited for the work they are doing;
- has few personal belongings;
- is dropped off and collected for work always in the same way, especially at unusual times (i.e. very early or late at night).

Black Lives Matter. Campaigners in June 2020 in Bristol protesting even in the midst of the coronavirus lockdown in order to show the strength of their feeling and the importance of dealing with continued racism.

The Survival of Slavery and Racist Attitudes

The advice given by experts is not to confront anyone but to report your concern to the police or Crimestoppers or the Modern Slavery Helpline or any specialist anti-slavery organisation.

There are a number of charities whose work in exposing and opposing slavery deserves more support. Two obvious ones are 'Anti-Slavery International' and the Bristol-based 'Unseen'. 'Anti-Slavery International' was founded in 1839 and it describes itself as the oldest human rights organisation in the world. It has been involved in the development of all major laws against slavery and it engages directly in the fight against slavery in many countries, as well as lobbying international institutions such as the United Nations, the International Labour Organisation, the European Union, the African Union, etc. 'Unseen' raises awareness, runs safe houses and a slavery helpline, works with local businesses, and co-chairs the South West Anti-Slavery Partnership which encourages police, businesses, charities, and NHS staff to collaborate more in tackling slavery. Both these charities have excellent websites which outline their work and how people can help.

The past can never be unwritten but how we live in the present writes our future. The toppling of Edward Colston's statue in June 2020 as part of the 'Black Lives Matter' protest may make a statement but it does not solve today's problems. Bristol's mayor Marvin Rees rightly commented to the press on the statue's removal:

> I know the removal of the Colston Statue will divide opinion, as the statue itself has done for many years. However, it's important to listen to those who found the statue to represent an affront to humanity. Let's make the legacy of today about the future of our city, tackling racism and inequality.

The more modern Bristolians engage in fighting racism generally and slavery in particular the more the city will make some atonement for its terrible role in the slave trade and for the racist behaviour that has so scarred and still scars its more recent history.

We can only move forward by confronting the racist legacy of slavery together
Antonio Guterres, Secretary-General of United Nations in message for International Day of Remembrance of the Victims of Slavery and the Transatlantic Slave Trade in 2020

The Survival of Slavery and Racist Attitudes

God speed the year of jubilee
The wide world o'er!
When from their galling chains set free,
Th' oppress'd shall vilely bend the knee,
And wear the yoke of tyranny
Like brutes no more.
That year will come, and freedom's reign,
To man his plundered rights again
Restore.

God speed the day when human blood
Shall cease to flow!
In every clime be understood,
The claims of human brotherhood,
And each return for evil, good,
Not blow for blow;
That day will come all feuds to end.
And change into a faithful friend
Each foe.

God speed the hour, the glorious hour,
When none on earth
Shall exercise a lordly power,
Nor in a tyrant's presence cower;
But all to manhood's stature tower,
By equal birth!
That hour will come, to each, to all,
And from his prison-house, the thrall
Go forth.

Until that year, day, hour, arrive,
With head, and heart, and hand I'll strive,
To break the rod, and rend the gyve,
The spoiler of his prey deprive —
So witness Heaven!
And never from my chosen post,
Whate'er the peril or the cost,
Be driven.

William Lloyd Garrison, prominent nineteenth-century American abolitionist and social reformer in his magazine *The Liberator* in 1845

Six of the most famous and influential of the nineteenth-century writers of 'slave narratives' after Frederick Douglass. Top left to right: William W. Brown, Solomon Northup, and Harriet Jacobs. Right: Booker T. Washington. Below left: Sojourner Truth. Below right: Harriet Tubman. Their stories helped win over many Americans to the anti-slavery cause just as Olaudah Equiano's autobiography had won over many British people.

Further Reading

The cause of freedom is not the cause of a race or a sect, a party or class – it is the cause of humankind, the very birthright of humanity
  Anna Julia Cooper American civil rights activist in *Woman versus the Indian* in 1892

This is not a bibliography for historical specialists. Anyone wanting that should get a copy of *Slavery, Abolition and Emancipation: A Reading List* produced by Bristol Reference Library in 2007. What follows is simply a list of books that might interest those who would like to know more.

1. Personal accounts of enslavement and suffering brought about by racial prejudice:

Olaudah Equiano's full autobiography is available in various editions and online. It encouraged others to write what became known as 'slave narratives'. There is therefore a rich source of first-hand accounts of slavery written in the nineteenth century by those who were enslaved, mostly African Americans. Here are six of the best of them in chronological order and all are available in various editions and online:

- *Narrative of the Life of Frederick Douglass, an American Slave written by himself* (1845): the most famous and influential of all the slave narrative books written in the nineteenth century. No book more vividly portrays the horror of American slavery and the importance of freedom.
- *Narrative of William W. Brown, a Fugitive Slave* (1847) : a memorable account second only to Douglass' book. It gives real insight into the mindset of the enslaved.
- *The Narrative of Sojourner Truth* (1850) : the autobiography of Isabella Baumfree, a woman's rights activist as well as an abolitionist. She was listed in 2014 by the Smithsonian Institute in Washington D.C. as one of the '100 Most Significant Americans of All Time'
- *Twelve Years a Slave : Narrative of Solomon Northup* (1853): a vivid account of a man kidnapped and sold into slavery and of life on the plantations and the slave markets of the Deep South. The book was turned into a memorable film in 2014.

- *Harriet Jacobs: Incidents in the Life of A Slave Girl* (1861) : a book that focuses on the sexual abuse of female slaves and the problems facing enslaved mothers. It includes an account of her hiding for seven years in an attic to escape capture.
- *Booker T. Washington: Up From Slavery* (1901). A book about the transforming power of education. Rated as being one of the best non-fiction books of the twentieth century.

Based on her telling her story, it is also worth reading *The Incredible Memoirs of Harriet Tubman American abolitionist born into slavery* (1868) and recently made into a film '*Harriet*' in 2019. It is also worth pointing out that in the 1930s 2,300 first person accounts of slavery and 500 black and white photographs of former slaves were collected as part of a Federal Writers Project in America and these were published in many volumes. These are now available downloadable on line free of charge from the Library of Congress under the heading *Born In Slavery*.

The racist legacy that developed out of slavery and the problems that has generated for defining what it means to be a black person has also been powerfully described in many novels. Here are just a few examples:

- Zora Neale Hurston: *Dust Tracks On A Road* (1942): a candid and poignant account of her rise from childhood poverty in the rural South to literary fame.
- Langston Hughes: *The Big Sea* (1940): a book about coming to terms with being of mixed race and life in the nightclubs of Harlem and Paris.
- Richard Wright: *Black Boy*(1945) : a profound and frequently shocking depiction of racism in the early twentieth century.
- James Baldwin: *The Fire Next Time* (1963): two essays, one on the central role of race in American history and one on race and religion.
- Anne Moody: *Coming of Age In Mississippi* (1968): an African-American woman struggles against racism among white people and sexism among black people.
- Maya Angelou: *I Know Why The Caged Bird Sings* (1969) a book about how a victim of racism and rape is transformed by a love of literature. The first of a seven-volume series.
- Margo Jefferson: *Negroland* (2015) about the ups and downs of black life within upper class African-American society in the 1950s and 1960s.

2. Secondary Sources

I would recommend the following:

- Ira Berlin: *Many Thousands Gone* 2000 Harvard University Press
- J. Black: *Slavery, a new Global History* 2011 Robinson Press
- M.Dresser & A.Hann: *Slavery and the British Country House* 2013 English Heritage
- P. Freyer: *The History of Black People in Britain* 1984 Pluto Press
- A. Hothschild: *Bury the Chains* 2004 Macmillan
- D. Olusoga : *Black and British: A Forgotten History* 2016 Macmillan
- M.Rediker: *The Slave Ship: A Human History* 2008 Penguin
- E.Reynolds: *Stand the Storm: A History of the Transatlantic Slave Trade* 1986 Allison & Busby
- S.Schama: *Rough Crossings* 2005 BBC Books
- Ronald Segal: *The Black Diaspora: Five centuries of the Black Experience Outside Africa* 1995 Farrar Straus & Giroux
- Ronad Segal : *Islam's Black Slaves* 2001 Farrar Straus & Giroux
- H.Thomas: *The Slave Trade* 1997 Macmillan
- J. Walvin: *Black Ivory: A History of British Slavery* 2005 Wiley-Blackwell

If you wish to learn more about individual figures, then I would suggest reading any of the following biographies:

- J. Aitkin: *John Newton: From Grace to Amazing Grace* 2007 Crossway Books
- V.Caretta: *Equiano the African* 2005 Univ. of Georgia Press
- V.Caretta: *Phillis Wheatley, Biography of a Genius in Bondage* 2011 Univ. of Georgia Press
- C.Eickelmann: *Pero, the life of a slave in eighteenth-century Bristol* 2004 Redcliffe Press
- D. Grant: *The Fortunate Slave: An Illustration of African Slavery in the early Eighteenth Century* OUP 1968.
- R.Hattersley: *A Brand Plucked FromThe Burning* (on John Wesley) 2002 Little Brown
- M.Jackson: *Let This Voice Be Heard: Antony Benezet, Father of Atlantic Abolitionism* 2010 Univ. of Pennsylvania Press
- S. Tomkin: *William Wilberforce: A Biography* 2007 Eerdmanns
- E. G. Wilson : *Thomas Clarkson* 1996 (2nd edition) William Sessions

- Marlon James: *The Book of Night Women* (2009)
- Tracy Chevalier: *The Last Runaway* (2013)
- David Pesci: *Amistad* (2014)
- Jacqueline Woodson: *Brown Girl Dreaming* (2014)
- Colson Whitehead: *The Underground Railroad* (2016)

For those who like poetry a good anthology is *Amazing Grace: An Anthology of Poems about Slavery 1660-1810* (edit. James Basker) 2005 Yale University Press.

4. Films

This may appear an odd category in a reading list but films are often based on great books and they are a powerful medium in their own right. There have been a small number of memorable films on the slave trade or slavery or the American Civil War. I would particularly recommend *Glory* (1989), *Amistad* (1997), *Beloved* (1998), *Amazing Grace* (2006), *Lincoln* (2012), *Twelve Years A Slave* (2013), and *Harriet* (2019).

There have been far more films made on the theme of continued racism towards black people. I would particularly recommend *The Defiant Ones* (1958), T*o Kill A Mockingbird* (1962), *The Colour Purple* (1985), *Mississippi Burning* (1998), *A Dry White Season* (1989), *Driving Miss Daisy* (1989), *The Long Walk Home* (1990), *Malcom X* (1992), *Cry the Beloved Country* (1995), *Cry Freedom* (1995), *The Watermelon Woman* (1996), *American History X* (1998), *Skin* (2008), *The Help* (2011), *Selma* (2014), *Mudbound* (2017), *BlacKkKlansman* (2018) and *Green Book* (2018).

Further Reading

The Brothers: an engraving based on French sculpture produced c1850 by Charles Cordier

INDEX

It is never too late to give up our prejudices
Henry David Thoreau, American philosopher and abolitionist in *Walden* in 1854

Red indicates a separate quotation. Blue indicates an illustration

Abbot Diane 436, 438
Abolition date in different countries 417, 421-422
Abolition of Slave Trade Act (1807) 386, 387
Abraham 26
Act of Assembly of Barbados 102
Afro-American and Afro-Caribbean (use of word) 41
African-American and African-Caribbean (use of word) 41-42
African Institution 389
African slavery compared to European 78
African tribes 51, 52 and alleged inferiority 281-285
African unnamed individuals as portrayed in art 27, 65, 68, 89, 91, 214, 219, 249, 253, 280, 335, 387, 390, 419
Africatown 420
Aldworth Robert and Thomas 29
Alleyne Captain 243, 270
Allwood family 272
Almshouse (on King Street) 155, 161, 263
Almshouse (on St Michael's Hill) 158, 161
Amherst Lord 136
Am I Not a Man and a Brother cameo 359, 360-361, 405
Ames Mary 398

Amo Anton Wilhelm 306-307, 309
Anayasi Ray 80
Anchor Society 164
Anderson Charles 198
Anderson John 196, 197, 198, 208, 262
Angelou Maya 42
Anglicanism and slavery 317-318, 320, 345-346, 350-354, 356, 369, 402
Anonymous 38, 43, 75, 183, 190 192, 204,213, 263, 306, 307, 391, 398, 405
Annis John 122-123, 136, 328
Anti-Slavery International 422, 424, 446
Anti-Slavery Society 402
Aristotle 13
Arne Thomas and *Rule Britannia* 298
Arnold James 357
Arnos Court 274, 275
Arundel Elisha 206
Asbury Francis 335, 336, 343
Ashley Court 186, 219
Ashley Lord 291
Ashmead George 393
Ashton Court 220
Assembly Rooms 263
Astry Arabella, Diana and Elizabeth 244
Atkins John 45-46
Atkins Michael 224
Auden W.H. 86

Baartman Sara (Hottentot Venus) 249, 252
Badminton House 274,276
Bahamas Motto 201
Bailey Guy 431, 433. 434
Baker Richard (Dick) 80, 82, 84,86,87,92
Baker Richard 93, 95
Baker Thomas 210
Baldwin James 246
Bailie Evan 222, 385, 386, 402, 405, 406, 408, 412, 414 and family 272, 415
Bailey Paul 434
Bales Kevin 424
Ball John 15
BAME 443
Bance Island Fort 45, 54
Banks Joseph 117
Baptist views on slavery 316, 346, 347, 362, 375, 379, 397,404, 411-412
Barber Francis 318
Barker Robert 213, 311
Barracoon 53, 54
Barrere Pierre 282
Bathurst Basin 194, 195
Bathurst Benjamin 194, 195
Bathurst Charles 194
Baxter Richard 286, 287-288
Beaufort House 268, 269
Becher Cranfield 187, 188, 264
Becher Edward and George 188
Becher John 184, 185, 186,188, 263, 264
Becher Michael 187, 188

457

Beck Joseph 362
Beckford Carmen 440, 441
Beckford William 228, 229, 230, 230, 276
Beckford's Tower 229, 230
Beddoes Thomas 222
Bedford Arthur 163
Behn Aphra 286, 290-291, 300, 314,316
Belefonte Harry 430
Belle Elizabeth (Dido) 319, 321
Benezet Anthony 322, 323, 324, 331,332, 344
Benn Tony 432
Bennett Roy 121
Berkeley Norbonne 272
Berkeley Square 273
Beswick Thomas 359
Bettiscombe Manor 278
Bevan James 324
Bicknell John 99
Biddulph Thomas 393
Bimbe Jack 208, 210
Black American (use of word) 42
Black British (use of word) 439
Black and White Cafe 435, 436, 437, 439
Black Castle 274
Black Christ 91
Black Dinah 240
Blackfacing 95, 453 and *Black and White Minstrel Show* 429-430
Black History Month 440
Black Lives Matter 9, 169, 170, 429, 446, 444-445
Black Mary 164, 165
Black Panther Movement 41, 438
Blackboy Hill 241
Blair Alexander 128
Blaise Castle Estate 263, 274, 275
Blake William 349, 371-372, 373
Bland Francis 146
Blathwayt William 276, 277
Blue School 220

Bonnie Prince Charlie 175, 299
Born in Slavery 450
Boscawen Edward (Vice-Admiral) 87,89, 92
Boswell James 376
Bradburn Samuel 377
Bragge Charles 272, 386
Brereton Colonel 409
Brickdale John 278
Brickdale Matthew 270, 278, 356, 365, 367, 368
Bright Henry 175, 190, 221-222, 262
Bright Henry (M.P.) 222, 402, 414
Bright Lowbridge 180, 222
Bright Richard 222,223, 279
Bristol and competition with Liverpool 171-176, 177, 178-183, 355
Bristol and Clifton Female Anti-Slavery Society 398-399, 404
Bristol Brass Company 259
Bristol Bus boycott 430-432, 433, 434
Bristol Cathedral 25, 26, 266
Bristol Corporation 176
Bristol Grammar School 24-25
Bristol Infirmary 219, 220
Bristol Old Vic (Theatre Royal) 264, 265
Bristol Riot of 1831 401, 408-409
Bristol University 232, 234
Bristol (views of) 150, 153
Bristol West Indian Parents and Friends Association 434
Brokenshire James 425
Bromley Henry 148
Brown Austin Channing 285
Brown William 93
Brown William Wells 170, 448, 449
Brunel Isambard Kingdom 416
Buehner Carl W. 130
Burchell Thomas 411

Burke Edmund 17, 205, 335, 336-340, 349, 368
Burton Paul 156
Bush Robert 274
Buxton Thomas Fowell 393, 395, 403
Byng John (Rear-Admiral) 83, 86

Cabot Circus 21, 22
Cabot John 20, 21
Cabot Sebastian 21, 22
Cabot Tower 21
Cafe Revival 237
Caledonia Place 272, 273
Campbell Alexander 348
Campbell Delores 441, 442
Campbell Sir Archibald 94
Camplin John 356, 362
Cann Robert 272
Capitein Jacobus 295, 296-297, 297
Caretta Vincent 57, 74, 136
Cary John 34,36, 160
Casamajor Clementia 190
Casamajor Lewis 190, 262, 264, 274
Cassidy John 166
Caton James 205
Cattellena 240
Cave family 272
Cervantes Miguel de 324
Challoner Wiliam 185, 186
Chambers Miles 168, 442
Champion Joseph 274
Champion Nehemiah 220, 259, 268
Champion Richard 208, 209, 220
Champion William 274, 311
Chaplin Charlie 291
Charles II 30,32, 32, 263,266, 287, 289, 291-2
Charlotte Queen 142
Chatterton Thomas 309, 316
Chauvin Derek 429
Chilcott John 198
Child Rebecca 274
Chocolate production 234, 235, 236
Chodrun Pema 299

Index

Christmas Steps 216, 218
Cicero Marcus 13
Cirencester Park 195
City of Sanctuary 442
Civil Rights Congress of Nigeria 46
Clapham Sect 369, 379
Clarkson Thomas 197, 318, 331, 332, 344, 347, 350 367, 376, 385, 388, 393, early life 345-346, and Wilberforce 350-52, visit to Bristol 353, 356-358, 369, 394
Claxton Christopher 401, 405-406, 408-409, 415
Clevedon Court 191, 193, 194
Cleve Hill House 272, 275
Clifton 268-272, 273
Clifton Court 268, 269
Clifton Hill House 268, 269
Clifton Suspension Bridge 157, 279
Clotilda 420, 423
Clutterbuck family 276
Coates Ta-Nehisi 199
Cobbett William 394, 396-397
Codd Robert 64, 66
Codrington Christopher Bethel 270, 276
Codrington John 272
Codrington William 276, 277
Coffee production and houses 235, 236-237
Coffles 48, 49
Coghlan John 198
Coke Thomas 335, 343
Coker Court 31
Coker Fanny and Kate 252
Cole Alyssa 259
Coleridge Samuel 218, 379, 380, 381, 382-384
Collingwood Luke 340
Colman Samuel 394, 395
Colonel Jack 294
Colston Edward 9,33, 158, 164, 264, early life 159, link with Royal African Company 159-160, links with Bristol 160, as religious benefactor 161-162, as school benefactor 162-163, as MP 163, death and bequests 163-164, Black Mary portrait 164, 165, reputation and statue 158, 165, 166-168, 169, 170, 446
Colston Girls' School 164
Colston's School for Boys 162, 165
Colston Society 164
Colston named streets and buildings 166,167
Columbus Christopher 18,19, 20, 23
Combe Henry 186, 263, 276
Combe William 334, 335
Commercial Rooms 266, 267
Commonwealth Co-ordinated Committee 431, 434, 440
Company of Adventurers Trading to the Ports of Africa 29, 176
Compensation paid to slave owners 415-416
Constantine Learie 432
Coon (use of word) 283-284
Cooper Anna Julia 449
Cooper David 342, 342
Cooper Thomas 358
Corn Exchange 266, 267
Corn Street 266
Cornwallis Crescent 272
Cornwell Richard 247
Coromantin slaves in Bristol 77-78
Cossins John 276
Costello Ray 110
Coster Thomas 190, 191, 192, 263, 264
Cosway Richard 348
Cote House 219, 220
Cottle Amos 379
Cottle Joseph 379-380, 381, 383
Cotton production 237-238
Council House 266, 267
Cowper William 320, 340, 364, 372, 374
Cox Thomas 172

Craven Matthew 241
Crimping 204-205
Cromwell Oliver 32
Cropper James 388, 393
Cruger Henry 365, 367, 368
Cugoano Ottobah 139, 140, 141, 142, 147, 220, 349, 348-350
Cullen Susannah 146-147, 148
Cullen Thomas 146
Cumberbatch Abraham 264, 265, 270
Cumberbatch Benedict 264, 265
Cunningham family 272
Curtis Michele 439, 440

Da Gama Vasco 18
Dampier Henry 188
Dampier Wiliam 200, 203
Daniel Thomas 226, 228, 229, 264, 415 and family 272
Darwin Charles 284
Davies Mark 264
Davis Angela Y. 134, 144
Davis Jefferson 26
Davis Richard Hart 391, 401, 402, 406
Davy Humphrey 222
Day James 185, 188
Day John 185
Day Nathaniel 252, 263
Day Peter 185
Day Thomas 36, 99
Dean John 357
Defoe Daniel 151, 200, 294
De Pauw Cornelius 282
Dettering Barbara 440, 441, 442
Deveraux Stephen 215
Dickinson family 276
Diderot Denis 314-315
Dillwyn William 332, 346, 347, 354
Doddington Park 276, 277
Dolben William 366-367
Dolphin Society 164
Doran James 98-100
Douglas Frederick 50, 74, 76 79, 108, 116, 117, 185, 289,

459

403, 418, 423, 449
Dower House 272, 275
Dowling Thomas 215
Dowry Parade 268, 271
Dowry Square 268, 271
Drake Francis 26, 27
Drake Judith 352
Drawbridge 216, 218
Dresser Madge 33, 240, 262, 268, 270, 278, 298, 322, 378
Drummond Clifford 431, 440, 441
Du Bois William 75, 76, 281, 412
Duckinfield Elizabeth 186
Duckinfield John 185, 186
Duckinfield Robert 186
Duddlestone John 186
Dukingfield Hall 184
Dundas Henry 338, 377
Durkin Hannah 69
Dutch East India Company 29
Dyrham Park 276, 277

Earle Joseph 262
Earnshill 276
Eaton Thomas 242
Eddo-Lodge Reni 431
Edmundson William 288-289
Edwards Mary and Thomas 163
Elbridge John 218, 220
Elbridge Thomas 219, 220
Elford William 367
Elton Abraham 191, 193
Elton Abraham II 193-194, 262
Elton Abraham III 194
Elton Issac 193,194, 262
Eton Jacob 193, 194
Elton Julia 194
Elton Margaret 193
Emerson Ralph Waldo 250
Engels Friedrich 394
Engusson Jane 186
Equiano Olaudah 8 37, 39, 97, 106, 143, 145, 296, captured and enslaved 43-44, 48-53, on the Middle Passage 57-64, sold as a slave 69-71,74-75, first experience of England 79-82, 83, sailor in Royal Navy 85-88, 89, 91, attitude to Africa 90, sold as slave in Caribbean 97-106, 107, buying his freedom 108-112, in London 112-114, as sailor 114,117-118, 119, 120–121, and John Annis 122-123, and Christianity 87, 88, 90, 91, 104, 121-128, as missionary 128, 129, 130-131, danger of re-enslavement 133-135, American War of Independence and afterwards 135-136, 138, and the *Zong* 136, 340-341, as His Majesty's Commissary 140-141, Sons of Africa 141-143, 148-149, autobiography 143-144, 145, 149, 368, 375 marriage and family 146-148, death 148
Equiano Anna Maria 145, 148
Equiano Joanna 39,148
Estlin John Prior 362
Evan Audley 431,440, 441
Evans Caleb 362
Evans Tony 421

Falconbridge Alexander 53, 54, 198, 357
Falconbridge Anna Maria 384
Fanon Fritz 146-147
Farley Elizabeth 313
Farley Felix 312
Farmer Paul 359
Farmer Thomas 100, 106, 108-110
Farr Richard 178, 188, 263
Farr Richard Jr 188, 270, 279
Farr Thomas 263, 274
Farr's Lane 261, 263
Ferdinand II of Spain 22
Feguson George 167
Fields John W. 418

Fisher Paul 220, 268
Floyd George 170, 428-429
Fonthill Abbey 228, 229, 230
Ford Benjamin 113
Fowler John 196, 196
Fox Charles James 375, 377
Fox George 286, 288 288,
Fox William 375
Frampton Court 278
Freeman Jonathan 270
Freke Philip 278
Freke Thomas 185, 186, 262
Fry Joseph 234
Fry Joseph Storrs (and J.S. Fry & Sons) 234, 235, 393
Full Moon 113

Gales Joseph 346
Gandhi Mahatma 96, 112, 410
Gandy Harry 243, 316, 343-344, 355, 362, 371
Garrison William Lloyd 455
Garvin John 346
George III 117, 142
George Prince 128, 130
Georgian House Museum 226, 227, 254
Gerbner Katherine 90
Ghezo King 45
Gibbs George 224, 279
Gibbs William 279
Gilbert Nathaniel 310
Goldney Hall 194
Goldney Thomas 191, 196, 268
Goldney Hall 191, 268, 271
Goldwin William 237
Gonglass 250
Gordon Peter 47
Gordon Robert 198
Gorge Elizabeth 272
Grainger James 71
Granderson Marcus 78
Grandy King George 251, 324, 325
Grant Abel 185, 186, 201
Grateful Society 164
Great House Henbury 244, 245
Great Western Cotton

Index

Factory 228, 234, 238
Great Western Railway 157, 279, 416
Green Sarah 247
Gregory of Nyssa 14
Grenville William 354, 386, 387
Griffiths Ralph 137
Grigg Jacob 346
Guerin Elizabeth 87, 88, 97, 112-113
Guerin Mary 87, 97, 112-113
Guerin Maynard 86 and family home 83
Guinea coin 266, 269
Guinea Company 27, 29, 30
Guinea Street 266, 269
Guterres Antonio 446

Hadfield Maria 348
Hackett Roy 431, 433, 434, 440, 441
Hackwood William 359
Hadspen House 187, 189
Hall family 272
Hallam John 362
Ham Green House 222, 223
Hamilton David 198
Hamilton Douglas 94
Hammon Briton 84-85
Hammond James Henry 237-238, 418, 420
Harding Richard 46
Hardy Thomas 147-148
Hare John 405
Hare William 188
Harford John Scandret 274
Harford Bank 274
Harper Harry 243
Harris James 252
Harris John 64, 66
Harris John (Baptist minister) 362
Harris Phillip 185, 186
Harris Rice 207
Hartman Saidiya 417
Hastings Selina, Countess of Huntingdon 307, 313, 326
Hawkins John 26, 27, 28
Haydon Robert 62, 64
Heard William 48, 49

Helyar Cary 31, 33
Helyar William 33, 221
Henley Robert 317
Henry II 15
Henry VIII 24, 26
Henry the Navigator 17, 19
Henry Owen 431, 440, 441
Henry Patrick 336
Henson Josiah 419
Henvill Richard 185
Heyrick Elizabeth 395, 399-400, 402
Hill Lawrence 70, 239
Hillhouse James 264
Hippisley John 309, 314, 315 and son 315
Hobhouse Arthur Lawrence 189
Hobhouse Emily 189
Hobhouse Henry 189, 270
Hobhouse Isaac 60, 188-189, 192, 262
Hobhouse Penelope 189
Holbrook Joseph 268
Hole In The Wall 205
Holmes Oliver Wendell 93
Holroyd John Baker 373, 374
Holt Sir John 286, 293
Hooke Abraham 184, 185, 186
Hooke Humphrey 276
Hope Allan 51
Hotwell Spa 268, 271
House Through Time 268
Howard Charles William 244
Hubbard Elbert 304
Huckleberry Finn 40, 453
Huggins Edward 226
Hughes Captain 133-134
Hughes Langston 40
Hume David 281-282, 308, 308
Hunt Henry 391, 392, 401
Hunt John 310
Hymand Kevin 428

Ibbetson Julius 270
Ibn-Hawkal 17
Iles Joseph 184, 188
Indentured labour 28-29
Interracial sex and marriage 101, 146-147, 246, 247-248
Irving Charles (Dr) 114, 117, 118, 121, 128, 130-131, 134-135
Irwin James 140, 141
Ismail Fozia 442
Ivie Gilman 239

Jacks Walter 243
Jackson Jesse 41
Jacob Samuel 160, 185
Jacobs Harriet Ann 247, 448, 450
Jamaican Riot 411
James II 287, 290, 292
Jayne John 207
Jefferis Joseph 185, 192, 262, 270
Jefferis William 185
Jefferson Thomas 333, 384, 388
Jenkins Robert 174
Jobson Richard 28
Johnson Elizabeth 327
Johnson family 272
Johnson James 378
Johnson Joseph 94, 95
Johnson Samuel 71, 74, 317-318, 318
Jolly John 114
Jones Christopher 189
Jones Pip 77, 190
Jones James 196, 197, 208
Jones Robert 206
Jones Thomas 66, 196, 197, 198, 206

Katherine 28, 240
Keller Helen 415
Kelsall James 340-341
Kennedy John 213, 215
Kennedy Thomas 201-202
Kimber John 214, 215, 377
King Boston 253, 255-257, 348
King Ken 361
King Martin Luther 41, 125, 127, 133, 432, 434, 438
King Robert 100-101, 106, 108-110
King Street 263-264

King William Alehouse 263, 265
Kings Weston House 186, 224, 225, 276
Kingswood School 253, 256
Kirkpatrick William 122
Knibb William 411-412, 413

Labour In Vain 82, 83
Ladies Society for the Relief of Negro Slaves 399-400
Lake Cleo 168
Lamb Charles 380
Landor Walter Savage 369
Laroche James 62, 190-192, 205, 208, 262, 264
Laroche James II 192-193, 196
Laroche John 190
Leadstone John 45
Lechmere Edmund 377
Leckington James 123
Lee Harper 432
Lee Robert E. 228
Leigh Court 224, 225
Lewin-Turner Tayo 166
Lewins Mead Sugar House 216, 218, 264
Lewis Cudjoe 420, 420, 423
Lewis C.S. 388
Lewis Richard Jeffrey 164
Lewis Thomas 313, 320
Lay Benjamin 295, 297-298, 298, 308
Library 264, 265
Lincoln Abraham 257, 293, 343, 357, 371
Lind James 117
Lines William 357
Lisle David 318
Llandoger Trow 200, 263-264, 265
Locke John 286, 287, 291-293
London Corresponding Society 147-148
Long Edward 280, 282-283, 284-285, 382
Lord Mayor's Chapel 184, 186
Lougher Richard and Walter 188
Louverture Toussant 381, 384
Lovell Robert 380
Lowell Robert 181
Lutwidge Skeffington 117

Macaulay Thomas Babington 348, 348
Macaulay Zachary 256-257, 346, 347, 348
Macnamara Matthias 135-136
Maillard Thomas 24
Malcolm X 41, 77, 237
Mandela Nelson 85, 122, 130, 349
Marchionni Bartolommeo 20
Marlborough 64, 65
Marsh William 402
Marsh Street 263
Matthew 21
Matthews William 181
Mbande Nzinga, Queen of Angola 48
McCloud Melony 42
McCrear Matilda 421, 423
McKay Claude 393
McTaggert James 198, 206, 264
Melville Herman 67
Merchant Venturers 26, 27, 154, 155, 156-7, 168, 174, 363, 367, and educational institutions 156-157; Old Vic 264, and Clifton 268
Methodism 119, 123, 124-125, 301, 312, 322, 376-377, 379, 411, 412, and printing/publishing 312, 329-331, 404, 411, 412, 420; see also entries on various Methodist leaders, notably the Wesleys and Whitefield
Meyler Richard 190, 221-222
Middle Passage 33, 56, 57-58, 59, 60, 61, 62-64, 65, 66-67, 204
Middleton Charles 351, 354
Miles Philip John 224, 225
Miles William 224, 368
Miller Walter 62

Mills family 270
Milmo Cahal 171
Milward Nathaniel 222, 246
Mingo Lewis 242
Mint Workhouse (St Peter Sugar House) 31, 34, 36, 160
Miskito Indians 128, 129, 130-131
Mitchell John 325
Modern Slavery Act 425, 428
Montagu George 138
Montagu John (Duke) 137, 306
Montesquieu Baron 301
More Hannah 242, 352, 353, 356, 364, 366, 369, 375, 379, 380, 399
Morrison Toni 71
Muslim traders 15, 16, 17, 19, 44-45, 49
Mulatto and its variations 283
Murray William, Earl of Mansfield 319, 320-321, 325, 341

Nancy (Pero's sister) 252
Napoleon Bonaparte 385
Napper John 33, 34
Neale Alexander 264
Neely Matthew 213
Negro (use of word) 38, 40-41
Negro History Week 439-440
Negroland 54
Negro spirituals 75-76
Nelson Horatio (Admiral) 93, 95, 118, 119, 384-385, 386
Newark Park 278
New Room 4, 7, 303, 308, 312, 327, 344, 364, 397
Newton James 207
Newton John 48, 58, 198, 207, 351, 352
Nicols Grace 81
Noah 26
Northrup Samuel 46, 57, 264, 448, 449

Obama Barack 140
Obama Michele 333

Index

Obi or Three Fingered Jack 378-379
Old Bank 266, 267
Old Duke 263. 265
Oglethorpe James Edward 305
Oliver Thomas and family 270, 272
Olusogo David 9, 268 268, 438 429-430
O'Neil Terence 325
Orchard Street 195, 264
Orwell George 40
Osborne Ann 138
Over Court (nr Almondsbury) 191, 192
Owens Jesse 243
Ozleworth Park 278

Paine Thomas 384, 388
Panah Peter 371-372
Parkes D'Arcy 167
Parkinson Leonard 281
Pascal Michael Henry 79, 82, 87, 88, 92, 96, 97-8, 112-113
Peach Samuel 274
Peaden Tom 252
Pedlar Thomas 268
Peloquin Stephen 264
Penn Sir William 30, 31
Pennington Thomas 188, 202
Penny Lane 167, 177
Perkins Doctor 106
Perkins John (Jack Punch) 94-96
Pero 226, 252, 254-255
Pero's Bridge 253
Perrin Sarah 8, 308
Peter, Paul and Mary (folk group) 316
Philip M. NourbeSe 341
Phillips Samuel 206
Phillips Trevor 435
Phipps John Constantine 117, 119
Pine William 312, 313, 333, 365
Pinney Charles 398, 401, 408, 409 and family 415
Pinney John 222, 224 226,

227, 228, 252, 278, 361, 363
Pirates and privateering 200-204
Pitt George (Colonel) 136
Pitt William 182 352, 354, 367, 367, 377, 386
Pittacus of Mytiene 55
Pitts Samuel 174
Plantation overseers 102, 221
Pocock Nicholas 208, 209
Pope Alexander 171, 293, 295
Porter Stephen 205
Porter William 410-411
Powder Monkeys 85-86,92-3
Powell John 196, 198
Power Thomas 188
Prescott William 112
Press gang 179, 205, 211
Prince (negro slave) 242, 245
Prince Street 184, 261, 263
Privilege Negroes 241
Protheroe Edward 391-392, 403-406, 407, 408, 412

Quaco John 78
Quaker attitudes to slavery 286, 288-290, 297-298, 308, 310-311, 316, 322, 332, 342, 343-344, 354, 355, 358, 362, 393, 399, 404, 406, 415, 420
Quaker Friars in Broadmead 298, 303
Queen Anne 293
Queen Elizabeth's Hospital 162,228
Queen's Square 258, 261, 262-263

Rascal Dizee 239
Racedown House 278
Ramsey James 345-345, 346, 346, 347, 351, 354, 368
Rankin Thomas 332-334, 335, 336
Redland High School 276
Red Maids School 228
Rees Marvin 442, 446
Reeve William 221, 274, 311
Reform Act 409-410
Reynal Abbe 336

Rice production 236
Richmond Terrace 272, 273
Robin John (Ancona Robin) 324-328 and letter 323
Robin John (Little Ephraim) 324-328
Robinson Mary Darby 365, 366
Rodda Martin 334
Rodney Walter 33, 176
Rodney Place 272
Rodway James 346
Rogers James 196, 197-198, 208, 213, 252
Rogers Woodes 200, 201,203, 262
Romaine William 119, 127
Romilly Samuel 391-392
Rouquet James 313
Rousseau Jean-Jacques 311, 314
Royal Adventurers into Africa 32
Royal African Company 32,33,34,36,45, 250
Royal Fort 268, 269
Royal York Crescent 272, 273
Ruddock Noblett 185, 186, 192, 231, 263
Rummer Tavern 216, 218
Rutter Thomas 362
Ryland John 346

Sailor punishments 211, 212-213, 214
St Bartholomew's Hospital 24, 25
St Nicholas Abbey, Barbados 31
St Paul 12, 14
St Paul's Carnival 434, 437
St Paul's riot 430, 435, 436, 437, 438
St Peter's Hospital 36
Sambo (use of word) 283
Sancho Ignatius 137-138, 139, 142, 306
Sanders Thomas 393
Sankey Emanuel 104
Sarpong June 141
Saunders Edward 185, 192,

266
Savage Richard 298-299, 303
Scarifying 46, 47
Schama Simon 37
Schiebinger Londa 400
Schimmelpennick Mary Anne 399, 401, 404
Scipio Africanus 240, 244, 245, 246
Selkirk Alexander (Robinson Crusoe) 200, 203, 213, 264
Seneca 12, 14
Serfdom 15,16, 421
Sessarakoo, Prince of Annamaboe 250
Seven Stars 353, 356-357
Shakespeare Tavern 184, 186, 263
Sharp Granville 9, 122-123, 129, 136, 140, 148, 243, 256, 319, 320, 321, 346, 369, 388; early life 317, legal cases 318-322, links with Benezet and Wesley 322, 331, 332, the Zong 341, the Sierra Leone project 346
Shape Samuel 411, 413
Sharp William 318
Sierra Leone scheme 140-141, 256, 346-348, 350, 379
Sims Thomas 198
Singh Raghbir 433, 434
Sketchley James 270
Slave captains and their crews 199-215
Slave names 75-78, in Bristol (pre1700) 239- 240, (in 1700-1750) 240-241,(1750-1800) 241-243, and named free 251
Slave plaques (images of) 195
Slave profit and the economy 259-262, 278-279
Slave punishments (images of) 23, 35, 47, 103, 111, 373
Slave ships in Bristol 171-172
Slave trader definition 152, 154
Slave treatment of women (visual images) 214, 249

Slavery Act 1833 413, 414-416
Slavery and British freedom 287, 292, 294, 296, 298-299, 317-325
Slavery in ancient times 12, 13-14
Slavery memorials (visual images) 249, 339, 426-427
Slavery (modern signs of) 443 and definition/ numbers 424-425
Slaves resident in Bristol 239-258
Sloane Hans 234, 235
Smith Marie-Antoinette 92
Smith Mychel Denzel 368
Smith Joseph 202, 268
Smith Redoshi 421, 423
Smith William 222, 346
Smollett Tobias 113
Smyth Florence 219
Smyth Jarrit 220
Smyth John Hugh 220, 244
Smyth Thomas 240
Society for Constitutional Information 346
Society for Effecting the Abolition of the Slave Trade 141, 147, 148, 354, 358-369, 376
Society for Mitigation and Gradual Abolition of Slavery 392-394, 398, 400, 402
Society for the Relief of Free Negroes Unlawfully Held in Bondage 333
Society of Merchant Venturers (see Merchant Venturers)
Solomon Job Ben 137, 305-306, 309
Somerset Coal Canal 260
Somerset Henry 274, 276, 373, 374
Somerset James 320-321
Sons of Africa 8, 140, 142. 148-149
Southerne Thomas 314
Southey Robert 218, 246, 379,

379, 380, 381, 382
Southwell Edward 276, 277
South Sea Company 293
Southwell 187
Spanish Requirement 22, 23
Spavins William 82, 115
S.S. Great Britain 416
Stedman John 238
Stephen James 378
Stephenson Paul 428, 431-432, 433, 434-435, 436
Sterne Laurence 279
Stevenson Bryan 422
Stevenson Robert Louis 264
Stoke's Croft Endowed School 184,186
Stoke House 272, 275
Stowe Harriet-Beecher 67, 101 331, 332, 366, 452-453
Strong Jonathan 318
Sturge Joseph 413
Sugar production 22, 24, 72, 216, 217-218, 230, 231, 373, 401
Sulgar Henry 356
Swift Jonathan 274
Swymmer Anthony 33,34
Swymmer Elizabeth 29
Swymmer William 33, 264
Syphax Jonathan 118

Tallmadge James 363
Teach Edward (Blackbeard) 200-201, 203
Teast Sydenham 172
Temple School 162-163
Testonites 351-352
Thackeray William Makepeace 186
The Royal Slave 286, 290-291
Thelwell John 384
Thomas Dalby 199, 217
Thomas Franklin 147
Thomas Hugh 388
Thompson John 325
Thompson William 356
Thoreau Henry David 443, 457
Thorne Nicholas 24, 25, 26
Thorne Robert 20, 24, 25
Thornton Henry 369

Index

Thoughts Upon Slavery 7, 323, 329-331
Tightpacking 58
Tobacco production 72, 231-232
Tobin James 374
Tockington Court 274
Todd Silas 210, 212
Tomba (rebel slave) 45-46
Tonge Henry 188, 263
Tooke John Horne 346
Tovey Samuel 166
Townsend Lucy 399-400
Tracey Park 274
Transatlantic Slave Trade Database numbers 35
Triangular Trade 32-33, 35
Trinity College 272
Trotman family 272
Trotsky Leon 251
Truth Sojourner 389, 448, 449
Tubman Harriet 51, 161, 251, 325, 448, 450
Tucker Josiah 318, 353, 355, 356, 357, 362
Tucker Timothy 208, 210
Tully George 9, 308
Tunbridge Robert 185, 186
Tutu Desmond 87, 349, 354
Twain Mark 40, 453
Tyndall Thomas 268 269
Tyndall's Park 270
Tyntesfield House 279

Uncle Ephraim 188
Uncle Tom's Cabin 68, 331, 419, 452-453
United Nations Declaration of Human Rights 422
Unseen 446
Unsworth Barry 62, 255

Vasa Anna Maria 148
Vassa Johanna 148
Vespucchi Amerigo 20
Venn Henry and John 369
Vidal family 272
Voltaire 24, 313-314
Vyvyan Richard 412-413, 414

Wadstrom Carl Bernhard 371
Wallace George 317
Walls Robert 263
Warburton William 135, 318
Waring Samuel 406
Warmley House 274, 275
Washington Eric 149
Washington Booker T. 252, 448, 450
Washington George 68, 167, 334
Waters Billy 93, 95
Watt James 222
Way Benjamin 186
Way Joseph 185, 186
Weaver Brigstock 202
Webb Harry 263
Webber Henry 359
Wedgwood Josiah 346, 353, 358
Wedgwood Thomas 226
Weekes Jane 227, 252
Wellington Duke of 406
Wesley Charles 105 303, 323, 324 336 ,early life 301-302, 312 , 355-356, views on slavery 304-305, 307, social connections 313, 320, 379, Calabar princes 324-328, and Wilberforce 352, death 355
Wesley John 7,105, 136, 137, 268, 279, 303, 336, 353, early life 301-302, views on slavery 305, 307, 308,310, influence of Benezet 322, 324,331, 332, Thoughts on Slavery 323, 329-331, 329, 331, abolition movement in America 332-334, 336, 342-343, abolition movement in Britain 355, 358-359, 363-364, 365, 372 death 375
West India Association 394, 400, 412
Westcott John 205
Weston William 20
Wetherell Charles 408
Wheatley John 326
Wheatley Phillis 323, 326,

326
Whipping 47
White Man's faith 68, 91
White slavery 239, 370 (see also William Cobbett)
Whitefield George 104, 104-105, 107, 301-302, 307, 309, 311-312, 313, 331, 332-333, 369
Whitwell Matthew 84
Wiesel Elie 115
Wilberforce William 7, 179, 254, 318, 347, 377, 375, 398 early life 351-352 and abolition pressure 363-369, 376-378, 385-389, 393-394, 414
William the Conqueror 14-15
Williams Eric 224
Williams Fannie 18
Williams Francis 137, 295, 296
Williams Joseph 208, 210
Wills Hall 233
Wills Henry Overton 232
Wills Henry Overton II 232, 233
Wills Henry Overton III 232
Wills Memorial Building 232, 233
Wills Tobacco Factory 233
Wills William Day 232, 233
Wilson Christopher 310
Wilson Harold 432
Windrush generation 430-431
Winslow John 84-85
Wolfe James(General) 87-88, 89
Wollstonecraft Mary 395, 398
Woodson Carter 439-440
Woolman John 310, 310
Woolnough Rebecca 220
Wordsworth William 379, 380
World Anti-Slavery Convention 417, 419
Wraxell Nathaniel 188
Wraxell Court 272, 275
Wright James 393, 402
Wright Joseph 393

Wright Matthew 362
Wright Thomas 362
Wulfstan, Bishop of
    Worcester 14, 16

Yate Robert 36

Yeamans John 30, 30, 31, 32
Yeamans Robert 30, 240
Yearsley Ann (Lactilla) 365, 366, 379
York Place 272, 273
Yorke Sir Philip 294, 295

Yorke Richard 118, 135
Young William 94

Zeno of Citium 14
Zong massacre 136, 339, 340-342

Attitude is a choice. Happiness is a choice. Optimism is a choice. Kindness is a choice. Giving is a choice. Respect is a choice. Whatever choice you make makes you. Choose wisely

Roy T. Bennett , writer on positive thinking in *The Light In The Heart* in 2020
